ALL GLORY TO ŚRĪ GURU AND GAURĀṄGA

ŚRĪMAD BHĀGAVATAM

of

KṚṢṆA-DVAIPĀYANA VYĀSA

ब्राह्मणा ऊचुः
त्वं क्रतुस्त्वं हविस्त्वं हुताशः स्वयं
त्वं हि मन्त्रः समिद्दर्भपात्राणि च ।
त्वं सदस्यर्त्विजो दम्पती देवता
अग्निहोत्रं स्वधा सोम आज्यं पशुः ॥

brāhmaṇā ūcuḥ
tvaṁ kratus tvaṁ havis tvaṁ hutāśaḥ svayaṁ
tvaṁ hi mantraḥ samid-darbha-pātrāṇi ca
tvaṁ sadasyartvijo dampatī devatā
agnihotraṁ svadhā soma ājyaṁ paśuḥ

(p. 291)

BOOKS by His Divine Grace A. C. Bhaktivedanta Swami Prabhupāda

Bhagavad-gītā As It Is
Śrīmad-Bhāgavatam, Cantos 1–10 (50 Vols.)
Śrī Caitanya-caritāmṛta (17 Vols.)
Teachings of Lord Caitanya
The Nectar of Devotion
The Nectar of Instruction
Śrī Īśopaniṣad
Easy Journey to Other Planets
Kṛṣṇa Consciousness: The Topmost Yoga System
Kṛṣṇa, the Supreme Personality of Godhead (3 Vols.)
Perfect Questions, Perfect Answers
Dialectical Spiritualism—A Vedic View of Western Philosophy
Teachings of Lord Kapila, the Son of Devahūti
Transcendental Teachings of Prahlād Mahārāja
Kṛṣṇa, the Reservoir of Pleasure
Life Comes From Life
The Perfection of Yoga
Beyond Birth and Death
On the Way to Kṛṣṇa
Geetār-gan (Bengali)
Rāja-vidyā: The King of Knowledge
Elevation to Kṛṣṇa Consciousness
Kṛṣṇa Consciousness: The Matchless Gift
Back to Godhead Magazine (Founder)

A complete catalog is available upon request.

Bhaktivedanta Book Trust
3764 Watseka Avenue
Los Angeles, California 90034

Endpapers: On the bank of the Ganges, Śukadeva Gosvāmī speaks *Śrīmad-Bhāgavatam* for the first time. Mahārāja Parīkṣit and other exalted saints and sages listen with rapt attention.

ŚRĪMAD BHĀGAVATAM

Fourth Canto

"The Creation of the Fourth Order"

(Part One—Chapters 1–8)

With the Original Sanskrit Text,
Its Roman Transliteration, Synonyms,
Translation and Elaborate Purports

by

His Divine Grace
A.C. Bhaktivedanta Swami Prabhupāda
Founder-*Ācārya* of the International Society for Krishna Consciousness

THE BHAKTIVEDANTA BOOK TRUST
New York · Los Angeles · London · Bombay

Readers interested in the subject matter of this book
are invited by the International Society for Krishna Consciousness
to correspond with its Secretary.

International Society for Krishna Consciousness
3764 Watseka Avenue
Los Angeles, California 90034

First Printing, 1974: 20,000 copies
Second Printing, 1977: 20,000 copies

Printed in the United States of America

Library of Congress Cataloging in Publication Data (Revised)

Puranas. Bhāgavatapurāna.
Śrīmad-Bhāgavatam.

Includes bibliographical references and indexes.
CONTENTS: Canto 1. Creation. 3 v.—Canto 2. The cosmic manifestation. 2 v.—Canto 3. The status quo. 4 v.—Canto 4. The creation of the Fourth Order. 4 v.—Canto 5. The creative impetus. 2 v.
1. Chaitanya, 1486-1534. I. Bhaktivedanta Swami, A. C., 1896- II. Title.
BL1135.P7A22 1972 73-169353
ISBN 0-912776-38-2

Table of Contents

CHAPTER EIGHT
Dhruva Mahārāja Leaves Home for the Forest

Preface

We must know the present need of human society. And what is that need? Human society is no longer bounded by geographical limits to particular countries or communities. Human society is broader than in the Middle Ages, and the world tendency is toward one state or one human society. The ideals of spiritual communism, according to *Śrīmad-Bhāgavatam*, are based more or less on the oneness of the entire human society, nay, of the entire energy of living beings. The need is felt by great thinkers to make this a successful ideology. *Śrīmad-Bhāgavatam* will fill this need in human society. It begins, therefore, with the aphorism of Vedānta philosophy *janmādy asya yataḥ* to establish the ideal of a common cause.

Human society, at the present moment, is not in the darkness of oblivion. It has made rapid progress in the field of material comforts, education and economic development throughout the entire world. But there is a pinprick somewhere in the social body at large, and therefore there are large-scale quarrels, even over less important issues. There is need of a clue as to how humanity can become one in peace, friendship and prosperity with a common cause. *Śrīmad-Bhāgavatam* will fill this need, for it is a cultural presentation for the respiritualization of the entire human society.

Śrīmad-Bhāgavatam should be introduced also in the schools and colleges, for it is recommended by the great student-devotee Prahlāda Mahārāja in order to change the demoniac face of society.

kaumāra ācaret prājño
dharmān bhāgavatān iha
durlabhaṁ mānuṣaṁ janma
tad apy adhruvam arthadam
(*Bhāg.* 7.6.1)

Disparity in human society is due to lack of principles in a godless civilization. There is God, or the Almighty One, from whom everything emanates, by whom everything is maintained and in whom everything is merged to rest. Material science has tried to find the ultimate source of creation very insufficiently, but it is a fact that there is one ultimate source of everything that be. This ultimate source is explained rationally and authoritatively in the beautiful *Bhāgavatam*, or *Śrīmad-Bhāgavatam.*

Śrīmad-Bhāgavatam is the transcendental science not only for knowing the ultimate source of everything but also for knowing our relation with Him and our duty toward perfection of the human society on the basis of this perfect knowledge. It is powerful reading matter in the Sanskrit language, and it is now rendered into English elaborately so that simply by a careful reading one will know God perfectly well, so much so that the reader will be sufficiently educated to defend himself from the onslaught of atheists. Over and above this, the reader will be able to convert others to accepting God as a concrete principle.

Śrīmad-Bhāgavatam begins with the definition of the ultimate source. It is a bona fide commentary on the *Vedānta-sūtra* by the same author, Śrīla Vyāsadeva, and gradually it develops into nine cantos up to the highest state of God realization. The only qualification one needs to study this great book of transcendental knowledge is to proceed step by step cautiously and not jump forward haphazardly like with an ordinary book. It should be gone through chapter by chapter, one after another. The reading matter is so arranged with its original Sanskrit text, its English transliteration, synonyms, translation and purports so that one is sure to become a God-realized soul at the end of finishing the first nine cantos.

The Tenth Canto is distinct from the first nine cantos because it deals directly with the transcendental activities of the Personality of Godhead Śrī Kṛṣṇa. One will be unable to capture the effects of the Tenth Canto without going through the first nine cantos. The book is complete in twelve cantos, each independent, but it is good for all to read them in small installments one after another.

I must admit my frailties in presenting *Śrīmad-Bhāgavatam*, but still I am hopeful of its good reception by the thinkers and leaders of society on the strength of the following statement of *Śrīmad-Bhāgavatam* (1.5.11):

tad-vāg-visargo janatāgha-viplavo
yasmin prati-ślokam abaddhavaty api

nāmāny anantasya yaśo 'ṅkitāni yac
chṛṇvanti gāyanti gṛṇanti sādhavaḥ

"On the other hand, that literature which is full with descriptions of the transcendental glories of the name, fame, form and pastimes of the unlimited Supreme Lord is a transcendental creation meant to bring about a revolution in the impious life of a misdirected civilization. Such transcendental literatures, even though irregularly composed, are heard, sung and accepted by purified men who are thoroughly honest."

Oṁ tat sat

A. C. Bhaktivedanta Swami

Introduction

"This *Bhāgavata Purāṇa* is as brilliant as the sun, and it has arisen just after the departure of Lord Kṛṣṇa to His own abode, accompanied by religion, knowledge, etc. Persons who have lost their vision due to the dense darkness of ignorance in the age of Kali shall get light from this *Purāṇa.*" (*Śrīmad-Bhāgavatam* 1.3.43)

The timeless wisdom of India is expressed in the *Vedas*, ancient Sanskrit texts that touch upon all fields of human knowledge. Originally preserved through oral tradition, the *Vedas* were first put into writing five thousand years ago by Śrīla Vyāsadeva, the "literary incarnation of God." After compiling the *Vedas*, Vyāsadeva set forth their essence in the aphorisms known as *Vedānta-sūtras. Śrīmad-Bhāgavatam* is Vyāsadeva's commentary on his own *Vedānta-sūtras.* It was written in the maturity of his spiritual life under the direction of Nārada Muni, his spiritual master. Referred to as "the ripened fruit of the tree of Vedic literature," *Śrīmad-Bhāgavatam* is the most complete and authoritative exposition of Vedic knowledge.

After compiling the *Bhāgavatam*, Vyāsa impressed the synopsis of it upon his son, the sage Śukadeva Gosvāmī. Śukadeva Gosvāmī subsequently recited the entire *Bhāgavatam* to Mahārāja Parīkṣit in an assembly of learned saints on the bank of the Ganges at Hastināpura (now Delhi). Mahārāja Parīkṣit was the emperor of the world and was a great *rājarṣi* (saintly king). Having received a warning that he would die within a week, he renounced his entire kingdom and retired to the bank of the Ganges to fast until death and receive spiritual enlightenment. The *Bhāgavatam* begins with Emperor Parīkṣit's sober inquiry to Śukadeva Gosvāmī: "You are the spiritual master of great saints and devotees. I am therefore begging you to show the way of perfection for all persons, and especially for one who is about to die. Please let me know what a man should hear, chant, remember and worship, and also what he should not do. Please explain all this to me."

Śukadeva Gosvāmī's answer to this question, and numerous other questions posed by Mahārāja Parīkṣit, concerning everything from the nature of the self to the origin of the universe, held the assembled sages in rapt attention continuously for the seven days leading to the King's death. The sage Sūta Gosvāmī, who was present on the bank of the Ganges when Śukadeva Gosvāmī first recited *Śrīmad-Bhāgavatam*, later repeated the *Bhāgavatam* before a gathering of sages in the forest of Naimiṣāraṇya. Those sages, concerned about the spiritual welfare of the people in general, had gathered to perform a long, continuous chain of sacrifices to counteract the degrading influence of the incipient age of Kali. In response to the sages' request that he speak the essence of Vedic wisdom, Sūta Gosvāmī repeated from memory the entire eighteen thousand verses of *Śrīmad-Bhāgavatam*, as spoken by Śukadeva Gosvāmī to Mahārāja Parīkṣit.

The reader of *Śrīmad-Bhāgavatam* hears Sūta Gosvāmī relate the questions of Mahārāja Parīkṣit and the answers of Śukadeva Gosvāmī. Also, Sūta Gosvāmī sometimes responds directly to questions put by Śaunaka Ṛṣi, the spokesman for the sages gathered at Naimiṣāraṇya. One therefore simultaneously hears two dialogues: one between Mahārāja Parīkṣit and Śukadeva Gosvāmī on the bank of the Ganges, and another at Naimiṣāraṇya between Sūta Gosvāmī and the sages at Naimiṣāraṇya Forest, headed by Śaunaka Ṛṣi. Furthermore, while instructing King Parīkṣit, Śukadeva Gosvāmī often relates historical episodes and gives accounts of lengthy philosophical discussions between such great souls as the saint Maitreya and his disciple Vidura. With this understanding of the history of the *Bhāgavatam*, the reader will easily be able to follow its intermingling of dialogues and events from various sources. Since philosophical wisdom, not chronological order, is most important in the text, one need only be attentive to the subject matter of *Śrīmad-Bhāgavatam* to appreciate fully its profound message.

The translator of this edition compares the *Bhāgavatam* to sugar candy—wherever you taste it, you will find it equally sweet and relishable. Therefore, to taste the sweetness of the *Bhāgavatam*, one may begin by reading any of its volumes. After such an introductory taste, however, the serious reader is best advised to go back to Volume One of the First Canto and then proceed through the *Bhāgavatam*, volume after volume, in its natural order.

This edition of the *Bhāgavatam* is the first complete English translation of this important text with an elaborate commentary, and it is the first widely available to the English-speaking public. It is the product of the scholarly and devotional effort of His Divine Grace A. C. Bhaktivedanta Swami Prabhupāda, the world's most distinguished teacher of Indian religious and philosophical thought. His consummate Sanskrit scholarship and intimate familiarity with Vedic culture and thought as well as the modern way of life combine to reveal to the West a magnificent exposition of this important classic.

Readers will find this work of value for many reasons. For those interested in the classical roots of Indian civilization, it serves as a vast reservoir of detailed information on virtually every one of its aspects. For students of comparative philosophy and religion, the *Bhāgavatam* offers a penetrating view into the meaning of India's profound spiritual heritage. To sociologists and anthropologists, the *Bhāgavatam* reveals the practical workings of a peaceful and scientifically organized Vedic culture, whose institutions were integrated on the basis of a highly developed spiritual world-view. Students of literature will discover the *Bhāgavatam* to be a masterpiece of majestic poetry. For students of psychology, the text provides important perspectives on the nature of consciousness, human behavior and the philosophical study of identity. Finally, to those seeking spiritual insight, the *Bhāgavatam* offers simple and practical guidance for attainment of the highest self-knowledge and realization of the Absolute Truth. The entire multivolume text, presented by the Bhaktivedanta Book Trust, promises to occupy a significant place in the intellectual, cultural and spiritual life of modern man for a long time to come.

—The Publishers

His Divine Grace
A. C. Bhaktivedanta Swami Prabhupāda
Founder-Ācārya of the International Society for Krishna Consciousness

PLATE ONE

After Atri Muni had married Anasūyā, Lord Brahmā ordered him to create generations of progeny. Thus Atri Muni and his wife went to perform severe austerities in the valley of Mount Ṛkṣa. There the great sage concentrated his mind by practicing the yogic breathing exercises. Completely controlling his senses, for one hundred years he remained standing on only one leg, eating nothing but air. While performing these severe austerities, Atri Muni prayed within his mind, "May the Lord of the universe, of whom I have taken shelter, kindly offer me a son exactly like Him." Eventually, Atri Muni's breathing exercise caused a blazing fire to emanate from his head, and that fire was seen by Lord Brahmā, Lord Viṣṇu and Lord Śiva, the three principal deities of the universe. They approached the muni's hermitage, accompanied by the denizens of the heavenly planets. As soon as he saw Brahmā, Viṣṇu and Śiva, Atri was extremely pleased, and he approached them on one leg despite great difficulty. (*pp. 17–22*)

PLATE TWO

Millions of years ago, soon after the creation of the universe, the expert progenitor Dakṣa and his wife Mūrti had Śrī Nara-Nārāyaṇa Ṛṣi as their son. Śrī Nara-Nārāyaṇa Ṛṣi is a partial expansion of Lord Kṛṣṇa, and on the occasion of His appearance the entire world became filled with joy. Everyone's mind became tranquil, and thus in all directions the air, the rivers and the mountains became pleasant. In the heavenly planets bands began to play, the Gandharvas and Kinnaras sang, beautiful damsels danced, and many demigods showered flowers upon the sacred scene below. On earth the pacified sages chanted Vedic prayers, and all signs of good fortune appeared. Then Lord Brahmā led the other demigods in prayer: "Let that Supreme Personality of Godhead Nara-Nārāyaṇa Ṛṣi, who has created peace and prosperity to destroy the calamities of this world, kindly bestow His glance upon us demigods. His merciful glance defeats the beauty of the spotless lotus flower, which is the home of the goddess of fortune." (*pp. 41–44*)

PLATE THREE

Lord Śiva's wife Satī was the daughter of the powerful progenitor Dakṣa. One day, hearing of a great, festive sacrifice to be held at her father's house, Satī asked Śiva to let her attend, though she had not been invited. Śiva reminded her that Dakṣa had recently offended him very severely: "O most worshipful Satī, although I am innocent, out of envy your father has insulted me with cruel words. Therefore it is clear that you will not be honored at his house because you are my wife. Rather, you will be so offended that you will regret your connection with me. It is said that if one is hurt by an enemy's arrows, he is not as aggrieved as when he is cut by a relative's unkind words. Such grief continues to rend his heart day and night. Thus I forbid you to see your father. If you go to your father's house despite my instructions, the future will not be good for you. And the insult from your relatives will be equal to death." (*pp. 108–18*)

PLATE FOUR

Disregarding her husband Śiva's warning, Satī went to her father's house to attend the great sacrifice. Thousands of Lord Śiva's disciples—ghosts, ghouls and demons—accompanied her. When Satī reached the sacrificial arena, her mother and sisters received her well, but her father, Dakṣa, snubbed her. Then, seeing that the *brāhmaṇas* were offering no oblations to her husband, Satī became extremely angry and said to Dakṣa, "Lord Śiva is the most beloved of all living entities. He has no rival, and he behaves equally towards everyone. No one but you could be envious of such a universal being, who is free from all enmity. My dear father, you are committing the greatest offense by envying Lord Śiva, whose very name purifies one of all sin. Because you have blasphemed him, I shall no longer bear this unworthy body, which I have received from you." Having said this, Satī sat down on the floor and absorbed herself in mystic yoga. Then, meditating on the fiery elements and Lord Śiva's lotus feet, Satī caused her body to ignite and burn to ashes. (*pp. 121–55*)

PLATE FIVE

After Satī's death, Lord Śiva's disciples killed Dakṣa and destroyed the sacrificial arena. At that time all the priests, demigods and other members of the sacrificial assembly, being defeated and injured by Lord Śiva's soldiers, approached Lord Brahmā in great distress. They offered him obeisances and described the events that had transpired. In response, Lord Brahmā said, "You have excluded Lord Śiva from taking his share of the sacrificial oblations, and therefore you are all offenders at his lotus feet. Still, if you go to him, fall down at his lotus feet and surrender to him without reservation, he will be very pleased with you." Having thus instructed the members of Dakṣa's sacrificial assembly, Lord Brahmā led them to Kailāsa Hill, the abode of Lord Śiva. Kailāsa Hill is full of auspicious plants, flowers and trees, and it is sanctified by the presence of many great mystics and *yogīs*. Heavenly damsels sing and dance there, and peacocks, bees and cuckoos create a pleasing symphony. In the midst of this auspicious atmosphere, Lord Brahmā and the other demigods and sages saw an eight-hundred-mile-high banyan tree, and beneath that tree they saw Lord Śiva, sitting in meditation. Surrounded by exalted persons like Kuvera (the treasurer of heaven) and the four saintly Kumāras, Lord Śiva looked as grave as eternal time. (*pp. 185–211*)

PLATE SIX

King Uttānapāda's two wives were named Sunīti and Suruci, and their respective sons were named Dhruva and Uttama. One day the King placed Uttama on his lap and began fondly patting him. But when Dhruva tried to join his brother, the King did not welcome him. While Dhruva was trying to get on his father's lap, Suruci became angry at him and said very proudly, "My dear child, because you are not born from my womb, you do not deserve to sit on either the King's lap or his throne. If you at all desire to rise to the throne, you must undergo severe austerities to satisfy the Supreme Personality of Godhead, Nārāyaṇa. Then, when you have achieved His favor, you shall have to take your next birth from my womb." Having been struck by the strong words of his stepmother, Dhruva became enraged and began to breathe very heavily, just as a snake breathes very heavily when struck by a stick. And when Dhruva saw that his father was silent and did not protest Suruci's words, he immediately left the palace and went to his mother, Sunīti. (*pp. 317–21*)

PLATE SEVEN

When Dhruva left home to perform severe austerities, the great sage Nārada approached him out of compassion. At first Nārada tried to dissuade the small child from the difficult path he had chosen, but then, seeing Dhruva's strong determination, Nārada said, "My dear boy, I wish all good fortune to you. Your mother Sunīti's instruction to execute devotional service to God is actually just suitable for you. Therefore you should go to the virtuous forest named Madhuvana, and there, on the bank of the Yamunā River, practice eightfold mystic *yoga.* First you should bathe in the Yamunā. Then perform the necessary regulative principles for mystic *yoga* and sit down on your sitting place in a calm and quiet position. Next, practice the three kinds of breathing exercises, and thus gradually control the life air, the mind and the senses. Completely free yourself from all material contamination, and with great patience begin to meditate on the beautiful form of Lord Viṣṇu in your heart. While meditating on this form of the Lord, you should also chant the *mantra oṁ namo bhagavate vāsudevāya* and think of the transcendental activities the Lord performs in His various incarnations. Anyone who sincerely worships the Lord in this way receives His blessing." Dhruva then entered Madhuvana forest to execute devotional service. At this time the great sage Nārada thought it wise to go visit King Uttānapāda and encourage him, for Nārada knew that the King was deeply worried about his son Dhruva's safety. (*pp. 331–76*)

CHAPTER ONE

Genealogical Table of the Daughters of Manu

TEXT 1

मैत्रेय उवाच

मनोस्तु शतरूपायां तिस्रः कन्याश्च जज्ञिरे ।
आकूतिर्देवहूतिश्च प्रसूतिरिति विश्रुताः ॥ १ ॥

maitreya uvāca
manos tu śatarūpāyāṁ
tisraḥ kanyāś ca jajñire
ākūtir devahūtiś ca
prasūtir iti viśrutāḥ

maitreyaḥ uvāca—the great sage Maitreya said; *manoḥ tu*—of Svāyambhuva Manu; *śatarūpāyām*—in his wife Śatarūpā; *tisraḥ*—three; *kanyāḥ ca*—daughters also; *jajñire*—gave birth; *ākūtiḥ*—named Ākūti; *devahūtiḥ*—named Devahūti; *ca*—also; *prasūtiḥ*—named Prasūti; *iti*—thus; *viśrutāḥ*—well known.

TRANSLATION

Śrī Maitreya said: Svāyambhuva Manu begot three daughters in his wife Śatarūpā, and their names were Ākūti, Devahūti and Prasūti.

PURPORT

First of all let us offer our respectful obeisances unto our spiritual master, Oṁ Viṣṇupāda Śrī Śrīmad Bhaktisiddhānta Sarasvatī Gosvāmī Prabhupāda, by whose order I am engaged in this herculean task of writing commentary on the *Śrīmad-Bhāgavatam* as the Bhaktivedanta purports. By his grace we have finished three cantos already, and we are just trying to begin the Fourth Canto. By his divine grace let us offer our respectful obeisances unto Lord Caitanya, who began this Kṛṣṇa consciousness movement of *Bhāgavata-dharma* five hundred years ago, and through His grace let us offer our obeisances to the six Gosvāmīs, and then let us offer our obeisances to Rādhā and Kṛṣṇa, the spiritual couple who enjoy eternally in Vṛndāvana with Their cowherd boys and damsels in Vrajabhūmi. Let us also offer our respectful obeisances to all the devotees and eternal servitors of the Supreme Lord.

In this Fourth Canto of *Śrīmad-Bhāgavatam* there are thirty-one chapters, and all these chapters describe the secondary creation by Brahmā and the Manus. The Supreme Lord Himself does the real creation by agitating His material energy, and then, by His order, Brahmā, the first living creature in the universe, attempts to create the different planetary systems and their inhabitants, expanding the population through his progeny, like Manu and other progenitors of living entities, who work perpetually under the order of the Supreme Lord. In the First Chapter of this Fourth Canto there are descriptions of the three daughters of Svāyambhuva Manu and their descendants. The next six chapters describe the sacrifice performed by King Dakṣa and how it was spoiled. Thereafter the activities of Mahārāja Dhruva are described in five chapters. Then, in eleven chapters, the activities of King Pṛthu are described, and the next eight chapters are devoted to the activities of the Pracetā kings.

As described in the first verse of this chapter, Svāyambhuva Manu had three daughters, named Ākūti, Devahūti and Prasūti. Of these three daughters, one daughter, Devahūti, has already been described, along with her husband, Kardama Muni, and her son, Kapila Muni. In this chapter the descendants of the first daughter, Ākūti, will specifically be described. Svāyambhuva Manu was the son of Brahmā. Brahmā had many other sons, but Manu's name is specifically mentioned first because he was a great devotee of the Lord. In this verse there is also the word *ca*, indicating that besides the three daughters mentioned, Svāyambhuva Manu also had two sons.

TEXT 2

आकूतिं रुचये प्रादादपि भ्रातृमतीं नृपः ।
पुत्रिकाधर्ममाश्रित्य शतरूपानुमोदितः ॥ २ ॥

ākūtiṁ rucaye prādād
api bhrātṛmatīṁ nṛpaḥ
putrikā-dharmam āśritya
śatarūpānumoditaḥ

ākūtim—Ākūti; *rucaye*—unto the great sage Ruci; *prādāt*—handed over; *api*—although; *bhrātṛ-matīm*—daughter having a brother; *nṛpaḥ*—the King; *putrikā*—get the resultant son; *dharmam*—religious rites; *āśritya*—taking shelter; *śatarūpā*—by the wife of Svāyambhuva Manu; *anumoditaḥ*—being sanctioned.

TRANSLATION

Ākūti had two brothers, but in spite of her brothers, King Svāyambhuva Manu handed her over to Prajāpati Ruci on the condition that the son born of her be returned to Manu as his son. This he did in consultation with his wife, Śatarūpā.

PURPORT

Sometimes a sonless person offers his daughter to a husband on the condition that his grandson be returned to him to be adopted as his son and inherit his property. This is called *putrikā-dharma*, which means that by execution of religious rituals one gets a son, although one is sonless by one's own wife. But here we see extraordinary behavior in Manu, for in spite of his having two sons, he handed over his first daughter to Prajāpati Ruci on the condition that the son born of his daughter be returned to him as his son. Śrīla Viśvanātha Cakravartī Ṭhākura comments in this connection that King Manu knew that the Supreme Personality of Godhead would take birth in the womb of Ākūti; therefore, in spite of having two sons, he wanted the particular son born of Ākūti because he was ambitious to have the Supreme Personality of Godhead appear as his son and grandson. Manu is the lawgiver of mankind, and since he personally executed the *putrikā-dharma*, we may accept that such a system may be adopted by mankind also. Thus, even though one has a son, if one wants to have a particular son from one's daughter, one may give one's daughter in charity on that condition. That is the opinion of Śrīla Jīva Gosvāmī.

TEXT 3

प्रजापतिः स भगवान् रुचिस्तस्यामजीजनत् ।
मिथुनं ब्रह्मवर्चस्वी परमेण समाधिना ॥ ३ ॥

prajāpatiḥ sa bhagavān
rucis tasyām ajījanat
mithunaṁ brahma-varcasvī
parameṇa samādhinā

prajāpatiḥ—one who is entrusted with begetting children; *saḥ*—he; *bhagavān*—the most opulent; *ruciḥ*—the great sage Ruci; *tasyām*—in her; *ajījanat*—gave birth; *mithunam*—couple; *brahma-varcasvī*—spiritually very much powerful; *parameṇa*—with great strength; *samādhinā*—in trance.

TRANSLATION

Ruci, who was very powerful in his brahminical qualifications and was appointed one of the progenitors of the living entities, begot one son and one daughter by his wife, Ākūti.

PURPORT

The word *brahma-varcasvī* is very significant. Ruci was a *brāhmaṇa*, and he executed the brahminical duties very rigidly. As stated in *Bhagavad-gītā*, the brahminical qualifications are control of the senses, control of the mind, cleanliness within and without, development of spiritual and material knowledge, simplicity, truthfulness, faith in the Supreme Personality of Godhead, etc. There are many qualities which indicate a brahminical personality, and it is understood that Ruci followed all the brahminical principles rigidly. Therefore he is specifically mentioned as *brahma-varcasvī*. One who is born of a *brāhmaṇa* father but does not act as a *brāhmaṇa* is called, in Vedic language, a *brahma-bandhu*, and is calculated to be on the level of *śūdras* and women. Thus in the *Bhāgavatam* we find that *Mahābhārata* was specifically compiled by Vyāsadeva for *strī-śūdra-brahma-bandhu*. *Strī* means women, *śūdra* means the lower class of civilized human society, and *brahma-bandhu* means persons who are born in the families of *brāhmaṇas* but do not follow the rules and regulations carefully. All of these three classes are called less intelligent; they have no access to the study of the *Vedas*, which are specifically meant for persons who have acquired the brahminical qualifications. This restriction is based not upon any sectarian distinction but upon qualification. The Vedic literatures cannot be understood unless one has developed the brahminical qualifications. It is regrettable, therefore, that persons who have no brahminical qualifications and have never been trained under a bona fide spiritual master nevertheless comment on Vedic literatures like the *Śrīmad-Bhāgavatam* and other *Purāṇas*, for such persons cannot deliver their real message. Ruci was considered a first-class *brāhmaṇa;* therefore he is mentioned here as *brahma-varcasvī*, one who had full prowess in brahminical strength.

TEXT 4

यस्तयोः पुरुषः साक्षाद्विष्णुर्यज्ञस्वरूपधृक् ।
या स्त्री सा दक्षिणा भूतेरंशभूतानपायिनी ॥ ४ ॥

yas tayoḥ puruṣaḥ sākṣād
viṣṇur yajña-svarūpa-dhṛk
yā strī sā dakṣiṇā bhūter
aṁśa-bhūtānapāyinī

yaḥ—one who; *tayoḥ*—out of them; *puruṣaḥ*—male; *sākṣāt*—directly; *viṣṇuḥ*—the Supreme Lord; *yajña*—Yajña; *svarūpa-dhṛk*—accepting the form; *yā*—the other; *strī*—female; *sā*—she; *dakṣiṇā*—Dakṣiṇā; *bhūteḥ*—of the goddess of fortune; *aṁśa-bhūtā*—being a plenary expansion; *anapāyinī*—never to be separated.

TRANSLATION

Of the two children born of Ākūti, the male child was directly an incarnation of the Supreme Personality of Godhead, and His name was Yajña, which is another name of Lord Viṣṇu. The female child was a partial incarnation of Lakṣmī, the goddess of fortune, the eternal consort of Lord Viṣṇu.

PURPORT

Lakṣmī, the goddess of fortune, is the eternal consort of Lord Viṣṇu. Here it is stated that both the Lord and Lakṣmī, who are eternal consorts, appeared from Ākūti simultaneously. Both the Lord and His consort are beyond this material creation, as confirmed by many authorities (*nārāyaṇaḥ paro 'vyaktāt*); therefore their eternal relationship cannot be changed, and Yajña, the boy born of Ākūti, later married the goddess of fortune.

TEXT 5

आनिन्ये स्वगृहं पुत्र्याः पुत्रं विततरोचिषम् ।
स्वायम्भुवो मुदा युक्तो रुचिर्जग्राह दक्षिणाम् ॥ ५ ॥

āninye sva-gṛhaṁ putryāḥ
putraṁ vitata-rociṣam
svāyambhuvo mudā yukto
rucir jagrāha dakṣiṇām

āninye—brought to; *sva-gṛham*—home; *putryāḥ*—born of the daughter; *putram*—the son; *vitata-rociṣam*—very powerful; *svāyambhuvaḥ*—the Manu named Svāyambhuva; *mudā*—being very pleased; *yuktaḥ*—with; *ruciḥ*—the great sage Ruci; *jagrāha*—kept; *dakṣiṇām*—the daughter named Dakṣiṇā.

TRANSLATION

Svāyambhuva Manu very gladly brought home the beautiful boy named Yajña, and Ruci, his son-in-law, kept with him the daughter, Dakṣiṇā.

PURPORT

Svāyambhuva Manu was very glad to see that his daughter Ākūti had given birth to both a boy and girl. He was afraid that he would take one son and that because of this his son-in-law Ruci might be sorry. Thus when he heard that a daughter was born along with the boy, he was very glad. Ruci, according to his promise, returned his male child to

Svāyambhuva Manu and decided to keep the daughter, whose name was Dakṣiṇā. One of Lord Viṣṇu's names is Yajña because He is the master of the *Vedas.* The name Yajña comes from *yajuṣāṁ patiḥ*, which means "Lord of all sacrifices." In the *Yajur Veda* there are different ritualistic prescriptions for performing *yajñas*, and the beneficiary of all such *yajñas* is the Supreme Lord, Viṣṇu. Therefore it is stated in *Bhagavad-gītā* (3.9), *yajñārthāt karmaṇaḥ:* one should act, but one should perform one's prescribed duties only for the sake of Yajña, or Viṣṇu. If one does not act for the satisfaction of the Supreme Personality of Godhead, or if one does not perform devotional service, then there will be reactions to all one's activities. It does not matter if the reaction is good or bad; if our activities are not dovetailed with the desire of the Supreme Lord, or if we do not act in Kṛṣṇa consciousness, then we shall be responsible for the results of all our activities. There is always a reaction to every kind of action, but if actions are performed for Yajña, there is no reaction. Thus if one acts for Yajña, or the Supreme Personality of Godhead, one is not entangled in the material condition, for it is mentioned in the *Vedas* and also in *Bhagavad-gītā* that the *Vedas* and the Vedic rituals are all meant for understanding the Supreme Personality of Godhead, Kṛṣṇa. From the very beginning one should try to act in Kṛṣṇa consciousness; that will free one from the reactions of material activities.

TEXT 6

तां कामयानां भगवानुवाह यजुषां पतिः ।
तुष्टायां तोषमापन्नोऽजनयद् द्वादशात्मजान् ॥ ६ ॥

tāṁ kāmayānāṁ bhagavān
uvāha yajuṣāṁ patiḥ
tuṣṭāyāṁ toṣam āpanno
'janayad dvādaśātmajān

tām—her; *kāmayānām*—desiring; *bhagavān*—the Lord; *uvāha*—married; *yajuṣām*—of all sacrifices; *patiḥ*—master; *tuṣṭāyām*—in His wife, who was very much pleased; *toṣam*—great pleasure; *āpannaḥ*—having obtained; *ajanayat*—gave birth; *dvādaśa*—twelve; *ātmajān*—sons.

TRANSLATION

The Lord of the ritualistic performance of yajña later married Dakṣiṇā, who was anxious to have the Personality of Godhead as her husband, and in this wife the Lord was also very much pleased to beget twelve children.

PURPORT

An ideal husband and wife are generally called Lakṣmī-Nārāyaṇa to compare them to the Lord and the goddess of fortune, for it is significant that Lakṣmī-Nārāyaṇa are forever happy as husband and wife. A wife should always remain satisfied with her husband, and a husband should always remain satisfied with his wife. In the *Cāṇakya-śloka*, the moral instructions of Cāṇakya Paṇḍita, it is said that if a husband and wife are always satisfied with one another, then the goddess of fortune automatically comes. In other words, where there is no disagreement between husband and wife, all material opulence is present, and good children are born. Generally, according to Vedic civilization, the wife is trained to be satisfied in all conditions, and the husband, according to Vedic instruction, is required to please the wife with sufficient food, ornaments and clothing. Then, if they are satisfied with their mutual dealings, good children are born. In this way the entire world can become peaceful, but unfortunately in this age of Kali there are no ideal husbands and wives; therefore unwanted children are produced, and there is no peace and prosperity in the present-day world.

TEXT 7

तोषः प्रतोषः संतोषो भद्रः शान्तिरिडस्पतिः ।
इध्मः कविर्विभुः स्वह्नः सुदेवो रोचनो द्विषट् ॥ ७ ॥

toṣaḥ pratoṣaḥ santoṣo
bhadraḥ śāntir iḍaspatiḥ
idhmaḥ kavir vibhuḥ svahnaḥ
sudevo rocano dvi-ṣaṭ

toṣaḥ—Toṣa; *pratoṣaḥ*—Pratoṣa; *santoṣaḥ*—Santoṣa; *bhadraḥ*—Bhadra; *śāntiḥ*—Śānti; *iḍaspatiḥ*—Iḍaspati; *idhmaḥ*—Idhma; *kaviḥ*—

Kavi; *vibhuḥ*—Vibhu; *svahnaḥ*—Svahna; *sudevaḥ*—Sudeva; *roca-naḥ*—Rocana; *dvi-ṣaṭ*—twelve.

TRANSLATION

The twelve boys born of Yajña and Dakṣiṇā were named Toṣa, Pratoṣa, Santoṣa, Bhadra, Śānti, Iḍaspati, Idhma, Kavi, Vibhu, Svahna, Sudeva and Rocana.

TEXT 8

तुषिता नाम ते देवा आसन् स्वायम्भुवान्तरे ।
मरीचिमिश्रा ऋषयो यज्ञः सुरगणेश्वरः ॥ ८ ॥

tuṣitā nāma te devā
āsan svāyambhuvāntare
marīci-miśrā ṛṣayo
yajñaḥ sura-gaṇeśvaraḥ

tuṣitāḥ—the category of the Tuṣitas; *nāma*—of the name; *te*—all of them; *devāḥ*—demigods; *āsan*—became; *svāyambhuva*—the name of the Manu; *antare*—at that period; *marīci-miśrāḥ*—headed by Marīci; *ṛṣayaḥ*—great sages; *yajñaḥ*—the incarnation of Lord Viṣṇu; *sura-gaṇa-īśvaraḥ*—the king of the demigods.

TRANSLATION

During the time of Svāyambhuva Manu, these sons all became the demigods collectively named the Tuṣitas. Marīci became the head of the seven ṛṣis, and Yajña became the king of the demigods, Indra.

PURPORT

During the life of Svāyambhuva Manu, six kinds of living entities were generated from the demigods known as the Tuṣitas, from the sages headed by Marīci, and from descendants of Yajña, king of the demigods, and all of them expanded their progeny to observe the order of the Lord to fill the universe with living entities. These six kinds of living entities are known as *manus, devas, manu-putras, aṁśāvatāras, sureśvaras* and *ṛṣis*. Yajña, being the incarnation of the Supreme Personality of Godhead, became the leader of the demigods, Indra.

TEXT 9

प्रियव्रतोत्तानपादौ मनुपुत्रौ महौजसौ ।
तत्पुत्रपौत्रनप्तॄणामनुवृत्तं तदन्तरम् ॥ ९ ॥

priyavratottānapādau
manu-putrau mahaujasau
tat-putra-pautra-naptṝṇām
anuvṛttaṁ tad-antaram

priyavrata—Priyavrata; *uttānapādau*—Uttānapāda; *manu-putrau*—sons of Manu; *mahā-ojasau*—very great, powerful; *tat*—their; *putra*—sons; *pautra*—grandsons; *naptṝṇām*—grandsons from the daughter; *anuvṛttam*—following; *tat-antaram*—in that Manu's period.

TRANSLATION

Svāyambhuva Manu's two sons, Priyavrata and Uttānapāda, became very powerful kings, and their sons and grandsons spread all over the three worlds during that period.

TEXT 10

देवहूतिमदात्तात कर्दमायात्मजां मनुः ।
तत्सम्बन्धि श्रुतप्रायं भवता गदतो मम ॥१०॥

devahūtim adāt tāta
kardamāyātmajāṁ manuḥ
tat-sambandhi śruta-prāyaṁ
bhavatā gadato mama

devahūtim—Devahūti; *adāt*—handed over; *tāta*—my dear son; *kardamāya*—unto the great sage Kardama; *ātmajām*—daughter; *manuḥ*—Lord Svāyambhuva Manu; *tat-sambandhi*—in that connection; *śruta-*

prāyam—heard almost in full; *bhavatā*—by you; *gadataḥ*—spoken; *mama*—by me.

TRANSLATION

My dear son, Svāyambhuva Manu handed over his very dear daughter Devahūti to Kardama Muni. I have already spoken to you about them, and you have heard about them almost in full.

TEXT 11

दक्षाय ब्रह्मपुत्राय प्रसूतिं भगवान्मनुः ।
प्रायच्छद्यत्कृतः सर्गस्त्रिलोक्यां विततो महान् ॥११॥

dakṣāya brahma-putrāya
prasūtiṁ bhagavān manuḥ
prāyacchad yat-kṛtaḥ sargas
tri-lokyāṁ vitato mahān

dakṣāya—unto Prajāpati Dakṣa; *brahma-putrāya*—the son of Lord Brahmā; *prasūtim*—Prasūti; *bhagavān*—the great personality; *manuḥ*—Svāyambhuva Manu; *prāyacchat*—handed over; *yat-kṛtaḥ*—done by whom; *sargaḥ*—creation; *tri-lokyām*—in the three worlds; *vitataḥ*—expanded; *mahān*—greatly.

TRANSLATION

Svāyambhuva Manu handed over his daughter Prasūti to the son of Brahmā named Dakṣa, who was also one of the progenitors of the living entities. The descendants of Dakṣa are spread throughout the three worlds.

TEXT 12

याः कर्दमसुताः प्रोक्ता नव ब्रह्मर्षिपत्नयः ।
तासां प्रसूतिप्रसवं प्रोच्यमानं निबोध मे ॥१२॥

yāḥ kardama-sutāḥ proktā
nava brahmarṣi-patnayaḥ

tāsāṁ prasūti-prasavaṁ
procyamānaṁ nibodha me

yāḥ—those who; *kardama-sutāḥ*—the daughters of Kardama; *proktāḥ*—were mentioned; *nava*—nine; *brahma-ṛṣi*—great sages of spiritual knowledge; *patnayaḥ*—wives; *tāsām*—their; *prasūti-prasavam*—generations of sons and grandsons; *procyamānam*—describing; *nibodha*—try to understand; *me*—from me.

TRANSLATION

You have already been informed about the nine daughters of Kardama Muni, who were handed over to nine different sages. I shall now describe the descendants of those nine daughters. Please hear from me.

PURPORT

The Third Canto has already described how Kardama Muni begot nine daughters in Devahūti and how all the daughters were later handed over to great sages like Marīci, Atri and Vasiṣṭha.

TEXT 13

पत्नी मरीचेस्तु कला सुषुवे कर्दमात्मजा ।
कश्यपं पूर्णिमानं च ययोरापूरितं जगत् ॥१३॥

patnī marīces tu kalā
suṣuve kardamātmajā
kaśyapaṁ pūrṇimānaṁ ca
yayor āpūritaṁ jagat

patnī—wife; *marīceḥ*—of the sage named Marīci; *tu*—also; *kalā*—named Kalā; *suṣuve*—gave birth; *kardama-ātmajā*—daughter of Kardama Muni; *kaśyapam*—of the name Kaśyapa; *pūrṇimānam ca*—and of the name Pūrṇimā; *yayoḥ*—by whom; *āpūritam*—spread all over; *jagat*—the world.

TRANSLATION

Kardama Muni's daughter Kalā, who was married to Marīci, gave birth to two children, whose names were Kaśyapa and Pūrṇimā. Their descendants are spread all over the world.

TEXT 14

पूर्णिमासूत विरजं विश्वगं च परंतप ।
देवकुल्यां हरेः पादशौचाद्याभूत्सरिद्दिवः ॥१४॥

pūrṇimāsūta virajaṁ
viśvagaṁ ca parantapa
devakulyāṁ hareḥ pāda-
śaucād yābhūt sarid divaḥ

pūrṇimā—Pūrṇimā; *asūta*—begot; *virajam*—a son named Viraja; *viśvagam ca*—and named Viśvaga; *param-tapa*—O annihilator of enemies; *devakulyām*—a daughter named Devakulyā; *hareḥ*—of the Supreme Personality of Godhead; *pāda-śaucāt*—by the water which washed His lotus feet; *yā*—she; *abhūt*—became; *sarit divaḥ*—the transcendental water within the banks of the Ganges.

TRANSLATION

My dear Vidura, of the two sons, Kaśyapa and Pūrṇimā, Pūrṇimā begot three children, namely Viraja, Viśvaga and Devakulyā. Of these three, Devakulyā was the water which washed the lotus feet of the Personality of Godhead and which later on transformed into the Ganges of the heavenly planets.

PURPORT

Of the two sons Kaśyapa and Pūrṇimā, herein Pūrṇimā's descendants are described. An elaborate description of these descendants will be given in the Sixth Canto. It is also understood herein that Devakulyā is the presiding deity of the River Ganges, which comes down from the heavenly planets to this planet and is accepted to be sanctified because it touched the lotus feet of the Supreme Personality of Godhead, Hari.

TEXT 15

अत्रेः पत्न्यनसूया त्रीञ्जज्ञे सुयशसः सुतान् ।
दत्तं दुर्वाससं सोममात्मेशब्रह्मसम्भवान् ॥१५॥

atreḥ patny anasūyā trīñ
jajñe suyaśasaḥ sutān
dattaṁ durvāsasaṁ somam
ātmeśa-brahma-sambhavān

atreḥ—of Atri Muni; *patnī*—wife; *anasūyā*—named Anasūyā; *trīn*—three; *jajñe*—bore; *su-yaśasaḥ*—very famous; *sutān*—sons; *dattam*—Dattātreya; *durvāsasam*—Durvāsā; *somam*—Soma (the moon-god); *ātma*—the Supersoul; *īśa*—Lord Śiva; *brahma*—Lord Brahmā; *sambhavān*—incarnations of.

TRANSLATION

Anasūyā, the wife of Atri Muni, gave birth to three very famous sons—Soma, Dattātreya and Durvāsā—who were partial representations of Lord Viṣṇu, Lord Śiva and Lord Brahmā. Soma was a partial representation of Lord Brahmā, Dattātreya was a partial representation of Lord Viṣṇu, and Durvāsā was a partial representation of Lord Śiva.

PURPORT

In this verse we find the words *ātma-īśa-brahma-sambhavān*. *Ātma* means the Supersoul, or Viṣṇu, *īśa* means Lord Śiva, and *brahma* means the four-headed Lord Brahmā. The three sons born of Anasūyā—Dattātreya, Durvāsā and Soma—were born as partial representations of these three demigods. *Ātma* is not in the category of the demigods or living entities because He is Viṣṇu; therefore He is described as *vibhinnāṁśa-bhūtānām*. The Supersoul, Viṣṇu, is the seed-giving father of all living entities, including Brahmā and Lord Śiva. Another meaning of the word *ātma* may be accepted in this way: the principle who is the Supersoul in every *ātmā*, or, one may say, the soul of everyone, became manifested as Dattātreya, because the word *aṁśa*, part and parcel, is used here.

In *Bhagavad-gītā* the individual souls are also described as parts of the Supreme Personality of Godhead, or Supersoul, so why not accept that Dattātreya was one of those parts? Lord Śiva and Lord Brahmā are also described here as parts, so why not accept all of them as ordinary individual souls? The answer is that the manifestations of Viṣṇu and those of the ordinary living entities are certainly all parts and parcels of the Supreme Lord, and no one is equal to Him, but among the parts and parcels there are different categories. In the *Varāha Purāṇa* it is nicely explained that some of the parts are *svāṁśa* and some are *vibhinnāṁśa. Vibhinnāṁśa* parts are called *jīvas*, and *svāṁśa* parts are in the Viṣṇu category. In the *jīva* category, the *vibhinnāṁśa* parts and parcels, there are also gradations. That is explained in the *Viṣṇu Purāṇa*, where it is clearly stated that the individual parts and parcels of the Supreme Lord are subject to being covered by the external energy, called illusion, or *māyā*. Such individual parts and parcels, who can travel to any part of the Lord's creation, are called *sarva-gata* and are suffering the pangs of material existence. They are proportionately freed from the coverings of ignorance under material existence according to different levels of work and under different influences of the modes of material nature. For example, the sufferings of *jīvas* situated in the mode of goodness are less than those of *jīvas* situated in the mode of ignorance. Pure Kṛṣṇa consciousness, however, is the birthright of all living entities because every living entity is part and parcel of the Supreme Lord. The consciousness of the Lord is also in the part and parcel, and according to the proportion to which that consciousness is cleared of material dirt, the living entities are differently situated. In the *Vedānta-sūtra*, the living entities of different gradations are compared to candles or lamps with different candle power. For example, some electric bulbs have the power of one thousand candles, some have the power of five hundred candles, some the power of one hundred candles, some fifty candles, etc., but all electric bulbs have light. Light is present in every bulb, but the gradations of light are different. Similarly, there are gradations of Brahman. The Viṣṇu *svāṁśa* expansions of the Supreme Lord in different Viṣṇu forms are like lamps, Lord Śiva is also like a lamp, and the supreme candle power, or the one-hundred-percent light, is Kṛṣṇa. The *viṣṇu-tattva* has ninety-four percent, the *śiva-tattva* has eighty-four percent, Lord Brahmā has seventy-eight percent, and the living entities are also like Brahmā, but in the conditioned state their power is still more dim. There are gradations of Brahman, and no one can deny this fact. Therefore the words *ātmeśa-brahma-sambhavān* indicate that Dattātreya was directly part and parcel of Viṣṇu, whereas Durvāsā and Soma were parts and parcels of Lord Śiva and Lord Brahmā.

TEXT 16

विदुर उवाच
अत्रेर्गृहे सुरश्रेष्ठाः स्थित्युत्पत्त्यन्तहेतवः ।
किञ्चिच्चिकीर्षवो जाता एतदाख्याहि मे गुरो ॥१६॥

vidura uvāca
atrer gṛhe sura-śreṣṭhāḥ
sthity-utpatty-anta-hetavaḥ
kiñcic cikīrṣavo jātā
etad ākhyāhi me guro

viduraḥ uvāca—Śrī Vidura said; *atreḥ gṛhe*—in the house of Atri; *sura-śreṣṭhāḥ*—chief demigods; *sthiti*—maintenance; *utpatti*—creation; *anta*—destruction; *hetavaḥ*—causes; *kiñcit*—something; *cikīrṣavaḥ*—desiring to do; *jātāḥ*—appeared; *etat*—this; *ākhyāhi*—tell; *me*—to me; *guro*—my dear spiritual master.

TRANSLATION

After hearing this, Vidura inquired from Maitreya: My dear master, how is it that the three deities Brahmā, Viṣṇu and Śiva, who are the creator, maintainer and destroyer of the whole creation, became the offspring of the wife of Atri Muni?

PURPORT

The inquisitiveness of Vidura was quite fitting, for he understood that when the Supersoul, Lord Brahmā and Lord Śiva all appeared through the person of Anasūyā, the wife of Atri Muni, there must have been some great purpose. Otherwise why should they have appeared in such a way?

TEXT 17

मैत्रेय उवाच
ब्रह्मणा चोदितः सृष्टावत्रिर्ब्रह्मविदां वरः ।
सह पत्न्या ययावृक्षं कुलाद्रिं तपसि स्थितः ॥१७॥

maitreya uvāca
brahmaṇā coditaḥ sṛṣṭāv
atrir brahma-vidāṁ varaḥ
saha patnyā yayāv ṛkṣaṁ
kulādriṁ tapasi sthitaḥ

maitreyaḥ uvāca—Śrī Maitreya Ṛṣi said; *brahmaṇā*—by Lord Brahmā; *coditaḥ*—being inspired; *sṛṣṭau*—for creation; *atriḥ*—Atri; *brahma-vidām*—of the persons learned in spiritual knowledge; *varaḥ*—the chief; *saha*—with; *patnyā*—wife; *yayau*—went; *ṛkṣam*—to the mountain named Ṛkṣa; *kula-adrim*—great mountain; *tapasi*—for austerities; *sthitaḥ*—remained.

TRANSLATION

Maitreya said: When Lord Brahmā ordered Atri Muni to create generations after marrying Anasūyā, Atri Muni and his wife went to perform severe austerities in the valley of the mountain known as Ṛkṣa.

TEXT 18

तस्मिन् प्रसूनस्तबकपलाशाशोककानने ।
वार्भिःस्रवद्भिरुद्घुष्टे निर्विन्ध्यायाः समन्ततः ॥१८॥

tasmin prasūna-stabaka-
palāśāśoka-kānane
vārbhiḥ sravadbhir udghuṣṭe
nirvindhyāyāḥ samantataḥ

tasmin—in that; *prasūna-stabaka*—bunches of flowers; *palāśa*—*palāśa* trees; *aśoka*—*aśoka* trees; *kānane*—in the forest garden;

vārbhiḥ—by the waters; *sravadbhiḥ*—flowing; *udghuṣṭe*—in sound; *nirvindhyāyāḥ*—of the River Nirvindhyā; *samantataḥ*—everywhere.

TRANSLATION

In that mountain valley flows a river named Nirvindhyā. On the bank of the river are many aśoka trees and other plants full of palāśa flowers, and there is always the sweet sound of water flowing from a waterfall. The husband and wife reached that beautiful place.

TEXT 19

प्राणायामेन संयम्य मनो वर्षशतं मुनिः ।
अतिष्ठदेकपादेन निर्द्वन्द्वोऽनिलभोजनः ॥१९॥

prāṇāyāmena saṁyamya
mano varṣa-śataṁ muniḥ
atiṣṭhad eka-pādena
nirdvandvo 'nila-bhojanaḥ

prāṇāyāmena—by practice of the breathing exercise; *saṁyamya*—controlling; *manaḥ*—mind; *varṣa-śatam*—one hundred years; *muniḥ*—the great sage; *atiṣṭhat*—remained there; *eka-pādena*—standing on one leg; *nirdvandvaḥ*—without duality; *anila*—air; *bhojanaḥ*—eating.

TRANSLATION

There the great sage concentrated his mind by the yogic breathing exercises, and thereby controlling all attachment, he remained standing on one leg only, eating nothing but air, and stood there on one leg for one hundred years.

TEXT 20

शरणं तं प्रपद्येऽहं य एव जगदीश्वरः ।
प्रजामात्मसमां मह्यं प्रयच्छत्विति चिन्तयन् ॥२०॥

śaraṇaṁ taṁ prapadye 'haṁ
ya eva jagad-īśvaraḥ

prajām ātma-samāṁ mahyaṁ
prayacchatv iti cintayan

śaraṇam—taking shelter; *tam*—unto Him; *prapadye*—surrender; *aham*—I; *yaḥ*—one who; *eva*—certainly; *jagat-īśvaraḥ*—master of the universe; *prajām*—son; *ātma-samām*—like Himself; *mahyam*—unto me; *prayacchatu*—let Him give; *iti*—thus; *cintayan*—thinking.

TRANSLATION

He was thinking: May the Lord of the universe, of whom I have taken shelter, kindly be pleased to offer me a son exactly like Him.

PURPORT

It appears that the great sage Atri Muni had no specific idea of the Supreme Personality of Godhead. Of course, he must have been conversant with the Vedic information that there is a Supreme Personality of Godhead who is the creator of the universe, from whom everything emanated, who maintains this created manifestation, and in whom the entire manifestation is conserved after dissolution. *Yato vā imāni bhūtāni* (*Taittirīya Upaniṣad* 3.1.1). The Vedic *mantras* give us information of the Supreme Personality of Godhead, so Atri Muni concentrated his mind upon that Supreme Personality of Godhead, even without knowing His name, just to beg from Him a child exactly on His level. This kind of devotional service, in which knowledge of God's name is lacking, is also described in *Bhagavad-gītā* where the Lord says that four kinds of men with backgrounds of pious activities come to Him asking for what they need. Atri Muni wanted a son exactly like the Lord, and therefore he is not supposed to have been a pure devotee, because he had a desire to be fulfilled, and that desire was material. Although he wanted a son exactly like the Supreme Personality of Godhead, this desire was material because he did not want the Personality of Godhead Himself, but only a child exactly like Him. If he had desired the Supreme Personality of Godhead as his child, he would have been completely free of material desires because he would have wanted the Supreme Absolute Truth, but because he wanted a similar child, his desire was material. Thus Atri Muni cannot be counted among the pure devotees.

TEXT 21

तप्यमानं त्रिभुवनं प्राणायामैधसाग्निना ।
निर्गतेन मुनेर्मूर्ध्नः समीक्ष्य प्रभवस्त्रयः ॥२१॥

tapyamānaṁ tri-bhuvanaṁ
prāṇāyāmaidhasāgninā
nirgatena muner mūrdhnaḥ
samīkṣya prabhavas trayaḥ

tapyamānam—while practicing austerities; *tri-bhuvanam*—the three worlds; *prāṇāyāma*—practice by breathing exercise; *edhasā*—fuel; *agninā*—by the fire; *nirgatena*—issuing out; *muneḥ*—of the great sage; *mūrdhnaḥ*—the top of the head; *samīkṣya*—looking over; *prabhavaḥ trayaḥ*—the three great gods (Brahmā, Viṣṇu and Maheśvara).

TRANSLATION

While Atri Muni was engaged in these severe austerities, a blazing fire came out of his head by virtue of his breathing exercise, and that fire was seen by the three principal deities of the three worlds.

PURPORT

According to Śrīla Jīva Gosvāmī, the fire of *prāṇāyāma* is mental satisfaction. That fire was perceived by the Supersoul, Viṣṇu, and thereby Lord Brahmā and Śiva also perceived it. Atri Muni, by his breathing exercise, concentrated on the Supersoul, or the Lord of the universe. As confirmed in *Bhagavad-gītā*, the Lord of the universe is Vāsudeva (*vāsudevaḥ sarvam iti*), and, by the direction of Vāsudeva, Lord Brahmā and Lord Śiva work. Therefore, on the direction of Vāsudeva, both Lord Brahmā and Lord Śiva perceived the severe penance adopted by Atri Muni, and thus they were pleased to come down, as stated in the next verse.

TEXT 22

अप्सरोमुनिगन्धर्वसिद्धविद्याधरोरगैः ।
वितायमानयशसस्तदाश्रमपदं ययुः ॥२२॥

apsaro-muni-gandharva-
siddha-vidyādharoragaiḥ
vitāyamāna-yaśasas
tad-āśrama-padaṁ yayuḥ

apsaraḥ—heavenly society women; *muni*—great sages; *gandharva*—inhabitants of the Gandharva planet; *siddha*—of Siddhaloka; *vidyādhara*—other demigods; *uragaiḥ*—the inhabitants of Nāgaloka; *vitāyamāna*—being spread; *yaśasaḥ*—fame, reputation; *tat*—his; *āśrama-padam*—hermitage; *yayuḥ*—went.

TRANSLATION

At that time, the three deities approached the hermitage of Atri Muni, accompanied by the denizens of the heavenly planets, such as the celestial beauties, the Gandharvas, the Siddhas, the Vidyādharas and the Nāgas. Thus they entered the āśrama of the great sage, who had become famous by his austerities.

PURPORT

It is advised in the Vedic literatures that one should take shelter of the Supreme Personality of Godhead, who is the Lord of the universe and the master of creation, maintenance and dissolution. He is known as the Supersoul, and when one worships the Supersoul, all other deities, such as Brahmā and Śiva, appear with Lord Viṣṇu because they are directed by the Supersoul.

TEXT 23

तत्प्रादुर्भावसंयोगविद्योतितमना मुनिः ।
उत्तिष्ठन्नेकपादेन ददर्श विबुधर्षभान् ॥२३॥

tat-prādurbhāva-saṁyoga-
vidyotita-manā muniḥ
uttiṣṭhann eka-pādena
dadarśa vibudharṣabhān

tat—their; *prādurbhāva*—appearance; *saṁyoga*—simultaneously; *vidyotita*—enlightened; *manāḥ*—in the mind; *muniḥ*—the great sage;

uttiṣṭhan—being awakened; *eka-pādena*—even on one leg; *dadarśa*—saw; *vibudha*—demigods; *ṛṣabhān*—the great personalities.

TRANSLATION

The sage was standing on one leg, but as soon as he saw that the three deities had appeared before him, he was so pleased to see them all together that despite great difficulty he approached them on one leg.

TEXT 24

प्रणम्य दण्डवद्भूमावुपतस्थेऽर्हणाञ्जलिः ।
वृषहंससुपर्णस्थान् स्वैः स्वैश्चिह्नैश्च चिह्नितान् ॥२४॥

praṇamya daṇḍavad bhūmāv
upatasthe 'rhaṇāñjaliḥ
vṛṣa-haṁsa-suparṇa-sthān
svaiḥ svaiś cihnaiś ca cihnitān

praṇamya—offering obeisances; *daṇḍa-vat*—like a rod; *bhūmau*—ground; *upatasthe*—fell down; *arhaṇa*—all paraphernalia for worship; *añjaliḥ*—folded hands; *vṛṣa*—bull; *haṁsa*—swan; *suparṇa*—the Garuḍa bird; *sthān*—situated; *svaiḥ*—own; *svaiḥ*—own; *cihnaiḥ*—by symbols; *ca*—and; *cihnitān*—being recognized.

TRANSLATION

Thereafter he began to offer prayers to the three deities, who were seated on different carriers—a bull, a swan and Garuḍa—and who held in their hands a drum, kuśa grass and a discus. The sage offered them his respects by falling down like a stick.

PURPORT

Daṇḍa means "a long rod," and *vat* means "like." Before a superior, one has to fall down on the ground just like a stick, and this sort of offering of respect is called *daṇḍavat.* Atri Ṛṣi offered his respect to the three deities in that way. They were identified by their different carriers and different symbolic representations. In that connection it is stated here that Lord Viṣṇu was sitting on Garuḍa, a big aquiline bird, and was carrying in His hand a disc, Brahmā was sitting on a swan and had in his hand *kuśa* grass, and Lord Śiva was sitting on a bull and carrying in his hand a small drum called a *ḍamaru.* Atri Ṛṣi recognized them by their symbolic representations and different carriers, and thus he offered them prayers and respects.

TEXT 25

कृपावलोकेन हसद्वदनेनोपलम्भितान् ।
तद्रोचिषा प्रतिहते निमील्य मुनिरक्षिणी ॥२५॥

kṛpāvalokena hasad-
vadanenopalambhitān
tad-rociṣā pratihate
nimīlya munir akṣiṇī

kṛpā-avalokena—glancing with mercy; *hasat*—smiling; *vadanena*—with faces; *upalambhitān*—appearing very much satisfied; *tat*—their; *rociṣā*—by the glaring effulgence; *pratihate*—being dazzled; *nimīlya*—closing; *muniḥ*—the sage; *akṣiṇī*—his eyes.

TRANSLATION

Atri Muni was greatly pleased to see that the three devas were gracious towards him. His eyes were dazzled by the effulgence of their bodies, and therefore he closed his eyes for the time being.

PURPORT

Since the deities were smiling, he could understand that they were pleased with him. Their glaring bodily effulgence was intolerable to his eyes, so he closed them for the time being.

TEXTS 26–27

चेतस्तत्प्रवणं युञ्जन्नस्तावीत्संहताञ्जलिः ।
श्लक्ष्णया सूक्तया वाचा सर्वलोकगरीयसः ॥२६॥

अत्रिरुवाच
विश्वोद्भवस्थितिलयेषु विभज्यमानै-
र्मायागुणैरनुयुगं विगृहीतदेहाः ।
ते ब्रह्मविष्णुगिरिशाः प्रणतोऽस्म्यहं व-
स्तेभ्यः क एव भवतां म इहोपहूतः ॥२७॥

cetas tat-pravaṇaṁ yuñjann
astāvīt saṁhatāñjaliḥ
ślakṣṇayā sūktayā vācā
sarva-loka-garīyasaḥ

atrir uvāca
viśvodbhava-sthiti-layeṣu vibhajyamānair
māyā-guṇair anuyugaṁ vigṛhīta-dehāḥ
te brahma-viṣṇu-giriśāḥ praṇato 'smy ahaṁ vas
tebhyaḥ ka eva bhavatāṁ ma ihopahūtaḥ

cetaḥ—heart; *tat-pravaṇam*—fixing on them; *yuñjan*—making; *astāvīt*—offered prayers; *saṁhata-añjaliḥ*—with folded hands; *ślakṣṇayā*—ecstatic; *sūktayā*—prayers; *vācā*—words; *sarva-loka*—all over the world; *garīyasaḥ*—honorable; *atriḥ uvāca*—Atri said; *viśva*—the universe; *udbhava*—creation; *sthiti*—maintenance; *layeṣu*—in destruction; *vibhajyamānaiḥ*—being divided; *māyā-guṇaiḥ*—by the external modes of nature; *anuyugam*—according to different millenniums; *vigṛhīta*—accepted; *dehāḥ*—bodies; *te*—they; *brahma*—Lord Brahmā; *viṣṇu*—Lord Viṣṇu; *giriśāḥ*—Lord Śiva; *praṇataḥ*—bowed; *asmi*—am; *aham*—I; *vaḥ*—unto you; *tebhyaḥ*—from them; *kaḥ*—who; *eva*—certainly; *bhavatām*—of you; *me*—by me; *iha*—here; *upahūtaḥ*—called for.

TRANSLATION

But since his heart was already attracted by the deities, somehow or other he gathered his senses, and with folded hands and sweet words he began to offer prayers to the predominating deities of the universe. The great sage Atri said: O Lord Brahmā, Lord Viṣṇu and Lord Śiva, you have divided yourself into three bodies by ac-

cepting the three modes of material nature, as you do in every millennium for the creation, maintenance and dissolution of the cosmic manifestation. I offer my respectful obeisances unto all of you and beg to inquire whom of you three I have called by my prayer.

PURPORT

Atri Ṛṣi called for the Supreme Personality of Godhead, *jagad-īśvara*, the Lord of the universe. The Lord must exist before the creation, otherwise how could He be its Lord? If someone constructs a big building, this indicates that he must have existed before the building was constructed. Therefore the Supreme Lord, the creator of the universe, must be transcendental to the material modes of nature. But it is known that Viṣṇu takes charge of the mode of goodness, Brahmā takes charge of the mode of passion, and Lord Śiva takes charge of the mode of ignorance. Therefore Atri Muni said, "That *jagad-īśvara*, the Lord of the universe, must be one of you, but since three of you have appeared, I cannot recognize whom I have called. You are all so kind. Please let me know who is actually *jagad-īśvara*, the Lord of the universe." In fact, Atri Ṛṣi was doubtful about the constitutional position of the Supreme Lord, Viṣṇu, but he was quite certain that the Lord of the universe cannot be one of the creatures created by *māyā*. His very inquiry about whom he had called indicates that he was in doubt about the constitutional position of the Lord. Therefore he prayed to all three, "Kindly let me know who is the transcendental Lord of the universe." He was certain, of course, that not all of them could be the Lord, but the Lord of the universe was one of the three.

TEXT 28

एको मयेह भगवान् विविधप्रधानै-
श्चित्तीकृतः प्रजननाय कथं नु यूयम् ।
अत्रागतास्तनुभृतां मनसोऽपि दूराद्
ब्रूत प्रसीदत महानिह विस्मयो मे ॥२८॥

eko mayeha bhagavān vividha-pradhānaiś
cittī-kṛtaḥ prajananāya kathaṁ nu yūyam

atrāgatās tanu-bhṛtāṁ manaso 'pi dūrād
brūta prasīdata mahān iha vismayo me

ekaḥ—one; *mayā*—by me; *iha*—here; *bhagavān*—great personality; *vividha*—various; *pradhānaiḥ*—by paraphernalia; *cittī-kṛtaḥ*—fixed in mind; *prajananāya*—for begetting a child; *katham*—why; *nu*—however; *yūyam*—all of you; *atra*—here; *āgatāḥ*—appeared; *tanu-bhṛtām*—of the embodied; *manasaḥ*—the minds; *api*—although; *dūrāt*—from far beyond; *brūta*—kindly explain; *prasīdata*—being merciful to me; *mahān*—very great; *iha*—this; *vismayaḥ*—doubt; *me*—of mine.

TRANSLATION

I called for the Supreme Personality of Godhead, desiring a son like Him, and I thought of Him only. But although He is far beyond the mental speculation of man, all three of you have come here. Kindly let me know how you have come, for I am greatly bewildered about this.

PURPORT

Atri Muni was confidently aware that the Supreme Personality of Godhead is the Lord of the universe, so he prayed for the one Supreme Lord. He was surprised, therefore, that three of them appeared.

TEXT 29

मैत्रेय उवाच
इति तस्य वचः श्रुत्वा त्रयस्ते विबुधर्षभाः ।
प्रत्याहुः श्लक्ष्णया वाचा प्रहस्य तमृषिं प्रभो ॥२९॥

maitreya uvāca
iti tasya vacaḥ śrutvā
trayas te vibudharṣabhāḥ
pratyāhuḥ ślakṣṇayā vācā
prahasya tam ṛṣiṁ prabho

maitreyaḥ uvāca—the sage Maitreya said; *iti*—thus; *tasya*—his; *vacaḥ*—words; *śrutvā*—after hearing; *trayaḥ te*—all three; *vibudha*—demigods; *ṛṣabhāḥ*—chiefs; *pratyāhuḥ*—replied; *ślakṣṇayā*—gentle; *vācā*—voices; *prahasya*—smiling; *tam*—unto him; *ṛṣim*—the great sage; *prabho*—O mighty one.

TRANSLATION

The great sage Maitreya continued: Upon hearing Atri Muni speak in that way, the three great deities smiled, and they replied in the following sweet words.

TEXT 30

देवा ऊचुः
यथा कृतस्ते सङ्कल्पो भाव्यं तेनैव नान्यथा ।
सत्सङ्कल्पस्य ते ब्रह्मन् यद्वै ध्यायति ते वयम् ॥३०॥

devā ūcuḥ
yathā kṛtas te saṅkalpo
bhāvyaṁ tenaiva nānyathā
sat-saṅkalpasya te brahman
yad vai dhyāyati te vayam

devāḥ ūcuḥ—the demigods replied; *yathā*—as; *kṛtaḥ*—done; *te*—by you; *saṅkalpaḥ*—determination; *bhāvyam*—to be done; *tena eva*—by that; *na anyathā*—not otherwise; *sat-saṅkalpasya*—one whose determination is never lost; *te*—of you; *brahman*—O dear *brāhmaṇa; yat*—that which; *vai*—certainly; *dhyāyati*—meditating; *te*—all of them; *vayam*—we are.

TRANSLATION

The three deities told Atri Muni: Dear brāhmaṇa, you are perfect in your determination, and therefore as you have decided, so it will happen; it will not happen otherwise. We are all the same person upon whom you were meditating, and therefore we have all come to you.

PURPORT

Atri Muni unspecifically thought of the Personality of Godhead, the Lord of the universe, although he had no clear idea of the Lord of the universe nor of His specific form. Mahā-Viṣṇu, from whose breathing millions of universes emanate and into whom they are again withdrawn, may be accepted as the Lord of the universe. Garbhodakaśāyī Viṣṇu, from whose abdomen sprouted the lotus flower which is the birthplace of Brahmā, may also be considered the Lord of the universe. Similarly, Kṣīrodakaśāyī Viṣṇu, who is the Supersoul of all living entities, may also be considered the Lord of the universe. Then, under the order of Kṣīrodakaśāyī Viṣṇu, the Viṣṇu form within this universe, Lord Brahmā and Lord Śiva may also be accepted as the Lords of the universe.

Viṣṇu is the Lord of the universe because He is its maintainer. Similarly, Brahmā creates the different planetary systems and the population, so he also may be considered the Lord of the universe. Or Lord Śiva, who is ultimately the destroyer of the universe, also may be considered its Lord. Therefore, since Atri Muni did not specifically mention whom he wanted, all three—Brahmā, Viṣṇu and Lord Śiva—came before him. They said, "Since you were thinking of having a son exactly like the Supreme Personality of Godhead, the Lord of the universe, your determination will be fulfilled." In other words, one's determination is fulfilled according to the strength of one's devotion. As stated in *Bhagavad-gītā* (9.25): *yānti deva-vratā devān pitṝn yānti pitṛ-vratāḥ*. If one is attached to a particular demigod, one is promoted to the abode of that demigod; if one is attached to the Pitās, or forefathers, one is promoted to their planet; and similarly if one is attached to the Supreme Personality of Godhead, Kṛṣṇa, one is promoted to the abode of Lord Kṛṣṇa. Atri Muni had no clear conception of the Lord of the universe; therefore the three presiding deities who are actually the lords of the universe in the three departments of the modes of nature all came before him. Now, according to the strength of his determination for a son, his desire would be fulfilled by the grace of the Lord.

TEXT 31

अथास्मदंशभूतास्ते आत्मजा लोकविश्रुताः ।
भवितारोऽङ्ग भद्रं ते विस्रप्स्यन्ति च ते यशः ॥३१॥

athāsmad-aṁśa-bhūtās te
ātmajā loka-viśrutāḥ
bhavitāro 'ṅga bhadraṁ te
visrapsyanti ca te yaśaḥ

atha—therefore; *asmat*—our; *aṁśa-bhūtāḥ*—plenary expansions; *te*—your; *ātmajāḥ*—sons; *loka-viśrutāḥ*—very famous in the world; *bhavitāraḥ*—in the future will be born; *aṅga*—dear great sage; *bhadram*—all good fortune; *te*—unto you; *visrapsyanti*—will spread; *ca*—also; *te*—your; *yaśaḥ*—reputation.

TRANSLATION

You will have sons who will represent a partial manifestation of our potency, and because we desire all good fortune for you, those sons will glorify your reputation throughout the world.

TEXT 32

एवं कामवरं दत्त्वा प्रतिजग्मुः सुरेश्वराः ।
सभाजितास्तयोः सम्यग्दम्पत्योर्मिषतोस्ततः ॥३२॥

evaṁ kāma-varaṁ dattvā
pratijagmuḥ sureśvarāḥ
sabhājitās tayoḥ samyag
dampatyor miṣatos tataḥ

evam—thus; *kāma-varam*—desired benediction; *dattvā*—offering; *pratijagmuḥ*—returned; *sura-īśvarāḥ*—the chief demigods; *sabhājitāḥ*—being worshiped; *tayoḥ*—while they; *samyak*—perfectly; *dampatyoḥ*—the husband and wife; *miṣatoḥ*—were looking on; *tataḥ*—from there.

TRANSLATION

Thus, while the couple looked on, the three deities Brahmā, Viṣṇu and Maheśvara disappeared from that place after bestowing upon Atri Muni the benediction.

TEXT 33

सोमोऽभूद्ब्रह्मणोंऽशेन दत्तो विष्णोस्तु योगवित् ।
दुर्वासाः शंकरस्यांशो निबोधाङ्गिरसः प्रजाः ॥३३॥

somo 'bhūd brahmaṇo 'ṁśena
datto viṣṇos tu yogavit
durvāsāḥ śaṅkarasyāṁśo
nibodhāṅgirasaḥ prajāḥ

somaḥ—the king of the moon planet; *abhūt*—appeared; *brahmaṇaḥ*—of Lord Brahmā; *aṁśena*—partial expansion; *dattaḥ*—Dattātreya; *viṣṇoḥ*—of Viṣṇu; *tu*—but; *yoga-vit*—very powerful *yogī; durvāsāḥ*—Durvāsā; *śaṅkarasya aṁśaḥ*—partial expansion of Lord Śiva; *nibodha*—just try to understand; *aṅgirasaḥ*—of the great sage Aṅgirā; *prajāḥ*—generations.

TRANSLATION

Thereafter, from the partial representation of Brahmā, the moon-god was born of them; from the partial representation of Viṣṇu, the great mystic Dattātreya was born; and from the partial representation of Śaṅkara [Lord Śiva], Durvāsā was born. Now you may hear from me of the many sons of Aṅgirā.

TEXT 34

श्रद्धा त्वङ्गिरसः पत्नी चतस्रोऽसूत कन्यकाः ।
सिनीवाली कुहू राका चतुर्थ्यनुमतिस्तथा ॥३४॥

śraddhā tv aṅgirasaḥ patnī
catasro 'sūta kanyakāḥ
sinīvālī kuhū rākā
caturthy anumatis tathā

śraddhā—Śraddhā; *tu*—but; *aṅgirasaḥ*—of Aṅgirā Ṛṣi; *patnī*—wife; *catasraḥ*—four; *asūta*—gave birth; *kanyakāḥ*—daughters; *sinīvālī*—Sinīvālī; *kuhūḥ*—Kuhū; *rākā*—Rākā; *caturthī*—the fourth one; *anumatiḥ*—Anumati; *tathā*—also.

TRANSLATION

Aṅgirā's wife, Śraddhā, gave birth to four daughters, named Sinīvālī, Kuhū, Rākā and Anumati.

TEXT 35

तत्पुत्रावपरावास्तां ख्यातौ स्वारोचिषेऽन्तरे ।
उतथ्यो भगवान् साक्षाद्ब्रह्मिष्ठश्च बृहस्पतिः ॥३५॥

tat-putrāv aparāv āstāṁ
khyātau svārociṣe 'ntare
utathyo bhagavān sākṣād
brahmiṣṭhaś ca bṛhaspatiḥ

tat—his; *putrau*—sons; *aparau*—others; *āstām*—were born; *khyātau*—very famous; *svārociṣe*—in the Svārociṣa millennium; *antare*—of the Manu; *utathyaḥ*—Utathya; *bhagavān*—very mighty; *sākṣāt*—directly; *brahmiṣṭhaḥ ca*—fully spiritually advanced; *bṛhaspatiḥ*—Bṛhaspati.

TRANSLATION

Besides these four daughters, she also had another two sons. One of them was known as Utathya, and the other was the learned scholar Bṛhaspati.

TEXT 36

पुलस्त्योऽजनयत्पत्न्यामगस्त्यं च हविर्भुवि ।
सोऽन्यजन्मनि दह्राग्निर्विश्रवाश्च महातपाः ॥३६॥

pulastyo 'janayat patnyām
agastyaṁ ca havirbhuvi
so 'nya-janmani dahrāgnir
viśravāś ca mahā-tapāḥ

pulastyaḥ—the sage Pulastya; *ajanayat*—begot; *patnyām*—in his wife; *agastyam*—the great sage Agastya; *ca*—also; *havirbhuvi*—in Havirbhū; *saḥ*—he (Agastya); *anya-janmani*—in the next birth;

dahra-agniḥ—the digesting fire; *viśravāḥ*—Viśravā; *ca*—and; *mahā-tapāḥ*—greatly powerful because of austerity.

TRANSLATION

Pulastya begot in his wife, Havirbhū, one son of the name Agastya, who in his next birth became Dahrāgni. Besides him, Pulastya begot another very great and saintly son, whose name was Viśravā.

TEXT 37

तस्य यक्षपतिर्देवः कुबेरस्त्विडविडासुतः ।
रावणः कुम्भकर्णश्च तथान्यस्यां विभीषणः ॥३७॥

tasya yakṣa-patir devaḥ
kuberas tv iḍaviḍā-sutaḥ
rāvaṇaḥ kumbhakarṇaś ca
tathānyasyāṁ vibhīṣaṇaḥ

tasya—his; *yakṣa-patiḥ*—the king of the Yakṣas; *devaḥ*—demigod; *kuberaḥ*—Kuvera; *tu*—and; *iḍaviḍā*—of Iḍaviḍā; *sutaḥ*—son; *rāvaṇaḥ*—Rāvaṇa; *kumbhakarṇaḥ*—Kumbhakarṇa; *ca*—also; *tathā*—so; *anyasyām*—in the other; *vibhīṣaṇaḥ*—Vibhīṣaṇa.

TRANSLATION

Viśravā had two wives. The first wife was Iḍaviḍā, from whom Kuvera, the master of all Yakṣas, was born, and the next wife was named Keśinī, from whom three sons were born—Rāvaṇa, Kumbhakarṇa and Vibhīṣaṇa.

TEXT 38

पुलहस्य गतिर्भार्या त्रीनसूत सती सुतान् ।
कर्मश्रेष्ठं वरीयांसं सहिष्णुं च महामते ॥३८॥

pulahasya gatir bhāryā
trīn asūta satī sutān

karmaśreṣṭhaṁ varīyāṁsaṁ
sahiṣṇuṁ ca mahā-mate

pulahasya—of Pulaha; *gatiḥ*—Gati; *bhāryā*—wife; *trīn*—three; *asūta*—gave birth; *satī*—chaste; *sutān*—sons; *karma-śreṣṭham*—very expert in fruitive activities; *varīyāṁsam*—very respectable; *sahiṣṇum*—very tolerant; *ca*—also; *mahā-mate*—O great Vidura.

TRANSLATION

Gati, the wife of the sage Pulaha, gave birth to three sons, named Karmaśreṣṭha, Varīyān and Sahiṣṇu, and all of them were great sages.

PURPORT

Gati, the wife of Pulaha, was the fifth daughter of Kardama Muni. She was very faithful to her husband, and all her sons were as good as he.

TEXT 39

क्रतोरपि क्रिया भार्या वालखिल्यानसूयत ।
ऋषीन्षष्टिसहस्राणि ज्वलतो ब्रह्मतेजसा ॥३९॥

krator api kriyā bhāryā
vālakhilyān asūyata
ṛṣīn ṣaṣṭi-sahasrāṇi
jvalato brahma-tejasā

kratoḥ—of the great sage Kratu; *api*—also; *kriyā*—Kriyā; *bhāryā*—wife; *vālakhilyān*—just like Vālakhilya; *asūyata*—begot; *ṛṣīn*—sages; *ṣaṣṭi*—sixty; *sahasrāṇi*—thousand; *jvalataḥ*—very brilliant; *brahma-tejasā*—by dint of the Brahman effulgence.

TRANSLATION

Kratu's wife, Kriyā, gave birth to sixty thousand great sages, named the Vālakhilyas. All these sages were greatly advanced in spiritual knowledge, and their bodies were illuminated by such knowledge.

PURPORT

Kriyā was the sixth daughter of Kardama Muni, and she produced sixty thousand sages, who were known as the Vālakhilyas because they all retired from family life as *vānaprasthas.*

TEXT 40

ऊर्जायां जज्ञिरे पुत्रा वसिष्ठस्य परन्तप ।
चित्रकेतुप्रधानास्ते सप्त ब्रह्मर्षयोऽमलाः ॥४०॥

ūrjāyāṁ jajñire putrā
vasiṣṭhasya parantapa
citraketu-pradhānās te
sapta brahmarṣayo 'malāḥ

ūrjāyām—in Ūrjā; *jajñire*—took birth; *putrāḥ*—sons; *vasiṣṭhasya*—of the great sage Vasiṣṭha; *parantapa*—O great one; *citraketu*—Citraketu; *pradhānāḥ*—headed by; *te*—all the sons; *sapta*—seven; *brahma-ṛṣayaḥ*—great sages with spiritual knowledge; *amalāḥ*—without contamination.

TRANSLATION

The great sage Vasiṣṭha begot in his wife, Ūrjā, sometimes called Arundhatī, seven spotlessly great sages, headed by the sage named Citraketu.

TEXT 41

चित्रकेतुः सुरोचिश्च विरजा मित्र एव च ।
उल्बणो वसुभृद्यानो द्युमान् शक्त्यादयोऽपरे ॥४१॥

citraketuḥ surociś ca
virajā mitra eva ca
ulbaṇo vasubhṛdyāno
dyumān śakty-ādayo 'pare

citraketuḥ—Citraketu; *surociḥ ca*—and Suroci; *virajāḥ*—Virajā; *mitraḥ*—Mitra; *eva*—also; *ca*—and; *ulbaṇaḥ*—Ulbaṇa; *vasubhṛdyā-*

naḥ—Vasubhṛdyāna; *dyumān*—Dyumān; *śakti-ādayaḥ*—sons headed by Śakti; *apare*—from his other wife.

TRANSLATION

The names of these seven sages are as follows: Citraketu, Suroci, Virajā, Mitra, Ulbaṇa, Vasubhṛdyāna and Dyumān. Some other very competent sons were born from Vasiṣṭha's other wife.

PURPORT

Ūrjā, who is sometimes known as Arundhatī and was the wife of Vasiṣṭha, was the ninth daughter of Kardama Muni.

TEXT 42

चित्तिस्त्वथर्वणः पत्नी लेभे पुत्रं धृतव्रतम् ।
दध्यञ्चमश्वशिरसं भृगोर्वंशं निबोध मे ॥४२॥

cittis tv atharvaṇaḥ patnī
lebhe putraṁ dhṛta-vratam
dadhyañcam aśvaśirasaṁ
bhṛgor vaṁśaṁ nibodha me

cittiḥ—Citti; *tu*—also; *atharvaṇaḥ*—of Atharvā; *patnī*—wife; *lebhe*—got; *putram*—son; *dhṛta-vratam*—completely dedicated to a vow; *dadhyañcam*—Dadhyañca; *aśvaśirasam*—Aśvaśirā; *bhṛgoḥ vaṁśam*—generations of Bhṛgu; *nibodha*—try to understand; *me*—from me.

TRANSLATION

Citti, wife of the sage Atharvā, gave birth to a son named Aśvaśirā by accepting a great vow called Dadhyañca. Now you may hear from me about the descendants of the sage Bhṛgu.

PURPORT

The wife of Atharvā known as Citti is also known as Śānti. She was the eighth daughter of Kardama Muni.

TEXT 43

भृगुः ख्यात्यां महाभागः पत्न्यां पुत्रानजीजनत् ।
धातारं च विधातारं श्रियं च भगवत्पराम् ॥४३॥

bhṛguḥ khyātyāṁ mahā-bhāgaḥ
patnyāṁ putrān ajījanat
dhātāraṁ ca vidhātāraṁ
śriyaṁ ca bhagavat-parām

bhṛguḥ—the great sage Bhṛgu; *khyātyām*—in his wife, Khyāti; *mahā-bhāgaḥ*—greatly fortunate; *patnyām*—unto the wife; *putrān*—sons; *ajījanat*—gave birth; *dhātāram*—Dhātā; *ca*—also; *vidhātāram*—Vidhātā; *śriyam*—a daughter named Śrī; *ca bhagavat-parām*—and a great devotee of the Lord.

TRANSLATION

The sage Bhṛgu was highly fortunate. In his wife, known as Khyāti, he begot two sons, named Dhātā and Vidhātā, and one daughter, named Śrī, who was very much devoted to the Supreme Personality of Godhead.

TEXT 44

आयतिं नियतिं चैव सुते मेरुस्तयोरदात् ।
ताभ्यां तयोरभवतां मृकण्डः प्राण एव च ॥४४॥

āyatiṁ niyatiṁ caiva
sute merus tayor adāt
tābhyāṁ tayor abhavatāṁ
mṛkaṇḍaḥ prāṇa eva ca

āyatim—Āyati; *niyatim*—Niyati; *ca eva*—also; *sute*—daughters; *meruḥ*—the sage Meru; *tayoḥ*—unto those two; *adāt*—gave in marriage; *tābhyām*—out of them; *tayoḥ*—both of them; *abhavatām*—appeared; *mṛkaṇḍaḥ*—Mṛkaṇḍa; *prāṇaḥ*—Prāṇa; *eva*—certainly; *ca*—and.

TRANSLATION

The sage Meru had two daughters, named Āyati and Niyati, whom he gave in charity to Dhātā and Vidhātā. Āyati and Niyati gave birth to two sons, Mṛkaṇḍa and Prāṇa.

TEXT 45

मार्कण्डेयो मृकण्डस्य प्राणाद्वेदशिरा मुनिः ।
कविश्च भार्गवो यस्य भगवानुशना सुतः ॥४५॥

mārkaṇḍeyo mṛkaṇḍasya
prāṇād vedaśirā muniḥ
kaviś ca bhārgavo yasya
bhagavān uśanā sutaḥ

mārkaṇḍeyaḥ—Mārkaṇḍeya; *mṛkaṇḍasya*—of Mṛkaṇḍa; *prāṇāt*—from Prāṇa; *vedaśirāḥ*—Vedaśirā; *muniḥ*—great sage; *kaviḥ ca*—of the name Kavi; *bhārgavaḥ*—of the name Bhārgava; *yasya*—whose; *bhagavān*—greatly powerful; *uśanā*—Śukrācārya; *sutaḥ*—son.

TRANSLATION

From Mṛkaṇḍa, Mārkaṇḍeya Muni was born, and from Prāṇa the sage Vedaśirā, whose son was Uśanā [Śukrācārya], also known as Kavi. Thus Kavi also belonged to the descendants of the Bhṛgu dynasty.

TEXTS 46–47

त एते मुनयः क्षत्तर्लोकान् सर्गैरभावयन् ।
एष कर्दमदौहित्रसंतानः कथितस्तव ॥४६॥
शृण्वतः श्रद्दधानस्य सद्यः पापहरः परः ।
प्रसूतिं मानवीं दक्ष उपयेमे ह्यजात्मजः ॥४७॥

ta ete munayaḥ kṣattar
lokān sargair abhāvayan
eṣa kardama-dauhitra-
santānaḥ kathitas tava

śṛṇvataḥ śraddadhānasya
sadyaḥ pāpa-haraḥ paraḥ
prasūtiṁ mānavīṁ dakṣa
upayeme hy ajātmajaḥ

te—they; *ete*—all; *munayaḥ*—great sages; *kṣattaḥ*—O Vidura; *lokān*—the three worlds; *sargaiḥ*—with their descendants; *abhāvayan*—filled; *eṣaḥ*—this; *kardama*—of the sage Kardama; *dauhitra*—grandsons; *santānaḥ*—offspring; *kathitaḥ*—already spoken; *tava*—unto you; *śṛṇvataḥ*—hearing; *śraddadhānasya*—of the faithful; *sadyaḥ*—immediately; *pāpa-haraḥ*—reducing all sinful activities; *paraḥ*—great; *prasūtim*—Prasūti; *mānavīm*—daughter of Manu; *dakṣaḥ*—King Dakṣa; *upayeme*—married; *hi*—certainly; *aja-ātmajaḥ*—son of Brahmā.

TRANSLATION

My dear Vidura, the population of the universe was thus increased by the descendants of these sages and the daughters of Kardama. Anyone who hears the descriptions of this dynasty with faith will be relieved from all sinful reactions. Another of Manu's daughters, known as Prasūti, married the son of Brahmā named Dakṣa.

TEXT 48

तस्यां ससर्ज दुहितॄः षोडशामललोचनाः ।
त्रयोदशादाद्धर्माय तथैकामग्नये विभुः ॥४८॥

tasyāṁ sasarja duhitṝḥ
ṣoḍaśāmala-locanāḥ
trayodaśādād dharmāya
tathaikām agnaye vibhuḥ

tasyām—unto her; *sasarja*—created; *duhitṝḥ*—daughters; *ṣoḍaśa*—sixteen; *amala-locanāḥ*—with lotuslike eyes; *trayodaśa*—thirteen; *adāt*—gave; *dharmāya*—to Dharma; *tathā*—so; *ekām*—one daughter; *agnaye*—to Agni; *vibhuḥ*—Dakṣa.

TRANSLATION

Dakṣa begot sixteen very beautiful daughters with lotuslike eyes in his wife Prasūti. Of these sixteen daughters, thirteen were given in marriage to Dharma, and one daughter was given to Agni.

TEXTS 49–52

पितृभ्य एकां युक्तेभ्यो भवायैकां भवच्छिदे ।
श्रद्धा मैत्री दया शान्तिस्तुष्टिः पुष्टिः क्रियोन्नतिः॥४९॥
बुद्धिर्मेधा तितिक्षा ह्रीर्मूर्तिर्धर्मस्य पत्नयः ।
श्रद्धासूत शुभं मैत्री प्रसादमभयं दया ॥५०॥
शान्तिः सुखं मुदं तुष्टिः स्मयं पुष्टिरसूयत ।
योगं क्रियोन्नतिर्दर्पमर्थं बुद्धिरसूयत ॥५१॥
मेधा स्मृतिं तितिक्षा तु क्षेमं ह्रीः प्रश्रयं सुतम् ।
मूर्तिः सर्वगुणोत्पत्तिर्नरनारायणावृषी ॥५२॥

pitṛbhya ekāṁ yuktebhyo
bhavāyaikāṁ bhava-cchide
śraddhā maitrī dayā śāntis
tuṣṭiḥ puṣṭiḥ kriyonnatiḥ

buddhir medhā titikṣā hrīr
mūrtir dharmasya patnayaḥ
śraddhāsūta śubhaṁ maitrī
prasādam abhayaṁ dayā

śāntiḥ sukhaṁ mudaṁ tuṣṭiḥ
smayaṁ puṣṭir asūyata
yogaṁ kriyonnatir darpam
arthaṁ buddhir asūyata

medhā smṛtiṁ titikṣā tu
kṣemaṁ hrīḥ praśrayaṁ sutam
mūrtiḥ sarva-guṇotpattir
nara-nārāyaṇāv ṛṣī

pitṛbhyaḥ—to the Pitās; *ekām*—one daughter; *yuktebhyaḥ*—the assembled; *bhavāya*—to Lord Śiva; *ekām*—one daughter; *bhava-chide*—who delivers from the material entanglement; *śraddhā, maitrī, dayā, śāntiḥ, tuṣṭiḥ, puṣṭiḥ, kriyā, unnatiḥ, buddhiḥ, medhā, titikṣā, hrīḥ, mūrtiḥ*—names of thirteen daughters of Dakṣa; *dharmasya*—of Dharma; *patnayaḥ*—the wives; *śraddhā*—Śraddhā; *asūta*—gave birth to; *śubham*—Śubha; *maitrī*—Maitrī; *prasādam*—Prasāda; *abhayam*—Abhaya; *dayā*—Dayā; *śāntiḥ*—Śānti; *sukham*—Sukha; *mudam*—Muda; *tuṣṭiḥ*—Tuṣṭi; *smayam*—Smaya; *puṣṭiḥ*—Puṣṭi; *asūyata*—gave birth to; *yogam*—Yoga; *kriyā*—Kriyā; *unnatiḥ*—Unnati; *darpam*—Darpa; *artham*—Artha; *buddhiḥ*—Buddhi; *asūyata*—begot; *medhā*—Medhā; *smṛtim*—Smṛti; *titikṣā*—Titikṣā; *tu*—also; *kṣemam*—Kṣema; *hrīḥ*—Hrī; *praśrayam*—Praśraya; *sutam*—son; *mūrtiḥ*—Mūrti; *sarva-guṇa*—of all respectable qualities; *utpattiḥ*—the reservoir; *nara-nārāyaṇau*—both Nara and Nārāyaṇa; *ṛṣī*—the two sages.

TRANSLATION

One of the remaining two daughters was given in charity to the Pitṛloka, where she resides very amicably, and the other was given to Lord Śiva, who is the deliverer of sinful persons from material entanglement. The names of the thirteen daughters of Dakṣa who were given to Dharma are Śraddhā, Maitrī, Dayā, Śānti, Tuṣṭi, Puṣṭi, Kriyā, Unnati, Buddhi, Medhā, Titikṣā, Hrī and Mūrti. These thirteen daughters produced the following sons: Śraddhā gave birth to Śubha, Maitrī produced Prasāda, Dayā gave birth to Abhaya, Śānti gave birth to Sukha, Tuṣṭi gave birth to Muda, Puṣṭi gave birth to Smaya, Kriyā gave birth to Yoga, Unnati gave birth to Darpa, Buddhi gave birth to Artha, Medhā gave birth to Smṛti, Titikṣā gave birth to Kṣema, and Hrī gave birth to Praśraya. Mūrti, a reservoir of all respectable qualities, gave birth to Śrī Nara-Nārāyaṇa, the Supreme Personality of Godhead.

TEXT 53

ययोर्जन्मन्यदो विश्वमभ्यनन्दत्सुनिर्वृतम् ।
मनांसि ककुभो वाताः प्रसेदुः सरितोऽद्रयः ॥५३॥

yayor janmany ado viśvam
abhyanandat sunirvṛtam
manāṁsi kakubho vātāḥ
praseduḥ sarito 'drayaḥ

yayoḥ—both of whom (Nara and Nārāyaṇa); *janmani*—on the appearance; *adaḥ*—that; *viśvam*—universe; *abhyanandat*—became glad; *su-nirvṛtam*—full of joy; *manāṁsi*—everyone's mind; *kakubhaḥ*—the directions; *vātāḥ*—the air; *praseduḥ*—became pleasant; *saritaḥ*—the rivers; *adrayaḥ*—the mountains.

TRANSLATION

On the occasion of the appearance of Nara-Nārāyaṇa, the entire world was full of joy. Everyone's mind became tranquil, and thus in all directions the air, the rivers and the mountains became pleasant.

TEXTS 54–55

दिव्यवाद्यन्त तूर्याणि पेतुः कुसुमवृष्टयः ।
मुनयस्तुष्टुवुस्तुष्टा जगुर्गन्धर्वकिन्नराः ॥५४॥
नृत्यन्ति स्म स्त्रियो देव्य आसीत्परममङ्गलम् ।
देवा ब्रह्मादयः सर्वे उपतस्थुरभिष्टवैः ॥५५॥

divy avādyanta tūryāṇi
petuḥ kusuma-vṛṣṭayaḥ
munayas tuṣṭuvus tuṣṭā
jagur gandharva-kinnarāḥ

nṛtyanti sma striyo devya
āsīt parama-maṅgalam
devā brahmādayaḥ sarve
upatasthur abhiṣṭavaiḥ

divi—in the heavenly planets; *avādyanta*—vibrated; *tūryāṇi*—a band of instruments; *petuḥ*—they showered; *kusuma*—of flowers; *vṛṣṭayaḥ*—showers; *munayaḥ*—the sages; *tuṣṭuvuḥ*—chanted Vedic prayers; *tuṣṭāḥ*—pacified; *jaguḥ*—began to sing; *gandharva*—the Gandharvas; *kinnarāḥ*—the Kinnaras; *nṛtyanti sma*—danced; *striyaḥ*—the beautiful damsels; *devyaḥ*—of the heavenly planets; *āsīt*—were visible; *parama-maṅgalam*—the highest good fortune; *devāḥ*—the demigods; *brahma-ādayaḥ*—Brahmā and others; *sarve*—all; *upatasthuḥ*—worshiped; *abhiṣṭavaiḥ*—with respectful prayers.

TRANSLATION

In the heavenly planets, bands began to play, and they showered flowers from the sky. The pacified sages chanted Vedic prayers, the denizens of heaven known as the Gandharvas and Kinnaras sang, the beautiful damsels of the heavenly planets danced, and in this way, at the time of the appearance of Nara-Nārāyaṇa, all signs of good fortune were visible. Just at that time, great demigods like Brahmā also offered their respectful prayers.

TEXT 56

देवा ऊचुः
यो मायया विरचितं निजयात्मनीदं
खे रूपभेदमिव तत्प्रतिचक्षणाय ।
एतेन धर्मसदने ऋषिमूर्तिनाद्य
प्रादुश्चकार पुरुषाय नमः परस्मै ॥५६॥

devā ūcuḥ
yo māyayā viracitaṁ nijayātmanīdaṁ
khe rūpa-bhedam iva tat-praticakṣaṇāya
etena dharma-sadane ṛṣi-mūrtinādya
prāduścakāra puruṣāya namaḥ parasmai

devāḥ—the demigods; *ūcuḥ*—said; *yaḥ*—who; *māyayā*—by the external energy; *viracitam*—was created; *nijayā*—by His own; *ātmani*—being situated in Him; *idam*—this; *khe*—in the sky; *rūpa-bhedam*—bunches of clouds; *iva*—as if; *tat*—of Himself; *praticakṣaṇāya*—for manifesting; *etena*—with this; *dharma-sadane*—in the house of Dharma; *ṛṣi-mūrtinā*—with the form of a sage; *adya*—today; *prā-*

duścakāra—appeared; *puruṣāya*—unto the Personality of Godhead; *namaḥ*—respectful obeisances; *parasmai*—the Supreme.

TRANSLATION

The demigods said: Let us offer our respectful obeisances unto the transcendental Personality of Godhead, who created as His external energy this cosmic manifestation, which is situated in Him as the air and clouds are situated in space, and who has now appeared in the form of Nara-Nārāyaṇa Ṛṣi in the house of Dharma.

PURPORT

The universal form of the Lord is the cosmic manifestation, which is an exhibition of the external energy of the Supreme Personality of Godhead. In space there are innumerable varieties of planets and also the air, and in the air there are variously colored clouds, and sometimes we see airplanes running from one place to another. Thus the entire cosmic manifestation is full of variety, but actually that variety is a manifestation of the external energy of the Supreme Lord, and that energy is situated in Him. Now the Lord Himself, after manifesting His energy, appeared within the creation of His energy, which is simultaneously one with and different from Himself, and therefore the demigods offered their respects to the Supreme Personality of Godhead, who manifests Himself in such varieties. There are some philosophers, called nondualists, who because of their impersonal conception think that varieties are false. In this verse it is specifically stated, *yo māyayā viracitam.* This indicates that the varieties are a manifestation of the energy of the Supreme Personality of Godhead. Thus because the energy is nondifferent from the Godhead, the varieties are also factual. The material varieties may be temporary, but they are not false. They are a reflection of the spiritual varieties. Here the word *praticakṣaṇāya*, "there are varieties," announces the glories of the Supreme Personality of Godhead, who appeared as Nara-Nārāyaṇa Ṛṣi and who is the origin of all varieties of material nature.

TEXT 57

सोऽयं स्थितिव्यतिकरोपशमाय सृष्टान्
सत्त्वेन नः सुरगणाननुमेयतत्त्वः ।

दृश्याददभ्रकरुणेन विलोकनेन
यच्छ्रीनिकेतममलं क्षिपतारविन्दम् ॥५७॥

so 'yaṁ sthiti-vyatikaropaśamāya sṛṣṭān
sattvena naḥ sura-gaṇān anumeya-tattvaḥ
dṛśyād adabhra-karuṇena vilokanena
yac chrī-niketam amalaṁ kṣipatāravindam

saḥ—that; *ayam*—He; *sthiti*—of the created world; *vyatikara*—calamities; *upaśamāya*—for destroying; *sṛṣṭān*—created; *sattvena*—by the mode of goodness; *naḥ*—us; *sura-gaṇān*—the demigods; *anumeya-tattvaḥ*—understood by the *Vedas; dṛśyāt*—glance over; *adabhra-karuṇena*—merciful; *vilokanena*—glance; *yat*—which; *śrī-niketam*—the home of the goddess of fortune; *amalam*—spotless; *kṣipata*—supersedes; *aravindam*—lotus.

TRANSLATION

Let that Supreme Personality of Godhead, who is understood by truly authorized Vedic literature and who has created peace and prosperity to destroy all calamities of the created world, be kind enough to bestow His glance upon the demigods. His merciful glance can supersede the beauty of the spotless lotus flower which is the home of the goddess of fortune.

PURPORT

The Supreme Personality of Godhead, who is the origin of the cosmic manifestation, is covered by the wonderful activities of material nature, just as outer space or the illumination of the sun and moon is sometimes covered by clouds or dust. It is very difficult to find the origin of the cosmic manifestation; therefore material scientists conclude that nature is the ultimate cause of all manifestations. But from *śāstra*, or authentic literature like *Bhagavad-gītā* and other Vedic scriptures, we understand that behind this wonderful cosmic manifestation is the Supreme Personality of Godhead, and in order to maintain the regular procedures of the cosmic manifestation and to be visible to the eyes of persons who are in the mode of goodness, the Lord appears. He is the cause of the creation and dissolution of the cosmic manifestation. The demigods therefore prayed for His merciful glance upon them in order to be blessed.

TEXT 58

एवं सुरगणैस्तात भगवन्तावभिष्टुतौ ।
लब्धावलोकैर्ययतुरर्चितौ गन्धमादनम् ॥५८॥

evaṁ sura-gaṇais tāta
bhagavantāv abhiṣṭutau
labdhāvalokair yayatur
arcitau gandhamādanam

evam—thus; *sura-gaṇaiḥ*—by the demigods; *tāta*—O Vidura; *bhagavantau*—the Supreme Personality of Godhead; *abhiṣṭutau*—having been praised; *labdha*—having obtained; *avalokaiḥ*—the glance (of mercy); *yayatuḥ*—departed; *arcitau*—having been worshiped; *gandha-mādanam*—to the Gandhamādana Hill.

TRANSLATION

[Maitreya said:] O Vidura, thus the demigods worshiped with prayers the Supreme Personality of Godhead appearing as the sage Nara-Nārāyaṇa. The Lord glanced upon them with mercy and then departed for Gandhamādana Hill.

TEXT 59

ताविमौ वै भगवतो हरेरंशाविहागतौ ।
भारव्ययाय च भुवः कृष्णौ यदुकुरूद्वहौ ॥५९॥

tāv imau vai bhagavato
harer aṁśāv ihāgatau
bhāra-vyayāya ca bhuvaḥ
kṛṣṇau yadu-kurūdvahau

tau—both; *imau*—these; *vai*—certainly; *bhagavataḥ*—of the Supreme Personality of Godhead; *hareḥ*—of Hari; *aṁśau*—part and parcel expansion; *iha*—here (in this universe); *āgatau*—has appeared; *bhāra-vyayāya*—for mitigation of the burden; *ca*—and; *bhuvaḥ*—of the world; *kṛṣṇau*—the two Kṛṣṇas (Kṛṣṇa and Arjuna); *yadu-kuru-udvahau*—who are the best of the Yadu and Kuru dynasties respectively.

TRANSLATION

That Nara-Nārāyaṇa Ṛṣi, who is a partial expansion of Kṛṣṇa, has now appeared in the dynasties of Yadu and Kuru, in the forms of Kṛṣṇa and Arjuna respectively, to mitigate the burden of the world.

PURPORT

Nārāyaṇa is the Supreme Personality of Godhead, and Nara is a part of the Supreme Personality of Godhead, Nārāyaṇa. Thus the energy and the energetic together are the Supreme Personality of Godhead. Maitreya informed Vidura that Nara, the portion of Nārāyaṇa, had appeared in the family of the Kurus and that Nārāyaṇa, the plenary expansion of Kṛṣṇa, had come as Kṛṣṇa, the Supreme Personality of Godhead, with the purpose of delivering suffering humanity from the pangs of material burdens. In other words, Nārāyaṇa Ṛṣi was now present in the world in the forms of Kṛṣṇa and Arjuna.

TEXT 60

स्वाहाभिमानिनश्चाग्नेरात्मजांस्त्रीनजीजनत् ।
पावकं पवमानं च शुचिं च हुतभोजनम् ॥६०॥

svāhābhimāninaś cāgner
ātmajāṁs trīn ajījanat
pāvakaṁ pavamānaṁ ca
śuciṁ ca huta-bhojanam

svāhā—Svāhā, the wife of Agni; *abhimāninaḥ*—the presiding deity of fire; *ca*—and; *agneḥ*—from Agni; *ātmajān*—sons; *trīn*—three; *ajījanat*—produced; *pāvakam*—Pāvaka; *pavamānam ca*—and Pavamāna; *śucim ca*—and Śuci; *huta-bhojanam*—eating the oblations of sacrifice.

TRANSLATION

The predominating deity of fire begot in his wife, Svāhā, three children, named Pāvaka, Pavamāna and Śuci, who exist by eating the oblations offered to the fire of sacrifice.

PURPORT

After describing the descendants of the thirteen wives of Dharma, who were all daughters of Dakṣa, Maitreya now describes the fourteenth daughter of Dakṣa, Svāhā, and her three sons. Oblations offered in the sacrificial fire are meant for the demigods, and on behalf of the demigods the three sons of Agni and Svāhā, namely Pāvaka, Pavamāna and Śuci, accept the oblations.

TEXT 61

तेभ्योऽग्नयः समभवन् चत्वारिंशच्च पञ्च च ।
त एवैकोनपञ्चाशत्साकं पितृपितामहैः ॥६१॥

tebhyo 'gnayaḥ samabhavan
catvāriṁśac ca pañca ca
ta evaikonapañcāśat
sākaṁ pitṛ-pitāmahaiḥ

tebhyaḥ—from them; *agnayaḥ*—fire-gods; *samabhavan*—were produced; *catvāriṁśat*—forty; *ca*—and; *pañca*—five; *ca*—and; *te*—they; *eva*—certainly; *ekona-pañcāśat*—forty-nine; *sākam*—along with; *pitṛ-pitāmahaiḥ*—with the fathers and grandfather.

TRANSLATION

From those three sons another forty-five descendants were generated, who are also fire-gods. The total number of fire-gods is therefore forty-nine, including the fathers and the grandfather.

PURPORT

The grandfather is Agni, and the sons are Pāvaka, Pavamāna and Śuci. Counting these four, plus forty-five grandsons, there are altogether forty-nine different fire-gods.

TEXT 62

वैतानिके कर्मणि यन्नामभिर्ब्रह्मवादिभिः ।
आग्नेय्य इष्टयो यज्ञे निरूप्यन्तेऽग्नयस्तु ते ॥६२॥

vaitānike karmaṇi yan-
nāmabhir brahma-vādibhiḥ
āgneyya iṣṭayo yajñe
nirūpyante 'gnayas tu te

vaitānike—offering of oblations; *karmaṇi*—the activity; *yat*—of the fire-gods; *nāmabhiḥ*—by the names; *brahma-vādibhiḥ*—by impersonalist *brāhmaṇas; āgneyyaḥ*—for Agni; *iṣṭayaḥ*—sacrifices; *yajñe*—in the sacrifice; *nirūpyante*—are the objective; *agnayaḥ*—the forty-nine fire-gods; *tu*—but; *te*—those.

TRANSLATION

These forty-nine fire-gods are the beneficiaries of the oblations offered in the Vedic sacrificial fire by impersonalist brāhmaṇas.

PURPORT

Impersonalists who perform Vedic fruitive sacrifices are attracted to the various fire-gods and offer oblations in their name. The forty-nine fire-gods are described herewith.

TEXT 63

अग्निष्वात्ता बर्हिषदः सोम्याः पितर आज्यपाः ।
साग्नयोऽनग्नयस्तेषां पत्नी दाक्षायणी स्वधा ॥६३॥

agniṣvāttā barhiṣadaḥ
saumyāḥ pitara ājyapāḥ
sāgnayo 'nagnayas teṣāṁ
patnī dākṣāyaṇī svadhā

agniṣvāttāḥ—the Agniṣvāttas; *barhiṣadaḥ*—the Barhiṣadas; *saumyāḥ*—the Saumyas; *pitaraḥ*—the forefathers; *ājyapāḥ*—the Ājyapas; *sa-agnayaḥ*—those whose means is by fire; *anagnayaḥ*—those whose means is without fire; *teṣām*—of them; *patnī*—the wife; *dākṣāyaṇī*—the daughter of Dakṣa; *svadhā*—Svadhā.

TRANSLATION

The Agniṣvāttas, the Barhiṣadas, the Saumyas and the Ājyapas are the Pitās. They are either sāgnika or niragnika. The wife of all these Pitās is Svadhā, who is the daughter of King Dakṣa.

TEXT 64

तेभ्यो दधार कन्ये द्वे वयुनां धारिणीं स्वधा ।
उभे ते ब्रह्मवादिन्यौ ज्ञानविज्ञानपारगे ॥६४॥

tebhyo dadhāra kanye dve
vayunāṁ dhāriṇīṁ svadhā
ubhe te brahma-vādinyau
jñāna-vijñāna-pārage

tebhyaḥ—from them; *dadhāra*—produced; *kanye*—daughters; *dve*—two; *vayunām*—Vayunā; *dhāriṇīm*—Dhāriṇī; *svadhā*—Svadhā; *ubhe*—both of them; *te*—they; *brahma-vādinyau*—impersonalists; *jñāna-vijñāna-pāra-ge*—expert in both transcendental and Vedic knowledge.

TRANSLATION

Svadhā, who was offered to the Pitās, begot two daughters named Vayunā and Dhāriṇī, both of whom were impersonalists and were expert in transcendental and Vedic knowledge.

TEXT 65

भवस्य पत्नी तु सती भवं देवमनुव्रता ।
आत्मनः सदृशं पुत्रं न लेभे गुणशीलतः ॥६५॥

bhavasya patnī tu satī
bhavaṁ devam anuvratā
ātmanaḥ sadṛśaṁ putraṁ
na lebhe guṇa-śīlataḥ

bhavasya—of Bhava (Lord Śiva); *patnī*—the wife; *tu*—but; *satī*—named Satī; *bhavam*—to Bhava; *devam*—a demigod; *anuvratā*—faithfully engaged in service; *ātmanaḥ*—of herself; *sadṛśam*—similar; *putram*—a son; *na lebhe*—did not obtain; *guṇa-śīlataḥ*—by good qualities and by character.

TRANSLATION

The sixteenth daughter, whose name was Satī, was the wife of Lord Śiva. She could not produce a child, although she always faithfully engaged in the service of her husband.

TEXT 66

पितर्यप्रतिरूपे स्वे भवायानागसे रुषा ।
अप्रौढैवात्मनात्मानमजहाद्योगसंयुता ॥६६॥

pitary apratirūpe sve
bhavāyānāgase ruṣā
aprauḍhaivātmanātmānam
ajahād yoga-saṁyutā

pitari—as a father; *apratirūpe*—unfavorable; *sve*—her own; *bhavāya*—unto Lord Śiva; *anāgase*—faultless; *ruṣā*—with anger; *aprauḍhā*—before attaining maturity; *eva*—even; *ātmanā*—by herself; *ātmānam*—the body; *ajahāt*—gave up; *yoga-saṁyutā*—by mystic *yoga.*

TRANSLATION

The reason is that Satī's father, Dakṣa, used to rebuke Lord Śiva in spite of Śiva's faultlessness. Consequently, before attaining a mature age, Satī gave up her body by dint of yogic mystic power.

PURPORT

Lord Śiva, being the head of all mystic *yogīs,* never even constructed a home for his residence. Satī was the daughter of a great king, Dakṣa, and because his youngest daughter, Satī, selected as her husband Lord Śiva, King Dakṣa was not very much satisfied with her. Therefore whenever she met her father, he unnecessarily criticized her husband, although

Lord Śiva was faultless. Because of this, before attaining a mature age Satī gave up the body given by her father, Dakṣa, and therefore she could not produce a child.

Thus end the Bhaktivedanta purports of the Fourth Canto, First Chapter, of the Śrīmad-Bhāgavatam, *entitled "Genealogical Table of the Daughters of Manu."*

CHAPTER TWO

Dakṣa Curses Lord Śiva

TEXT 1

विदुर उवाच
भवे शीलवतां श्रेष्ठे दक्षो दुहितृवत्सलः ।
विद्वेषमकरोत्कस्मादनादृत्यात्मजां सतीम् ॥ १ ॥

vidura uvāca
bhave śīlavatāṁ śreṣṭhe
dakṣo duhitṛ-vatsalaḥ
vidveṣam akarot kasmād
anādṛtyātmajāṁ satīm

viduraḥ uvāca—Vidura said; *bhave*—towards Lord Śiva; *śīla-vatām*—among the gentle; *śreṣṭhe*—the best; *dakṣaḥ*—Dakṣa; *duhitṛ-vatsalaḥ*—being affectionate towards his daughter; *vidveṣam*—enmity; *akarot*—did exhibit; *kasmāt*—why; *anādṛtya*—neglecting; *ātmajām*—his own daughter; *satīm*—Satī.

TRANSLATION

Vidura inquired: Why was Dakṣa, who was so affectionate towards his daughter, envious of Lord Śiva, who is the best among the gentle? Why did he neglect his daughter Satī?

PURPORT

In the Second Chapter of the Fourth Canto, the cause of the dissension between Lord Śiva and Dakṣa, which was due to a great sacrifice arranged by Dakṣa for the pacification of the entire universe, is explained. Lord Śiva is described here as the best of the gentle because he is not envious of anyone, he is equal to all living entities, and all other good qualities are present in his personality. The word *śiva* means "all-auspicious." No one can be an enemy of Lord Śiva's, for he is so peaceful and renounced that he does not even construct a house for his residence, but lives underneath a tree, always detached from all worldly things. The personality of Lord Śiva symbolizes the best of gentleness. Why, then, was Dakṣa, who offered his beloved daughter to such a gentle personality, inimical towards Lord Śiva so intensely that Satī, the daughter of Dakṣa and wife of Lord Śiva, gave up her body?

TEXT 2

कस्तं चराचरगुरुं निर्वैरं शान्तविग्रहम् ।
आत्मारामं कथं द्वेष्टि जगतो दैवतं महत् ॥ २ ॥

kas taṁ carācara-guruṁ
nirvairaṁ śānta-vigraham
ātmārāmaṁ kathaṁ dveṣṭi
jagato daivataṁ mahat

kaḥ—who (Dakṣa); *tam*—him (Lord Śiva); *cara-acara*—of the whole world (both animate and inanimate); *gurum*—the spiritual master; *nirvairam*—without enmity; *śānta-vigraham*—having a peaceful personality; *ātma-ārāmam*—satisfied in himself; *katham*—how; *dveṣṭi*—hates; *jagataḥ*—of the universe; *daivatam*—demigod; *mahat*—the great.

TRANSLATION

Lord Śiva, the spiritual master of the entire world, is free from enmity, is a peaceful personality, and is always satisfied in himself. He is the greatest among the demigods. How is it possible that Dakṣa could be inimical towards such an auspicious personality?

PURPORT

Lord Śiva is described here as *carācara-guru*, the spiritual master of all animate and inanimate objects. He is sometimes known as Bhūtanātha, which means "the worshipable deity of the dull-headed." *Bhūta* is also sometimes taken to indicate the ghosts. Lord Śiva takes charge of reforming persons who are ghosts and demons, not to speak of others, who are godly; therefore he is the spiritual master of everyone, both the dull and demoniac and the highly learned Vaiṣṇavas. It is also stated, *vaiṣṇavānāṁ yathā śambhuḥ:* Śambhu, Lord Śiva, is the greatest of all Vaiṣṇavas. On one hand he is the worshipable object of the dull demons, and on the other he is the best of all Vaiṣṇavas, or devotees, and he has a *sampradāya* called the Rudra-sampradāya. Even if he is an enemy or is sometimes angry, such a personality cannot be the object of envy, so Vidura, in astonishment, asked why he was taken as such, especially by Dakṣa. Dakṣa is also not an ordinary person. He is a Prajāpati, in charge of fathering population, and all his daughters are highly elevated, especially Satī. The word *satī* means "the most chaste." Whenever there is consideration of chastity, Satī, this wife of Lord Śiva and daughter of Dakṣa, is considered first. Vidura, therefore, was astonished. "Dakṣa is such a great man," he thought, "and is the father of Satī. And Lord Śiva is the spiritual master of everyone. How then could there possibly be so much enmity between them that Satī, the most chaste goddess, could give up her body because of their quarrel?"

TEXT 3

एतदाख्याहि मे ब्रह्मन् जामातुः श्वशुरस्य च ।
विद्वेषस्तु यतः प्राणांस्तत्यजे दुस्त्यजान्सती ॥ ३ ॥

etad ākhyāhi me brahman
jāmātuḥ śvaśurasya ca
vidveṣas tu yataḥ prāṇāṁs
tatyaje dustyajān satī

etat—thus; *ākhyāhi*—please tell; *me*—to me; *brahman*—O *brāhmaṇa; jāmātuḥ*—of the son-in-law (Lord Śiva); *śvaśurasya*—of the father-in-law (Dakṣa); *ca*—and; *vidveṣaḥ*—quarrel; *tu*—as to; *yataḥ*—from what cause; *prāṇān*—her life; *tatyaje*—gave up; *dustyajān*—which is impossible to give up; *satī*—Satī.

TRANSLATION

My dear Maitreya, to part with one's life is very difficult. Would you kindly explain to me how such a son-in-law and father-in-law

could quarrel so bitterly that the great goddess Satī could give up her life?

TEXT 4

मैत्रेय उवाच
पुरा विश्वसृजां सत्रे समेताः परमर्षयः ।
तथामरगणाः सर्वे सानुगा मुनयोऽग्नयः ॥ ४ ॥

maitreya uvāca
purā viśva-sṛjāṁ satre
sametāḥ paramarṣayaḥ
tathāmara-gaṇāḥ sarve
sānugā munayo 'gnayaḥ

maitreyaḥ uvāca—the sage Maitreya said; *purā*—formerly (at the time of Svāyambhuva Manu); *viśva-sṛjām*—of the creators of the universe; *satre*—at a sacrifice; *sametāḥ*—were assembled; *paramarṣayaḥ*—the great sages; *tathā*—and also; *amara-gaṇāḥ*—the demigods; *sarve*—all; *sa-anugāḥ*—along with their followers; *munayaḥ*—the philosophers; *agnayaḥ*—the fire-gods.

TRANSLATION

The sage Maitreya said: In a former time, the leaders of the universal creation performed a great sacrifice in which all the great sages, philosophers, demigods and fire-gods assembled with their followers.

PURPORT

Upon being asked by Vidura, the sage Maitreya began to explain the cause of the misunderstanding between Lord Śiva and Dakṣa, because of which the goddess Satī gave up her body. Thus begins the history of a great sacrifice performed by the leaders of the universal creation, namely Marīci, Dakṣa and Vasiṣṭha. These great personalities arranged for a great sacrifice, for which demigods like Indra and the fire-gods assembled with their followers. Lord Brahmā and Lord Śiva were also present.

TEXT 5

तत्र प्रविष्टमृषयो दृष्ट्वार्कमिव रोचिषा ।
भ्राजमानं वितिमिरं कुर्वन्तं तन्महत्सदः ॥ ५ ॥

tatra praviṣṭam ṛṣayo
dṛṣṭvārkam iva rociṣā
bhrājamānaṁ vitimiraṁ
kurvantaṁ tan mahat sadaḥ

tatra—there; *praviṣṭam*—having entered; *ṛṣayaḥ*—the sages; *dṛṣṭvā*—seeing; *arkam*—the sun; *iva*—just like; *rociṣā*—with luster; *bhrājamānam*—shining; *vitimiram*—free from darkness; *kurvantam*—making; *tat*—that; *mahat*—great; *sadaḥ*—assembly.

TRANSLATION

When Dakṣa, the leader of the Prajāpatis, entered that assembly, his personal bodily luster as bright as the effulgence of the sun, the entire assembly was illuminated, and all the assembled personalities became insignificant in his presence.

TEXT 6

उदतिष्ठन् सदस्यास्ते स्वधिष्ण्येभ्यः सहाग्नयः ।
ऋते विरिञ्चां शर्वं च तद्भासाक्षिप्तचेतसः ॥ ६ ॥

udatiṣṭhan sadasyās te
sva-dhiṣṇyebhyaḥ sahāgnayaḥ
ṛte viriñcāṁ śarvaṁ ca
tad-bhāsākṣipta-cetasaḥ

udatiṣṭhan—stood up; *sadasyāḥ*—the members of the assembly; *te*—they; *sva-dhiṣṇyebhyaḥ*—from their own seats; *saha-agnayaḥ*—along with the fire-gods; *ṛte*—except for; *viriñcām*—Brahmā; *śarvam*—Śiva; *ca*—and; *tat*—his (Dakṣa's); *bhāsa*—by the luster; *ākṣipta*—are influenced; *cetasaḥ*—those whose minds.

TRANSLATION

Influenced by his personal bodily luster, all the fire-gods and other participants in that great assembly, with the exceptions of Lord Brahmā and Lord Śiva, gave up their own sitting places and stood in respect for Dakṣa.

TEXT 7

सदसस्पतिभिर्दक्षो भगवान् साधु सत्कृतः ।
अजं लोकगुरुं नत्वा निषसाद तदाज्ञया ॥ ७ ॥

sadasas-patibhir dakṣo
bhagavān sādhu sat-kṛtaḥ
ajaṁ loka-guruṁ natvā
niṣasāda tad-ājñayā

sadasaḥ—of the assembly; *patibhiḥ*—by the leaders; *dakṣaḥ*—Dakṣa; *bhagavān*—the possessor of all opulences; *sādhu*—properly; *sat-kṛtaḥ*—was welcomed; *ajam*—to the unborn (Brahmā); *loka-gurum*—to the teacher of the universe; *natvā*—making obeisances; *niṣasāda*—sat down; *tat-ājñayā*—by his (Brahmā's) order.

TRANSLATION

Dakṣa was adequately welcomed by the president of the great assembly, Lord Brahmā. After offering Lord Brahmā respect, Dakṣa, by the order of Brahmā, properly took his seat.

TEXT 8

प्राङ्निषण्णं मृडं दृष्ट्वा नामृष्यत्तदनादृतः ।
उवाच वामं चक्षुर्भ्यामभिवीक्ष्य दहन्निव ॥ ८ ॥

prāṅ-niṣaṇṇaṁ mṛḍaṁ dṛṣṭvā
nāmṛṣyat tad-anādṛtaḥ
uvāca vāmaṁ cakṣurbhyām
abhivīkṣya dahann iva

prāk—before; *niṣaṇṇam*—being seated; *mṛḍam*—Lord Śiva; *dṛṣṭvā*—seeing; *na amṛṣyat*—did not tolerate; *tat*—by him (Śiva); *anādṛtaḥ*—not being respected; *uvāca*—said; *vāmam*—dishonest; *cakṣurbhyām*—with both eyes; *abhivīkṣya*—looking at; *dahan*—burning; *iva*—as if.

TRANSLATION

Before taking his seat, however, Dakṣa was very much offended to see Lord Śiva sitting and not showing him any respect. At that time, Dakṣa became greatly angry, and, his eyes glowing, he began to speak very strongly against Lord Śiva.

PURPORT

Lord Śiva, being the son-in-law of Dakṣa, was expected to show his father-in-law respect by standing with the others, but because Lord Brahmā and Lord Śiva are the principal demigods, their positions are greater than Dakṣa's. Dakṣa, however, could not tolerate this, and he took it as an insult by his son-in-law. Previously, also, he was not very much satisfied with Lord Śiva, for Śiva looked very poor and was niggardly in dress.

TEXT 9

श्रूयतां ब्रह्मर्षयो मे सहदेवाः सहाग्नयः ।
साधूनां ब्रुवतो वृत्तं नाज्ञानान्न च मत्सरात् ॥ ९ ॥

śrūyatāṁ brahmarṣayo me
saha-devāḥ sahāgnayaḥ
sādhūnāṁ bruvato vṛttaṁ
nājñānān na ca matsarāt

śrūyatām—hear; *brahma-ṛṣayaḥ*—O sages among the *brāhmaṇas; me*—unto me; *saha-devāḥ*—O demigods; *saha-agnayaḥ*—O fire-gods; *sādhūnām*—of the gentle; *bruvataḥ*—speaking; *vṛttam*—the manners; *na*—not; *ajñānāt*—from ignorance; *na ca*—and not; *matsarāt*—from envy.

TRANSLATION

All sages, brāhmaṇas and fire-gods present, please hear me with attention, for I speak about the manners of gentle persons. I do not speak out of ignorance or envy.

PURPORT

In speaking against Lord Śiva, Dakṣa tried to pacify the assembly by presenting in a very tactful way that he was going to speak about the manners of gentle persons, although naturally this might affect some unmannerly upstarts and the assembly might be unhappy because they did not want even unmannerly persons to be offended. In other words, he was in complete knowledge that he was speaking against Lord Śiva in spite of Śiva's spotless character. As far as envy is concerned, from the very beginning he was envious of Lord Śiva; therefore he could not distinguish his own particular envy. Although he spoke like a man in ignorance, he wanted to cover his statements by saying that he was not speaking for impudent and envious reasons.

TEXT 10

अयं तु लोकपालानां यशोघ्नो निरपत्रपः ।
सद्भिराचरितः पन्था येन स्तब्धेन दूषितः ॥१०॥

ayaṁ tu loka-pālānāṁ
yaśo-ghno nirapatrapaḥ
sadbhir ācaritaḥ panthā
yena stabdhena dūṣitaḥ

ayam—he (Śiva); *tu*—but; *loka-pālānām*—of the governors of the universe; *yaśaḥ-ghnaḥ*—spoiling the fame; *nirapatrapaḥ*—shameless; *sadbhiḥ*—by those of gentle manner; *ācaritaḥ*—followed; *panthāḥ*—the path; *yena*—by whom (Śiva); *stabdhena*—being devoid of proper actions; *dūṣitaḥ*—is polluted.

TRANSLATION

Śiva has spoiled the name and fame of the governors of the universe and has polluted the path of gentle manners. Because he is shameless, he does not know how to act.

PURPORT

Dakṣa wanted to impress upon the minds of all the great sages assembled in that meeting that Śiva, being one of the demigods, had ruined the good reputations of all the demigods by his unmannerly behavior. The words used against Lord Śiva by Dakṣa can also be understood in a different way, in a good sense. For example, he stated that Śiva is *yaśo-ghna*, which means "one who spoils name and fame." So this can also be interpreted to mean that he was so famous that his fame killed all other fame. Again, Dakṣa used the word *nirapatrapa*, which also can be used in two senses. One sense is "one who is stunted," and another sense is "one who is the maintainer of persons who have no other shelter." Generally Lord Śiva is known as the lord of the *bhūtas*, or lower grade of living creatures. They take shelter of Lord Śiva because he is very kind to everyone and is very quickly satisfied. Therefore he is called Āśutoṣa. To such men, who cannot approach other demigods or Viṣṇu, Lord Śiva gives shelter. Therefore the word *nirapatrapa* can be used in that sense.

TEXT 11

एष मे शिष्यतां प्राप्तो यन्मे दुहितुरग्रहीत् ।
पाणिं विप्राग्निमुखतः सावित्र्या इव साधुवत् ॥११॥

eṣa me śiṣyatāṁ prāpto
yan me duhitur agrahīt
pāṇiṁ viprāgni-mukhataḥ
sāvitryā iva sādhuvat

eṣaḥ—he (Śiva); *me*—my; *śiṣyatām*—subordinate position; *prāptaḥ*—accepted; *yat*—because; *me duhituḥ*—of my daughter; *agrahīt*—he took; *pāṇim*—the hand; *vipra-agni*—of *brāhmaṇas* and fire; *mukhataḥ*—in the presence; *sāvitryāḥ*—Gāyatrī; *iva*—like; *sādhuvat*—like an honest person.

TRANSLATION

He has already accepted himself as my subordinate by marrying my daughter in the presence of fire and brāhmaṇas. He has married my daughter, who is equal to Gāyatrī, and has pretended to be just like an honest person.

PURPORT

Dakṣa's statement that Lord Śiva pretended to be an honest person means that Śiva was dishonest because in spite of accepting the position of Dakṣa's son-in-law, he was not respectful to Dakṣa.

TEXT 12

गृहीत्वा मृगशावाक्ष्याः पाणिं मर्कटलोचनः ।
प्रत्युत्थानाभिवादार्हे वाचाप्यकृत नोचितम् ॥१२॥

gṛhītvā mṛga-śāvākṣyāḥ
pāṇiṁ markaṭa-locanaḥ
pratyutthānābhivādārhe
vācāpy akṛta nocitam

gṛhītvā—taking; *mṛga-śāva*—like a deer cub; *akṣyāḥ*—of her who has eyes; *pāṇim*—the hand; *markaṭa*—of a monkey; *locanaḥ*—he who has the eyes; *pratyutthāna*—of rising from one's seat; *abhivāda*—the honor; *arhe*—to me, who deserves; *vācā*—with sweet words; *api*—even; *akṛta na*—he did not do; *ucitam*—honor.

TRANSLATION

He has eyes like a monkey's, yet he has married my daughter, whose eyes are just like those of a deer cub. Nevertheless he did not stand up to receive me, nor did he think it fit to welcome me with sweet words.

TEXT 13

लुप्तक्रियायाशुचये मानिने भिन्नसेतवे ।
अनिच्छन्नप्यदां बालां शूद्रायेवोशतीं गिरम् ॥१३॥

lupta-kriyāyāśucaye
mānine bhinna-setave
anicchann apy adāṁ bālāṁ
śūdrāyevośatīṁ giram

lupta-kriyāya—not observing rules and regulations; *aśucaye*—impure; *mānine*—proud; *bhinna-setave*—having broken all rules of civility; *anicchan*—not desiring; *api*—although; *adām*—handed over; *bālām*—my daughter; *śūdrāya*—unto a *śūdra; iva*—as; *uśatīm giram*—the message of the *Vedas.*

TRANSLATION

I had no desire to give my daughter to this person, who has broken all rules of civility. Because of not observing the required rules and regulations, he is impure, but I was obliged to hand over my daughter to him just as one teaches the messages of the Vedas to a śūdra.

PURPORT

A *śūdra* is forbidden to take lessons from the *Vedas* because a *śūdra,* due to his unclean habits, is not worthy to hear such instructions. This restriction, that unless one has acquired the brahminical qualifications one should not read the Vedic literatures, is like the restriction that a law student should not enter a law college unless he has been graduated from all lower grades. According to the estimation of Dakṣa, Śiva was unclean in habits and not worthy to have the hand of his daughter, Satī, who was so enlightened, beautiful and chaste. The word used in this connection is *bhinna-setave*, which refers to one who has broken all the regulations for good behavior by not following the Vedic principles. In other words, according to Dakṣa the entire transaction of the marriage of his daughter with Śiva was not in order.

TEXTS 14–15

प्रेतावासेषु घोरेषु प्रेतैर्भूतगणैर्वृतः ।
अटत्युन्मत्तवन्नग्नो व्युप्तकेशो हसन् रुदन् ॥१४॥
चिताभस्मकृतस्नानः प्रेतस्रङ्न्रस्थिभूषणः ।
शिवापदेशो ह्यशिवो मत्तो मत्तजनप्रियः ।
पतिः प्रमथनाथानां तमोमात्रात्मकात्मनाम् ॥१५॥

pretāvāseṣu ghoreṣu
pretair bhūta-gaṇair vṛtaḥ

aṭaty unmattavan nagno
vyupta-keśo hasan rudan

citā-bhasma-kṛta-snānaḥ
preta-sraṅ-nrasthi-bhūṣaṇaḥ
śivāpadeśo hy aśivo
matto matta-jana-priyaḥ
patiḥ pramatha-nāthānāṁ
tamo-mātrātmakātmanām

preta-āvāseṣu—at the burning places of dead bodies; *ghoreṣu*—horrible; *pretaiḥ*—by the Pretas; *bhūta-gaṇaiḥ*—by the Bhūtas; *vṛtaḥ*—accompanied by; *aṭati*—he wanders; *unmatta-vat*—like a madman; *nagnaḥ*—naked; *vyupta-keśaḥ*—having scattered hair; *hasan*—laughing; *rudan*—crying; *citā*—of the funeral pyre; *bhasma*—with the ashes; *kṛta-snānaḥ*—taking bath; *preta*—of the skulls of dead bodies; *srak*—having a garland; *nṛ-asthi-bhūṣaṇaḥ*—ornamented with dead men's bones; *śiva-apadeśaḥ*—who is *śiva*, or auspicious, only in name; *hi*—for; *aśivaḥ*—inauspicious; *mattaḥ*—crazy; *matta-jana-priyaḥ*—very dear to the crazy beings; *patiḥ*—the leader; *pramatha-nāthānām*—of the lords of the Pramathas; *tamaḥ-mātra-ātmaka-ātmanām*—of those grossly in the mode of ignorance.

TRANSLATION

He lives in filthy places like crematoriums, and his companions are the ghosts and demons. Naked like a madman, sometimes laughing and sometimes crying, he smears crematorium ashes all over his body. He does not bathe regularly, and he ornaments his body with a garland of skulls and bones. Therefore only in name is he Śiva, or auspicious; actually, he is the most mad and inauspicious creature. Thus he is very dear to crazy beings in the gross mode of ignorance, and he is their leader.

PURPORT

Those who do not regularly bathe are supposed to be in association with ghosts and crazy creatures. Lord Śiva appeared to be like that, but his name, Śiva, is actually fitting, for he is very kind to persons who are in the darkness of the mode of ignorance, such as unclean drunkards who do not regularly bathe. Lord Śiva is so kind that he gives shelter to such creatures and gradually elevates them to spiritual consciousness. Although it is very difficult to raise such creatures to spiritual understanding, Lord Śiva takes charge of them, and therefore, as stated in the *Vedas*, Lord Śiva is all-auspicious. Thus by his association even such fallen souls can be elevated. Sometimes it is seen that great personalities meet with fallen souls, not for any personal interest but for the benefit of those souls. In the creation of the Lord there are different kinds of living creatures. Some of them are in the mode of goodness, some are in the mode of passion, and some are in the mode of ignorance. Lord Viṣṇu takes charge of persons who are advanced Kṛṣṇa conscious Vaiṣṇavas, and Lord Brahmā takes charge of persons who are very much attached to material activities, but Lord Śiva is so kind that he takes charge of persons who are in gross ignorance and whose behavior is lower that that of the animals. Therefore Lord Śiva is especially called auspicious.

TEXT 16

तस्मा उन्मादनाथाय नष्टशौचाय दुर्हृदे ।
दत्ता बत मया साध्वी चोदिते परमेष्ठिना ॥१६॥

tasmā unmāda-nāthāya
naṣṭa-śaucāya durhṛde
dattā bata mayā sādhvī
codite parameṣṭhinā

tasmai—to him; *unmāda-nāthāya*—to the lord of ghosts; *naṣṭa-śaucāya*—being devoid of all cleanliness; *durhṛde*—heart filled with nasty things; *dattā*—was given; *bata*—alas; *mayā*—by me; *sādhvī*—Satī; *codite*—being requested; *parameṣṭhinā*—by the supreme teacher (Brahmā).

TRANSLATION

On the request of Lord Brahmā I handed over my chaste daughter to him, although he is devoid of all cleanliness and his heart is filled with nasty things.

PURPORT

It is the duty of parents to hand over their daughters to suitable persons just befitting their family tradition in cleanliness, gentle behavior, wealth, social position, etc. Dakṣa was repentant that on the request of Brahmā, who was his father, he had handed over his daughter to a person who, according to his calculation, was nasty. He was so angry that he did not acknowledge that the request was from his father. Instead, he referred to Brahmā as *parameṣṭhī*, the supreme teacher in the universe; because of his temperament of gross anger, he was not even prepared to accept Brahmā as his father. In other words, he accused even Brahmā of being less intelligent because he had advised Dakṣa to hand over his beautiful daughter to such a nasty fellow. In anger one forgets everything, and thus Dakṣa, in anger, not only accused the great Lord Śiva, but criticized his own father, Lord Brahmā, for his not very astute advice that Dakṣa hand over his daughter to Lord Śiva.

TEXT 17

मैत्रेय उवाच

विनिन्द्यैवं स गिरिशमप्रतीपमवस्थितम् ।
दक्षोऽथाप उपस्पृश्य क्रुद्धः शप्तुं प्रचक्रमे ॥१७॥

maitreya uvāca
vinindyaivaṁ sa giriśam
apratīpam avasthitam
dakṣo 'thāpa upaspṛśya
kruddhaḥ śaptuṁ pracakrame

maitreyaḥ uvāca—Maitreya said; *vinindya*—abusing; *evam*—thus; *saḥ*—he (Dakṣa); *giriśam*—Śiva; *apratīpam*—without any hostility; *avasthitam*—remaining; *dakṣaḥ*—Dakṣa; *atha*—now; *apaḥ*—water; *upaspṛśya*—washing hands and mouth; *kruddhaḥ*—angry; *śaptum*—to curse; *pracakrame*—began to.

TRANSLATION

The sage Maitreya continued: Thus Dakṣa, seeing Lord Śiva sitting as if against him, washed his hands and mouth and cursed him in the following words.

TEXT 18

अयं तु देवयजन इन्द्रोपेन्द्रादिभिर्भवः ।
सह भागं न लभतां देवैर्देवगणाधमः ॥१८॥

ayaṁ tu deva-yajana
indropendrādibhir bhavaḥ
saha bhāgaṁ na labhatāṁ
devair deva-gaṇādhamaḥ

ayam—that; *tu*—but; *deva-yajane*—in the sacrifice of the demigods; *indra-upendra-ādibhiḥ*—with Indra, Upendra and the others; *bhavaḥ*—Śiva; *saha*—along with; *bhāgam*—a portion; *na*—not; *labhatām*—should obtain; *devaiḥ*—with the demigods; *deva-gaṇa-adhamaḥ*—the lowest of all the demigods.

TRANSLATION

The demigods are eligible to share in the oblations of sacrifice, but Lord Śiva, who is the lowest of all the demigods, should not have a share.

PURPORT

Because of this curse, Śiva was deprived of his share in the oblations of Vedic sacrifices. It was due to the curse of Dakṣa, Śrī Viśvanātha Cakravartī comments in this connection, that Lord Śiva was saved from the calamity of taking part with other demigods, who were all materialistic. Lord Śiva is the greatest devotee of the Supreme Personality of Godhead, and it is not fitting for him to eat or sit with materialistic persons like the demigods. Thus the curse of Dakṣa was indirectly a blessing, for Śiva would not have to eat or sit with other demigods, who were too materialistic. There is a practical example set for us by Gaurakiśora dāsa Bābājī Mahārāja, who used to sit on the side of a latrine to chant Hare Kṛṣṇa. Many materialistic persons used to come and bother him and disturb his daily routine of chanting, so to avoid their company he used to sit by the side of a latrine, where materialistic persons would not go because of the filth and the obnoxious smell. However, Gaurakiśora dāsa Bābājī Mahārāja was so great that he was accepted as the spiritual master of such a great personality as His Divine Grace Oṁ Viṣṇupāda Śrī Śrīmad

Bhaktisiddhānta Sarasvatī Gosvāmī Mahārāja. The conclusion is that Lord Śiva behaved in his own way to avoid materialistic persons who might disturb him in his prosecution of devotional service.

TEXT 19

निषिध्यमानः स सदस्यमुख्यै-
र्दक्षो गिरित्राय विसृज्य शापम् ।
तस्माद्विनिष्क्रम्य विवृद्धमन्यु-
र्जगाम कौरव्य निजं निकेतनम् ॥१९॥

niṣidhyamānaḥ sa sadasya-mukhyair
dakṣo giritrāya visṛjya śāpam
tasmād viniṣkramya vivṛddha-manyur
jagāma kauravya nijaṁ niketanam

niṣidhyamānaḥ—being requested not to; *saḥ*—he (Dakṣa); *sadasya-mukhyaiḥ*—by the members of the sacrifice; *dakṣaḥ*—Dakṣa; *giri-trāya*—to Śiva; *visṛjya*—giving; *śāpam*—a curse; *tasmāt*—from that place; *viniṣkramya*—going out; *vivṛddha-manyuḥ*—being exceedingly angry; *jagāma*—went; *kauravya*—O Vidura; *nijam*—to his own; *niketanam*—home.

TRANSLATION

Maitreya continued: My dear Vidura, in spite of the requests of all the members of the sacrificial assembly, Dakṣa, in great anger, cursed Lord Śiva and then left the assembly and went back to his home.

PURPORT

Anger is so detrimental that even a great personality like Dakṣa, out of anger, left the arena where Brahmā was presiding and all the great sages and pious and saintly persons were assembled. All of them requested him not to leave, but, infuriated, he left, thinking that the auspicious place was not fit for him. Puffed up by his exalted position, he thought that no one was greater than he in argument. It appears that all the members of the assembly, including Lord Brahmā, requested him not to be angry and leave their company, but in spite of all these requests, he left. That is the effect of cruel anger. In *Bhagavad-gītā*, therefore, it is advised that one who desires to make tangible advancement in spiritual consciousness must avoid three things—lust, anger and the mode of passion. Actually we can see that lust, anger and passion make a man crazy, even though he be as great as Dakṣa. The very name Dakṣa suggests that he was expert in all material activities, but still, because of his aversion towards such a saintly personality as Śiva, he was attacked by these three enemies—anger, lust and passion. Lord Caitanya, therefore, advised that one be very careful not to offend Vaiṣṇavas. He compared offenses toward a Vaiṣṇava to a mad elephant. As a mad elephant can do anything horrible, so when a person offends a Vaiṣṇava he can perform any abominable action.

TEXT 20

विज्ञाय शापं गिरिशानुगाग्रणी-
नन्दीश्वरो रोषकषायदूषितः ।
दक्षाय शापं विससर्ज दारुणं
ये चान्वमोदंस्तदवाच्यतां द्विजाः ॥२०॥

vijñāya śāpaṁ giriśānugāgraṇīr
nandīśvaro roṣa-kaṣāya-dūṣitaḥ
dakṣāya śāpaṁ visasarja dāruṇaṁ
ye cānvamodaṁs tad-avācyatāṁ dvijāḥ

vijñāya—understanding; *śāpam*—the curse; *giriśa*—of Śiva; *anuga-agraṇīḥ*—one of the principal associates; *nandīśvaraḥ*—Nandīśvara; *roṣa*—anger; *kaṣāya*—red; *dūṣitaḥ*—blinded; *dakṣāya*—to Dakṣa; *śāpam*—a curse; *visasarja*—gave; *dāruṇam*—harsh; *ye*—who; *ca*—and; *anvamodan*—tolerated; *tat-avācyatām*—the cursing of Śiva; *dvijāḥ*—*brāhmaṇas*.

TRANSLATION

Upon understanding that Lord Śiva had been cursed, Nandīśvara, one of Lord Śiva's principal associates, became greatly angry. His eyes became red, and he prepared to curse Dakṣa and all the brāhmaṇas present there who had tolerated Dakṣa's cursing Śiva in harsh words.

PURPORT

There is a long-standing dissension among some of the neophyte Vaiṣṇavas and Śaivites; they are always at loggerheads. When Dakṣa cursed Lord Śiva in harsh words, some of the *brāhmaṇas* present might have enjoyed it because some *brāhmaṇas* do not very much admire Lord Śiva. This is due to their ignorance of Lord Śiva's position. Nandīśvara was affected by the cursing, but he did not follow the example of Lord Śiva, who was also present there. Although Lord Śiva could also have cursed Dakṣa in a similar way, he was silent and tolerant; but Nandīśvara, his follower, was not tolerant. Of course, as a follower it was right for him not to tolerate an insult to his master, but he should not have cursed the *brāhmaṇas* who were present. The entire issue was so complicated that those who were not strong enough forgot their positions, and thus cursing and countercursing went on in that great assembly. In other words, the material field is so unsteady that even personalities like Nandīśvara, Dakṣa and many of the *brāhmaṇas* present were infected by the atmosphere of anger.

TEXT 21

य एतन्मर्त्यमुद्दिश्य भगवत्यप्रतिद्रुहि ।
द्रुह्यत्यज्ञः पृथग्दृष्टिस्तत्त्वतो विमुखो भवेत् ॥२१॥

ya etan martyam uddiśya
bhagavaty apratidruhi
druhyaty ajñaḥ pṛthag-dṛṣṭis
tattvato vimukho bhavet

yaḥ—who (Dakṣa); *etat martyam*—this body; *uddiśya*—with reference to; *bhagavati*—to Śiva; *apratidruhi*—who is not envious;

druhyati—bears envy; *ajñaḥ*—less intelligent persons; *pṛthak-dṛṣṭiḥ*—the vision of duality; *tattvataḥ*—from transcendental knowledge; *vimukhaḥ*—bereft; *bhavet*—may become.

TRANSLATION

Anyone who has accepted Dakṣa as the most important personality and neglected Lord Śiva because of envy is less intelligent and, because of visualizing in duality, will be bereft of transcendental knowledge.

PURPORT

The first curse by Nandīśvara was that anyone supporting Dakṣa was foolishly identifying himself with the body, and therefore, because Dakṣa had no transcendental knowledge, supporting him would deprive one of transcendental knowledge. Dakṣa, Nandīśvara said, identified himself with the body like other materialistic persons and was trying to derive all kinds of facilities in relationship with the body. He had excessive attachment for the body and, in relation to the body, with wife, children, home and other such things, which are different from the soul. Therefore Nandīśvara's curse was that anyone who supported Dakṣa would be bereft of transcendental knowledge of the soul and thus also be deprived of knowledge of the Supreme Personality of Godhead.

TEXT 22

गृहेषु कूटधर्मेषु सक्तो ग्राम्यसुखेच्छया ।
कर्मतन्त्रं वितनुते वेदवादविपन्नधीः ॥२२॥

gṛheṣu kūṭa-dharmeṣu
sakto grāmya-sukhecchayā
karma-tantraṁ vitanute
veda-vāda-vipanna-dhīḥ

gṛheṣu—in householder life; *kūṭa-dharmeṣu*—of pretentious religiosity; *saktaḥ*—being attracted; *grāmya-sukha-icchayā*—by desire for material happiness; *karma-tantram*—fruitive activities; *vitanute*—he performs; *veda-vāda*—by the explanations of the *Vedas; vipanna-dhīḥ*—intelligence being lost.

TRANSLATION

Pretentiously religious householder life, in which one is attracted to material happiness and thus also attracted to the superficial explanation of the Vedas, robs one of all intelligence and attaches one to fruitive activities as all in all.

PURPORT

Persons who identify with bodily existence are attached to the fruitive activities described in the Vedic literature. For example, in the *Vedas* it is said that one who observes the *cāturmāsya* vow will attain eternal happiness in the heavenly kingdom. In *Bhagavad-gītā*, it is said that this flowery language of the *Vedas* mostly attracts persons who identify with the body. To them such happiness as that of the heavenly kingdom is everything; they do not know that beyond that is the spiritual kingdom, or kingdom of God, and they have no knowledge that one can go there. Thus they are bereft of transcendental knowledge. Such persons are very careful in observing the rules and regulations of household life in order to be promoted in the next life to the moon or other heavenly planets. It is stated here that such persons are attached to *grāmya-sukha*, which means "material happiness," without knowledge of eternal, blissful spiritual life.

TEXT 23

बुद्ध्या पराभिध्यायिन्या विस्मृतात्मगतिः पशुः ।
स्त्रीकामः सोऽस्त्वतितरां दक्षो बस्तमुखोऽचिरात् ॥२३॥

buddhyā parābhidhyāyinyā
vismṛtātma-gatiḥ paśuḥ
strī-kāmaḥ so 'stv atitarāṁ
dakṣo basta-mukho 'cirāt

buddhyā—by intelligence; *para-abhidhyāyinyā*—by accepting the body as the self; *vismṛta-ātma-gatiḥ*—having forgotten the knowledge of Viṣṇu; *paśuḥ*—an animal; *strī-kāmaḥ*—attached to sex life; *saḥ*—he (Dakṣa); *astu*—let; *atitarām*—excessive; *dakṣaḥ*—Dakṣa; *basta-mukhaḥ*—the face of a goat; *acirāt*—in a very short time.

TRANSLATION

Dakṣa has accepted the body as all in all. Therefore, since he has forgotten the viṣṇu-pāda, or viṣṇu-gati, and is attached to sex life only, within a short time he will have the face of a goat.

TEXT 24

विद्याबुद्धिरविद्यायां कर्ममय्यामसौ जडः ।
संसरन्त्विह ये चामुमनु शर्वावमानिनम् ॥२४॥

vidyā-buddhir avidyāyāṁ
karmamayyām asau jaḍaḥ
saṁsarantv iha ye cāmum
anu śarvāvamāninam

vidyā-buddhiḥ—materialistic education and intelligence; *avidyā-yām*—in nescience; *karma-mayyām*—formed of fruitive activities; *asau*—he (Dakṣa); *jaḍaḥ*—dull; *saṁsarantu*—let them take birth again and again; *iha*—here in this world; *ye*—who; *ca*—and; *amum*—Dakṣa; *anu*—following; *śarva*—Śiva; *avamāninam*—insulting.

TRANSLATION

Those who have become as dull as matter by cultivating materialistic education and intelligence are nesciently involved in fruitive activities. Such men have purposely insulted Lord Śiva. May they continue in the cycle of repeated birth and death.

PURPORT

The three curses mentioned above are sufficient to make one as dull as stone, void of spiritual knowledge and preoccupied with materialistic education, which is nescience. After uttering these curses, Nandīśvara then cursed the *brāhmaṇas* to continue in the cycle of birth and death because of their supporting Dakṣa in blaspheming Lord Śiva.

TEXT 25

गिरः श्रुतायाः पुष्पिण्या मधुगन्धेन भूरिणा ।
मथ्ना चोन्मथितात्मानः सम्मुह्यन्तु हरद्विषः ॥२५॥

giraḥ śrutāyāḥ puṣpiṇyā
madhu-gandhena bhūriṇā
mathnā conmathitātmānaḥ
sammuhyantu hara-dviṣaḥ

giraḥ—words; *śrutāyāḥ*—of the *Vedas; puṣpiṇyāḥ*—flowery; *madhu-gandhena*—with the scent of honey; *bhūriṇā*—profuse; *mathnā*—enchanting; *ca*—and; *unmathita-ātmānaḥ*—whose minds have become dull; *sammuhyantu*—let them remain attached; *hara-dviṣaḥ*—envious of Lord Śiva.

TRANSLATION

May those who are envious of Lord Śiva, being attracted by the flowery language of the enchanting Vedic promises, and who have thus become dull, always remain attached to fruitive activities.

PURPORT

The Vedic promises of elevation to higher planets for a better standard of materialistic life are compared to flowery language because in a flower there is certainly an aroma but that aroma does not last for a very long time. In a flower there is honey, but that honey is not eternal.

TEXT 26

सर्वभक्षा द्विजा वृत्त्यै धृतविद्यातपोव्रताः ।
वित्तदेहेन्द्रियारामा याचका विचरन्त्विह ॥२६॥

sarva-bhakṣā dvijā vṛttyai
dhṛta-vidyā-tapo-vratāḥ

vitta-dehendriyārāmā
yācakā vicarantv iha

sarva-bhakṣāḥ—eating everything; *dvijāḥ*—the *brāhmaṇas; vṛttyai*—for maintaining the body; *dhṛta-vidyā*—having taken to education; *tapaḥ*—austerity; *vratāḥ*—and vows; *vitta*—money; *deha*—the body; *indriya*—the senses; *ārāmāḥ*—the satisfaction; *yācakāḥ*—as beggars; *vicarantu*—let them wander; *iha*—here.

TRANSLATION

These brāhmaṇas take to education, austerity and vows only for the purpose of maintaining the body. They shall be devoid of discrimination between what to eat and what not to eat. They will acquire money, begging from door to door, simply for the satisfaction of the body.

PURPORT

The third curse inflicted by Nandīśvara on the *brāhmaṇas* who supported Dakṣa is completely functioning in the age of Kali. The so-called *brāhmaṇas* are no longer interested in understanding the nature of the Supreme Brahman, although a *brāhmaṇa* means one who has attained knowledge about Brahman. In the *Vedānta-sūtra* also it is stated, *athāto brahma-jijñāsā:* this human form of life is meant for realization of the Supreme Brahman, the Absolute Truth, or, in other words, human life is meant for one's elevation to the post of a *brāhmaṇa*. Unfortunately the modern *brāhmaṇas*, or so-called *brāhmaṇas* who come in originally brahminical families, have left their own occupational duties, but they do not allow others to occupy the posts of *brāhmaṇas*. The qualifications for *brāhmaṇas* are described in the scriptures, in *Śrīmad-Bhāgavatam*, *Bhagavad-gītā* and all other Vedic literatures. *Brāhmaṇa* is not a hereditary title or position. If someone from a non-*brāhmaṇa* family (for example, one born in a family of *śūdras*) tries to become a *brāhmaṇa* by being properly qualified under the instruction of a bona fide spiritual master, these so-called *brāhmaṇas* will object. Such *brāhmaṇas*, having been cursed by Nandīśvara, are actually in a position where they have no discrimination between eatables and noneatables and simply live to maintain the perishable material body and its family. Such fallen conditioned souls are not worthy to be called *brāhmaṇas*, but in Kali-yuga they claim to be *brāhmaṇas*, and if a person actually tries to attain the brahminical qualifications, they try to hinder his progress. This is the situation in the present age. Caitanya Mahāprabhu condemned this principle very strongly. During His conversation with Rāmānanda Rāya, He said that regardless of whether a person is born in a *brāhmaṇa* family or *śūdra* family, regardless of whether he is a householder or a *sannyāsī*, if he knows the science of Kṛṣṇa he must be a spiritual master. Caitanya Mahāprabhu had many so-called *śūdra* disciples like Haridāsa Ṭhākura and Rāmānanda Rāya. Even the Gosvāmīs, who were principal students of Lord Caitanya, were also ostracized from *brāhmaṇa* society, but Caitanya Mahāprabhu, by His grace, made them first-class Vaiṣṇavas.

TEXT 27

तस्यैवं वदतः शापं श्रुत्वा द्विजकुलाय वै ।
भृगुः प्रत्यसृजच्छापं ब्रह्मदण्डं दुरत्ययम् ॥२७॥

tasyaivaṁ vadataḥ śāpaṁ
śrutvā dvija-kulāya vai
bhṛguḥ pratyasṛjac chāpaṁ
brahma-daṇḍam duratyayam

tasya—his (Nandīśvara's); *evam*—thus; *vadataḥ*—words; *śāpam*—the curse; *śrutvā*—hearing; *dvija-kulāya*—unto the *brāhmaṇas; vai*—indeed; *bhṛguḥ*—Bhṛgu; *pratyasṛjat*—made; *śāpam*—a curse; *brahma-daṇḍam*—the punishment of a *brāhmaṇa; duratyayam*—insurmountable.

TRANSLATION

When all the hereditary brāhmaṇas were thus cursed by Nandīśvara, the sage Bhṛgu, as a reaction, condemned the followers of Lord Śiva with this very strong brahminical curse.

PURPORT

The word *duratyaya* is particularly used in reference to a *brahma-daṇḍa*, or curse by a *brāhmaṇa*. A curse by a *brāhmaṇa* is very strong; therefore it is called *duratyaya*, or insurmountable. As the Lord states in

Bhagavad-gītā, the stringent laws of nature are insurmountable; similarly, if a curse is uttered by a *brāhmaṇa*, that curse is also insurmountable. But *Bhagavad-gītā* also says that the curses or benedictions of the material world are, after all, material creations. The *Caitanya-caritāmṛta* confirms that that which is accepted in this material world to be a benediction and that which is taken to be a curse are both on the same platform because they are material. To get out of this material contamination, one should take shelter of the Supreme Personality of Godhead, as recommended in *Bhagavad-gītā* (7.14): *mām eva ye prapadyante māyām etāṁ taranti te.* The best path is to transcend all material curses and benedictions and take shelter of the Supreme Lord, Kṛṣṇa, and remain in a transcendental position. Persons who have taken shelter of Kṛṣṇa are always peaceful; they are never cursed by anyone, nor do they attempt to curse anyone. That is a transcendental position.

TEXT 28

भवव्रतधरा ये च ये च तान् समनुव्रताः ।
पाषण्डिनस्ते भवन्तु सच्छास्त्रपरिपन्थिनः ॥२८॥

bhava-vrata-dharā ye ca
ye ca tān samanuvratāḥ
pāṣaṇḍinas te bhavantu
sac-chāstra-paripanthinaḥ

bhava-vrata-dharāḥ—taking a vow to satisfy Lord Śiva; *ye*—who; *ca*—and; *ye*—who; *ca*—and; *tān*—such principles; *samanuvratāḥ*—following; *pāṣaṇḍinaḥ*—atheists; *te*—they; *bhavantu*—let them become; *sat-śāstra-paripanthinaḥ*—diverted from transcendental scriptural injunctions.

TRANSLATION

One who takes a vow to satisfy Lord Śiva or who follows such principles will certainly become an atheist and be diverted from transcendental scriptural injunctions.

PURPORT

It is sometimes seen that devotees of Lord Śiva imitate the characteristics of Lord Śiva. For example, Lord Śiva drank an ocean of poison, so some of the followers of Lord Śiva imitate him and try to take intoxicants like *gāñjā* (marijuana). Here the curse is that if someone follows such principles he must become an infidel and turn against the principles of Vedic regulation. It is said that such devotees of Lord Śiva will be *sac-chāstra-paripanthinaḥ*, which means "opposed to the conclusion of *śāstra*, or scripture." This is confirmed in the *Padma Purāṇa* also. Lord Śiva was ordered by the Supreme Personality of Godhead to preach the impersonal, or Māyāvāda, philosophy for a particular purpose, just as Lord Buddha preached the philosophy of voidness for particular purposes mentioned in the *śāstras*.

Sometimes it is necessary to preach a philosophical doctrine which is against the Vedic conclusion. In the *Śiva Purāṇa* it is stated that Lord Śiva said to Pārvatī that in the Kali-yuga, in the body of a *brāhmaṇa*, he would preach the Māyāvāda philosophy. Thus it is generally found that the worshipers of Lord Śiva are Māyāvādī followers. Lord Śiva himself says, *māyāvādam asac-chāstram. Asat-śāstra*, as explained here, means the doctrine of Māyāvāda impersonalism, or becoming one with the Supreme. Bhṛgu Muni cursed that persons who worshiped Lord Śiva would become followers of this Māyāvāda *asat-śāstra*, which attempts to establish that the Supreme Personality of Godhead is impersonal. Besides that, among the worshipers of Lord Śiva there is a section who live a devilish life. *Śrīmad-Bhāgavatam* and *Nārada-pañcarātra* are authorized scriptures that are considered *sat-śāstra*, or scriptures which lead one to the path of God realization. *Asat-śāstras* are just the opposite.

TEXT 29

नष्टशौचा मूढधियो जटाभस्मास्थिधारिणः ।
विशन्तु शिवदीक्षायां यत्र दैवं सुरासवम् ॥२९॥

naṣṭa-śaucā mūḍha-dhiyo
jaṭā-bhasmāsthi-dhāriṇaḥ
viśantu śiva-dīkṣāyāṁ
yatra daivaṁ surāsavam

naṣṭa-śaucāḥ—cleanliness being abandoned; *mūḍha-dhiyaḥ*—foolish; *jaṭā-bhasma-asthi-dhāriṇaḥ*—wearing long hair, ashes and bones;

viśantu—may enter; *śiva-dīkṣāyām*—into initiation of worship of Śiva; *yatra*—where; *daivam*—are spiritual; *sura-āsavam*—wine and liquor.

TRANSLATION

Those who vow to worship Lord Śiva are so foolish that they imitate him by keeping long hair on their heads. When initiated into worship of Lord Śiva, they prefer to live on wine, flesh and other such things.

PURPORT

Indulging in wine and meat, keeping long hair on one's head, not bathing daily, and smoking *gāñjā* (marijuana) are some of the habits which are accepted by foolish creatures who do not have regulated lives. By such behavior one becomes devoid of transcendental knowledge. In the initiation into the Śiva *mantra* there are *mudrikāṣṭaka*, in which it is sometimes recommended that one make his sitting place on the vagina and thus desire *nirvāṇa*, or dissolution of existence. In that process of worship, wine is needed, or sometimes, in place of wine, palm tree juice which is converted into an intoxicant. This is also offered according to *Śiva-āgama*, a scripture on the method of worshiping Lord Śiva.

TEXT 30

ब्रह्म च ब्राह्मणांश्चैव यद्यूयं परिनिन्दथ ।
सेतुं विधारणं पुंसामतः पाषण्डमाश्रिताः ॥३०॥

brahma ca brāhmaṇāṁś caiva
yad yūyaṁ parinindatha
setuṁ vidhāraṇaṁ puṁsām
ataḥ pāṣaṇḍam āśritāḥ

brahma—the *Vedas; ca*—and; *brāhmaṇān*—the *brāhmaṇas; ca*—and; *eva*—certainly; *yat*—because; *yūyam*—you; *parinindatha*—blaspheme; *setum*—Vedic principles; *vidhāraṇam*—holding; *puṁsām*—of mankind; *ataḥ*—therefore; *pāṣaṇḍam*—atheism; *āśritāḥ*—have taken shelter.

TRANSLATION

Bhṛgu Muni continued: Since you blaspheme the Vedas and the brāhmaṇas, who are followers of the Vedic principles, it is understood that you have already taken shelter of the doctrine of atheism.

PURPORT

Bhṛgu Muni, in cursing Nandīśvara, said that not only would they be degraded as atheists because of this curse, but they had already fallen to the standard of atheism because they had blasphemed the *Vedas*, which are the source of human civilization. Human civilization is based on the qualitative divisions of social order, namely the intelligent class, the martial class, the productive class and the laborer class. The *Vedas* provide the right direction for advancing in spiritual cultivation and economic development and regulating the principle of sense gratification, so that ultimately one may be liberated from material contamination to his real state of spiritual identification (*ahaṁ brahmāsmi*). As long as one is in the contamination of material existence, one changes bodies from the aquatics up to the position of Brahmā, but the human form of life is the highest perfectional life in the material world. The *Vedas* give directions by which to elevate oneself in the next life. The *Vedas* are the mother for such instructions, and the *brāhmaṇas*, or persons who are in knowledge of the *Vedas*, are the father. Thus if one blasphemes the *Vedas* and *brāhmaṇas*, naturally one goes down to the status of atheism. The exact word used in Sanskrit is *nāstika*, which refers to one who does not believe in the *Vedas* but manufactures some concocted system of religion. Śrī Caitanya Mahāprabhu has said that the followers of the Buddhist system of religion are *nāstikas*. In order to establish his doctrine of nonviolence, Lord Buddha flatly refused to believe in the *Vedas*, and thus, later on, Śaṅkarācārya stopped this system of religion in India and forced it to go outside India. Here it is stated, *brahma ca brāhmaṇān*. *Brahma* means the *Vedas*. *Ahaṁ brahmāsmi* means "I am in full knowledge." The Vedic assertion is that one should think that he is Brahman, for actually he is Brahman. If *brahma*, or the Vedic spiritual science, is condemned, and the masters of the spiritual science, the *brāhmaṇas*, are condemned, then where does human civilization stand? Bhṛgu Muni said, "It is not due to my cursing that you shall become atheists; you are already situated in the principle of atheism. Therefore you are condemned."

TEXT 31

एष एव हि लोकानां शिवः पन्थाः सनातनः ।
यं पूर्वे चानुसंतस्थुर्यत्प्रमाणं जनार्दनः ॥३१॥

eṣa eva hi lokānāṁ
śivaḥ panthāḥ sanātanaḥ
yaṁ pūrve cānusantasthur
yat-pramāṇaṁ janārdanaḥ

eṣaḥ—the *Vedas; eva*—certainly; *hi*—for; *lokānām*—of all people; *śivaḥ*—auspicious; *panthāḥ*—path; *sanātanaḥ*—eternal; *yam*—which (Vedic path); *pūrve*—in the past; *ca*—and; *anusantasthuḥ*—was rigidly followed; *yat*—in which; *pramāṇam*—the evidence; *janārdanaḥ*—Janārdana.

TRANSLATION

The Vedas give the eternal regulative principles for auspicious advancement in human civilization which have been rigidly followed in the past. The strong evidence of this principle is the Supreme Personality of Godhead, who is called Janārdana, the well-wisher of all living entities.

PURPORT

In the *Bhagavad-gītā* the Supreme Personality of Godhead, Kṛṣṇa, has claimed that He is the father of all living entities, regardless of form. There are 8,400,000 different species of life forms, and Lord Kṛṣṇa claims that He is the father of all. Because the living entities are parts and parcels of the Supreme Personality of Godhead, they are all sons of the Lord, and for their benefit, because they are hovering under the impression that they can lord it over material nature, the *Vedas* are given to them for their guidance. Therefore the *Vedas* are called *apauruṣeya*, for they are not written by any man or demigod, including the first living creature, Brahmā. Brahmā is not the creator or author of the *Vedas*. He is also one of the living beings in this material world; therefore he does not have the power to write or speak the *Vedas* independently. Every living entity within this material world is subject to four deficiencies: he commits mistakes, he accepts one thing for another, he cheats, and he has imperfect senses. The *Vedas*, however, are not written by any living creature within this material world. Therefore they are said to be *apauruṣeya.* No one can trace out the history of the *Vedas.* Of course, modern human civilization has no chronological history of the world or the universe, and it cannot present actual historical facts older than three thousand years. But no one has traced out when the *Vedas* were written, because they were never written by any living being within this material world. All other systems of knowledge are defective because they have been written or spoken by men or demigods who are products of this material creation, but *Bhagavad-gītā* is *apauruṣeya,* for it was not spoken by any human being or any demigod of this material creation; it was spoken by Lord Kṛṣṇa, who is beyond the material creation. That is accepted by such stalwart scholars as Śaṅkarācārya, not to speak of other *ācāryas* such as Rāmānujācārya and Madhvācārya. Śaṅkarācārya has accepted that Nārāyaṇa and Kṛṣṇa are transcendental, and in *Bhagavad-gītā* also Lord Kṛṣṇa has established, *ahaṁ sarvasya prabhavo mattaḥ sarvaṁ pravartate:* "I am the origin of everything; everything emanates from Me." This material creation, including Brahmā and Śiva and all the demigods, has been created by Him, for everything has emanated from Him. He also says that the purpose of all the *Vedas* is to understand Him (*vedaiś ca sarvair aham eva vedyaḥ*). He is the original *veda-vit,* or knower of the *Vedas,* and *vedānta-kṛt,* or compiler of *Vedānta.* Brahmā is not the compiler of the *Vedas.*

In the beginning of *Śrīmad-Bhāgavatam* it is established, *tene brahma hṛdā:* the Supreme Absolute Truth, the Personality of Godhead, instructed Brahmā in the Vedic knowledge through his heart. Therefore the evidence that Vedic knowledge is free from the defects of mistakes, illusions, cheating and imperfection is that it is spoken by the Supreme Personality of Godhead, Janārdana, and has thus been followed from time immemorial, beginning from Brahmā. The Vedic religion or the principles of the *Vedas* have been followed by the highly cultured population of India since time immemorial; no one can trace out the history of Vedic religion. Therefore it is *sanātana,* and any blasphemy against the *Vedas* is calculated to be atheism. The *Vedas* are described as *setu*, which means "a bridge." If one wants to attain his spiritual existence, one has to cross an ocean of nescience. The *Vedas* are the bridge by which to cross such a great ocean.

The *Vedas* describe how to divide the human race into four divisions according to quality and working capacity. This is a very scientific system, and it is also *sanātana*, for no one can trace out its history and it has no dissolution. No one can stop the system of *varṇa* and *āśrama*, or the castes and divisions. For example, whether or not one accepts the name *brāhmaṇa*, there is a class in society which is known as the intelligent class and which is interested in spiritual understanding and philosophy. Similarly, there is a class of men who are interested in administration and in ruling others. In the Vedic system these martially spirited men are called *kṣatriyas*. Similarly, everywhere there is a class of men who are interested in economic development, business, industry and moneymaking; they are called *vaiśyas*. And there is another class who are neither intelligent nor martially spirited nor endowed with the capacity for economic development but who simply can serve others. They are called *śūdras*, or the laborer class. This system is *sanātana*—it comes from time immemorial, and it will continue in the same way. There is no power in the world which can stop it. Therefore, since this *sanātana-dharma* system is eternal, one can elevate himself to the highest standard of spiritual life by following the Vedic principles.

It is stated that formerly the sages followed this system; therefore to follow the Vedic system is to follow the standard etiquette of society. But the followers of Lord Śiva, who are drunkards, who are addicted to intoxicants and sex life, who do not bathe and who smoke *gāñjā*, are against all human etiquette. The conclusion is that persons who rebel against the Vedic principles are themselves the evidence that the *Vedas* are authoritative, because by not following the Vedic principles they become like animals. Such animalistic persons are themselves evidence of the supremacy of the Vedic regulations.

TEXT 32

तद्ब्रह्म परमं शुद्धं सतां वर्त्म सनातनम् ।
विगर्ह्य यात पाषण्डं दैवं वो यत्र भूतराट् ॥३२॥

tad brahma paramaṁ śuddhaṁ
satāṁ vartma sanātanam
vigarhya yāta pāṣaṇḍaṁ
daivaṁ vo yatra bhūta-rāṭ

tat—that; *brahma*—*Veda;* *paramam*—supreme; *śuddham*—pure; *satām*—of the saintly persons; *vartma*—path; *sanātanam*—eternal; *vigarhya*—blaspheming; *yāta*—should go; *pāṣaṇḍam*—to atheism; *daivam*—deity; *vaḥ*—your; *yatra*—where; *bhūta-rāṭ*—the lord of the *bhūtas.*

TRANSLATION

By blaspheming the principles of the Vedas, which are the pure and supreme path of the saintly persons, certainly you followers of Bhūtapati, Lord Śiva, will descend to the standard of atheism without a doubt.

PURPORT

Lord Śiva is described here as *bhūta-rāṭ.* The ghosts and those who are situated in the material mode of ignorance are called *bhūtas,* so *bhūta-rāṭ* refers to the leader of the creatures who are in the lowest standard of the material modes of nature. Another meaning of *bhūta* is anyone who has taken birth or anything which is produced, so in that sense Lord Śiva may be accepted as the father of this material world. Here, of course, Bhṛgu Muni takes Lord Śiva as the leader of the lowest creatures. The characteristics of the lowest class of men have already been described—they do not bathe, they have long hair on their heads, and they are addicted to intoxicants. In comparison with the path followed by the followers of Bhūtarāṭ, the Vedic system is certainly excellent, for it promotes people to spiritual life as the highest eternal principle of human civilization. If one decries or blasphemes the Vedic principles, then he falls to the standard of atheism.

TEXT 33

मैत्रेय उवाच

तस्यैवं वदतः शापं भृगोः स भगवान् भवः ।
निश्चक्राम ततः किञ्चिद्विमना इव सानुगः ॥३३॥

maitreya uvāca
tasyaivaṁ vadataḥ śāpaṁ
bhṛgoḥ sa bhagavān bhavaḥ
niścakrāma tataḥ kiñcid
vimanā iva sānugaḥ

maitreyaḥ uvāca—Maitreya said; *tasya*—of him; *evam*—thus; *vadataḥ*—being spoken; *śāpam*—curse; *bhṛgoḥ*—of Bhṛgu; *saḥ*—he; *bhagavān*—the possessor of all opulences; *bhavaḥ*—Lord Śiva; *niścakrāma*—went; *tataḥ*—from there; *kiñcit*—somewhat; *vimanāḥ*—morose; *iva*—as; *sa-anugaḥ*—followed by his disciples.

TRANSLATION

The sage Maitreya said: When such cursing and countercursing was going on between Lord Śiva's followers and the parties of Dakṣa and Bhṛgu, Lord Śiva became very morose. Not saying anything, he left the arena of the sacrifice, followed by his disciples.

PURPORT

Here Lord Śiva's excellent character is described. In spite of the cursing and countercursing between the parties of Dakṣa and Śiva, because he is the greatest Vaiṣṇava he was so sober that he did not say anything. A Vaiṣṇava is always tolerant, and Lord Śiva is considered the topmost Vaiṣṇava, so his character, as shown in this scene, is excellent. He became morose because he knew that these people, both his men and Dakṣa's, were unnecessarily cursing and countercursing one another, without any interest in spiritual life. From his point of view, he did not see anyone as lower or higher, because he is a Vaiṣṇava. As stated in *Bhagavad-gītā* (5.18), *paṇḍitāḥ sama-darśinaḥ:* one who is perfectly learned does not see anyone as lesser or greater, because he sees everyone from the spiritual platform. Thus the only alternative left to Lord Śiva was to leave in order to stop his follower, Nandīśvara, as well as Bhṛgu Muni, from cursing and countercursing in that way.

TEXT 34

तेऽपि विश्वसृजः सत्रं सहस्रपरिवत्सरान् ।
संविधाय महेष्वास यत्रेज्य ऋषभो हरिः ॥३४॥

te 'pi viśva-sṛjaḥ satraṁ
sahasra-parivatsarān
saṁvidhāya maheṣvāsa
yatrejya ṛṣabho hariḥ

te—those; *api*—even; *viśva-sṛjaḥ*—progenitors of the universal population; *satram*—the sacrifice; *sahasra*—one thousand; *parivat-sarān*—years; *saṁvidhāya*—performing; *maheṣvāsa*—O Vidura; *yatra*—in which; *ijyaḥ*—to be worshiped; *ṛṣabhaḥ*—the presiding Deity of all demigods; *hariḥ*—Hari.

TRANSLATION

The sage Maitreya continued: O Vidura, all the progenitors of the universal population thus executed a sacrifice for thousands of years, for sacrifice is the best way to worship the Supreme Lord, Hari, the Personality of Godhead.

PURPORT

It is clearly stated here that the stalwart personalities who generate the entire population of the world are interested in satisfying the Supreme Personality of Godhead by offering sacrifices. The Lord also says in *Bhagavad-gītā* (5.29), *bhoktāraṁ yajña-tapasām.* One may engage in performing sacrifices and severe austerities for perfection, but they are all meant to satisfy the Supreme Lord. If such activities are performed for personal satisfaction, one is involved in *pāṣaṇḍa,* or atheism; but when they are performed for the satisfaction of the Supreme Lord, one is following the Vedic principle. All the assembled sages performed sacrifices for one thousand years.

TEXT 35

आप्लुत्यावभृथं यत्र गङ्गा यमुनयान्विता ।
विरजेनात्मना सर्वे स्वं स्वं धाम ययुस्ततः ॥३५॥

āplutyāvabhṛthaṁ yatra
gaṅgā yamunayānvitā
virajenātmanā sarve
svaṁ svaṁ dhāma yayus tataḥ

āplutya—taking a bath; *avabhṛtham*—the bath which is taken after performing sacrifices; *yatra*—where; *gaṅgā*—the River Ganges; *yamunayā*—by the River Yamunā; *anvitā*—mixed; *virajena*—without infection; *ātmanā*—by the mind; *sarve*—all; *svam svam*—their respective; *dhāma*—abodes; *yayuḥ*—went; *tataḥ*—from there.

TRANSLATION

My dear Vidura, carrier of bows and arrows, all the demigods who were performing the sacrifice took their bath at the confluence of the Ganges and the Yamunā after completing the yajña performance. Such a bath is called avabhṛtha-snāna. After thus becoming purified in heart, they departed for their respective abodes.

PURPORT

After Lord Śiva and, previously, Dakṣa, left the arena of sacrifice, the sacrifice was not stopped; the sages went on for many years in order to satisfy the Supreme Lord. The sacrifice was not destroyed for want of Śiva and Dakṣa, and the sages went on with their activities. In other words, it may be assumed that if one does not worship the demigods, even up to Lord Śiva and Brahmā, one can nevertheless satisfy the Supreme Personality of Godhead. This is also confirmed in *Bhagavad-gītā* (7.20). *Kāmais tais tair hṛta-jñānāḥ prapadyante 'nya-devatāḥ.* Persons who are impelled by lust and desire go to the demigods to derive some material benefit. *Bhagavad-gītā* uses the very specific words *nāsti buddhiḥ,* meaning "persons who have lost their sense or intelligence." Only such persons care for demigods and want to derive material benefit from them. Of course, this does not mean that one should not show respect to the demigods; but there is no need to worship them. One who is honest may be faithful to the government, but he does not need to bribe the government servants. Bribery is illegal; one does not bribe a government servant, but that does not mean that one does not show him respect. Similarly, one who engages in the transcendental loving service of the Supreme Lord does not need to worship any demigod, nor does he have any tendency to show disrespect to the demigods. Elsewhere in *Bhagavad-gītā* (9.23) it is stated, *ye 'py anya-devatā-bhaktā yajante śraddhayānvitāḥ.* The Lord says that anyone who worships the demigods is also worshiping Him, but he is worshiping *avidhi-pūrvakam,* which means "without following the regulative principles." The regulative principle is to worship the Supreme Personality of Godhead. Worship of demigods may indirectly be worship of the Personality of Godhead, but it is not regulated. By worshiping the Supreme Lord, one automatically serves all the demigods because they are parts and parcels of the whole. If one supplies water to the root of a tree, all the parts of the tree, such as the leaves and branches, are automatically satisfied, and if one supplies food to the stomach, all the limbs of the body—the hands, legs, fingers, etc.—are nourished. Thus by worshiping the Supreme Personality of Godhead one can satisfy all the demigods, but by worshiping all the demigods one does not completely worship the Supreme Lord. Therefore worship of the demigods is irregular, and it is disrespectful to the scriptural injunctions.

In this age of Kali it is practically impossible to perform the *deva-yajña*, or sacrifices to the demigods. As such, in this age *Śrīmad-Bhāgavatam* recommends *saṅkīrtana-yajña. Yajñaiḥ saṅkīrtana-prāyair yajanti hi sumedhasaḥ* (*Bhāg.* 11.5.32). "In this age the intelligent person completes the performances of all kinds of *yajñas* simply by chanting Hare Kṛṣṇa, Hare Kṛṣṇa, Kṛṣṇa Kṛṣṇa, Hare Hare/ Hare Rāma, Hare Rāma, Rāma Rāma, Hare Hare." *Tasmin tuṣṭe jagat tuṣṭaḥ:* "When Lord Viṣṇu is satisfied, all the demigods, who are parts and parcels of the Supreme Lord, are satisfied."

Thus end the Bhaktivedanta purports of the Fourth Canto, Second Chapter, of the Śrīmad-Bhāgavatam, *entitled "Dakṣa Curses Lord Śiva."*

CHAPTER THREE

Talks Between Lord Śiva and Satī

TEXT 1

मैत्रेय उवाच
सदा विद्विषतोरेवं कालो वै ध्रियमाणयोः ।
जामातुः श्वशुरस्यापि सुमहानतिचक्रमे ॥ १ ॥

maitreya uvāca
sadā vidviṣator evaṁ
kālo vai dhriyamāṇayoḥ
jāmātuḥ śvaśurasyāpi
sumahān aticakrame

maitreyaḥ uvāca—Maitreya said; *sadā*—constantly; *vidviṣatoḥ*—the tension; *evam*—in this manner; *kālaḥ*—time; *vai*—certainly; *dhriyamāṇayoḥ*—continued to bear; *jāmātuḥ*—of the son-in-law; *śvaśurasya*—of the father-in-law; *api*—even; *su-mahān*—a very great; *aticakrame*—passed.

TRANSLATION

Maitreya continued: In this manner the tension between the father-in-law and son-in-law, Dakṣa and Lord Śiva, continued for a considerably long period.

PURPORT

The previous chapter has already explained that Vidura questioned the sage Maitreya as to the cause of the misunderstanding between Lord Śiva and Dakṣa. Another question is why the strife between Dakṣa and his son-in-law caused Satī to destroy her body. The chief reason for Satī's giving up her body was that her father, Dakṣa, began another sacrificial performance, to which Lord Śiva was not invited at all. Generally, when any sacrifice is performed, although each and every sacrifice is intended to pacify the Supreme Personality of Godhead, Viṣṇu, all the demigods, especially Lord Brahmā and Lord Śiva and the other principal demigods, such as Indra and Candra, are invited, and they take part. It is said that unless all the demigods are present, no sacrifice is complete. But in the tension between the father-in-law and son-in-law, Dakṣa began another *yajña* performance, to which Lord Śiva was not invited. Dakṣa was the chief progenitor employed by Lord Brahmā, and he was a son of Brahmā, so he had a high position and was also very proud.

TEXT 2

यदाभिषिक्तो दक्षस्तु ब्रह्मणा परमेष्ठिना ।
प्रजापतीनां सर्वेषामाधिपत्ये स्मयोऽभवत् ॥ २ ॥

yadābhiṣikto dakṣas tu
brahmaṇā parameṣṭhinā
prajāpatīnāṁ sarveṣām
ādhipatye smayo 'bhavat

yadā—when; *abhiṣiktaḥ*—appointed; *dakṣaḥ*—Dakṣa; *tu*—but; *brahmaṇā*—by Brahmā; *parameṣṭhinā*—the supreme teacher; *prajāpatīnām*—of the Prajāpatis; *sarveṣām*—of all; *ādhipatye*—as the chief; *smayaḥ*—puffed up; *abhavat*—he became.

TRANSLATION

When Lord Brahmā appointed Dakṣa the chief of all the Prajāpatis, the progenitors of population, Dakṣa became very much puffed up.

PURPORT

Although he was envious and was inimical towards Lord Śiva, Dakṣa was appointed the chief of all Prajāpatis. That was the cause of his excessive pride. When a man becomes too proud of his material possessions, he can perform any disastrous act, and therefore Dakṣa acted out of false prestige. That is described in this chapter.

TEXT 3

इष्ट्वा स वाजपेयेन ब्रह्मिष्ठानभिभूय च ।
बृहस्पतिसवं नाम समारेभे क्रतूत्तमम् ॥ ३ ॥

iṣṭvā sa vājapeyena
brahmiṣṭhān abhibhūya ca
bṛhaspati-savaṁ nāma
samārebhe kratūttamam

iṣṭvā—after performing; *saḥ*—he (Dakṣa); *vājapeyena*—with a *vājapeya* sacrifice; *brahmiṣṭhān*—Śiva and his followers; *abhibhūya*—neglecting; *ca*—and; *bṛhaspati-savam*—the *bṛhaspati-sava; nāma*—called; *samārebhe*—began; *kratu-uttamam*—the best of sacrifices.

TRANSLATION

Dakṣa began a sacrifice named vājapeya, and he became excessively confident of his support by Lord Brahmā. He then performed another great sacrifice, named bṛhaspati-sava.

PURPORT

In the *Vedas* it is prescribed that before performing a *bṛhaspati-sava* sacrifice, one should perform the sacrifice named *vājapeya.* While performing these sacrifices, however, Dakṣa neglected great devotees like Lord Śiva. According to Vedic scriptures, the demigods are eligible to participate in *yajñas* and share the oblations, but Dakṣa wanted to avoid them. All sacrifices are intended to pacify Lord Viṣṇu, but Lord Viṣṇu includes all His devotees. Brahmā, Lord Śiva and the other demigods are all obedient servants of Lord Viṣṇu; therefore Lord Viṣṇu is never satisfied without them. But Dakṣa, being puffed up with his power, wanted to deprive Lord Brahmā and Lord Śiva of participation in the sacrifice, understanding that if one satisfies Viṣṇu, it is not necessary to satisfy His followers. But that is not the process. Viṣṇu wants His followers to be satisfied first. Lord Kṛṣṇa says, *mad-bhakta-pūjābhyadhikā:* "The worship of My devotees is better than worship of Me." Similarly, in the *Śiva Purāṇa,* it is stated that the best mode of worship is to offer oblations to Viṣṇu, but better than that is to worship the devotees of Kṛṣṇa. Thus Dakṣa's determination to neglect Lord Śiva in the sacrifices was not fitting.

TEXT 4

तस्मिन् ब्रह्मर्षयः सर्वे देवर्षिपितृदेवताः ।
आसन् कृतस्वस्त्ययनास्तत्पत्न्यश्च सभर्तृकाः ॥ ४ ॥

tasmin brahmarṣayaḥ sarve
devarṣi-pitṛ-devatāḥ
āsan kṛta-svastyayanās
tat-patnyaś ca sa-bhartṛkāḥ

tasmin—in that (sacrifice); *brahma-ṛṣayaḥ*—the *brahmarṣis; sarve*—all; *devarṣi*—the *devarṣis; pitṛ*—ancestors; *devatāḥ*—demigods; *āsan*—were; *kṛta-svasti-ayanāḥ*—were very nicely decorated with ornaments; *tat-patnyaḥ*—their wives; *ca*—and; *sa-bhartṛkāḥ*—along with their husbands.

TRANSLATION

While the sacrifice was being performed, many brahmarṣis, great sages, ancestral demigods and other demigods, their wives all very nicely decorated with ornaments, attended from different parts of the universe.

PURPORT

In any auspicious ceremony, such as a marriage ceremony, sacrificial ceremony or *pūjā* ceremony, it is auspicious for married women to decorate themselves very nicely with ornaments, fine clothing and cosmetics. These are auspicious signs. Many heavenly women assembled with their husbands, the *devarṣis*, demigods and *rājarṣis*, in that great sacrifice named *bṛhaspati-sava.* It is specifically mentioned in this verse that they approached with their husbands, for when a woman is decorated nicely, her husband becomes more cheerful. The nice decorations, ornaments and dress of the wives of the demigods and sages and the cheerfulness of the demigods and sages themselves were all auspicious signs for the ceremony.

TEXTS 5–7

तदुपश्रुत्य नभसि खेचराणां प्रजल्पताम् ।
सती दाक्षायणी देवी पितृयज्ञमहोत्सवम् ॥ ५ ॥
व्रजन्तीः सर्वतो दिग्भ्य उपदेववरस्त्रियः ।
विमानयानाः सप्रेष्ठा निष्ककण्ठीः सुवाससः॥ ६ ॥
दृष्ट्वा स्वनिलयाभ्याशे लोलाक्षीर्मृष्टकुण्डलाः ।
पतिं भूतपतिं देवमौत्सुक्यादभ्यभाषत ॥ ७ ॥

tad upaśrutya nabhasi
khe-carāṇāṁ prajalpatām
satī dākṣāyaṇī devī
pitṛ-yajña-mahotsavam

vrajantīḥ sarvato digbhya
upadeva-vara-striyaḥ
vimāna-yānāḥ sa-preṣṭhā
niṣka-kaṇṭhīḥ suvāsasaḥ

dṛṣṭvā sva-nilayābhyāśe
lolākṣīr mṛṣṭa-kuṇḍalāḥ
patiṁ bhūta-patiṁ devam
autsukyād abhyabhāṣata

tat—then; *upaśrutya*—hearing; *nabhasi*—in the sky; *khe-carāṇām*—of those who were flying in the air (the Gandharvas); *prajalpatām*—the conversation; *satī*—Satī; *dākṣāyaṇī*—the daughter of Dakṣa; *devī*—the wife of Śiva; *pitṛ-yajña-mahā-utsavam*—the great festival of sacrifice performed by her father; *vrajantīḥ*—were going; *sarvataḥ*—from all; *digbhyaḥ*—directions; *upadeva-vara-striyaḥ*—the beautiful wives of the demigods; *vimāna-yānāḥ*—flying in their airplanes; *sa-preṣṭhāḥ*—along with their husbands; *niṣka-kaṇṭhīḥ*—having nice necklaces with lockets; *su-vāsasaḥ*—dressed in fine clothing; *dṛṣṭvā*—seeing; *sva-nilaya-abhyāśe*—near her residence; *lola-akṣīḥ*—having beautiful glittering eyes; *mṛṣṭa-kuṇḍalāḥ*—nice ear-rings; *patim*—her husband; *bhūta-patim*—the master of the *bhūtas;*

devam—the demigod; *autsukyāt*—from great anxiety; *abhyabhāṣata*—she spoke.

TRANSLATION

The chaste lady Satī, the daughter of Dakṣa, heard the heavenly denizens flying in the sky conversing about the great sacrifice being performed by her father. When she saw that from all directions the beautiful wives of the heavenly denizens, their eyes very beautifully glittering, were near her residence and were going to the sacrifice dressed in fine clothing and ornamented with earrings and necklaces with lockets, she approached her husband, the master of the bhūtas, in great anxiety, and spoke as follows.

PURPORT

It appears that the residence of Lord Śiva was not on this planet but somewhere in outer space, otherwise how could Satī have seen the airplanes coming from different directions towards this planet and heard the passengers talking about the great sacrifice being performed by Dakṣa? Satī is described here as Dākṣāyaṇī because she was the daughter of Dakṣa. The mention of *upadeva-vara* refers to inferior demigods like the Gandharvas, Kinnaras and Uragas, who are not exactly demigods but between the demigods and human beings. They were also coming in planes. The word *sva-nilayābhyāśe* indicates that they were passing right near her residential quarters. The dresses and bodily features of the wives of the heavenly denizens are very nicely described here. Their eyes moved, their earrings and other ornaments glittered and glared, their dresses were the nicest possible, and all of them had special lockets on their necklaces. Each woman was accompanied by her husband. Thus they looked so beautiful that Satī, Dākṣāyaṇī, was impelled to dress similarly and go to the sacrifice with her husband. That is the natural inclination of a woman.

TEXT 8

सत्युवाच

प्रजापतेस्ते श्वशुरस्य साम्प्रतं
निर्यापितो यज्ञमहोत्सवः किल ।

वयं च तत्राभिसराम वाम ते
यद्यर्थितामी विबुधा व्रजन्ति हि ॥ ८ ॥

saty uvāca
prajāpates te śvaśurasya sāmpratam
niryāpito yajña-mahotsavaḥ kila
vayaṁ ca tatrābhisarāma vāma te
yady arthitāmī vibudhā vrajanti hi

satī uvāca—Satī said; *prajāpateḥ*—of Dakṣa; *te*—your; *śvaśurasya*—of your father-in-law; *sāmpratam*—nowadays; *niryāpitaḥ*—has been started; *yajña-mahā-utsavaḥ*—a great sacrifice; *kila*—certainly; *vayam*—we; *ca*—and; *tatra*—there; *abhisarāma*—may go; *vāma*—O my dear Lord Śiva; *te*—your; *yadi*—if; *arthitā*—desire; *amī*—these; *vibudhāḥ*—demigods; *vrajanti*—are going; *hi*—because.

TRANSLATION

Satī said: My dear Lord Śiva, your father-in-law is now executing great sacrifices, and all the demigods, having been invited by him, are going there. If you desire, we may also go.

PURPORT

Satī knew of the tension between her father and her husband, but still she expressed to her husband, Lord Śiva, that since such sacrifices were going on at her father's house and so many demigods were going, she also desired to go. But she could not express her willingness directly, and so she told her husband that if he desired to go, then she could also accompany him. In other words, she submitted her desire very politely to her husband.

TEXT 9

तस्मिन् भगिन्यो मम भर्तृभिः स्वकै-
र्ध्रुवं गमिष्यन्ति सुहृद्दिदृक्षवः ।
अहं च तस्मिन् भवताभिकामये
सहोपनीतं परिबर्हमर्हितुम् ॥ ९ ॥

tasmin bhaginyo mama bhartṛbhiḥ svakair
dhruvaṁ gamiṣyanti suhṛd-didṛkṣavaḥ
ahaṁ ca tasmin bhavatābhikāmaye
sahopanītaṁ paribarham arhitum

tasmin—in that sacrifice; *bhaginyaḥ*—sisters; *mama*—my; *bhartṛbhiḥ*—with their husbands; *svakaiḥ*—their own; *dhruvam*—surely; *gamiṣyanti*—will go; *suhṛt-didṛkṣavaḥ*—desiring to meet the relatives; *aham*—I; *ca*—and; *tasmin*—in that assembly; *bhavatā*—with you (Lord Śiva); *abhikāmaye*—I desire; *saha*—with; *upanītam*—given; *paribarham*—ornaments of decoration; *arhitum*—to accept.

TRANSLATION

I think that all my sisters must have gone to this great sacrificial ceremony with their husbands just to see their relatives. I also desire to decorate myself with the ornaments given to me by my father and go there with you to participate in that assembly.

PURPORT

It is a woman's nature to want to decorate herself with ornaments and nice dresses and accompany her husband to social functions, meet friends and relatives, and enjoy life in that way. This propensity is not unusual, for woman is the basic principle of material enjoyment. Therefore in Sanskrit the word for woman is *strī*, which means "one who expands the field of material enjoyment." In the material world there is an attraction between woman and man. This is the arrangement of conditional life. A woman attracts a man, and in that way the scope of material activities, involving house, wealth, children and friendship, increases, and thus instead of decreasing one's material demands, one becomes entangled in material enjoyment. Lord Śiva, however, is different; therefore his name is Śiva. He is not at all attracted by material enjoyment, although his wife, Satī, was the daughter of a very great leader and was given to him by the request of Brahmā. Lord Śiva was reluctant, but Satī, as a woman, the daughter of a king, wanted enjoyment. She wanted to go to her father's house, just as her other sisters might have done, and meet them and enjoy social life. Here, she specifically indicated that she would decorate herself with the ornaments given by her father. She did not say that she would decorate herself with the ornaments given by her husband because her husband was callous about all such matters. He did not know how to decorate his wife and take part in social life because he was always in ecstasy with thoughts of the Supreme Personality of Godhead. According to the Vedic system, a daughter is given a sufficient dowry at the time of her marriage, and therefore Satī was also given a dowry by her father, and ornaments were included. It is also the custom that the husband gives some ornaments, but here it is particularly mentioned that her husband, being materially almost nothing, could not do so; therefore she wanted to decorate herself with the ornaments given by her father. It was fortunate for Satī that Lord Śiva did not take the ornaments from his wife and spend them for *gāñjā*, because those who imitate Lord Śiva in smoking *gāñjā* exploit everything from household affairs; they take all of their wives' property and spend on smoking, intoxication and similar other activities.

TEXT 10

तत्र स्वसॄर्मे ननु भर्तृसम्मिता
मातृष्वसॄः क्लिन्नधियं च मातरम् ।
द्रक्ष्ये चिरोत्कण्ठमना महर्षिभि-
रुन्नीयमानं च मृडाध्वरध्वजम् ॥१०॥

tatra svasṝr me nanu bhartṛ-sammitā
mātṛ-ṣvasṝḥ klinna-dhiyaṁ ca mātaram
drakṣye cirotkaṇṭha-manā maharṣibhir
unnīyamānaṁ ca mṛḍādhvara-dhvajam

tatra—there; *svasṝḥ*—own sisters; *me*—my; *nanu*—surely; *bhartṛ-sammitāḥ*—along with their husbands; *mātṛ-svasṝḥ*—the sisters of my mother; *klinna-dhiyam*—affectionate; *ca*—and; *mātaram*—mother; *drakṣye*—I shall see; *cira-utkaṇṭha-manāḥ*—being very anxious for a long time; *mahā-ṛṣibhiḥ*—by great sages; *unnīyamānam*—being raised; *ca*—and; *mṛḍa*—O Śiva; *adhvara*—sacrifice; *dhvajam*—flags.

TRANSLATION

My sisters, my mother's sisters and their husbands, and other affectionate relatives must be assembled there, so if I go I shall be

able to see them, and I shall be able to see the flapping flags and the performance of the sacrifice by the great sages. For these reasons, my dear husband, I am very much anxious to go.

PURPORT

As stated before, the tension between the father-in-law and son-in-law persisted for a considerable time. Satī, therefore, had not gone to her father's house for a long while. Thus she was very anxious to go to her father's house, particularly because on that occasion her sisters and their husbands and her mother's sisters would be there. As is natural for a woman, she wanted to dress equally to her other sisters and also be accompanied by her husband. She did not, of course, want to go alone.

TEXT 11

त्वय्येतदाश्चर्यमजात्ममायया
विनिर्मितं भाति गुणत्रयात्मकम् ।
तथाप्यहं योषिदतत्त्वविच्च ते
दीना दिदृक्षे भव मे भवक्षितिम् ॥११॥

tvayy etad āścaryam ajātma-māyayā
vinirmitaṁ bhāti guṇa-trayātmakam
tathāpy ahaṁ yoṣid atattva-vic ca te
dīnā didṛkṣe bhava me bhava-kṣitim

tvayi—in you; *etat*—this; *āścaryam*—wonderful; *aja*—O Lord Śiva; *ātma-māyayā*—by the external energy of the Supreme Lord; *vinirmitam*—created; *bhāti*—appears; *guṇa-traya-ātmakam*—being an interaction of the three modes of material nature; *tathā api*—even so; *aham*—I; *yoṣit*—woman; *atattva-vit*—not conversant with the truth; *ca*—and; *te*—your; *dīnā*—poor; *didṛkṣe*—I wish to see; *bhava*—O Lord Śiva; *me*—my; *bhava-kṣitim*—place of birth.

TRANSLATION

This manifested cosmos is a wonderful creation of the interaction of the three material modes, or the external energy of the

Supreme Lord. This truth is fully known to you. Yet I am but a poor woman, and, as you know, I am not conversant with the truth. Therefore I wish to see my birthplace once more.

PURPORT

Dākṣāyaṇī, Satī, knew very well that her husband, Lord Śiva, was not very much interested in the glaring manifestation of the material world, which is caused by the interaction of the three modes of nature. Therefore she addressed her husband as *aja*, which refers to one who has transcended the bondage of birth and death, or one who has realized his eternal position. She stated, "The illusion of accepting the perverted reflection, the material or cosmic manifestation, to be real is not present in you, because you are self-realized. For you the attraction of social life and the consideration that someone is father, someone is mother and someone is sister, which are illusory relationships, is already over; but because I am a poor woman, I am not so advanced in transcendental realization. Therefore naturally these appear to me as real." Only less intelligent persons accept this perverted reflection of the spiritual world to be real. Those who are under the spell of the external energy accept this manifestation to be fact, whereas those who are advanced in spiritual realization know that it is illusion. Actual reality is elsewhere, in the spiritual world. "But as far as I am concerned," Satī said, "I do not have much knowledge about self-realization. I am poor because I do not know the actual facts. I am attracted by my birthplace, and I want to see it." One who has attraction for his birthplace, for his body, and for other such items mentioned in the *Bhāgavatam* is considered to be like an ass or a cow. Satī might have heard all this many times from her husband, Lord Śiva, but because she was a woman, *yoṣit*, she still hankered after the same material objects of affection. The word *yoṣit* means "one who is enjoyed." Therefore woman is called *yoṣit.* In spiritual advancement, association with *yoṣit* is always restricted because if one is like a play doll in the hands of *yoṣit,* then all his spiritual advancement is at once stopped. It is said, "Those who are just like playthings in the hands of a woman (*yoṣit-krīḍā-mṛgeṣu*) cannot make any advancement in spiritual realization."

TEXT 12

पश्य प्रयान्तीरभवान्ययोषितो
ऽप्यलंकृताः कान्तसखा वरूथशः ।
यासां व्रजद्भिः शितिकण्ठ मण्डितं
नभो विमानैः कलहंसपाण्डुभिः ॥१२॥

paśya prayāntīr abhavānya-yoṣito
'py alaṅkṛtāḥ kānta-sakhā varūthaśaḥ
yāsāṁ vrajadbhiḥ śiti-kaṇṭha maṇḍitaṁ
nabho vimānaiḥ kala-haṁsa-pāṇḍubhiḥ

paśya—just see; *prayāntīḥ*—going; *abhava*—O never-born; *anya-yoṣitaḥ*—other women; *api*—certainly; *alaṅkṛtāḥ*—ornamented; *kānta-sakhāḥ*—with their husbands and friends; *varūthaśaḥ*—in large numbers; *yāsām*—of them; *vrajadbhiḥ*—flying; *śiti-kaṇṭha*—O blue-throated one; *maṇḍitam*—decorated; *nabhaḥ*—the sky; *vimānaiḥ*—with airplanes; *kala-haṁsa*—swans; *pāṇḍubhiḥ*—white.

TRANSLATION

O never-born, O blue-throated one, not only my relatives but also other women, dressed in nice clothes and decorated with ornaments, are going there with their husbands and friends. Just see how their flocks of white airplanes have made the entire sky very beautiful.

PURPORT

Here Lord Śiva is addressed as *abhava*, which means "one who is never born," although generally he is known as *bhava*, "one who is born." Rudra, Lord Śiva, is actually born from between the eyes of Brahmā, who is called Svayambhū because he is not born of any human being or material creature but is born directly from the lotus flower which grows from the abdomen of Viṣṇu. When Lord Śiva is addressed here as *abhava*, this may be taken to mean "one who has never felt material miseries." Satī wanted to impress upon her husband that even those who were not related to her father were also going, to say nothing of herself, who was intimately related with him. Lord Śiva is addressed here as blue throated. Lord Śiva drank an ocean of poison and kept it in his throat, not swallowing it or allowing it to go down to his stomach, and thus his throat became blue. Since then he has been known as *nīlakaṇṭha*, or blue throated. The reason that Lord Śiva drank an ocean of poison was for others' benefit. When the ocean was churned by the demigods and the demons, the churning at first produced poison, so because the poisonous ocean might have affected others who were not so advanced, Lord Śiva drank all the ocean water. In other words, he could drink such a great amount of poison for others' benefit, and now, since his wife was personally requesting him to go to her father's house, even if he did not wish to give that permission, he should do so out of his great kindness.

TEXT 13

कथं सुतायाः पितृगेहकौतुकं
निशम्य देहः सुरवर्य नेङ्गते ।
अनाहुता अप्यभियन्ति सौहृदं
भर्तुर्गुरोर्देहकृतश्च केतनम् ॥१३॥

kathaṁ sutāyāḥ pitṛ-geha-kautukaṁ
niśamya dehaḥ sura-varya neṅgate
anāhutā apy abhiyanti sauhṛdaṁ
bhartur guror deha-kṛtaś ca ketanam

katham—how; *sutāyāḥ*—of a daughter; *pitṛ-geha-kautukam*—the festival in the house of her father; *niśamya*—hearing; *dehaḥ*—the body; *sura-varya*—O best of the demigods; *na*—not; *iṅgate*—disturbed; *anāhutāḥ*—without being called; *api*—even; *abhiyanti*—goes; *sauhṛdam*—a friend; *bhartuḥ*—of the husband; *guroḥ*—of the spiritual master; *deha-kṛtaḥ*—of the father; *ca*—and; *ketanam*—the house.

TRANSLATION

O best of the demigods, how can the body of a daughter remain undisturbed when she hears that some festive event is taking place in her father's house? Even though you may be considering that I

have not been invited, there is no harm if one goes to the house of one's friend, husband, spiritual master or father without invitation.

TEXT 14

तन्मे प्रसीदेदममर्त्य वाञ्छितं
कर्तुं भवान्कारुणिको बतार्हति ।
त्वयात्मनोऽर्धेऽहमदभ्रचक्षुषा
निरूपिता मानुगृहाण याचितः ॥१४॥

tan me prasīdedam amartya vāñchitaṁ
kartuṁ bhavān kāruṇiko batārhati
tvayātmano 'rdhe 'ham adabhra-cakṣuṣā
nirūpitā mānugṛhāṇa yācitaḥ

tat—therefore; *me*—unto me; *prasīda*—please be kind; *idam*—this; *amartya*—O immortal lord; *vāñchitam*—desire; *kartum*—to do; *bhavān*—Your Honor; *kāruṇikaḥ*—kind; *bata*—O lord; *arhati*—is able; *tvayā*—by you; *ātmanaḥ*—of your own body; *ardhe*—in the half; *aham*—I; *adabhra-cakṣuṣā*—having all knowledge; *nirūpitā*—am situated; *mā*—to me; *anugṛhāṇa*—please show kindness; *yācitaḥ*—requested.

TRANSLATION

O immortal Śiva, please be kind towards me and fulfill my desire. You have accepted me as half of your body; therefore please show kindness towards me and accept my request.

TEXT 15

ऋषिरुवाच

एवं गिरित्रः प्रिययाभिभाषितः
प्रत्यभ्यधत्त प्रहसन् सुहृत्प्रियः ।
संस्मारितो मर्मभिदः कुवागिषून्
यानाह को विश्वसृजां समक्षतः ॥१५॥

ṛṣir uvāca
evaṁ giritraḥ priyayābhibhāṣitaḥ
pratyabhyadhatta prahasan suhṛt-priyaḥ
saṁsmārito marma-bhidaḥ kuvāg-iṣūn
yān āha ko viśva-sṛjāṁ samakṣataḥ

ṛṣiḥ uvāca—the great sage Maitreya said; *evam*—thus; *giritraḥ*—Lord Śiva; *priyayā*—by his dear wife; *abhibhāṣitaḥ*—being spoken to; *pratyabhyadhatta*—replied; *prahasan*—while smiling; *suhṛt-priyaḥ*—dear to the relatives; *saṁsmāritaḥ*—remembering; *marma-bhidaḥ*—heart piercing; *kuvāk-iṣūn*—malicious words; *yān*—which (words); *āha*—said; *kaḥ*—who (Dakṣa); *viśva-sṛjām*—of the creators of the universal manifestation; *samakṣataḥ*—in the presence.

TRANSLATION

The great sage Maitreya said: Lord Śiva, the deliverer of the hill Kailāsa, having thus been addressed by his dear wife, replied smilingly, although at the same time he remembered the malicious, heart-piercing speeches delivered by Dakṣa before the guardians of the universal affairs.

PURPORT

When Lord Śiva heard from his wife about Dakṣa, the psychological effect was that he immediately remembered the strong words spoken against him in the assembly of the guardians of the universe, and, remembering those words, he was sorry at heart, although to please his wife he smiled. In *Bhagavad-gītā* it is said that a liberated person is always in mental equilibrium in both the distress and the happiness of this material world. Therefore the question may now be raised why a liberated personality like Lord Śiva was so unhappy because of the words of Dakṣa. The answer is given by Śrīla Viśvanātha Cakravartī Ṭhākura. Lord Śiva is *ātmārāma*, or situated in complete self-realization, but because he is the incarnation in charge of the material mode of ignorance, *tamo-guṇa*, he is sometimes affected by the pleasure and pain of the material world. The difference between the pleasure and pain of this material world and that of the spiritual world is that in the spiritual world the effect is qualitatively absolute. Therefore one may feel sorry in the absolute world, but the manifestation of so-called pain is always full of bliss. For instance, once Lord Kṛṣṇa, in His childhood, was chastised by His mother, Yaśodā, and Lord Kṛṣṇa cried. But although He shed tears from His eyes, this is not to be considered a reaction of the mode of ignorance, for the incident was full of transcendental pleasure. When Kṛṣṇa was playing in so many ways, sometimes it appeared that He caused distress to the *gopīs*, but actually such dealings were full of transcendental bliss. That is the difference between the material and spiritual worlds. The spiritual world, where everything is pure, is pervertedly reflected in this material world. Since everything in the spiritual world is absolute, in the spiritual varieties of apparent pleasure and pain there is no perception other than eternal bliss, whereas in the material world, because everything is contaminated by the modes of material nature, there are feelings of pleasure and pain. Therefore because Lord Śiva, although a fully self-realized person, was in charge of the material mode of ignorance, he felt sorrow.

TEXT 16

श्रीभगवानुवाच

त्वयोदितं शोभनमेव शोभने
अनाहुता अप्यभियन्ति बन्धुषु ।
ते यद्यनुत्पादितदोषदृष्टयो
बलीयसानात्म्यमदेन मन्युना ॥१६॥

śrī-bhagavān uvāca
tvayoditaṁ śobhanam eva śobhane
anāhutā apy abhiyanti bandhuṣu
te yady anutpādita-doṣa-dṛṣṭayo
balīyasānātmya-madena manyunā

śrī-bhagavān uvāca—the great lord replied; *tvayā*—by you; *uditam*—said; *śobhanam*—is true; *eva*—certainly; *śobhane*—my dear beautiful wife; *anāhutāḥ*—without being invited; *api*—even; *abhiyanti*—go; *bandhuṣu*—among friends; *te*—those (friends); *yadi*—if; *anutpādita-doṣa-dṛṣṭayaḥ*—not finding fault; *balīyasā*—more important; *anātmya-madena*—by pride caused by identification with the body; *manyunā*—by anger.

TRANSLATION

The great lord replied: My dear beautiful wife, you have said that one may go to a friend's house without being invited, and this is true, provided such a friend does not find fault with the guest because of bodily identification and thereby become angry towards him.

PURPORT

Lord Śiva could foresee that as soon as Satī reached her father's house, her father, Dakṣa, being too puffed up because of bodily identification, would be angry at her presence, and although she was innocent and faultless, he would be mercilessly angry towards her. Lord Śiva warned that since her father was too puffed up by his material possessions, he would be angry, and this would be intolerable for her. Therefore it was better that she not go. This fact was already experienced by Lord Śiva because although Lord Śiva was faultless, Dakṣa had cursed him in so many harsh words.

TEXT 17

विद्यातपोवित्तवपुर्वयःकुलैः
सतां गुणैः षड्भिरसत्तमेतरैः ।
स्मृतौ हतायां भृतमानदुर्दृशः
स्तब्धा न पश्यन्ति हि धाम भूयसाम् ॥१७॥

vidyā-tapo-vitta-vapur-vayaḥ-kulaiḥ
satāṁ guṇaiḥ ṣaḍbhir asattametaraiḥ
smṛtau hatāyāṁ bhṛta-māna-durdṛśaḥ
stabdhā na paśyanti hi dhāma bhūyasām

vidyā—education; *tapaḥ*—austerity; *vitta*—wealth; *vapuḥ*—beauty of body, etc.; *vayaḥ*—youth; *kulaiḥ*—with heritage; *satām*—of the pious; *guṇaiḥ*—by such qualities; *ṣaḍbhiḥ*—six; *asattama-itaraiḥ*—having the opposite result to those who are not great souls; *smṛtau*—

good sense; *hatāyām*—being lost; *bhṛta-māna-durdṛśaḥ*—blind due to pride; *stabdhāḥ*—being proud; *na*—not; *paśyanti*—see; *hi*—for; *dhāma*—the glories; *bhūyasām*—of the great souls.

TRANSLATION

Although the six qualities education, austerity, wealth, beauty, youth and heritage are for the highly elevated, one who is proud of possessing them becomes blind, and thus he loses his good sense and cannot appreciate the glories of great personalities.

PURPORT

It may be argued that since Dakṣa was very learned, wealthy and austere and had descended from a very exalted heritage, how could he be unnecessarily angry towards another? The answer is that when the qualities of good education, good parentage, beauty and sufficient wealth are misplaced in a person who is puffed up by all these possessions, they produce a very bad result. Milk is a very nice food, but when milk is touched by an envious serpent it becomes poisonous. Similarly, material assets such as education, wealth, beauty and good parentage are undoubtedly nice, but when they decorate persons of a malicious nature, then they act adversely. Another example, given by Cāṇakya Paṇḍita, is that a serpent that has a jewel on its head is still fearful because it is a serpent. A serpent, by nature, is envious of other living entities, even though they be faultless. When a serpent bites another creature, it is not necessarily because the other creature is at fault; it is the habit of the serpent to bite innocent creatures. Similarly, although Dakṣa was qualified by many material assets, because he was proud of his possessions and because he was envious, all those qualities were polluted. It is sometimes, therefore, detrimental for a person advancing in spiritual consciousness, or Kṛṣṇa consciousness, to possess such material assets. Kuntīdevī, while offering prayers to Kṛṣṇa, addressed Him as *akiñcana-gocara*, one who is easily approached by those who are bereft of all material acquisitions. Material exhaustion is an advantage for advancement in Kṛṣṇa consciousness, although if one is conscious of his eternal relationship with the Supreme Personality of Godhead, one can utilize one's material assets, such as great learning and beauty and exalted ancestry, for the service of the Lord; then such assets become glorious. In other words, unless one is Kṛṣṇa conscious, all his material possessions are zero, but when this zero is by the side of the Supreme One, it at once increases in value to ten. Unless situated by the side of the Supreme One, zero is always zero; one may add one hundred zeros, but the value will still remain zero. Unless one's material assets are used in Kṛṣṇa consciousness, they may play havoc and degrade the possessor.

TEXT 18

नैतादृशानां स्वजनव्यपेक्षया
गृहान् प्रतीयादनवस्थितात्मनाम् ।
येऽभ्यागतान् वक्रधियाभिचक्षते
आरोपितभ्रूभिरमर्षणाक्षिभिः ॥१८॥

naitādṛśānāṁ sva-jana-vyapekṣayā
gṛhān pratīyād anavasthitātmanām
ye 'bhyāgatān vakra-dhiyābhicakṣate
āropita-bhrūbhir amarṣaṇākṣibhiḥ

na—not; *etādṛśānām*—like this; *sva-jana*—kinsmen; *vyapekṣayā*—depending on that; *gṛhān*—in the house of; *pratīyāt*—one should go; *anavasthita*—disturbed; *ātmanām*—mind; *ye*—those; *abhyāgatān*—guests; *vakra-dhiyā*—with a cold reception; *abhicakṣate*—looking at; *āropita-bhrūbhiḥ*—with raised eyebrows; *amarṣaṇa*—angry; *akṣibhiḥ*—with the eyes.

TRANSLATION

One should not go to anyone's house, even on the consideration of his being a relative or a friend, when the man is disturbed in his mind and looks upon the guest with raised eyebrows and angry eyes.

PURPORT

However low a person may be, he is never unkind to his children, wife and nearest kin; even a tiger is kind to its cubs, for within the animal kingdom the cubs are treated very nicely. Since Satī was the daughter of Dakṣa, however cruel and contaminated he might be, naturally it was expected that he would receive her very nicely. But here it is indicated by the word *anavasthita* that such a person cannot be trusted. Tigers are very kind to their cubs, but it is also known that sometimes they eat them. Malicious persons should not be trusted, because they are always unsteady. Thus Satī was advised not to go to her father's house because to accept such a father as a relative and to go to his house without being properly invited was not suitable.

TEXT 19

तथारिभिर्न व्यथते शिलीमुखैः
शेतेऽर्दिताङ्गो हृदयेन दूयता ।
स्वानां यथा वक्रधियां दुरुक्तिभि-
र्दिवानिशं तप्यति मर्मताडितः ॥१९॥

tathāribhir na vyathate śilīmukhaiḥ
śete 'rditāṅgo hṛdayena dūyatā
svānāṁ yathā vakra-dhiyāṁ duruktibhir
divā-niśaṁ tapyati marma-tāḍitaḥ

tathā—so; *aribhiḥ*—enemy; *na*—not; *vyathate*—is hurt; *śilīmukhaiḥ*—by the arrows; *śete*—rests; *ardita*—aggrieved; *aṅgaḥ*—a part; *hṛdayena*—by the heart; *dūyatā*—grieving; *svānām*—of relatives; *yathā*—as; *vakra-dhiyām*—deceitful; *duruktibhiḥ*—by harsh words; *divā-niśam*—day and night; *tapyati*—suffers; *marma-tāḍitaḥ*—one whose feelings are hurt.

TRANSLATION

Lord Śiva continued: If one is hurt by the arrows of an enemy, one is not as aggrieved as when cut by the unkind words of a relative, for such grief continues to rend one's heart day and night.

PURPORT

Satī might have concluded that she would take the risk of going to her father's house, and even if her father spoke unkindly against her she would be tolerant, as a son sometimes tolerates the reproaches of his parents. But Lord Śiva reminded her that she would not be able to tolerate such unkind words because natural psychology dictates that although one can suffer harm from an enemy and not mind so much because pain inflicted by an enemy is natural, when one is hurt by the strong words of a relative, one suffers the effects continually, day and night, and sometimes the injury becomes so intolerable that one commits suicide.

TEXT 20

व्यक्तं त्वमुत्कृष्टगतेः प्रजापतेः
प्रियात्मजानामसि सुभ्रु मे मता ।
तथापि मानं न पितुः प्रपत्स्यसे
मदाश्रयात्कः परितप्यते यतः ॥२०॥

vyaktaṁ tvam utkṛṣṭa-gateḥ prajāpateḥ
priyātmajānām asi subhru me matā
tathāpi mānaṁ na pituḥ prapatsyase
mad-āśrayāt kaḥ paritapyate yataḥ

vyaktam—it is clear; *tvam*—you; *utkṛṣṭa-gateḥ*—having the best behavior; *prajāpateḥ*—of Prajāpati Dakṣa; *priyā*—the pet; *ātmajānām*—of the daughters; *asi*—you are; *subhru*—O you with the beautiful eyebrows; *me*—my; *matā*—considered; *tathā api*—yet; *mānam*—honor; *na*—not; *pituḥ*—from your father; *prapatsyase*—you will meet with; *mat-āśrayāt*—from connection with me; *kaḥ*—Dakṣa; *paritapyate*—is feeling pain; *yataḥ*—from whom.

TRANSLATION

My dear white-complexioned wife, it is clear that of the many daughters of Dakṣa you are the pet, yet you will not be honored at his house because of your being my wife. Rather, you will be sorry that you are connected with me.

PURPORT

Lord Śiva put forward the argument that even if Satī proposed to go alone, without her husband, still she would not be received well because she was his wife. There was every chance of a catastrophe, even if she wanted to go alone. Therefore Lord Śiva indirectly requested her not to go to her father's house.

TEXT 21

पापच्यमानेन हृदातुरेन्द्रियः
समृद्धिभिः पूरुषबुद्धिसाक्षिणाम् ।
अकल्प एषामधिरोढुमञ्जसा
परं पदं द्वेष्टि यथासुरा हरिम् ॥२१॥

pāpacyamānena hṛdāturendriyaḥ
samṛddhibhiḥ pūruṣa-buddhi-sākṣiṇām
akalpa eṣām adhiroḍhum añjasā
paraṁ padaṁ dveṣṭi yathāsurā harim

pāpacyamānena—burning; *hṛdā*—with a heart; *ātura-indriyaḥ*—who is distressed; *samṛddhibhiḥ*—by the pious reputation, etc.; *pūruṣa-buddhi-sākṣiṇām*—of those who are always absorbed in thought of the Supreme Lord; *akalpaḥ*—being unable; *eṣām*—of those persons; *adhiroḍhum*—to rise; *añjasā*—quickly; *param*—merely; *padam*—to the standard; *dveṣṭi*—envy; *yathā*—as much as; *asurāḥ*—the demons; *harim*—the Supreme Personality of Godhead.

TRANSLATION

One who is conducted by false ego and thus always distressed, both mentally and sensually, cannot tolerate the opulence of self-realized persons. Being unable to rise to the standard of self-realization, he envies such persons as much as demons envy the Supreme Personality of Godhead.

PURPORT

The real reason for the enmity between Lord Śiva and Dakṣa is explained here. Dakṣa was envious of Lord Śiva because of Śiva's high position as an incarnation of a quality of the Supreme Personality of Godhead and because Śiva was directly in contact with the Supersoul and was therefore honored and given a better sitting place than he. There were many other reasons also. Dakṣa, being materially puffed up, could not tolerate the high position of Lord Śiva, so his anger at Lord Śiva's not standing up in his presence was only the final manifestation of his envy. Lord Śiva is always in meditation and always perceives the Supersoul, as expressed here by the words *pūruṣa-buddhi-sākṣiṇām*. The position of one whose intelligence is always absorbed in meditation upon the Supreme Personality of Godhead is very great and cannot be imitated by anyone, especially an ordinary person. When Dakṣa entered the arena of *yajña*, Lord Śiva was in meditation and might not have seen Dakṣa enter, but Dakṣa took the opportunity to curse him because Dakṣa had maintained an envious attitude towards Lord Śiva for a long time. Those who are actually self-realized see every individual body as a temple of the Supreme Personality of Godhead because the Supreme Personality of Godhead, in His Paramātmā feature, is residing in everyone's body.

When one offers respect to the body, it is not to the material body but to the presence of the Supreme Lord. Thus one who is always in meditation upon the Supreme Lord is always offering Him obeisances. But since Dakṣa was not very elevated, he thought that obeisances were offered to the material body, and because Lord Śiva did not offer respect to his material body, Dakṣa became envious. Such persons, being unable to rise to the standard of self-realized souls like Lord Śiva, are always envious. The example given here is very suitable. *Asuras*, demons or atheists, are always envious of the Supreme Personality of Godhead; they simply want to kill Him. Even in this age we find some so-called scholars commenting on *Bhagavad-gītā* who are envious of Kṛṣṇa. When Kṛṣṇa says, *man-manā bhava mad-bhaktaḥ* (Bg. 18.65)—"Always think of Me, become My devotee, and surrender unto Me"—the so-called scholars comment that it is not to Kṛṣṇa that we have to surrender. That is envy. The *asuras* or atheists, the demons, without reason or cause, are envious of the Supreme Personality of Godhead. Similarly, instead of offering respect to self-realized persons, foolish men who cannot approach the highest standard of self-realization are always envious, although there is no reason.

TEXT 22

प्रत्युद्गमप्रश्रयणाभिवादनं
विधीयते साधु मिथः सुमध्यमे ।

प्राज्ञैः परस्मै पुरुषाय चेतसा
गुहाशयायैव न देहमानिने ॥२२॥

pratyudgama-praśrayaṇābhivādanaṁ
vidhīyate sādhu mithaḥ sumadhyame
prājñaiḥ parasmai puruṣāya cetasā
guhā-śayāyaiva na deha-mānine

pratyudgama—standing up from one's seat; *praśrayaṇa*—welcoming; *abhivādanam*—obeisances; *vidhīyate*—are intended; *sādhu*—proper; *mithaḥ*—mutually; *su-madhyame*—my dear young wife; *prājñaiḥ*—by the wise; *parasmai*—unto the Supreme; *puruṣāya*—unto the Supersoul; *cetasā*—with the intelligence; *guhā-śayāya*—sitting within the body; *eva*—certainly; *na*—not; *deha-mānine*—to the person identifying with the body.

TRANSLATION

My dear young wife, certainly friends and relatives offer mutual greetings by standing up, welcoming one another and offering obeisances. But those who are elevated to the transcendental platform, being intelligent, offer such respects to the Supersoul, who is sitting within the body, not to the person who identifies with the body.

PURPORT

It may be argued that since Dakṣa was the father-in-law of Lord Śiva, it was certainly the duty of Lord Śiva to offer him respect. In answer to that argument it is explained here that when a learned person stands up or offers obeisances in welcome, he offers respect to the Supersoul, who is sitting within everyone's heart. It is seen, therefore, among Vaiṣṇavas, that even when a disciple offers obeisances to his spiritual master, the spiritual master immediately returns the obeisances because they are mutually offered not to the body but to the Supersoul. Therefore the spiritual master also offers respect to the Supersoul situated in the body of the disciple. The Lord says in *Śrīmad-Bhāgavatam* that offering respect to His devotee is more valuable than offering respect to Him. Devotees do not identify with the body, so offering respect to a Vaiṣṇava means offering respect to Viṣṇu. It is stated also that as a matter of etiquette as soon as one sees a Vaiṣṇava one must immediately offer him respect, indicating the Supersoul sitting within. A Vaiṣṇava sees the body as a temple of Viṣṇu. Since Lord Śiva had already offered respect to the Supersoul in Kṛṣṇa consciousness, offering respect to Dakṣa, who identified with his body, was already performed. There was no need to offer respect to his body, for that is not directed by any Vedic injunction.

TEXT 23

सत्त्वं विशुद्धं वसुदेवशब्दितं
यदीयते तत्र पुमानपावृतः ।
सत्त्वे च तस्मिन् भगवान् वासुदेवो
ह्यधोक्षजो मे नमसा विधीयते ॥२३॥

sattvaṁ viśuddhaṁ vasudeva-śabditaṁ
yad īyate tatra pumān apāvṛtaḥ
sattve ca tasmin bhagavān vāsudevo
hy adhokṣajo me namasā vidhīyate

sattvam—consciousness; *viśuddham*—pure; *vasudeva*—Vasudeva; *śabditam*—known as; *yat*—because; *īyate*—is revealed; *tatra*—there; *pumān*—the Supreme Person; *apāvṛtaḥ*—without any covering; *sattve*—in consciousness; *ca*—and; *tasmin*—in that; *bhagavān*—the Supreme Personality of Godhead; *vāsudevaḥ*—Vāsudeva; *hi*—because; *adhokṣajaḥ*—transcendental; *me*—by me; *namasā*—with obeisances; *vidhīyate*—worshiped.

TRANSLATION

I am always engaged in offering obeisances to Lord Vāsudeva in pure Kṛṣṇa consciousness. Kṛṣṇa consciousness is always pure consciousness, in which the Supreme Personality of Godhead, known as Vāsudeva, is revealed without any covering.

PURPORT

The living entity is constitutionally pure. *Asaṅgo hy ayaṁ puruṣaḥ.* In the Vedic literature it is said that the soul is always pure and uncontaminated by material attachment. The identification of the body with the soul is due to misunderstanding. As soon as one is fully Kṛṣṇa conscious it is to be understood that one is in his pure, original constitutional position. This state of existence is called *śuddha-sattva,* which means that it is transcendental to the material qualities. Since this *śuddha-sattva* existence is under the direct action of the internal potency, in this state the activities of material consciousness stop. For example, when iron is put into a fire, it becomes warm, and when red-hot, although it is iron, it acts like fire. Similarly, when copper is surcharged with electricity, its action as copper stops; it acts as electricity. *Bhagavad-gītā* (14.26) also confirms that anyone who engages in unadulterated devotional service to the Lord is at once elevated to the position of pure Brahman:

māṁ ca yo 'vyabhicāreṇa
bhakti-yogena sevate
sa guṇān samatītyaitān
brahma-bhūyāya kalpate

Therefore *śuddha-sattva,* as described in this verse, is the transcendental position, which is technically called *vasudeva.* Vasudeva is also the name of the person from whom Kṛṣṇa appears. This verse explains that the pure state is called *vasudeva* because in that state Vāsudeva, the Supreme Personality of Godhead, is revealed without any covering. To execute unadulterated devotional service, therefore, one must follow the rules and regulations of devotional service without desire to gain material profit by fruitive activities or mental speculation.

In pure devotional service one simply serves the Supreme Personality of Godhead as a matter of duty, without reason and without being impeded by material conditions. That is called *śuddha-sattva,* or *vasudeva,* because in that stage the Supreme Person, Kṛṣṇa, is revealed in the heart of the devotee. Śrīla Jīva Gosvāmī has very nicely described this *vasudeva,* or *śuddha-sattva,* in his *Bhagavat-sandarbha.* He explains that *aṣṭottara-śata* (108) is added to the name of the spiritual master to indicate one who is situated in *śuddha-sattva,* or in the transcendental state of *vasudeva.* The word *vasudeva* is also used for other purposes. For example, *vasudeva* also means one who is everywhere, or all-pervading.

The sun is also called *vasudeva-śabditam.* The word *vasudeva* may be utilized for different purposes, but whatever purpose we adopt, Vāsudeva means the all-pervading or localized Supreme Personality of Godhead. In *Bhagavad-gītā* (7.19) it is also stated, *vāsudevaḥ sarvam iti.* Factual realization is to understand Vāsudeva, the Supreme Personality of Godhead, and surrender unto Him. *Vasudeva* is the ground wherein Vāsudeva, the Supreme Personality of Godhead, is revealed. When one is free from the contamination of material nature and is situated in pure Kṛṣṇa consciousness, or in the *vasudeva* state, Vāsudeva, the Supreme Person, is revealed. This state is also called *kaivalya,* which means "pure consciousness." *Jñānaṁ sāttvikaṁ kaivalyam.* When one is situated in pure, transcendental knowledge, one is situated in *kaivalya.* Therefore *vasudeva* also means *kaivalya,* a word which is generally used by impersonalists. Impersonal *kaivalya* is not the last stage of realization, but in Kṛṣṇa consciousness *kaivalya,* when one understands the Supreme Personality of Godhead, then one is successful. In that pure state, by hearing, chanting, remembering, etc., because of the development of knowledge of the science of Kṛṣṇa, one can understand the Supreme Personality of Godhead. All these activities are under the guidance of the internal energy of the Supreme Lord.

The action of the internal potency is also described in this verse as *apāvṛtaḥ,* free from any covering. Because the Supreme Personality of Godhead, His name, His form, His quality, His paraphernalia, etc., being transcendental, are beyond material nature, it is not possible to understand any one of them with the materialistic senses. When the senses are purified by the discharge of pure devotional service (*hṛṣīkeṇa hṛṣīkeśa-sevanaṁ bhaktir ucyate*), the pure senses can see Kṛṣṇa without covering. Now one may inquire that since factually the devotee has the same material existential body, how is it possible that the same materialistic eyes become purified by devotional service? The example, as stated by Lord Caitanya, is that devotional service cleanses the mirror of the mind. In a clean mirror one can see one's face very distinctly. Similarly, simply by cleansing the mirror of the mind one can have a clear conception of the Supreme Personality of Godhead. It is stated in *Bhagavad-gītā* (8.8), *abhyāsa-yoga-yuktena.* By executing one's prescribed duties in devotional service, *cetasā nānya-gāminā,* or simply by hearing about God and chanting about Him, if one's mind is always engaged in chanting and hearing and is not allowed to go elsewhere, one can realize the Supreme Personality of Godhead. As confirmed by Lord Caitanya, by the *bhakti-yoga* process, beginning from hearing and chanting, one can cleanse the heart and mind, and thus one can clearly see the face of the Supreme Personality of Godhead.

Lord Śiva said that since his heart was always filled with the conception of Vāsudeva, the Supreme Personality of Godhead, because of the Supreme Lord's presence within his mind and heart, he was always offering obeisances unto that Supreme Godhead. In other words, Lord Śiva is always in trance, *samādhi.* This *samādhi* is not under the control of the devotee; it is under the control of Vāsudeva, for the entire internal energy of the Supreme Personality of Godhead acts under His order. Of course, the material energy also acts by His order, but His direct will is specifically executed through the spiritual energy. Thus by His spiritual energy He reveals Himself. It is stated in *Bhagavad-gītā* (4.6), *sambhavāmy ātma-māyayā. Ātma-māyayā* means "internal potency." By His sweet will He reveals Himself by His internal potency, being satisfied by the transcendental loving service of the devotee. The devotee never commands, "My dear Lord, please come here so that I can see You." It is not the position of the devotee to command the Supreme Personality of Godhead to come before him or to dance before him. There are many so-called devotees who command the Lord to come before them dancing. The Lord, however, is not subject to anyone's command, but if He is satisfied by one's pure devotional activities, He reveals Himself. Therefore a meaningful word in this verse is *adhokṣaja,* for it indicates that the activities of our material senses will fail to realize the Supreme Personality of Godhead. One cannot realize the Supreme Personality of Godhead simply by the attempt of one's speculative mind, but if one desires he can subdue all the material activities of his senses, and the Lord, by manifesting His spiritual energy, can reveal Himself to the pure devotee. When the Supreme Personality of Godhead reveals Himself to the pure devotee, the devotee has no other duty than to offer Him respectful obeisances. The Absolute Truth reveals Himself to the devotee in His form. He is not formless. Vāsudeva is not formless, for it is stated in this verse that as soon as the Lord reveals Himself, the devotee offers his obeisances. Obeisances are offered to a person, not to anything impersonal. One should not accept the Māyāvāda interpretation that Vāsudeva is impersonal. As stated in *Bhagavad-gītā*, *prapadyate*, one surrenders. One surrenders to a person, not to impersonal nonduality. Whenever there is a question of surrendering or offering obeisances, there must be an object of surrender or obeisances.

TEXT 24

तत्ते निरीक्ष्यो न पितापि देहकृद्
दक्षो मम द्विट् तदनुव्रताश्च ये ।
यो विश्वसृग्यज्ञगतं वरोरु मा-
मनागसं दुर्वचसाकरोत्तिरः ॥२४॥

tat te nirīkṣyo na pitāpi deha-kṛd
dakṣo mama dviṭ tad-anuvratāś ca ye
yo viśvasṛg-yajña-gataṁ varoru mām
anāgasaṁ durvacasākarot tiraḥ

tat—therefore; *te*—your; *nirīkṣyaḥ*—to be seen; *na*—not; *pitā*—your father; *api*—although; *deha-kṛt*—the giver of your body; *dakṣaḥ*—Dakṣa; *mama*—my; *dviṭ*—envious; *tat-anuvratāḥ*—his (Dakṣa's) followers; *ca*—also; *ye*—who; *yaḥ*—who (Dakṣa); *viśva-sṛk*—of the Viśvasṛks; *yajña-gatam*—being present at the sacrifice; *vara-ūru*—O Satī; *mām*—me; *anāgasam*—being innocent; *durvacasā*—with cruel words; *akarot tiraḥ*—has insulted.

TRANSLATION

Therefore you should not see your father, although he is the giver of your body, because he and his followers are envious of me. Because of his envy, O most worshipful one, he has insulted me with cruel words although I am innocent.

PURPORT

For a woman, both the husband and the father are equally worshipable. The husband is the protector of a woman during her youthful life, whereas the father is her protector during her childhood. Thus both are worshipable, but especially the father because he is the giver of the body.

Lord Śiva reminded Satī, "Your father is undoubtedly worshipable, even more than I am, but take care, for although he is the giver of your body, he may also be the taker of your body because when you see your father, because of your association with me, he may insult you. An insult from a relative is worse than death, especially when one is well situated."

TEXT 25

यदि व्रजिष्यस्यतिहाय मद्वचो
भद्रं भवत्या न ततो भविष्यति ।
सम्भावितस्य स्वजनात्पराभवो
यदा स सद्यो मरणाय कल्पते ॥२५॥

yadi vrajiṣyasy atihāya mad-vaco
bhadraṁ bhavatyā na tato bhaviṣyati
sambhāvitasya sva-janāt parābhavo
yadā sa sadyo maraṇāya kalpate

yadi—if; *vrajiṣyasi*—you will go; *atihāya*—neglecting; *mat-vacaḥ*—my words; *bhadram*—good; *bhavatyāḥ*—your; *na*—not; *tataḥ*—then; *bhaviṣyati*—will become; *sambhāvitasya*—most respectable; *sva-janāt*—by your own relative; *parābhavaḥ*—are insulted; *yadā*—when; *saḥ*—that insult; *sadyaḥ*—immediately; *maraṇāya*—to death; *kalpate*—is equal.

TRANSLATION

If in spite of this instruction you decide to go, neglecting my words, the future will not be good for you. You are most respectable, and when you are insulted by your relative, this insult will immediately be equal to death.

Thus end the Bhaktivedanta purports of the Fourth Canto, Third Chapter, of the Śrīmad-Bhāgavatam, *entitled "Talks Between Lord Śiva and Satī."*

CHAPTER FOUR

Satī Quits Her Body

TEXT 1

मैत्रेय उवाच
एतावदुक्त्वा विरराम शंकरः
पत्न्यङ्गनाशं ह्युभयत्र चिन्तयन् ।
सुहृद्दिदृक्षुः परिशङ्किता भवा-
न्निष्क्रामती निर्विशती द्विधास सा ॥१॥

maitreya uvāca
etāvad uktvā virarāma śaṅkaraḥ
patny-aṅga-nāśaṁ hy ubhayatra cintayan
suhṛd-didṛkṣuḥ pariśaṅkitā bhavān
niṣkrāmatī nirviśatī dvidhāsa sā

maitreyaḥ uvāca—Maitreya said; *etāvat*—so much; *uktvā*—after speaking; *virarāma*—was silent; *śaṅkaraḥ*—Lord Śiva; *patnī-aṅga-nāśam*—the destruction of the body of his wife; *hi*—since; *ubhayatra*—in both cases; *cintayan*—understanding; *suhṛt-didṛkṣuḥ*—being anxious to see her relatives; *pariśaṅkitā*—being afraid; *bhavāt*—of Śiva; *niṣkrāmatī*—moving out; *nirviśatī*—moving in; *dvidhā*—divided; *āsa*—was; *sā*—she (Satī).

TRANSLATION

The sage Maitreya said: Lord Śiva was silent after speaking to Satī, seeing her between decisions. Satī was very much anxious to see her relatives at her father's house, but at the same time she was afraid of Lord Śiva's warning. Her mind unsettled, she moved in and out of the room as a swing moves this way and that.

PURPORT

Satī's mind was divided about whether to go to her father's house or obey the orders of Lord Śiva. The struggle between the two decisions was so strong that she was pushed from one side of the room to another, and she began to move just like the pendulum of a clock.

TEXT 2

सुहृद्दिदृक्षाप्रतिघातदुर्मनाः
स्नेहाद्रुदत्यश्रुकलातिविह्वला ।
भवं भवान्यप्रतिपूरुषं रुषा
प्रधक्ष्यतीवैक्षत जातवेपथुः ॥ २ ॥

suhṛd-didṛkṣā-pratighāta-durmanāḥ
snehād rudaty aśru-kalātivihvalā
bhavaṁ bhavāny apratipūruṣaṁ ruṣā
pradhakṣyatīvaikṣata jāta-vepathuḥ

suhṛt-didṛkṣā—of the desire to see her relatives; *pratighāta*—the prevention; *durmanāḥ*—feeling sorry; *snehāt*—from affection; *rudatī*—crying; *aśru-kalā*—by drops of tears; *ativihvalā*—very much afflicted; *bhavam*—Lord Śiva; *bhavānī*—Satī; *aprati-pūruṣam*—without an equal or rival; *ruṣā*—with anger; *pradhakṣyatī*—to blast; *iva*—as if; *aikṣata*—looked at; *jāta-vepathuḥ*—shaking.

TRANSLATION

Satī felt very sorry at being forbidden to go see her relatives at her father's house, and due to affection for them, tears fell from her eyes. Shaking and very much afflicted, she looked at her uncommon husband, Lord Śiva, as if she were going to blast him with her vision.

PURPORT

The word *apratipūruṣam,* used in this verse, means "one who has no equal." Lord Śiva has no equal in the material world in regard to equality towards everyone. His wife, Satī, knew that her husband was equal towards everyone, so why in this case was he so unkind to his wife that he did not allow her to go to her father's house? This distressed her more than she could tolerate, and she looked at her husband as if she were ready to blast him with her vision. In other words, since Lord Śiva is the *ātmā* (*śiva* also means *ātmā*), it is indicated here that Satī was prepared to commit suicide. Another meaning of the word *apratipūruṣa* is "the personality who has no rival." Since Lord Śiva could not be persuaded to give her permission, Satī took shelter of a woman's last weapon, weeping, which forces a husband to agree to the proposal of his wife.

TEXT 3

ततो विनिःश्वस्य सती विहाय तं
शोकेन रोषेण च दूयता हृदा ।
पित्रोरगात्स्त्रैणविमूढधीर्गृहान्
प्रेम्णात्मनो योऽर्धमदात्सतां प्रियः ॥३॥

tato viniḥśvasya satī vihāya taṁ
śokena roṣeṇa ca dūyatā hṛdā
pitror agāt straiṇa-vimūḍha-dhīr gṛhān
premṇātmano yo 'rdham adāt satāṁ priyaḥ

tataḥ—then; *viniḥśvasya*—breathing very heavily; *satī*—Satī; *vihāya*—leaving; *tam*—him (Lord Śiva); *śokena*—by bereavement; *roṣeṇa*—by anger; *ca*—and; *dūyatā*—afflicted; *hṛdā*—with the heart; *pitroḥ*—of her father; *agāt*—she went; *straiṇa*—by her womanly nature; *vimūḍha*—deluded; *dhīḥ*—intelligence; *gṛhān*—to the house; *premṇā*—due to affection; *ātmanaḥ*—of his body; *yaḥ*—who; *ardham*—half; *adāt*—gave; *satām*—to the saintly; *priyaḥ*—dear.

TRANSLATION

Thereafter Satī left her husband, Lord Śiva, who had given her half his body due to affection. Breathing very heavily because of anger and bereavement, she went to the house of her father. This less intelligent act was due to her being a weak woman.

PURPORT

According to the Vedic conception of family life, the husband gives half his body to his wife, and the wife gives half of her body to her husband. In other words, a husband without a wife or a wife without a husband is incomplete. Vedic marital relationship existed between Lord Śiva and Satī, but sometimes, due to weakness, a woman becomes very much attracted by the members of her father's house, and this happened to Satī. In this verse it is specifically mentioned that she wanted to leave such a great husband as Śiva because of her womanly weakness. In other words, womanly weakness exists even in the relationship between husband and wife. Generally, separation between husband and wife is due to womanly behavior; divorce takes place due to womanly weakness. The best course for a woman is to abide by the orders of her husband. That makes family life very peaceful. Sometimes there may be misunderstandings between husband and wife, as found even in such an elevated family relationship as that of Satī and Lord Śiva, but a wife should not leave her husband's protection because of such a misunderstanding. If she does so, it is understood to be due to her womanly weakness.

TEXT 4

तामन्वगच्छन् द्रुतविक्रमां सती-
मेकां त्रिनेत्रानुचराः सहस्रशः ।
सपार्षदयक्षा मणिमन्मदादयः
पुरोवृषेन्द्रास्तरसा गतव्यथाः ॥ ४ ॥

tām anvagacchan druta-vikramāṁ satīm
ekāṁ tri-netrānucarāḥ sahasraśaḥ
sa-pārṣada-yakṣā maṇiman-madādayaḥ
puro-vṛṣendrās tarasā gata-vyathāḥ

tām—her (Satī); *anvagacchan*—followed; *druta-vikramām*—leaving rapidly; *satīm*—Satī; *ekām*—alone; *tri-netra*—of Lord Śiva (who has three eyes); *anucarāḥ*—the followers; *sahasraśaḥ*—by thousands; *sa-pārṣada-yakṣāḥ*—accompanied by his personal associates and the

Yakṣas; *maṇimat-mada-ādayaḥ*—Maṇimān, Mada, etc.; *puraḥ-vṛṣa-indrāḥ*—having the Nandī bull in front; *tarasā*—swiftly; *gata-vyathāḥ*—without fear.

TRANSLATION

When they saw Satī leaving alone very rapidly, thousands of Lord Śiva's disciples, headed by Maṇimān and Mada, quickly followed her with his bull Nandī in front and accompanied by the Yakṣas.

PURPORT

Satī was going very fast so that she might not be checked by her husband, but she was immediately followed by the many thousands of disciples of Lord Śiva, headed by the Yakṣas, Maṇimān and Mada. The word *gata-vyathāḥ*, used in this connection, means "without fear." Satī did not care that she was going alone; therefore she was almost fearless. The word *anucarāḥ* is also significant, for it indicates that Lord Śiva's disciples were always ready to sacrifice anything for Lord Śiva. All of them could understand the desire of Śiva, who did not want Satī to go alone. *Anucarāḥ* means "those who can immediately understand the purpose of their master."

TEXT 5

तां सारिकाकन्दुकदर्पणाम्बुज-
श्वेतातपत्रव्यजनस्रगादिभिः ।
गीतायनैर्दुन्दुभिशङ्खवेणुभि-
र्वृषेन्द्रमारोप्य विटङ्किता ययुः ॥ ५ ॥

tāṁ sārikā-kanduka-darpaṇāmbuja-
śvetātapatra-vyajana-srag-ādibhiḥ
gītāyanair dundubhi-śaṅkha-veṇubhir
vṛṣendram āropya viṭaṅkitā yayuḥ

tām—her (Satī); *sārikā*—pet bird; *kanduka*—ball; *darpaṇa*—mirror; *ambuja*—lotus flower; *śveta-ātapatra*—white umbrella; *vyajana*—chowrie; *srak*—garland; *ādibhiḥ*—and others; *gīta-ayanaiḥ*—accompanied with music; *dundubhi*—drums; *śaṅkha*—conchshells;

veṇubhiḥ—with flutes; *vṛṣa-indram*—on the bull; *āropya*—placing; *viṭaṅkitāḥ*—decorated; *yayuḥ*—they went.

TRANSLATION

The disciples of Lord Śiva arranged for Satī to be seated on the back of a bull and gave her the bird which was her pet. They bore a lotus flower, a mirror and all such paraphernalia for her enjoyment and covered her with a great canopy. Followed by a singing party with drums, conchshells and bugles, the entire procession was as pompous as a royal parade.

TEXT 6

आब्रह्मघोषोर्जितयज्ञवैशसं
विप्रर्षिजुष्टं विबुधैश्च सर्वशः ।
मृद्दार्वयःकाञ्चनदर्भचर्मभि-
र्निसृष्टभाण्डं यजनं समाविशत् ॥ ६ ॥

ābrahma-ghoṣorjita-yajña-vaiśasaṁ
viprarṣi-juṣṭaṁ vibudhaiś ca sarvaśaḥ
mṛd-dārv-ayaḥ-kāñcana-darbha-carmabhir
nisṛṣṭa-bhāṇḍaṁ yajanaṁ samāviśat

ā—from all sides; *brahma-ghoṣa*—with the sounds of the Vedic hymns; *ūrjita*—decorated; *yajña*—sacrifice; *vaiśasam*—destruction of animals; *viprarṣi-juṣṭam*—attended by the great sages; *vibudhaiḥ*—with demigods; *ca*—and; *sarvaśaḥ*—on all sides; *mṛt*—clay; *dāru*—wood; *ayaḥ*—iron; *kāñcana*—gold; *darbha*—*kuśa* grass; *carmabhiḥ*—skins; *nisṛṣṭa*—made of; *bhāṇḍam*—sacrificial animals and pots; *yajanam*—sacrifice; *samāviśat*—entered.

TRANSLATION

She then reached her father's house, where the sacrifice was being performed, and entered the arena where everyone was chanting the Vedic hymns. The great sages, brāhmaṇas and demigods were all assembled there, and there were many sacrificial

animals, as well as pots made of clay, stone, gold, grass and skin, which were all requisite for the sacrifice.

PURPORT

When learned sages and *brāhmaṇas* assemble to chant Vedic *mantras*, some of them also engage in arguing about the conclusion of the scriptures. Thus some of the sages and *brāhmaṇas* were arguing, and some of them were chanting the Vedic *mantras*, so the entire atmosphere was surcharged with transcendental sound vibration. This transcendental sound vibration has been simplified in the transcendental vibration Hare Kṛṣṇa, Hare Kṛṣṇa, Kṛṣṇa Kṛṣṇa, Hare Hare/ Hare Rāma, Hare Rāma, Rāma Rāma, Hare Hare. In this age, no one is expected to be highly educated in the Vedic ways of understanding because people are very slow, lazy and unfortunate. Therefore Lord Caitanya has recommended the sound vibration Hare Kṛṣṇa, and in the *Śrīmad-Bhāgavatam* (11.5.32) it is also recommended: *yajñaiḥ saṅkīrtana-prāyair yajanti hi sumedhasaḥ.* At the present moment it is impossible to gather sacrificial necessities because of the poverty of the population and their lack of knowledge in Vedic *mantras.* Therefore for this age it is recommended that people gather together and chant the Hare Kṛṣṇa *mantra* to satisfy the Supreme Personality of Godhead, who is accompanied by His associates. Indirectly this indicates Lord Caitanya, who is accompanied by His associates Nityānanda, Advaita and others. That is the process of performing *yajña* in this age.

Another significant point in this verse is that there were animals for sacrifice. That these animals were meant for sacrifice does not mean that they were meant to be killed. The great sages and realized souls assembled were performing *yajñas*, and their realization was tested by animal sacrifice, just as, in modern science, tests are made on animals to determine the effectiveness of a particular medicine. The *brāhmaṇas* entrusted with the performance of *yajña* were very realized souls, and to test their realization an old animal was offered in the fire and rejuvenated. That was the test of a Vedic *mantra.* The animals gathered were not meant to be killed and eaten. The real purpose of a sacrifice was not to replace a slaughterhouse but to test a Vedic *mantra* by giving an animal new life. Animals were used to test the power of Vedic *mantras*, not for meat.

TEXT 7

तामागतां तत्र न कश्चनाद्रियद्
विमानितां यज्ञकृतो भयाज्जनः ।
ऋते स्वसॄर्वै जननीं च सादराः
प्रेमाश्रुकण्ठ्यः परिषस्वजुर्मुदा ॥ ७ ॥

tām āgatāṁ tatra na kaścanādriyad
vimānitāṁ yajña-kṛto bhayāj janaḥ
ṛte svasṝr vai jananīṁ ca sādarāḥ
premāśru-kaṇṭhyaḥ pariṣasvajur mudā

tām—her (Satī); *āgatām*—having arrived; *tatra*—there; *na*—not; *kaścana*—anyone; *ādriyat*—received; *vimānitām*—not receiving respect; *yajña-kṛtaḥ*—of the performer of the sacrifice (Dakṣa); *bhayāt*—from fear; *janaḥ*—person; *ṛte*—except; *svasṝḥ*—her own sisters; *vai*—indeed; *jananīm*—mother; *ca*—and; *sa-ādarāḥ*—with respect; *prema-aśru-kaṇṭhyaḥ*—whose throats were filled with tears of affection; *pariṣasvajuḥ*—embraced; *mudā*—with glad faces.

TRANSLATION

When Satī, with her followers, reached the arena, because all the people assembled were afraid of Dakṣa, none of them received her well. No one welcomed her but her mother and sisters, who, with tears in their eyes and with glad faces, welcomed her and talked with her very pleasingly.

PURPORT

The mother and sisters of Satī could not follow the others, who did not receive Satī very well. Due to natural affection, they immediately embraced her with tears in their eyes and with loving feelings. This shows that women as a class are very softhearted; their natural affection and love cannot be checked by artificial means. Although the men present were very learned *brāhmaṇas* and demigods, they were afraid of their superior, Dakṣa, and because they knew that their welcoming Satī would displease him, although in their minds they wanted to receive her, they could not do so. Women are naturally softhearted, but men are sometimes very hardhearted.

TEXT 8

सौदर्यसम्प्रश्नसमर्थवार्तया
मात्रा च मातृष्वसृभिश्च सादरम् ।
दत्तां सपर्यां वरमासनं च सा
नादत्त पित्राप्रतिनन्दिता सती ॥८॥

saudarya-sampraśna-samartha-vārtayā
mātrā ca mātṛ-ṣvasṛbhiś ca sādaram
dattāṁ saparyāṁ varam āsanaṁ ca sā
nādatta pitrāpratinanditā satī

saudarya—of her sisters; *sampraśna*—with the greetings; *samartha*—proper; *vārtayā*—tidings; *mātrā*—by her mother; *ca*—and; *mātṛ-svasṛbhiḥ*—by her aunts; *ca*—and; *sa-ādaram*—along with respect; *dattām*—which was offered; *saparyām*—worship, adoration; *varam*—presents; *āsanam*—a seat; *ca*—and; *sā*—she (Satī); *na ādatta*—did not accept; *pitrā*—by her father; *apratinanditā*—not being welcomed; *satī*—Satī.

TRANSLATION

Although she was received by her sisters and mother, she did not reply to their words of reception, and although she was offered a seat and presents, she did not accept anything, for her father neither talked with her nor welcomed her by asking about her welfare.

PURPORT

Satī did not accept the greetings offered by her sisters and mother, for she was not at all satisfied by her father's silence. Satī was the youngest child of Dakṣa, and she knew that she was his pet. But now, because of her association with Lord Śiva, Dakṣa forgot all his affection for his daughter, and this very much aggrieved her. The material bodily conception is so polluted that even upon slight provocation all our relationships of love and affection are nullified. Bodily relationships are so transient that even though one is affectionate towards someone in a bodily relationship, a slight provocation terminates this intimacy.

TEXT 9

अरुद्रभागं तमवेक्ष्य चाध्वरं
पित्रा च देवे कृतहेलनं विभौ ।
अनादृता यज्ञसदस्यधीश्वरी
चुकोप लोकानिव धक्ष्यती रुषा ॥ ९ ॥

arudra-bhāgaṁ tam avekṣya cādhvaraṁ
pitrā ca deve kṛta-helanaṁ vibhau
anādṛtā yajña-sadasy adhīśvarī
cukopa lokān iva dhakṣyatī ruṣā

arudra-bhāgam—having no oblations for Lord Śiva; *tam*—that; *avekṣya*—seeing; *ca*—and; *adhvaram*—place of sacrifice; *pitrā*—by her father; *ca*—and; *deve*—to Lord Śiva; *kṛta-helanam*—contempt having been shown; *vibhau*—to the lord; *anādṛtā*—not being received; *yajña-sadasi*—in the assembly of the sacrifice; *adhīśvarī*—Satī; *cukopa*—became greatly angry; *lokān*—the fourteen worlds; *iva*—as if; *dhakṣyatī*—burning; *ruṣā*—with anger.

TRANSLATION

Present in the arena of sacrifice, Satī saw that there were no oblations for her husband, Lord Śiva. Next she realized that not only had her father failed to invite Lord Śiva, but when he saw Lord Śiva's exalted wife, Dakṣa did not receive her either. Thus she became greatly angry, so much so that she looked at her father as if she were going to burn him with her eyes.

PURPORT

By offering oblations in the fire while chanting the Vedic *mantra svāhā*, one offers respect to all the demigods, great sages and Pitās, including Lord Brahmā, Lord Śiva and Lord Viṣṇu. It is customary that Śiva is one of those who are offered respects, but Satī, while personally present in the arena, saw that the *brāhmaṇas* did not utter the *mantra* offering oblations to Lord Śiva, *namaḥ śivāya svāhā.* She was not sorry for herself, for she was ready to come to her father's house without being invited, but she wanted to see whether or not her husband was being respected. To see her relatives, her sisters and mother, was not so important; even when she was received by her mother and sisters she did not care, for she was most concerned that her husband was being insulted in the sacrifice. When she marked the insult, she became greatly angry, and she looked at her father so angrily that Dakṣa appeared to burn in her vision.

TEXT 10

जगर्ह सामर्षविपन्नया गिरा
शिवद्विषं धूमपथश्रमस्मयम् ।
स्वतेजसा भूतगणान् समुत्थितान्
निगृह्य देवी जगतोऽभिश‍ृण्वतः ॥१०॥

jagarha sāmarṣa-vipannayā girā
śiva-dviṣaṁ dhūma-patha-śrama-smayam
sva-tejasā bhūta-gaṇān samutthitān
nigṛhya devī jagato 'bhiśṛṇvataḥ

jagarha—began to condemn; *sā*—she; *amarṣa-vipannayā*—indistinct through anger; *girā*—with words; *śiva-dviṣam*—the enemy of Lord Śiva; *dhūma-patha*—in sacrifices; *śrama*—by troubles; *smayam*—very proud; *sva-tejasā*—by her order; *bhūta-gaṇān*—the ghosts; *samutthitān*—ready (to injure Dakṣa); *nigṛhya*—stopped; *devī*—Satī; *jagataḥ*—in the presence of all; *abhiśṛṇvataḥ*—being heard.

TRANSLATION

The followers of Lord Śiva, the ghosts, were ready to injure or kill Dakṣa, but Satī stopped them by her order. She was very angry and sorrowful, and in that mood she began to condemn the process of sacrificial fruitive activities and persons who are very proud of such unnecessary and troublesome sacrifices. She especially condemned her father, speaking against him in the presence of all.

PURPORT

The process of offering sacrifices is especially meant to satisfy Viṣṇu, who is called Yajñeśa because He is the enjoyer of the fruits of all sacrifice. *Bhagavad-gītā* (5.29) also confirms this fact. The Lord says, *bhoktāraṁ yajña-tapasām*. He is the actual beneficiary of all sacrifices. Not knowing this fact, less intelligent men offer sacrifices for some material benefit. To derive personal material benefits for sense gratification is the reason persons like Dakṣa and his followers perform sacrifices. Such sacrifices are condemned here as a labor of love without actual profit. This is confirmed in *Śrīmad-Bhāgavatam*. One may prosecute the Vedic injunctions of offering sacrifices and other fruitive activities, but if by such activities one does not develop attraction for Viṣṇu, they are useless labors. One who has developed love for Viṣṇu must develop love and respect for Viṣṇu's devotees. Lord Śiva is considered the foremost personality amongst the Vaiṣṇavas. *Vaiṣṇavānāṁ yathā śambhuḥ*. Thus when Satī saw that her father was performing great sacrifices but had no respect for the greatest devotee, Lord Śiva, she was very angry. This is fitting; when Viṣṇu or a Vaiṣṇava is insulted, one should be angry. Lord Caitanya, who always preached nonviolence, meekness and humility, also became angry when Nityānanda was offended by Jagāi and Mādhāi, and He wanted to kill them. When Viṣṇu or a Vaiṣṇava is blasphemed or dishonored, one should be very angry. Narottama dāsa Ṭhākura said, *krodha bhakta-dveṣi jane*. We have anger, and that anger can be a great quality when directed against a person who is envious of the Supreme Personality of Godhead or His devotee. One should not be tolerant when a person is offensive towards Viṣṇu or a Vaiṣṇava. The anger of Satī towards her father was not objectionable, for although he was her father, he was trying to insult the greatest Vaiṣṇava. Thus Satī's anger against her father was quite applaudable.

TEXT 11

देव्युवाच

न यस्य लोकेऽस्त्यतिशायनः प्रिय-
स्तथाप्रियो देहभृतां प्रियात्मनः ।
तस्मिन् समस्तात्मनि मुक्तवैरके
ऋते भवन्तं कतमः प्रतीपयेत् ॥११॥

devy uvāca
na yasya loke 'sty atiśāyanaḥ priyas
tathāpriyo deha-bhṛtāṁ priyātmanaḥ
tasmin samastātmani mukta-vairake
ṛte bhavantaṁ katamaḥ pratīpayet

devī uvāca—the blessed goddess said; *na*—not; *yasya*—of whom; *loke*—in the material world; *asti*—is; *atiśāyanaḥ*—having no rival; *priyaḥ*—dear; *tathā*—so; *apriyaḥ*—enemy; *deha-bhṛtām*—bearing material bodies; *priya-ātmanaḥ*—who is the most beloved; *tasmin*—towards Lord Śiva; *samasta-ātmani*—the universal being; *mukta-vairake*—who is free from all enmity; *ṛte*—except; *bhavantam*—for you; *katamaḥ*—who; *pratīpayet*—would be envious.

TRANSLATION

The blessed goddess said: Lord Śiva is the most beloved of all living entities. He has no rival. No one is very dear to him, and no one is his enemy. No one but you could be envious of such a universal being, who is free from all enmity.

PURPORT

In *Bhagavad-gītā* (9.29) the Lord says, *samo 'haṁ sarva-bhūteṣu:* "I am equal to all living entities." Similarly, Lord Śiva is a qualitative incarnation of the Supreme Personality of Godhead, so he has almost the same qualities as the Supreme Lord. Therefore he is equal to everyone; no one is his enemy, and no one is his friend, but one who is envious by nature can become the enemy of Lord Śiva. Therefore Satī accused her father, "No one but you could be envious of Lord Śiva or be his enemy." Other sages and learned *brāhmaṇas* were present, but they were not envious of Lord Śiva, although they were all dependent on Dakṣa. Therefore no one but Dakṣa could be envious of Lord Śiva. That was the accusation of Satī.

TEXT 12

दोषान् परेषां हि गुणेषु साधवो
गृह्णन्ति केचिन्न भवादृशो द्विज ।

गुणांश्च फल्गून् बहुलीकरिष्णवो
महत्तमास्तेष्वविदद्भवानघम् ॥१२॥

doṣān pareṣāṁ hi guṇeṣu sādhavo
gṛhṇanti kecin na bhavādṛśo dvija
guṇāṁś ca phalgūn bahulī-kariṣṇavo
mahattamās teṣv avidad bhavān agham

doṣān—faults; *pareṣām*—of others; *hi*—for; *guṇeṣu*—in the qualities; *sādhavaḥ*—*sādhus;* *gṛhṇanti*—find; *kecit*—some; *na*—not; *bhavādṛśaḥ*—like you; *dvija*—O twice-born; *guṇān*—qualities; *ca*—and; *phalgūn*—small; *bahulī-kariṣṇavaḥ*—greatly magnifies; *mahattamāḥ*—the greatest persons; *teṣu*—among them; *avidat*—find; *bhavān*—you; *agham*—the fault.

TRANSLATION

Twice-born Dakṣa, a man like you can simply find fault in the qualities of others. Lord Śiva, however, not only finds no faults with others' qualities, but if someone has a little good quality, he magnifies it greatly. Unfortunately, you have found fault with such a great soul.

PURPORT

King Dakṣa is addressed here by his daughter Satī as *dvija*, twice-born. Twice-born refers to the higher classes of men, namely the *brāhmaṇas, kṣatriyas* and *vaiśyas.* In other words, a *dvija* is not an ordinary man but one who has studied the Vedic literature from a spiritual master and can discriminate between good and bad. Therefore it is supposed that he understands logic and philosophy. Satī, Dakṣa's daughter, put before him sound arguments. There are some highly qualified persons who accept only the good qualities of others. Just as a bee is always interested in the honey in the flower and does not consider the thorns and colors, highly qualified persons, who are uncommon, accept only the good qualities of others, not considering their bad qualities, whereas the common man can judge what are good qualities and what are bad qualities.

Among the uncommonly good souls there are still gradations, and the best good soul is one who accepts an insignificant asset of a person and magnifies that good quality. Lord Śiva is also called Āśutoṣa, which refers to one who is satisfied very easily and who offers to any person the highest level of benediction. For example, once a devotee of Lord Śiva wanted the benediction that whenever he touched someone on the head, that person's head would at once be separated from his trunk. Lord Śiva agreed. Although the benediction asked was not very commendable because the devotee wanted to kill his enemy, Lord Śiva considered the devotee's good quality in worshiping and satisfying him and granted the benediction. Thus Lord Śiva accepted his bad qualities as magnificently good qualities. But Satī accused her father, "You are just the opposite. Although Lord Śiva has so many good qualities and no bad qualities at all, you have accepted him as bad and found fault with him. Because of your accepting his good qualities to be bad, instead of your becoming the most exalted soul you have become the most fallen. A man becomes the greatest soul by accepting the goodness of others' qualities, but by unnecessarily considering others' good qualities to be bad, you have become the lowest of the fallen souls."

TEXT 13

नाश्चर्यमेतद्यदसत्सु सर्वदा
महद्विनिन्दा कुणपात्मवादिषु ।
सेर्ष्यं महापूरुषपादपांसुभि-
र्निरस्ततेजःसु तदेव शोभनम् ॥१३॥

nāścaryam etad yad asatsu sarvadā
mahad-vinindā kuṇapātma-vādiṣu
serṣyaṁ mahāpūruṣa-pāda-pāṁsubhir
nirasta-tejaḥsu tad eva śobhanam

na—not; *āścaryam*—wonderful; *etat*—this; *yat*—which; *asatsu*—evil; *sarvadā*—always; *mahat-vinindā*—the deriding of great souls; *kuṇapa-ātma-vādiṣu*—among those who have accepted the dead body as the self; *sa-īrṣyam*—envy; *mahā-pūruṣa*—of great personalities; *pāda-pāṁsubhiḥ*—by the dust of the feet; *nirasta-tejaḥsu*—whose glory is diminished; *tat*—that; *eva*—certainly; *śobhanam*—very good.

TRANSLATION

It is not wonderful for persons who have accepted the transient material body as the self to engage always in deriding great souls. Such envy on the part of materialistic persons is very good because that is the way they fall down. They are diminished by the dust of the feet of great personalities.

PURPORT

Everything depends on the strength of the recipient. For example, due to the scorching sunshine many vegetables and flowers dry up, and many grow luxuriantly. Thus it is the recipient that causes growth and dwindling. Similarly, *mahīyasāṁ pāda-rajo-'bhiṣekam:* the dust of the lotus feet of great personalities offers all good to the recipient, but the same dust can also do harm. Those who are offenders at the lotus feet of a great personality dry up; their godly qualities diminish. A great soul may forgive offenses, but Kṛṣṇa does not excuse offenses to the dust of that great soul's feet, just as one can tolerate the scorching sunshine on one's head but cannot tolerate the scorching sunshine on one's feet. An offender glides down more and more; therefore he naturally continues to commit offenses at the feet of the great soul. Offenses are generally committed by persons who falsely identify with the impermanent body. King Dakṣa was deeply engrossed in a misconception because he identified the body with the soul. He offended the lotus feet of Lord Śiva because he thought that his body, being the father of the body of Satī, was superior to Lord Śiva's. Generally, less intelligent men misidentify in that way, and they act in the bodily concept of life. Thus they are subject to commit more and more offenses at the lotus feet of great souls. One who has such a concept of life is considered to be in the class of animals like cows and asses.

TEXT 14

यद् द्व्यक्षरं नाम गिरेरितं नृणां
सकृत्प्रसङ्गादघमाशु हन्ति तत् ।
पवित्रकीर्तिं तमलङ्घ्यशासनं
भवानहो द्वेष्टि शिवं शिवेतरः ॥१४॥

yad dvy-akṣaraṁ nāma gireritaṁ nṛṇāṁ
sakṛt prasaṅgād agham āśu hanti tat
pavitra-kīrtiṁ tam alaṅghya-śāsanaṁ
bhavān aho dveṣṭi śivaṁ śivetaraḥ

yat—which; *dvi-akṣaram*—consisting of two letters; *nāma*—named; *girā īritam*—merely being pronounced by the tongue; *nṛṇām*—persons; *sakṛt*—once; *prasaṅgāt*—from the heart; *agham*—sinful activities; *āśu*—immediately; *hanti*—destroys; *tat*—that; *pavitra-kīrtim*—whose fame is pure; *tam*—him; *alaṅghya-śāsanam*—whose order is never neglected; *bhavān*—you; *aho*—oh; *dveṣṭi*—envy; *śivam*—Lord Śiva; *śiva-itaraḥ*—who are inauspicious.

TRANSLATION

Satī continued: My dear father, you are committing the greatest offense by envying Lord Śiva, whose very name, consisting of two syllables, śi and va, purifies one of all sinful activities. His order is never neglected. Lord Śiva is always pure, and no one but you envies him.

PURPORT

Since Lord Śiva is the greatest soul among the living entities within this material world, his name, Śiva, is very auspicious for persons who identify the body with the soul. If such persons take shelter of Lord Śiva, gradually they will understand that they are not the material body but are spirit soul. *Śiva* means *maṅgala,* or auspicious. Within the body the soul is auspicious. *Ahaṁ brahmāsmi:* "I am Brahman." This realization is auspicious. As long as one does not realize his identity as the soul, whatever he does is inauspicious. *Śiva* means "auspicious," and devotees of Lord Śiva gradually come to the platform of spiritual identification, but that is not all. Auspicious life begins from the point of spiritual identification. But there are still more duties—one has to understand one's relationship with the Supreme Soul. If one is actually a devotee of Lord Śiva, he comes to the platform of spiritual realization, but if he is not intelligent enough, then he stops at that point, only realizing that he is spirit soul (*ahaṁ brahmāsmi*). If he is intelligent enough, however, he should continue to act in the way of Lord Śiva, for Lord Śiva is always absorbed in the thought of Vāsudeva. As previously explained, *sattvaṁ viśuddhaṁ vasudeva-śabditam:* Lord Śiva is always in meditation on the lotus feet of Vāsudeva, Śrī Kṛṣṇa. Thus the auspicious position of Lord Śiva is realized if one takes to the worship of Viṣṇu, because Lord Śiva says in the *Śiva Purāṇa* that the topmost worship is worship of Lord Viṣṇu. Lord Śiva is worshiped because he is the greatest devotee of Lord Viṣṇu. One should not, however, make the mistake of considering Lord Śiva and Lord Viṣṇu to be on the same level. That is also an atheistic idea. It is also enjoined in the *Vaiṣṇavīya Purāṇa* that Viṣṇu, or Nārāyaṇa, is the exalted Supreme Personality of Godhead, and no one should be compared to Him as equal, even Lord Śiva or Lord Brahmā, not to speak of other demigods.

TEXT 15

यत्पादपद्मं महतां मनोऽलिभि-
र्निषेवितं ब्रह्मरसासवार्थिभिः ।
लोकस्य यद्वर्षति चाशिषोऽर्थिन-
स्तस्मै भवान् द्रुह्यति विश्वबन्धवे ॥१५॥

yat-pāda-padmaṁ mahatāṁ mano-'libhir
niṣevitaṁ brahma-rasāsavārthibhiḥ
lokasya yad varṣati cāśiṣo 'rthinas
tasmai bhavān druhyati viśva-bandhave

yat-pāda-padmam—the lotus feet of whom; *mahatām*—of the higher personalities; *manaḥ-alibhiḥ*—by the bees of the mind; *niṣevitam*—being engaged at; *brahma-rasa*—of transcendental bliss (*brahmānanda*); *āsava-arthibhiḥ*—seeking the nectar; *lokasya*—of the common man; *yat*—which; *varṣati*—he fulfills; *ca*—and; *āśiṣaḥ*—desires; *arthinaḥ*—seeking; *tasmai*—towards him (Lord Śiva); *bhavān*—you; *druhyati*—are envious; *viśva-bandhave*—unto the friend of all living entities within the three worlds.

TRANSLATION

You are envious of Lord Śiva, who is the friend of all living entities within the three worlds. For the common man he fulfills all

desires, and because of their engagement in thinking of his lotus feet, he also blesses higher personalities who are seeking after brahmānanda [transcendental bliss].

PURPORT

Ordinarily there are two classes of men. One class, who are grossly materialistic, want material prosperity, and their desires are fulfilled if they worship Lord Śiva. Lord Śiva, being very quickly satisfied, satisfies the material desires of the common man very quickly; therefore it is seen that ordinary men are very much apt to worship him. Next, those who are disgusted or frustrated with the materialistic way of life worship Lord Śiva to attain salvation, which entails freedom from material identification. One who understands that he is not the material body but is spirit soul is liberated from ignorance. Lord Śiva also offers that facility. People generally practice religion for economic development, to get some money, for by getting money they can satisfy their senses. But when they are frustrated they want spiritual *brahmānanda*, or merging into the Supreme. These four principles of material life—religion, economic development, sense gratification and liberation—exist, and Lord Śiva is the friend of both the ordinary man and the man who is elevated in spiritual knowledge. Thus it was not good for Dakṣa to create enmity towards him. Even Vaiṣṇavas, who are above both the ordinary and the elevated men in this world, also worship Lord Śiva as the greatest Vaiṣṇava. Thus he is the friend of everyone—the common men, the elevated men and the devotees of the Lord—so no one should disrespect or create enmity towards Lord Śiva.

TEXT 16

किं वा शिवाख्यमशिवं न विदुस्त्वदन्ये
ब्रह्मादयस्तमवकीर्य जटाः श्मशाने ।
तन्माल्यभस्मनृकपाल्यवसत्पिशाचै-
र्ये मूर्धभिर्दधति तच्चरणावसृष्टम् ॥१६॥

kiṁ vā śivākhyam aśivaṁ na vidus tvad anye
brahmādayas tam avakīrya jaṭāḥ śmaśāne

tan-mālya-bhasma-nṛkapāly avasat piśācair
ye mūrdhabhir dadhati tac-caraṇāvasṛṣṭam

kim vā—whether; *śiva-ākhyam*—named Śiva; *aśivam*—inauspicious; *na viduḥ*—do not know; *tvat anye*—other than you; *brahma-ādayaḥ*—Brahmā and others; *tam*—him (Lord Śiva); *avakīrya*—scattered; *jaṭāḥ*—having twisted hair; *śmaśāne*—in the crematorium; *tat-mālya-bhasma-nṛ-kapālī*—who is garlanded with human skulls and smeared with ashes; *avasat*—associated; *piśācaiḥ*—with demons; *ye*—who; *mūrdhabhiḥ*—with the head; *dadhati*—place; *tat-caraṇa-avasṛṣṭam*—fallen from his lotus feet.

TRANSLATION

Do you think that greater, more respectable personalities than you, such as Lord Brahmā, do not know this inauspicious person who goes under the name Lord Śiva? He associates with the demons in the crematorium, his locks of hair are scattered all over his body, he is garlanded with human skulls and smeared with ashes from the crematorium, but in spite of all these inauspicious qualities, great personalities like Brahmā honor him by accepting the flowers offered to his lotus feet and placing them with great respect on their heads.

PURPORT

It is useless to condemn a great personality like Lord Śiva, and this is being stated by his wife, Satī, to establish the supremacy of her husband. First she said, "You call Lord Śiva inauspicious because he associates with demons in crematoriums, covers his body with the ashes of the dead, and garlands himself with the skulls of human beings. You have shown so many defects, but you do not know that his position is always transcendental. Although he appears inauspicious, why do personalities like Brahmā respect the dust of his lotus feet and place on their heads with great respect those very garlands which are condemned by you?" Since Satī was a chaste woman and the wife of Lord Śiva, it was her duty to establish the elevated position of Lord Śiva, not only by sentiment but by facts. Lord Śiva is not an ordinary living entity. This is the conclusion of Vedic scripture. He is neither on the level of the Supreme Personality of Godhead nor on the level of the ordinary living entities. Brahmā is in almost all cases an ordinary living entity. Sometimes, when there is no ordinary living entity available, the post of Brahmā is occupied by an expansion of Lord Viṣṇu, but generally this post is occupied by a greatly pious living entity within this universe. Thus Lord Śiva's position is constitutionally higher than that of Lord Brahmā, although Lord Śiva appeared as the son of Brahmā. Here it is mentioned that even personalities like Brahmā accept the so-called inauspicious flowers and the dust of the lotus feet of Lord Śiva. Great sages like Marīci, Atri, Bhṛgu and the others among the nine great sages who are descendants of Brahmā also respect Lord Śiva in such a way because they all know that Lord Śiva is not an ordinary living entity.

In many *Purāṇas* it is sometimes asserted that a demigod is elevated to such a high position that he is almost on an equal level with the Supreme Personality of Godhead, but the conclusion that Lord Viṣṇu is the Supreme Personality of Godhead is confirmed in every scripture. Lord Śiva is described in the *Brahma-saṁhitā* to be like curd or yogurt. Curd is not different from milk. Since milk is transformed into curd, in one sense curd is also milk. Similarly, Lord Śiva is in one sense the Supreme Personality of Godhead, but in another sense he is not, just as curd is milk although we have to distinguish between the two. These descriptions are in the Vedic literature. Whenever we find that a demigod occupies a position apparently more elevated than that of the Supreme Personality of Godhead, it is just to draw the devotee's attention to that particular demigod. It is also stated in the *Bhagavad-gītā* (9.25) that if one wants to worship a particular demigod, the Supreme Personality of Godhead, who is sitting in everyone's heart, gives one greater and greater attachment for that demigod so that one may be elevated to the demigod's abode. *Yānti deva-vratā devān.* By worshiping demigods one can elevate himself to the abodes of the demigods; similarly, by worshiping the Supreme Personality of Godhead one can be elevated to the spiritual kingdom. This is stated in different places in Vedic literature. Here Lord Śiva is praised by Satī, partially due to her personal respect for Lord Śiva, since he is her husband, and partially due to his exalted position, which exceeds that of ordinary living entities, even Lord Brahmā.

The position of Lord Śiva is accepted by Lord Brahmā, so Dakṣa, Satī's father, should also recognize him. That was the point of Satī's statement.

She did not actually come to her father's house to participate in the function, although before coming she pleaded with her husband that she wanted to see her sisters and her mother. That was a plea only, for actually at heart she maintained the idea that she would convince her father, Dakṣa, that it was useless to continue being envious of Lord Śiva. That was her main purpose. When she was unable to convince her father, she gave up the body he had given her, as will be seen in the following verses.

TEXT 17

कर्णौ पिधाय निरयाद्यदकल्प ईशे
धर्मावितर्यसृणिभिर्नृभिरस्यमाने ।
छिन्द्यात्प्रसह्य रुशतीमसतीं प्रभुश्चे-
ज्जिह्वामसूनपि ततो विसृजेत्स धर्मः ॥१७॥

karṇau pidhāya nirayād yad akalpa īśe
dharmāvitary asṛṇibhir nṛbhir asyamāne
chindyāt prasahya ruśatīm asatīṁ prabhuś cej
jihvām asūn api tato visṛjet sa dharmaḥ

karṇau—both ears; *pidhāya*—blocking; *nirayāt*—one should go away; *yat*—if; *akalpaḥ*—unable; *īśe*—the master; *dharma-avitari*—the controller of religion; *asṛṇibhiḥ*—by irresponsible; *nṛbhiḥ*—persons; *asyamāne*—being blasphemed; *chindyāt*—he should cut; *prasahya*—by force; *ruśatīm*—vilifying; *asatīm*—of the blasphemer; *prabhuḥ*—one is able; *cet*—if; *jihvām*—tongue; *asūn*—(his own) life; *api*—certainly; *tataḥ*—then; *visṛjet*—should give up; *saḥ*—that; *dharmaḥ*—is the process.

TRANSLATION

Satī continued: If one hears an irresponsible person blaspheme the master and controller of religion, one should block his ears and go away if unable to punish him. But if one is able to kill, then one should by force cut out the blasphemer's tongue and kill the offender, and after that one should give up his own life.

PURPORT

The argument offered by Satī is that a person who vilifies a great personality is the lowest of all creatures. But, by the same argument, Dakṣa could also defend himself by saying that since he was a Prajāpati, the master of many living creatures and one of the great officers of the great universal affairs, his position was so exalted that Satī should accept his good qualities instead of vilifying him. The answer to that argument is that Satī was not vilifying but defending. If possible she should have cut out Dakṣa's tongue because he blasphemed Lord Śiva. In other words, since Lord Śiva is the protector of religion, a person who vilifies him should be killed at once, and after killing such a person, one should give up one's life. That is the process, but because Dakṣa happened to be the father of Satī, she decided not to kill him but to give up her own life in order to compensate for the great sin she had committed by hearing blasphemy of Lord Śiva. The instruction set forth here in *Śrīmad-Bhāgavatam* is that one should not tolerate at any cost the activities of a person who vilifies or blasphemes an authority. If one is a *brāhmaṇa* he should not give up his body because by doing so he would be responsible for killing a *brāhmaṇa;* therefore a *brāhmaṇa* should leave the place or block his ears so that he will not hear the blasphemy. If one happens to be a *kṣatriya* he has the power to punish any man; therefore a *kṣatriya* should at once cut out the tongue of the vilifier and kill him. But as far as the *vaiśyas* and *śūdras* are concerned, they should immediately give up their bodies. Satī decided to give up her body because she thought herself to be among the *śūdras* and *vaiśyas.* As stated in *Bhagavad-gītā* (9.32), *striyo vaiśyās tathā śūdrāḥ.* Women, laborers and the mercantile class are on the same level. Thus since it is recommended that *vaiśyas* and *śūdras* should immediately give up their bodies upon hearing blasphemy of an exalted person like Lord Śiva, she decided to give up her life.

TEXT 18

अतस्तवोत्पन्नमिदं कलेवरं
न धारयिष्ये शितिकण्ठगर्हिणः ।
जग्धस्य मोहाद्धि विशुद्धिमन्धसो
जुगुप्सितस्योद्धरणं प्रचक्षते ॥१८॥

atas tavotpannam idaṁ kalevaraṁ
na dhārayiṣye śiti-kaṇṭha-garhiṇaḥ
jagdhasya mohād dhi viśuddhim andhaso
jugupsitasyoddharaṇaṁ pracakṣate

ataḥ—therefore; *tava*—from you; *utpannam*—received; *idam*—this; *kalevaram*—body; *na dhārayiṣye*—I shall not bear; *śiti-kaṇṭha-garhiṇaḥ*—who have blasphemed Lord Śiva; *jagdhasya*—which has been eaten; *mohāt*—by mistake; *hi*—because; *viśuddhim*—the purification; *andhasaḥ*—of food; *jugupsitasya*—poisonous; *uddharaṇam*—vomiting; *pracakṣate*—declare.

TRANSLATION

Therefore I shall no longer bear this unworthy body, which has been received from you, who have blasphemed Lord Śiva. If someone has taken food which is poisonous, the best treatment is to vomit.

PURPORT

Since Satī was the representation of the external potency of the Lord, it was in her power to vanquish many universes, including many Dakṣas, but in order to save her husband from the charge that he employed his wife, Satī, to kill Dakṣa because he could not do so due to his inferior position, she decided to give up her body.

TEXT 19

न वेदवादाननुवर्तते मतिः
स्व एव लोके रमतो महामुनेः ।
यथा गतिर्देवमनुष्ययोः पृथक्
स्व एव धर्मे न परं क्षिपेत्स्थितः ॥१९॥

na veda-vādān anuvartate matiḥ
sva eva loke ramato mahā-muneḥ
yathā gatir deva-manuṣyayoḥ pṛthak
sva eva dharme na paraṁ kṣipet sthitaḥ

na—not; *veda-vādān*—rules and regulations of the *Vedas; anuvartate*—follow; *matiḥ*—the mind; *sve*—in his own; *eva*—certainly; *loke*—in the self; *ramataḥ*—enjoying; *mahā-muneḥ*—of elevated transcendentalists; *yathā*—as; *gatiḥ*—the way; *deva-manuṣyayoḥ*—of the men and the demigods; *pṛthak*—separately; *sve*—in your own; *eva*—alone; *dharme*—occupational duty; *na*—not; *param*—another; *kṣipet*—should criticize; *sthitaḥ*—being situated.

TRANSLATION

It is better to execute one's own occupational duty than to criticize others'. Elevated transcendentalists may sometimes forgo the rules and regulations of the Vedas, since they do not need to follow them, just as the demigods travel in space whereas ordinary men travel on the surface of the earth.

PURPORT

The behavior of the most elevated transcendentalist and that of the most fallen conditioned soul appears to be the same. The elevated transcendentalist can surpass all the regulations of the *Vedas*, just as the demigods traveling in space surpass all the jungles and rocks on the surface of the globe, although a common man, who has no such ability to travel in space, has to face all those impediments. Although the most dear Lord Śiva appears not to observe all the rules and regulations of the *Vedas*, he is not affected by such disobedience, but a common man who wants to imitate Lord Śiva is mistaken. A common man must observe all the rules and regulations of the *Vedas* which a person who is in the transcendental position does not need to observe. Dakṣa found fault with Lord Śiva for not observing all the strict rules and regulations of the *Vedas*, but Satī asserted that he had no need to observe such rules. It is said that for one who is powerful like the sun or the fire, there is no consideration of purity or impurity. The sunshine can sterilize an impure place, whereas if someone else were to pass such a place he would be affected. One should not try to imitate Lord Śiva; rather, one should strictly follow one's prescribed occupational duties. One should never vilify a great personality like Lord Śiva.

TEXT 20

कर्म प्रवृत्तं च निवृत्तमप्यृतं
वेदे विविच्योभयलिङ्गमाश्रितम् ।
विरोधि तद्यौगपदैककर्तरि
द्वयं तथा ब्रह्मणि कर्म नर्च्छति ॥२०॥

karma pravṛttaṁ ca nivṛttam apy ṛtaṁ
vede vivicyobhaya-liṅgam āśritam
virodhi tad yaugapadaika-kartari
dvayaṁ tathā brahmaṇi karma narcchati

karma—activities; *pravṛttam*—attached to material enjoyment; *ca*—and; *nivṛttam*—materially detached; *api*—certainly; *ṛtam*—true; *vede*—in the *Vedas;* *vivicya*—distinguished; *ubhaya-liṅgam*—symptoms of both; *āśritam*—directed; *virodhi*—contradictory; *tat*—that; *yaugapada-eka-kartari*—both activities in one person; *dvayam*—two; *tathā*—so; *brahmaṇi*—in one who is transcendentally situated; *karma*—activities; *na ṛcchati*—are neglected.

TRANSLATION

In the Vedas there are directions for two kinds of activities—activities for those who are attached to material enjoyment and activities for those who are materially detached. In consideration of these two kinds of activities, there are two kinds of people, who have different symptoms. If one wants to see two kinds of activities in one person, that is contradictory. But both kinds of activities may be neglected by a person who is transcendentally situated.

PURPORT

The Vedic activities are so designed that the conditioned soul who has come to enjoy the material world may do so under direction so that at the end he becomes detached from such material enjoyment and is eligible to enter into the transcendental position. The four different social orders—*brahmacarya, gṛhastha, vānaprastha* and *sannyāsa*—gradually train a person to come to the platform of transcendental life. The activities and dress of a *gṛhastha*, or householder, are different from those of a *sannyāsī*, one in the renounced order of life. It is impossible for one person to adopt both orders. A *sannyāsī* cannot act like a householder, nor can a householder act like a *sannyāsī*, but above these two kinds of persons, one who engages in material activities and one who has renounced material activities, there is the person who is transcendental to both. Lord Śiva is in the transcendental position because, as stated before, he is always absorbed in the thought of Lord Vāsudeva within himself. Therefore neither the activities of the *gṛhastha* nor those of the *sannyāsī* in the renounced order can be applicable for him. He is in the *paramahaṁsa* stage, the highest perfectional stage of life. The transcendental position of Lord Śiva is also explained in *Bhagavad-gītā* (2.52–53). It is stated there that when one fully engages in the transcendental service of the Lord by performing activities without fruitive results, one is elevated to the transcendental position. At that time he has no obligation to follow the Vedic injunctions or the different rules and regulations of the *Vedas.* When one is above the directions of the Vedic ritualistic injunctions for attaining different allurements and is fully absorbed in transcendental thought, which means thought of the Supreme Personality of Godhead in devotional service, one is in the position called *buddhi-yoga*, or *samādhi*, ecstasy. For a person who has attained this stage, neither the Vedic activities for realizing material enjoyment nor those for renunciation are applicable.

TEXT 21

मा वः पदव्यः पितरस्मदास्थिता
या यज्ञशालासु न धूमवर्त्मभिः ।
तदन्नतृप्तैरसुभृद्भिरीडिता
अव्यक्तलिङ्गा अवधूतसेविताः ॥२१॥

mā vaḥ padavyaḥ pitar asmad-āsthitā
yā yajña-śālāsu na dhūma-vartmabhiḥ
tad-anna-tṛptair asu-bhṛdbhir īḍitā
avyakta-liṅgā avadhūta-sevitāḥ

mā—are not; *vaḥ*—yours; *padavyaḥ*—opulences; *pitaḥ*—O father; *asmat-āsthitāḥ*—possessed by us; *yāḥ*—which (opulences); *yajña-śālāsu*—in the sacrificial fire; *na*—not; *dhūma-vartmabhiḥ*—by the path of sacrifices; *tat-anna-tṛptaiḥ*—satisfied by the foodstuff of the sacrifice; *asu-bhṛdbhiḥ*—satisfying bodily necessities; *īḍitāḥ*—praised; *avyakta-liṅgāḥ*—whose cause is unmanifested; *avadhūta-sevitāḥ*—achieved by the self-realized souls.

TRANSLATION

My dear father, the opulence we possess is impossible for either you or your flatterers to imagine, for persons who engage in fruitive activities by performing great sacrifices are concerned with satisfying their bodily necessities by eating foodstuff offered as a sacrifice. We can exhibit our opulences simply by desiring to do so. This can be achieved only by great personalities who are renounced, self-realized souls.

PURPORT

Satī's father was under the impression that he was exalted in both prestige and opulence and that he had offered his daughter to a person who was not only poor but devoid of all culture. Her father might have been thinking that although she was a chaste woman, greatly adherent to her husband, her husband was in a deplorable condition. To counteract such thoughts, Satī said that the opulence possessed by her husband could not be understood by materialistic persons like Dakṣa and his followers, who were flatterers and were engaged in fruitive activities. Her husband's position was different. He possessed all opulences, but he did not like to exhibit them. Therefore such opulences are called *avyakta*, or unmanifested. But if required, simply by willing, Lord Śiva can show his wonderful opulences, and such an event is predicted here, for it would soon occur. The opulence Lord Śiva possesses is enjoyable in renunciation and love of God, not in material exhibition of sense gratificatory methods. Such opulences are possessed by personalities like the Kumāras, Nārada and Lord Śiva, not by others.

In this verse the performers of the Vedic rituals are condemned. They have been described here as *dhūma-vartmabhiḥ*, those who maintain themselves on the remnants of sacrificial foodstuff. There are two kinds of foodstuff offered in sacrifice. One kind is food offered in fruitive ritualistic sacrifices, and the other, the best, is food offered to Viṣṇu. Although in all cases Viṣṇu is the chief Deity on the sacrificial altar, the performers of fruitive rituals aim to satisfy various demigods to achieve in return some material prosperity. Real sacrifice, however, is to satisfy Lord Viṣṇu, and the remnants of such sacrifices are beneficial for advancement in devotional service. The process of elevation by performing sacrifices other than those aimed at Viṣṇu is very slow, and therefore it has been condemned in this verse. Viśvanātha Cakravartī has described the ritualistic performers to be like crows because crows delight in eating the remnants of food which has been thrown into the dustbin. All the *brāhmaṇas* who were present for the sacrifice were also condemned by Satī.

Whether or not King Dakṣa and his flatterers could understand the position of Lord Śiva, Satī wanted to impress upon her father that he should not think her husband to be without opulence. Satī, being the devoted wife of Lord Śiva, offers all kinds of material opulences to the worshipers of Lord Śiva. This fact is explained in the *Śrīmad-Bhāgavatam,* in the Tenth Canto. Lord Śiva's worshipers sometimes appear more opulent than the worshipers of Lord Viṣṇu because Durgā, or Satī, being the superintendent in charge of material affairs, can offer all material opulences to the worshipers of Lord Śiva in order to glorify her husband, whereas the worshipers of Viṣṇu are meant for spiritual elevation, and therefore their material opulence is sometimes found to decrease. These points are very nicely discussed in the Tenth Canto.

TEXT 22

नैतेन देहेन हरे कृतागसो
देहोद्भवेनालमलं कुजन्मना ।
व्रीडा ममाभूत्कुजनप्रसङ्गत-
स्तज्जन्म धिग् यो महतामवद्यकृत् ॥२२॥

naitena dehena hare kṛtāgaso
dehodbhavenālam alaṁ kujanmanā
vrīḍā mamābhūt kujana-prasaṅgatas
taj janma dhig yo mahatām avadya-kṛt

na—not; *etena*—by this; *dehena*—by the body; *hare*—to Lord Śiva; *kṛta-āgasaḥ*—having committed offenses; *deha-udbhavena*—produced from your body; *alam alam*—enough, enough; *ku-janmanā*—with a contemptible birth; *vrīḍā*—shame; *mama*—my; *abhūt*—was; *ku-jana-prasaṅgataḥ*—from a relationship with a bad person; *tat janma*—that birth; *dhik*—shameful; *yaḥ*—who; *mahatām*—of the great personalities; *avadya-kṛt*—an offender.

TRANSLATION

You are an offender at the lotus feet of Lord Śiva, and unfortunately I have a body produced from yours. I am very much ashamed of our bodily relationship, and I condemn myself because my body is contaminated by a relationship with a person who is an offender at the lotus feet of the greatest personality.

PURPORT

Lord Śiva is the greatest of all devotees of Lord Viṣṇu. It is stated, *vaiṣṇavānāṁ yathā śambhuḥ*. Śambhu, Lord Śiva, is the greatest of all devotees of Lord Viṣṇu. In the previous verses, Satī has described that Lord Śiva is always in a transcendental position because he is situated in pure *vasudeva*. *Vasudeva* is that state from which Kṛṣṇa, Vāsudeva, is born, so Lord Śiva is the greatest devotee of Lord Kṛṣṇa, and Satī's behavior is exemplary because no one should tolerate blasphemy against Lord Viṣṇu or His devotee. Satī is aggrieved not for her personal association with Lord Śiva but because her body is related with that of Dakṣa, who is an offender at Lord Śiva's lotus feet. She feels herself to be condemned because of the body given by her father, Dakṣa.

TEXT 23

गोत्रं त्वदीयं भगवान् वृषध्वजो
दाक्षायणीत्याह यदा सुदुर्मनाः ।
व्यपेतनर्मस्मितमाशु तदाऽहं
व्युत्स्रक्ष्य एतत्कुणपं त्वदङ्गजम् ॥२३॥

gotraṁ tvadīyaṁ bhagavān vṛṣadhvajo
dākṣāyaṇīty āha yadā sudurmanāḥ

vyapeta-narma-smitam āśu tadā 'haṁ
vyutsrakṣya etat kuṇapaṁ tvad-aṅgajam

gotram—family relationship; *tvadīyam*—your; *bhagavān*—the possessor of all opulences; *vṛṣadhvajaḥ*—Lord Śiva; *dākṣāyaṇī*—Dākṣāyaṇī (the daughter of Dakṣa); *iti*—thus; *āha*—calls; *yadā*—when; *sudurmanāḥ*—very morose; *vyapeta*—disappear; *narma-smitam*—my jolliness and smile; *āśu*—immediately; *tadā*—then; *aham*—I; *vyutsrakṣye*—I shall give up; *etat*—this (body); *kuṇapam*—dead body; *tvat-aṅga-jam*—produced from your body.

TRANSLATION

Because of our family relationship, when Lord Śiva addresses me as Dākṣāyaṇī I at once become morose, and my jolliness and my smile at once disappear. I feel very much sorry that my body, which is just like a bag, has been produced by you. I shall therefore give it up.

PURPORT

The word *dākṣāyaṇī* means "the daughter of King Dakṣa." Sometimes, when there was relaxed conversation between husband and wife, Lord Śiva used to call Satī "the daughter of King Dakṣa," and because this very word reminded her about her family relationship with King Dakṣa, she at once became ashamed because Dakṣa was an incarnation of all offenses. Dakṣa was the embodiment of envy, for he unnecessarily blasphemed a great personality, Lord Śiva. Simply upon hearing the word *dākṣāyaṇī*, she felt afflicted because of reference to the context because her body was the symbol of all the offensiveness with which Dakṣa was endowed. Since her body was constantly a source of unhappiness, she decided to give it up.

TEXT 24

मैत्रेय उवाच

इत्यध्वरे दक्षमनूद्य शत्रुहन्
क्षितावुदीचीं निषसाद शान्तवाक् ।
स्पृष्ट्वा जलं पीतदुकूलसंवृता
निमील्य दृग्योगपथं समाविशत् ॥२४॥

maitreya uvāca
ity adhvare dakṣam anūdya śatru-han
kṣitāv udīcīṁ niṣasāda śānta-vāk
spṛṣṭvā jalaṁ pīta-dukūla-saṁvṛtā
nimīlya dṛg yoga-pathaṁ samāviśat

maitreyaḥ uvāca—Maitreya said; *iti*—thus; *adhvare*—in the arena of sacrifice; *dakṣam*—to Dakṣa; *anūdya*—speaking; *śatru-han*—O annihilator of enemies; *kṣitau*—on the ground; *udīcīm*—facing north; *niṣasāda*—sat down; *śānta-vāk*—in silence; *spṛṣṭvā*—after touching; *jalam*—water; *pīta-dukūla-saṁvṛtā*—dressed in yellow garments; *nimīlya*—closing; *dṛk*—the vision; *yoga-patham*—the mystic *yoga* process; *samāviśat*—became absorbed.

TRANSLATION

Maitreya the sage told Vidura: O annihilator of enemies, while thus speaking to her father in the arena of sacrifice, Satī sat down on the ground and faced north. Dressed in saffron garments, she sanctified herself with water and closed her eyes to absorb herself in the process of mystic yoga.

PURPORT

It is said that when a man desires to quit his body he dresses in saffron garments. Therefore it appears that Satī changed her dress, indicating that she was going to quit the body given her by Dakṣa. Dakṣa was Satī's father, so instead of killing Dakṣa she decided that it would be better to destroy the part of his body which was hers. Thus she decided to give up the body of Dakṣa by the yogic process. Satī was the wife of Lord Śiva, who is known as Yogeśvara, the best among all *yogīs*, because he knows all the mystic processes of *yoga*, so it appeared that Satī also knew them. Either she learned *yoga* from her husband or she was enlightened because she was the daughter of such a great king as Dakṣa. The perfection of *yoga* is that one can give up one's body or release oneself from the embodiment of material elements according to one's desire. *Yogīs* who have attained perfection are not subject to death by natural laws; such perfect *yogīs* can leave the body whenever they desire. Generally the *yogī* first of all becomes mature in controlling the air passing within the body, thus bringing the soul to the top of the brain. Then when the body bursts into flames, the *yogī* can go anywhere he likes. This *yoga* system recognizes the soul, and thus it is distinct from the so-called *yoga* process for controlling the cells of the body, which has been discovered in the modern age. The real *yoga* process accepts the transmigration of the soul from one planet to another or one body to another; and it appears from this incident that Satī wanted to transfer her soul to another body or sphere.

TEXT 25

कृत्वा समानावनिलौ जितासना
सोदानमुत्थाप्य च नाभिचक्रतः ।
शनैर्हृदि स्थाप्य धियोरसि स्थितं
कण्ठाद् भ्रुवोर्मध्यमनिन्दितानयत् ॥२५॥

kṛtvā samānāv anilau jitāsanā
sodānam utthāpya ca nābhi-cakrataḥ
śanair hṛdi sthāpya dhiyorasi sthitaṁ
kaṇṭhād bhruvor madhyam aninditānayat

kṛtvā—after placing; *samānau*—in equilibrium; *anilau*—the *prāṇa* and *apāna* airs; *jita-āsanā*—having controlled the sitting posture; *sā*—Satī; *udānam*—the life air; *utthāpya*—raising; *ca*—and; *nābhi-cakrataḥ*—at the circle in the navel; *śanaiḥ*—gradually; *hṛdi*—in the heart; *sthāpya*—placing; *dhiyā*—with the intelligence; *urasi*—towards the pulmonary passage; *sthitam*—having been placed; *kaṇṭhāt*—through the throat; *bhruvoḥ*—of the eyebrows; *madhyam*—to the middle; *aninditā*—the blameless (Satī); *ānayat*—raised.

TRANSLATION

First of all she sat in the required sitting posture, and then she carried the life air upwards and placed it in the position of equilibrium near the navel. Then she raised her life air, mixed

with intelligence, to the heart and then gradually towards the pulmonary passage and from there to between her eyebrows.

PURPORT

The yogic process is to control the air passing within the body in different places called *ṣaṭ-cakra,* the six circles of air circulation. The air is raised from the abdomen to the navel, from the navel to the heart, from the heart to the throat, from the throat to between the eyebrows and from between the eyebrows to the top of the cerebrum. That is the sum and substance of practicing *yoga.* Before practicing the real *yoga* system, one has to practice the sitting postures because this helps in the breathing exercises which control the airs going upwards and downwards. This is a great technique which one has to practice to attain the highest perfectional stage of *yoga,* but such practice is not meant for this age. No one in this age can attain the perfectional stage of such *yoga,* but people indulge in practicing sitting postures, which is more or less a gymnastic process. By such bodily gymnastics one may develop good circulation and may therefore keep one's body fit, but if one simply restricts oneself to that gymnastic process one cannot attain the highest perfectional stage. The *yoga* process, as described in the *Keśava-śruti,* prescribes how one can control his living force according to his desire and transmigrate from one body to another or from one place to another. In other words, *yoga* practice is not meant to keep the body fit. Any transcendental process of spiritual realization automatically helps one to keep the body fit, for it is the spirit soul that keeps the body always fresh. As soon as the spirit soul is out of the body, the material body immediately begins to decompose. Any spiritual process keeps the body fit without separate endeavor, but if one takes it that the ultimate aim of *yoga* is to maintain the body, then he is mistaken. The real perfection of *yoga* is elevation of the soul to a higher position or the liberation of the soul from material entanglement. Some *yogīs* try to elevate the soul to higher planetary systems, where the standard of life is different from that of this planet and where the material comforts, life-span and other facilities for self-realization are greater, and some *yogīs* endeavor to elevate the soul to the spiritual world, the spiritual Vaikuṇṭha planets. The *bhakti-yoga* process directly elevates the soul to the spiritual planets, where life is eternally blissful and full of knowledge; therefore *bhakti-yoga* is considered to be the greatest of all *yoga* systems.

TEXT 26

एवं स्वदेहं महतां महीयसा
मुहुः समारोपितमङ्कमादरात् ।
जिहासती दक्षरुषा मनस्विनी
दधार गात्रेष्वनिलाग्निधारणाम् ॥२६॥

evaṁ sva-dehaṁ mahatāṁ mahīyasā
muhuḥ samāropitam aṅkam ādarāt
jihāsatī dakṣa-ruṣā manasvinī
dadhāra gātreṣv anilāgni-dhāraṇām

evam—thus; *sva-deham*—her own body; *mahatām*—of the great saints; *mahīyasā*—most worshipful; *muhuḥ*—again and again; *samāropitam*—seated; *aṅkam*—on the lap; *ādarāt*—respectfully; *jihāsatī*—wishing to give up; *dakṣa-ruṣā*—due to anger towards Dakṣa; *manasvinī*—voluntarily; *dadhāra*—placed; *gātreṣu*—on the limbs of the body; *anila-agni-dhāraṇām*—meditation on the fire and air.

TRANSLATION

Thus, in order to give up her body, which had been so respectfully and affectionately seated on the lap of Lord Śiva, who is worshiped by great sages and saints, Satī, due to anger towards her father, began to meditate on the fiery air within the body.

PURPORT

Lord Śiva is described herein as the best of all great souls. Although Satī's body was born of Dakṣa, Lord Śiva used to adore her by sitting her on his lap. This is considered a great token of respect. Thus Satī's body was not ordinary, but still she decided to give it up because it was the source of unhappiness because of its connection with Dakṣa. This severe example set by Satī is to be followed. One should be extremely careful about associating with persons who are not respectful to the higher authorities. It is instructed, therefore, in the Vedic literature that one should always be free from the association of atheists and nondevotees and should try to associate with devotees, for by the association of a devotee one can be elevated to the platform of self-realization. This injunction is stressed in many places in *Śrīmad-Bhāgavatam;* if one wants to be liberated from the clutches of material existence, then one has to associate with great souls, and if one wants to continue one's material existential life, then one may associate with persons who are materialistic. The materialistic way of life is based on sex life. Thus both becoming addicted to sex life and associating with persons who are addicted to sex life are condemned in the Vedic literature because such association will simply interfere with one's spiritual progress. However, association with great personalities, devotees who are great souls, will elevate one to the spiritual platform. Satīdevī decided to quit the body she had obtained from Dakṣa's body, and she wanted to transfer herself to another body so that she might have completely uncontaminated association with Lord Śiva. Of course, it is understood that in her next life she would take birth as the daughter of the Himalayas, Pārvatī, and then she would again accept Lord Śiva as her husband. Satī and Lord Śiva are eternally related; even after she changes her body, their relationship is never broken.

TEXT 27

ततः स्वभर्तुश्चरणाम्बुजासवं
जगद्गुरोश्चिन्तयती न चापरम् ।
ददर्श देहो हतकल्मषः सती
सद्यः प्रजज्वाल समाधिजाग्निना ॥२७॥

tataḥ sva-bhartuś caraṇāmbujāsavaṁ
jagad-guroś cintayatī na cāparam
dadarśa deho hata-kalmaṣaḥ satī
sadyaḥ prajajvāla samādhijāgninā

tataḥ—there; *sva-bhartuḥ*—of her husband; *caraṇa-ambuja-āsavam*—on the nectar of the lotus feet; *jagat-guroḥ*—of the supreme spiritual teacher of the universe; *cintayatī*—meditating; *na*—not; *ca*—and;

aparam—not other (than her husband); *dadarśa*—saw; *dehaḥ*—her body; *hata-kalmaṣaḥ*—taints of sin being destroyed; *satī*—Satī; *sadyaḥ*—soon; *prajajvāla*—burned; *samādhi-ja-agninā*—by fire produced by meditation.

TRANSLATION

Satī concentrated all her meditation on the holy lotus feet of her husband, Lord Śiva, who is the supreme spiritual master of all the world. Thus she became completely cleansed of all taints of sin and quit her body in a blazing fire by meditation on the fiery elements.

PURPORT

Satī at once thought of the lotus feet of her husband, Lord Śiva, who is one of the three great personalities of Godhead in charge of the management of the material world, and simply by meditating on his lotus feet she derived such great pleasure that she forgot everything in relationship with her body. This pleasure was certainly material because she gave up her body for another body that was also material, but by this example we can appreciate the devotee's pleasure in concentrating his mind and attention on the lotus feet of the Supreme Lord, Viṣṇu, or Kṛṣṇa. There is such transcendental bliss in simply meditating on the lotus feet of the Lord that one can forget everything but the Lord's transcendental form. This is the perfection of yogic *samādhi,* or ecstasy. In this verse it is stated that by such meditation she became free from all contamination. What was that contamination? The contamination was her concept of the body derived from Dakṣa, but she forgot that bodily relationship in trance. The purport is that when one becomes free from all bodily relationships within this material world and simply places himself in the position of an eternal servant of the Supreme Lord, it is to be understood that all the contamination of his material attachment has been burned by the blazing fires of transcendental ecstasy. It is not necessary for one to manifest a blazing fire externally, for if one forgets all his bodily relationships within this material world and becomes situated in his spiritual identity, it is said that one has been freed from all material contamination by the blazing fire of yogic *samādhi,* or ecstasy. That is the topmost perfection of *yoga.* If one keeps his bodily relationships within this material world and poses himself as a great *yogī,* he is not a bona fide *yogī*. In *Śrīmad-Bhāgavatam* (2.4.15) it is stated, *yat-kīrtanaṁ yat-smaraṇaṁ*. Simply by chanting the holy name of the Supreme Personality of Godhead, simply by remembering the lotus feet of Kṛṣṇa, simply by offering prayers to the Supreme Personality of Godhead, one is immediately freed from material contamination, the material bodily concept, by the blazing fire of ecstasy. This effect takes place immediately, without a second's delay.

According to Śrī Jīva Gosvāmī, that Satī quit her body means that she gave up within her heart her relationship with Dakṣa. Śrī Viśvanātha Cakravartī Ṭhākura also comments that since Satī is the superintendent deity of the external potency, when she quit her body she did not get a spiritual body but simply transferred from the body she had received from Dakṣa. Other commentators also say that she immediately transferred herself into the womb of Menakā, her future mother. She gave up the body she had received from Dakṣa and immediately transferred herself to another, better body, but this does not mean that she got a spiritual body.

TEXT 28

तत्पश्यतां खे भुवि चाद्भुतं महद्
हाहेति वादः सुमहानजायत ।
हन्त प्रिया दैवतमस्य देवी
जहावसून् केन सती प्रकोपिता ॥२८॥

tat paśyatāṁ khe bhuvi cādbhutaṁ mahad
hā heti vādaḥ sumahān ajāyata
hanta priyā daivatamasya devī
jahāv asūn kena satī prakopitā

tat—that; *paśyatām*—of those who had seen; *khe*—in the sky; *bhuvi*—on the earth; *ca*—and; *adbhutam*—wonderful; *mahat*—great; *hā hā*—oh, oh; *iti*—thus; *vādaḥ*—roar; *su-mahān*—tumultuous; *ajāyata*—occurred; *hanta*—alas; *priyā*—the beloved; *daiva-tamasya*—of the most respectable demigod (Lord Śiva); *devī*—Satī; *jahau*—quit; *asūn*—her life; *kena*—by Dakṣa; *satī*—Satī; *prakopitā*—angered.

TRANSLATION

When Satī annihilated her body in anger, there was a tumultuous roar all over the universe. Why had Satī, the wife of the most respectable demigod, Lord Śiva, quit her body in such a manner?

PURPORT

There was a tumultuous roaring all over the universe in the societies of the demigods of different planets because Satī was the daughter of Dakṣa, the greatest of all kings, and the wife of Lord Śiva, the greatest of all demigods. Why did she become so angry that she gave up her body? Since she was the daughter of a great personality and wife of a great personality, she had nothing to desire, but still she gave up her body in dissatisfaction. Certainly this was astonishing. One cannot attain complete satisfaction even if one is situated in the greatest material opulence. There was nothing Satī could not achieve either from her relationship with her father or from her relationship with the greatest of the demigods, but still, for some reason, she was dissatisfied. Therefore, *Śrīmad-Bhāgavatam* (1.2.6) explains that one has to achieve real satisfaction (*yayātmā suprasīdati*), but *ātmā*—the body, mind and soul—all become completely satisfied only if one develops devotional service to the Absolute Truth. *Sa vai puṁsāṁ paro dharmo yato bhaktir adhokṣaje. Adhokṣaja* means the Absolute Truth. If one can develop his unflinching love for the transcendental Supreme Personality of Godhead, that can give complete satisfaction, otherwise there is no possibility of satisfaction in the material world or anywhere else.

TEXT 29

अहो अनात्म्यं महदस्य पश्यत
प्रजापतेर्यस्य चराचरं प्रजाः ।
जहावसन्न् यद्विमतात्मजा सती
मनस्विनी मानमभीक्ष्णमर्हति ॥२९॥

aho anātmyaṁ mahad asya paśyata
prajāpater yasya carācaraṁ prajāḥ

jahāv asūn yad-vimatātmajā satī
manasvinī mānam abhīkṣṇam arhati

aho—oh; *anātmyam*—neglect; *mahat*—great; *asya*—of Dakṣa; *paśyata*—just see; *prajāpateḥ*—of the Prajāpati; *yasya*—of whom; *cara-acaram*—all living entities; *prajāḥ*—offspring; *jahau*—gave up; *asūn*—her body; *yat*—by whom; *vimatā*—disrespected; *ātma-jā*—his own daughter; *satī*—Satī; *manasvinī*—voluntarily; *mānam*—respect; *abhīkṣṇam*—repeatedly; *arhati*—deserved.

TRANSLATION

It was astonishing that Dakṣa, who was Prajāpati, the maintainer of all living entities, was so disrespectful to his own daughter, Satī, who was not only chaste but was also a great soul, that she gave up her body because of his neglect.

PURPORT

The word *anātmya* is significant. *Ātmya* means "the life of the soul," so this word indicates that although Dakṣa appeared to be living, actually he was a dead body, otherwise how could he neglect Satī, who was his own daughter? It was the duty of Dakṣa to look after the maintenance and comforts of all living entities because he was situated as Prajāpati, the governor of all living entities. Therefore how is it that he neglected his own daughter, who was the most exalted and chaste woman, a great soul, and who therefore deserved the most respectful treatment from her father? The death of Satī because of her being neglected by Dakṣa, her father, was most astonishing to all the great demigods of the universe.

TEXT 30

सोऽयं दुर्मर्षहृदयो ब्रह्मध्रुक् च
लोकेऽपकीर्तिं महतीमवाप्स्यति ।
यदङ्गजां स्वां पुरुषद्विड्डुद्यतां
न प्रत्यषेधन्मृतयेऽपराधतः ॥३०॥

so 'yaṁ durmarṣa-hṛdayo brahma-dhruk ca
loke 'pakīrtiṁ mahatīm avāpsyati

yad-aṅgajāṁ svāṁ puruṣa-dviḍ udyatāṁ
na pratyaṣedhan mṛtaye 'parādhataḥ

saḥ—he; *ayam*—that; *durmarṣa-hṛdayaḥ*—hardhearted; *brahma-dhruk*—unworthy to be a *brāhmaṇa; ca*—and; *loke*—in the world; *apakīrtim*—ill fame; *mahatīm*—extensive; *avāpsyati*—will gain; *yat-aṅga-jām*—the daughter of whom; *svām*—own; *puruṣa-dviṭ*—the enemy of Lord Śiva; *udyatām*—who was preparing; *na pratyaṣedhat*—did not prevent; *mṛtaye*—for death; *aparādhataḥ*—because of his offenses.

TRANSLATION

Dakṣa, who is so hardhearted that he is unworthy to be a brāhmaṇa, will gain extensive ill fame because of his offenses to his daughter, because of not having prevented her death, and because of his great envy of the Supreme Personality of Godhead.

PURPORT

Dakṣa is described here as most hardhearted and therefore unqualified to be a *brāhmaṇa. Brahma-dhruk* is described by some commentators to mean *brahma-bandhu,* or friend of the *brāhmaṇas.* A person who is born in a *brāhmaṇa* family but has no brahminical qualifications is called a *brahma-bandhu. Brāhmaṇas* are generally very softhearted and forbearing because they have the power to control the senses and the mind. Dakṣa, however, was not forbearing. For the simple reason that his son-in-law, Lord Śiva, did not stand up to show him the formality of respect, he became so angry and hardhearted that he tolerated even the death of his dearest daughter. Satī tried her best to mitigate the misunderstanding between the son-in-law and the father-in-law by coming to her father's house, even without an invitation, and at that time Dakṣa should have received her, forgetting all past misunderstandings. But he was so hardhearted that he was unworthy to be called an Āryan or *brāhmaṇa.* Thus his ill fame still continues. *Dakṣa* means "expert," and he was given this name because of his ability to beget many hundreds and thousands of children. Persons who are too sexually inclined and materialistic become so hardhearted because of a slight loss of prestige that they can tolerate even the death of their children.

TEXT 31

वदत्येवं जने सत्या दृष्ट्वासुत्यागमद्भुतम् ।
दक्षं तत्पार्षदा हन्तुमुदतिष्ठन्नुदायुधाः ॥३१॥

vadaty evaṁ jane satyā
dṛṣṭvāsu-tyāgam adbhutam
dakṣaṁ tat-pārṣadā hantum
udatiṣṭhann udāyudhāḥ

vadati—were talking; *evam*—thus; *jane*—while the people; *satyāḥ*—of Satī; *dṛṣṭvā*—after seeing; *asu-tyāgam*—the death; *adbhutam*—wonderful; *dakṣam*—Dakṣa; *tat-pārṣadāḥ*—the attendants of Lord Śiva; *hantum*—to kill; *udatiṣṭhan*—stood up; *udāyudhāḥ*—with uplifted weapons.

TRANSLATION

While people were talking among themselves about the wonderful voluntary death of Satī, the attendants who had come with her readied themselves to kill Dakṣa with their weapons.

PURPORT

The attendants who came with Satī were meant to protect her from calamities, but since they were unable to protect their master's wife, they decided to die for her, and before dying they wanted to kill Dakṣa. It is the duty of attendants to give protection to their master, and in case of failure it is their duty to die.

TEXT 32

तेषामापततां वेगं निशाम्य भगवान् भृगुः ।
यज्ञघ्नघ्नेन यजुषा दक्षिणाग्नौ जुहाव ह ॥३२॥

teṣām āpatatāṁ vegaṁ
niśāmya bhagavān bhṛguḥ
yajña-ghna-ghnena yajuṣā
dakṣiṇāgnau juhāva ha

teṣām—of them; *āpatatām*—who were approaching; *vegam*—the impulse; *niśāmya*—after seeing; *bhagavān*—the possessor of all opulences; *bhṛguḥ*—Bhṛgu Muni; *yajña-ghna-ghnena*—for killing the destroyers of the *yajña; yajuṣā*—with hymns of the *Yajur Veda; dakṣiṇa-agnau*—in the southern side of the sacrificial fire; *juhāva*—offered oblations; *ha*—certainly.

TRANSLATION

They came forward forcibly, but Bhṛgu Muni saw the danger and, offering oblations into the southern side of the sacrificial fire, immediately uttered mantric hymns from the Yajur Veda by which the destroyers of yajñic performances could be killed immediately.

PURPORT

Here is one example of powerful hymns in the *Vedas* which, when chanted, could perform wonderful acts. In the present age of Kali it is not possible to find expert *mantra* chanters; therefore all the sacrifices recommended in the *Vedas* are forbidden in this age. The only sacrifice recommended in this age is the chanting of the Hare Kṛṣṇa *mantra* because in this age it is not possible to accumulate the needed funds for performing sacrifices, not to speak of finding expert *brāhmaṇas* who can chant the *mantras* perfectly.

TEXT 33

अध्वर्युणा ह्यमाने देवा उत्पेतुरोजसा ।
ऋभवो नाम तपसा सोमं प्राप्ताः सहस्रशः ॥३३॥

adhvaryuṇā hūyamāne
devā utpetur ojasā
ṛbhavo nāma tapasā
somaṁ prāptāḥ sahasraśaḥ

adhvaryuṇā—by the priest, Bhṛgu; *hūyamāne*—oblations being offered; *devāḥ*—demigods; *utpetuḥ*—became manifested; *ojasā*—with great strength; *ṛbhavaḥ*—the Ṛbhus; *nāma*—named; *tapasā*—by penance; *somam*—Soma; *prāptāḥ*—having achieved; *sahasraśaḥ*—by the thousands.

TRANSLATION

When Bhṛgu Muni offered oblations in the fire, immediately many thousands of demigods named Ṛbhus became manifested. All of them were powerful, having achieved strength from Soma, the moon.

PURPORT

It is stated here that many thousands of demigods named Ṛbhus became manifested because of the oblations offered in the fire and the chanting of the hymns from the *Yajur Veda. Brāhmaṇas* like Bhṛgu Muni were so powerful that they could create such powerful demigods simply by chanting the Vedic *mantras.* Vedic *mantras* are still available, but the chanters are not. By chanting Vedic *mantras* or chanting the Gāyatrī or *ṛg-mantra* one can attain the results one desires. In the present age of Kali it is recommended by Lord Caitanya that simply by chanting Hare Kṛṣṇa one can attain all perfection.

TEXT 34

तैरलातायुधैः सर्वे प्रमथाः सहगुह्यकाः
हन्यमाना दिशो भेजुरुशद्भिर्ब्रह्मतेजसा ॥३४॥

tair alātāyudhaiḥ sarve
pramathāḥ saha-guhyakāḥ
hanyamānā diśo bhejur
uśadbhir brahma-tejasā

taiḥ—by them; *alāta-āyudhaiḥ*—with weapons of firebrands; *sarve*—all; *pramathāḥ*—the ghosts; *saha-guhyakāḥ*—along with the Guhyakas; *hanyamānāḥ*—being attacked; *diśaḥ*—in different directions; *bhejuḥ*—fled; *uśadbhiḥ*—glowing; *brahma-tejasā*—by brahminical power.

TRANSLATION

When the Ṛbhu demigods attacked the ghosts and Guhyakas with half-burned fuel from the yajña fire, all these attendants of

Satī fled in different directions and disappeared. This was possible simply because of brahma-tejas, brahminical power.

PURPORT

The word *brahma-tejasā*, used in this verse, is significant. In those days, *brāhmaṇas* were so powerful that simply by desiring and by chanting a Vedic *mantra*, they could accomplish very wonderful effects. But in the present age of degradation there are no such *brāhmaṇas*. According to the *Pāñcarātrika* system, in this age the entire population is supposed to consist of *śūdras* because the brahminical culture has been lost. But if anyone displays the signs of understanding Kṛṣṇa consciousness, he should be accepted, according to Vaiṣṇava *smṛti* regulations, as a prospective *brāhmaṇa* and should be given all facilities to achieve the highest perfection. The most magnanimous gift of Lord Caitanya's is that the highest perfection of life is available in this fallen age if one simply adopts the process of chanting Hare Kṛṣṇa, which is able to bring about the fulfillment of all activities in self-realization.

Thus end the Bhaktivedanta purports of the Fourth Canto, Fourth Chapter, of the Śrīmad-Bhāgavatam, *entitled "Satī Quits Her Body."*

CHAPTER FIVE

Frustration of the Sacrifice of Dakṣa

TEXT 1

मैत्रेय उवाच
भवो भवान्या निधनं प्रजापते-
रसत्कृताया अवगम्य नारदात् ।
स्वपार्षदसैन्यं च तदध्वरर्भुभि-
र्विद्रावितं क्रोधमपारमादधे ॥ १ ॥

maitreya uvāca
bhavo bhavānyā nidhanaṁ prajāpater
asat-kṛtāyā avagamya nāradāt
sva-pārṣada-sainyaṁ ca tad-adhvararbhubhir
vidrāvitaṁ krodham apāram ādadhe

maitreyaḥ uvāca—Maitreya said; *bhavaḥ*—Lord Śiva; *bhavānyāḥ*—of Satī; *nidhanam*—the death; *prajāpateḥ*—because of Prajāpati Dakṣa; *asat-kṛtāyāḥ*—having been insulted; *avagamya*—hearing about; *nāradāt*—from Nārada; *sva-pārṣada-sainyam*—the soldiers of his own associates; *ca*—and; *tat-adhvara*—(produced from) his (Dakṣa's) sacrifice; *ṛbhubhiḥ*—by the Ṛbhus; *vidrāvitam*—were driven away; *krodham*—anger; *apāram*—unbounded; *ādadhe*—showed.

TRANSLATION

Maitreya said: When Lord Śiva heard from Nārada that Satī, his wife, was now dead because of Prajāpati Dakṣa's insult to her and that his soldiers had been driven away by the Ṛbhu demigods, he became greatly angry.

PURPORT

Lord Śiva understood that Satī, being the youngest daughter of Dakṣa, could present the case of Lord Śiva's purity of purpose and would thus be able to mitigate the misunderstanding between Dakṣa and himself. But such a compromise was not attained, and Satī was deliberately insulted by her father by not being received properly when she visited his house without being invited. Satī herself could have killed her father, Dakṣa, because she is the personified material energy and has immense power to kill and create within this material universe. In the *Brahma-saṁhitā* her strength is described: she is capable of creating and dissolving many universes. But although she is so powerful, she acts under the direction of the Supreme Personality of Godhead, Kṛṣṇa, as His shadow. It would not have been difficult for Satī to punish her father, but she thought that since she was his daughter, it was not proper for her to kill him. Thus she decided to give up her own body, which she had obtained from his, and Dakṣa did not even check her.

When Satī passed away, giving up her body, the news was conveyed by Nārada to Lord Śiva. Nārada always carries the news of such events because he knows their import. When Lord Śiva heard that his chaste wife, Satī, was dead, he naturally became exceedingly angry. He also understood that Bhṛgu Muni had created the Ṛbhudeva demigods by uttering the *mantras* of the *Yajur Veda* and that these demigods had driven away all of his soldiers who were present in the arena of sacrifice. Therefore, he wanted to reply to this insult, and thus he decided to kill Dakṣa because he was the cause of the death of Satī.

TEXT 2

क्रुद्धः सुदष्टौष्ठपुटः स धूर्जटि-
जटां तडिद्वह्निसटोग्ररोचिषम् ।
उत्कृत्य रुद्रः सहसोत्थितो हसन्
गम्भीरनादो विससर्ज तां भुवि ॥ २ ॥

kruddhaḥ sudaṣṭauṣṭha-puṭaḥ sa dhūr-jaṭir
jaṭāṁ taḍid-vahni-saṭogra-rociṣam
utkṛtya rudraḥ sahasotthito hasan
gambhīra-nādo visasarja tāṁ bhuvi

kruddhaḥ—very angry; *su-daṣṭa-oṣṭha-puṭaḥ*—pressing his lips with his teeth; *saḥ*—he (Lord Śiva); *dhūḥ-jaṭiḥ*—having a cluster of hair on his head; *jaṭām*—one hair; *taḍit*—of electricity; *vahni*—of fire; *saṭā*—a flame; *ugra*—terrible; *rociṣam*—blazing; *utkṛtya*—snatching; *rudraḥ*—Lord Śiva; *sahasā*—at once; *utthitaḥ*—stood up; *hasan*—laughing; *gambhīra*—deep; *nādaḥ*—sound; *visasarja*—dashed; *tām*—that (hair); *bhuvi*—on the ground.

TRANSLATION

Thus Lord Śiva, being extremely angry, pressed his lips with his teeth and immediately snatched from his head a strand of hair which blazed like electricity or fire. He stood up at once, laughing like a madman, and dashed the hair to the ground.

TEXT 3

ततोऽतिकायस्तनुवा स्पृशन्दिवं
सहस्रबाहुर्घनरुक् त्रिसूर्यदृक् ।
करालदंष्ट्रो ज्वलदग्निमूर्धजः
कपालमाली विविधोद्यतायुधः ॥ ३ ॥

tato 'tikāyas tanuvā spṛśan divaṁ
sahasra-bāhur ghana-ruk tri-sūrya-dṛk
karāla-daṁṣṭro jvalad-agni-mūrdhajaḥ
kapāla-mālī vividhodyatāyudhaḥ

tataḥ—at this time; *atikāyaḥ*—a great personality (Vīrabhadra); *tanuvā*—with his body; *spṛśan*—touching; *divam*—the sky; *sahasra*—a thousand; *bāhuḥ*—arms; *ghana-ruk*—of black color; *tri-sūrya-dṛk*—as bright as three suns combined; *karāla-daṁṣṭraḥ*—having very fearful teeth; *jvalat-agni*—(like) burning fire; *mūrdhajaḥ*—having hair on his head; *kapāla-mālī*—garlanded with men's heads; *vividha*—various kinds; *udyata*—upraised; *āyudhaḥ*—equipped with weapons.

TRANSLATION

A fearful black demon as high as the sky and as bright as three suns combined was thereby created, his teeth very fearful and the hairs on his head like burning fire. He had thousands of arms,

equipped with various weapons, and he was garlanded with the heads of men.

TEXT 4

तं किं करोमीति गृणन्तमाह
बद्धाञ्जलिं भगवान् भूतनाथः ।
दक्षं सयज्ञं जहि मद्भटानां
त्वमग्रणी रुद्र भटांशको मे ॥ ४ ॥

taṁ kiṁ karomīti gṛṇantam āha
baddhāñjaliṁ bhagavān bhūta-nāthaḥ
dakṣaṁ sa-yajñaṁ jahi mad-bhaṭānāṁ
tvam agraṇī rudra bhaṭāṁśako me

tam—to him (Vīrabhadra); *kim*—what; *karomi*—shall I do; *iti*—thus; *gṛṇantam*—asking; *āha*—ordered; *baddha-añjalim*—with folded hands; *bhagavān*—the possessor of all opulences (Lord Śiva); *bhūta-nāthaḥ*—the lord of the ghosts; *dakṣam*—Dakṣa; *sa-yajñam*—along with his sacrifice; *jahi*—kill; *mat-bhaṭānām*—of all my associates; *tvam*—you; *agraṇīḥ*—the chief; *rudra*—O Rudra; *bhaṭa*—O expert in battle; *aṁśakaḥ*—born of my body; *me*—my.

TRANSLATION

When that gigantic demon asked with folded hands, "What shall I do, my lord?" Lord Śiva, who is known as Bhūtanātha, directly ordered, "Because you are born from my body, you are the chief of all my associates. Therefore, kill Dakṣa and his soldiers at the sacrifice."

PURPORT

Here is the beginning of competition between *brahma-tejas* and *śiva-tejas*. By *brahma-tejas*, brahminical strength, Bhṛgu Muni had created the Ṛbhu demigods, who had driven away the soldiers of Lord Śiva stationed in the arena. When Lord Śiva heard that his soldiers had been driven away, he created the tall black demon Vīrabhadra to retaliate. There is sometimes a competition between the mode of goodness and the mode of ignorance. That is the way of material existence. Even when one is situated in the mode of goodness, there is every possibility that his position will be mixed with or attacked by the mode of passion or ignorance. That is the law of material nature. Although pure goodness, or *śuddha-sattva*, is the basic principle in the spiritual world, pure manifestation of goodness is not possible in this material world. Thus, the struggle for existence between different material qualities is always present. This quarrel between Lord Śiva and Bhṛgu Muni, centering around Prajāpati Dakṣa, is the practical example of such competition between the different qualitative modes of material nature.

TEXT 5

आज्ञप्त एवं कुपितेन मन्युना
स देवदेवं परिचक्रमे विभुम् ।
मेने तदात्मानमसङ्गरंहसा
महीयसां तात सहः सहिष्णुम् ॥ ५ ॥

ājñapta evaṁ kupitena manyunā
sa deva-devaṁ paricakrame vibhum
mene tadātmānam asaṅga-raṁhasā
mahīyasāṁ tāta sahaḥ sahiṣṇum

ājñaptaḥ—being ordered; *evam*—in this manner; *kupitena*—angry; *manyunā*—by Lord Śiva (who is anger personified); *saḥ*—he (Vīrabhadra); *deva-devam*—he who is worshiped by the demigods; *paricakrame*—circumambulated; *vibhum*—Lord Śiva; *mene*—considered; *tadā*—at that time; *ātmānam*—himself; *asaṅga-raṁhasā*—with the power of Lord Śiva that cannot be opposed; *mahīyasām*—of the most powerful; *tāta*—my dear Vidura; *sahaḥ*—strength; *sahiṣṇum*—capable of coping with.

TRANSLATION

Maitreya continued: My dear Vidura, that black person was the personified anger of the Supreme Personality of Godhead, and he was prepared to execute the orders of Lord Śiva. Thus, considering himself capable of coping with any power offered against him, he circumambulated Lord Śiva.

TEXT 6

अन्वीयमानः स तु रुद्रपार्षदै-
भृशं नदद्भिर्व्यनदत्सुभैरवम् ।
उद्यम्य शूलं जगदन्तकान्तकं
सम्प्राद्रवद् घोषणभूषणाङ्घ्रिः ॥ ६ ॥

anvīyamānaḥ sa tu rudra-pārṣadair
bhṛśaṁ nadadbhir vyanadat subhairavam
udyamya śūlaṁ jagad-antakāntakaṁ
samprādravad ghoṣaṇa-bhūṣaṇāṅghriḥ

anvīyamānaḥ—being followed; *saḥ*—he (Vīrabhadra); *tu*—but; *rudra-pārṣadaiḥ*—by the soldiers of Lord Śiva; *bhṛśam*—tumultuously; *nadadbhiḥ*—roaring; *vyanadat*—sounded; *su-bhairavam*—very fearful; *udyamya*—carrying; *śūlam*—a trident; *jagat-antaka*—death; *antakam*—killing; *samprādravat*—hurried towards (the sacrifice of Dakṣa); *ghoṣaṇa*—roaring; *bhūṣaṇa-aṅghriḥ*—with bangles on his legs.

TRANSLATION

Many other soldiers of Lord Śiva followed the fierce personality in a tumultuous uproar. He carried a great trident, fearful enough to kill even death, and on his legs he wore bangles which seemed to roar.

TEXT 7

अथर्त्विजो यजमानः सदस्याः
ककुभ्युदीच्यां प्रसमीक्ष्य रेणुम् ।
तमः किमेतत्कुत एतद्रजोऽभू-
दिति द्विजा द्विजपत्न्यश्च दध्युः ॥ ७ ॥

athartvijo yajamānaḥ sadasyāḥ
kakubhy udīcyāṁ prasamīkṣya reṇum
tamaḥ kim etat kuta etad rajo 'bhūd
iti dvijā dvija-patnyaś ca dadhyuḥ

atha—at that time; *ṛtvijaḥ*—the priests; *yajamānaḥ*—the chief person performing the sacrifice (Dakṣa); *sadasyāḥ*—all the persons assembled in the sacrificial arena; *kakubhi udīcyām*—in the northern direction; *prasamīkṣya*—seeing; *reṇum*—the dust storm; *tamaḥ*—darkness; *kim*—what; *etat*—this; *kutaḥ*—from where; *etat*—this; *rajaḥ*—dust; *abhūt*—has come; *iti*—thus; *dvijāḥ*—the *brāhmaṇas; dvija-patnyaḥ*—the wives of the *brāhmaṇas; ca*—and; *dadhyuḥ*—began to speculate.

TRANSLATION

At that time, all the persons assembled in the sacrificial arena—the priests, the chief of the sacrificial performance, and the brāhmaṇas and their wives—wondered where the darkness was coming from. Later they could understand that it was a dust storm, and all of them were full of anxiety.

TEXT 8

वाता न वान्ति न हि सन्ति दस्यवः
प्राचीनबर्हिर्जीवति होग्रदण्डः ।
गावो न काल्यन्त इदं कुतो रजो
लोकोऽधुना किं प्रलयाय कल्पते ॥ ८ ॥

vātā na vānti na hi santi dasyavaḥ
prācīna-barhir jīvati hogra-daṇḍaḥ
gāvo na kālyanta idaṁ kuto rajo
loko 'dhunā kiṁ pralayāya kalpate

vātāḥ—the winds; *na vānti*—are not blowing; *na*—not; *hi*—because; *santi*—are possible; *dasyavaḥ*—plunderers; *prācīna-barhiḥ*—old King Barhi; *jīvati*—is living; *ha*—still; *ugra-daṇḍaḥ*—who would sternly punish; *gāvaḥ*—the cows; *na kālyante*—are not being driven; *idam*—this; *kutaḥ*—from where; *rajaḥ*—dust; *lokaḥ*—the planet; *adhunā*—now; *kim*—is it; *pralayāya*—for dissolution; *kalpate*—to be considered ready.

TRANSLATION

Conjecturing on the origin of the storm, they said: There is no wind blowing, and no cows are passing, nor is it possible that this dust storm could be raised by plunderers, for there is still the strong King Barhi, who would punish them. Where is this dust storm blowing from? Is the dissolution of the planet now to occur?

PURPORT

Specifically significant in this verse is *prācīna-barhir jīvati.* The king of that part of the land was known as Barhi, and although he was old, he was still living, and he was a very strong ruler. Thus there was no possibility of an invasion by thieves and plunderers. Indirectly it is stated here that thieves, plunderers, rogues and unwanted population can exist only in a state or kingdom where there is no strong ruler. When, in the name of justice, thieves are allowed liberty, the state and kingdom are disturbed by such plunderers and unwanted population. The dust storm created by the soldiers and assistants of Lord Śiva resembled the situation at the time of the dissolution of this world. When there is a need for the dissolution of the material creation, this function is conducted by Lord Śiva. Therefore the situation now created by him resembled the dissolution of the cosmic manifestation.

TEXT 9

प्रसूतिमिश्राः स्त्रिय उद्विग्नचित्ता
ऊचुर्विपाको वृजिनस्यैव तस्य ।
यत्पश्यन्तीनां दुहितॄणां प्रजेशः
सुतां सतीमवदध्यावनागाम् ॥ ९ ॥

prasūti-miśrāḥ striya udvigna-cittā
ūcur vipāko vṛjinasyaiva tasya
yat paśyantīnāṁ duhitṝṇāṁ prajeśaḥ
sutāṁ satīm avadadhyāv anāgām

prasūti-miśrāḥ—headed by Prasūti; *striyaḥ*—the women; *udvigna-cittāḥ*—being very anxious; *ūcuḥ*—said; *vipākaḥ*—the resultant danger; *vṛjinasya*—of the sinful activity; *eva*—indeed; *tasya*—his (Dakṣa's); *yat*—because; *paśyantīnām*—who were looking on; *duhitṝṇām*—of her sisters; *prajeśaḥ*—the lord of the created beings (Dakṣa); *sutām*—his daughter; *satīm*—Satī; *avadadhyau*—insulted; *anāgām*—completely innocent.

TRANSLATION

Prasūti, the wife of Dakṣa, along with the other women assembled, became very anxious and said: This danger has been created by Dakṣa because of the death of Satī, who, even though completely innocent, quit her body as her sisters looked on.

PURPORT

Prasūti, being a softhearted woman, could immediately understand that the imminent danger approaching was due to the impious activity of hardhearted Prajāpati Dakṣa. He was so cruel that he would not save her youngest daughter, Satī, from the act of committing suicide in the presence of her sisters. Satī's mother could understand how much Satī had been pained by the insult of her father. Satī had been present along with the other daughters, and Dakṣa had purposely received all of them but her because she happened to be the wife of Lord Śiva. This consideration convinced the wife of Dakṣa of the danger which was now ahead, and thus she knew that Dakṣa must be prepared to die for his heinous act.

TEXT 10

यस्त्वन्तकाले व्युप्तजटाकलापः
स्वशूलसूच्यर्पितदिग्गजेन्द्रः ।
वितत्य नृत्यत्युदितास्त्रदोर्ध्वजा-
नुच्चाट्टहासस्तनयित्नुभिन्नदिक् ॥१०॥

yas tv anta-kāle vyupta-jaṭā-kalāpaḥ
sva-śūla-sūcy-arpita-dig-gajendraḥ
vitatya nṛtyaty uditāstra-dor-dhvajān
uccāṭṭa-hāsa-stanayitnu-bhinna-dik

yaḥ—who (Lord Śiva); *tu*—but; *anta-kāle*—at the time of dissolution; *vyupta*—having scattered; *jaṭā-kalāpaḥ*—his bunch of hair; *sva-śūla*—his own trident; *sūci*—on the points; *arpita*—pierced; *dik-gajendraḥ*—the rulers of the different directions; *vitatya*—scattering; *nṛtyati*—dances; *udita*—upraised; *astra*—weapons; *doḥ*—hands; *dhvajān*—flags; *ucca*—loud; *aṭṭa-hāsa*—laughing; *stanayitnu*—by the thundering sound; *bhinna*—divided; *dik*—the directions.

TRANSLATION

At the time of dissolution, Lord Śiva's hair is scattered, and he pierces the rulers of the different directions with his trident. He laughs and dances proudly, scattering their hands like flags, as thunder scatters the clouds all over the world.

PURPORT

Prasūti, who appreciated the power and strength of her son-in-law, Lord Śiva, is describing what he does at the time of dissolution. This description indicates that the strength of Lord Śiva is so great that Dakṣa's power could not be set in comparison to it. At the time of dissolution, Lord Śiva, with his trident in hand, dances over the rulers of the different planets, and his hair is scattered, just as the clouds are scattered over all directions in order to plunge the different planets into incessant torrents of rain. In the last phase of dissolution, all the planets become inundated with water, and that inundation is caused by the dancing of Lord Śiva. This dance is called the *pralaya* dance, or dance of dissolution. Prasūti could understand that the dangers ahead resulted not only from Dakṣa's having neglected her daughter, but also because of his neglecting the prestige and honor of Lord Śiva.

TEXT 11

अमर्षयित्वा तमसह्यतेजसं
मन्युप्लुतं दुर्निरीक्ष्यं भ्रुकुट्या ।
करालदंष्ट्राभिरुदस्तभागणं
स्यात्स्वस्ति किं कोपयतो विधातुः ॥११॥

amarṣayitvā tam asahya-tejasaṁ
manyu-plutaṁ durnirīkṣyaṁ bhru-kuṭyā
karāla-daṁṣṭrābhir udasta-bhāgaṇaṁ
syāt svasti kiṁ kopayato vidhātuḥ

amarṣayitvā—after causing to become angry; *tam*—him (Lord Śiva); *asahya-tejasam*—with an unbearable effulgence; *manyu-plutam*—filled with anger; *durnirīkṣyam*—not able to be looked at; *bhru-kuṭyā*—by the movement of his brows; *karāla-daṁṣṭrābhiḥ*—by his fearful teeth; *udasta-bhāgaṇam*—having scattered the luminaries; *syāt*—there should be; *svasti*—good fortune; *kim*—how; *kopayataḥ*—causing (Lord Śiva) to be angry; *vidhātuḥ*—of Brahmā.

TRANSLATION

The gigantic black man bared his fearful teeth. By the movements of his brows he scattered the luminaries all over the sky, and he covered them with his strong, piercing effulgence. Because of the misbehavior of Dakṣa, even Lord Brahmā, Dakṣa's father, could not have been saved from the great exhibition of anger.

TEXT 12

बह्वेवमुद्विग्नदृशोच्यमाने
जनेन दक्षस्य मुहुर्महात्मनः ।
उत्पेतुरुत्पाततमाः सहस्रशो
भयावहा दिवि भूमौ च पर्यक् ॥१२॥

bahv evam udvigna-dṛśocyamāne
janena dakṣasya muhur mahātmanaḥ
utpetur utpātatamāḥ sahasraśo
bhayāvahā divi bhūmau ca paryak

bahu—much; *evam*—in this manner; *udvigna-dṛśā*—with nervous glances; *ucyamāne*—while this was being said; *janena*—by the persons (assembled at the sacrifice); *dakṣasya*—of Dakṣa; *muhuḥ*—again and again; *mahā-ātmanaḥ*—stronghearted; *utpetuḥ*—appeared; *utpāta-tamāḥ*—very powerful symptoms; *sahasraśaḥ*—by the thousands;

bhaya-āvahāḥ—producing fear; *divi*—in the sky; *bhūmau*—on the earth; *ca*—and; *paryak*—from all sides.

TRANSLATION

While all the people talked amongst themselves, Dakṣa saw dangerous omens from all sides, from the earth and from the sky.

PURPORT

In this verse Dakṣa has been described as *mahātmā.* The word *mahātmā* has been commented upon by different commentators in various manners. Vīrarāghava Ācārya has indicated that this word *mahātmā* means "steady in heart." That is to say that Dakṣa was so stronghearted that even when his beloved daughter was prepared to lay down her life, he was steady and unshaken. But in spite of his being so stronghearted, he was perturbed when he saw the various disturbances created by the gigantic black demon. Viśvanātha Cakravartī Ṭhākura remarks in this connection that even if one is called *mahātmā,* a great soul, unless he exhibits the symptoms of a *mahātmā,* he should be considered a *durātmā,* or a degraded soul. In *Bhagavad-gītā* (9.13) the word *mahātmā* describes the pure devotee of the Lord: *mahātmānas tu māṁ pārtha daivīṁ prakṛtim āśritāḥ.* A *mahātmā* is always under the guidance of the internal energy of the Supreme Personality of Godhead, and thus how could such a misbehaved person as Dakṣa be a *mahātmā*? A *mahātmā* is supposed to have all the good qualities of the demigods, and thus Dakṣa, lacking those qualities, could not be called a *mahātmā;* he should instead be called *durātmā,* a degraded soul. The word *mahātmā* to describe the qualifications of Dakṣa is used sarcastically.

TEXT 13

तावत्स रुद्रानुचरैर्महामखो
नानायुधैर्वामनकैरुदायुधैः ।
पिङ्गैः पिशङ्गैर्मकरोदराननैः
पर्याद्रवद्भिर्विदुरान्वरुध्यत ॥१३॥

tāvat sa rudrānucarair mahā-makho
nānāyudhair vāmanakair udāyudhaiḥ

piṅgaiḥ piśaṅgair makarodarānanaiḥ
paryādravadbhir vidurānvarudhyata

tāvat—very quickly; *saḥ*—that; *rudra-anucaraiḥ*—by the followers of Lord Śiva; *mahā-makhaḥ*—the arena of the great sacrifice; *nānā*—various kinds; *āyudhaiḥ*—with weapons; *vāmanakaiḥ*—of short stature; *udāyudhaiḥ*—upraised; *piṅgaiḥ*—blackish; *piśaṅgaiḥ*—yellowish; *makara-udara-ānanaiḥ*—with bellies and faces like sharks'; *paryādravadbhiḥ*—running all around; *vidura*—O Vidura; *anvarudhyata*—was surrounded.

TRANSLATION

My dear Vidura, all the followers of Lord Śiva surrounded the arena of sacrifice. They were of short stature and were equipped with various kinds of weapons; their bodies appeared to be like those of sharks, blackish and yellowish. They ran all around the sacrificial arena and thus began to create disturbances.

TEXT 14

केचिद्बभञ्जुः प्राग्वंशं पत्नीशालां तथापरे ।
सद आग्नीध्रशालां च तद्विहारं महानसम् ॥१४॥

kecid babhañjuḥ prāg-vaṁśaṁ
patnī-śālāṁ tathāpare
sada āgnīdhra-śālāṁ ca
tad-vihāraṁ mahānasam

kecit—some; *babhañjuḥ*—pulled down; *prāk-vaṁśam*—the pillars of the sacrificial pandal; *patnī-śālām*—the female quarters; *tathā*—also; *apare*—others; *sadaḥ*—the sacrificial arena; *āgnīdhra-śālām*—the house of the priests; *ca*—and; *tat-vihāram*—the house of the chief of the sacrifice; *mahā-anasam*—the house of the kitchen department.

TRANSLATION

Some of the soldiers pulled down the pillars which were supporting the pandal of sacrifice, some of them entered the female

quarters, some began destroying the sacrificial arena, and some entered the kitchen and the residential quarters.

TEXT 15

रुरुजुर्यज्ञपात्राणि तथैकेऽग्नीननाशयन् ।
कुण्डेष्वमूत्रयन् केचिद्बिभिदुर्वेदिमेखलाः ॥१५॥

rurujur yajña-pātrāṇi
tathaike 'gnīn anāśayan
kuṇḍeṣv amūtrayan kecid
bibhidur vedi-mekhalāḥ

rurujuḥ—broke; *yajña-pātrāṇi*—the pots used in the sacrifice; *tathā*—so; *eke*—some; *agnīn*—the sacrificial fires; *anāśayan*—extinguished; *kuṇḍeṣu*—on the sacrificial arenas; *amūtrayan*—passed urine; *kecit*—some; *bibhiduḥ*—tore down; *vedi-mekhalāḥ*—the boundary lines of the sacrificial arena.

TRANSLATION

They broke all the pots made for use in the sacrifice, and some of them began to extinguish the sacrificial fire. Some tore down the boundary line of the sacrificial arena, and some passed urine on the arena.

TEXT 16

अबाधन्त मुनीनन्ये एके पत्नीरतर्जयन् ।
अपरे जगृहुर्देवान् प्रत्यासन्नान् पलायितान् ॥१६॥

abādhanta munīn anye
eke patnīr atarjayan
apare jagṛhur devān
pratyāsannān palāyitān

abādhanta—blocked the way; *munīn*—the sages; *anye*—others; *eke*—some; *patnīḥ*—the women; *atarjayan*—threatened; *apare*—others; *jagṛhuḥ*—arrested; *devān*—the demigods; *pratyāsannān*—near at hand; *palāyitān*—who were fleeing.

TRANSLATION

Some blocked the way of the fleeing sages, some threatened the women assembled there, and some arrested the demigods who were fleeing the pandal.

TEXT 17

भृगुं बबन्ध मणिमान् वीरभद्रः प्रजापतिम् ।
चण्डेशः पूषणं देवं भगं नन्दीश्वरोऽग्रहीत् ॥१७॥

bhṛguṁ babandha maṇimān
vīrabhadraḥ prajāpatim
caṇḍeśaḥ pūṣaṇaṁ devaṁ
bhagaṁ nandīśvaro 'grahīt

bhṛgum—Bhṛgu Muni; *babandha*—arrested; *maṇimān*—Maṇimān; *vīrabhadraḥ*—Vīrabhadra; *prajāpatim*—Prajāpati Dakṣa; *caṇḍeśaḥ*—Caṇḍeśa; *pūṣaṇam*—Pūṣā; *devam*—the demigod; *bhagam*—Bhaga; *nandīśvaraḥ*—Nandīśvara; *agrahīt*—arrested.

TRANSLATION

Maṇimān, one of the followers of Lord Śiva, arrested Bhṛgu Muni, and Vīrabhadra, the black demon, arrested Prajāpati Dakṣa. Another follower, who was named Caṇḍeśa, arrested Pūṣā. Nandīśvara arrested the demigod Bhaga.

TEXT 18

सर्व एवर्त्विजो दृष्ट्वा सदस्याः सदिवौकसः ।
तैरर्द्यमानाः सुभृशं ग्रावभिर्नैकधाद्रवन् ॥१८॥

sarva evartvijo dṛṣṭvā
sadasyāḥ sa-divaukasaḥ
tair ardyamānāḥ subhṛśaṁ
grāvabhir naikadhā 'dravan

sarve—all; *eva*—certainly; *ṛtvijaḥ*—the priests; *dṛṣṭvā*—after seeing; *sadasyāḥ*—all the members assembled in the sacrifice; *sa-divaukasaḥ*—

along with the demigods; *taiḥ*—by those (stones); *ardyamānāḥ*—being disturbed; *su-bhṛśam*—very greatly; *grāvabhiḥ*—by stones; *na ekadhā*—in different directions; *adravan*—began to disperse.

TRANSLATION

There was a continuous shower of stones, and all the priests and other members assembled at the sacrifice were put into immense misery. For fear of their lives, they dispersed in different directions.

TEXT 19

जुह्वतः स्रुवहस्तस्य श्मश्रूणि भगवान् भवः ।
भृगोर्लुलुञ्चे सदसि योऽहसच्छ्मश्रु दर्शयन् ॥१९॥

juhvataḥ sruva-hastasya
śmaśrūṇi bhagavān bhavaḥ
bhṛgor luluñce sadasi
yo 'hasac chmaśru darśayan

juhvataḥ—offering sacrificial oblations; *sruva-hastasya*—with the sacrificial ladle in his hand; *śmaśrūṇi*—the mustache; *bhagavān*—the possessor of all opulences; *bhavaḥ*—Vīrabhadra; *bhṛgoḥ*—of Bhṛgu Muni; *luluñce*—tore out; *sadasi*—in the midst of the assembly; *yaḥ*—who (Bhṛgu Muni); *ahasat*—had smiled; *śmaśru*—his mustache; *darśayan*—showing.

TRANSLATION

Vīrabhadra tore off the mustache of Bhṛgu, who was offering the sacrificial oblations with his hands in the fire.

TEXT 20

भगस्य नेत्रे भगवान् पातितस्य रुषा भुवि ।
उज्जहार सदस्थोऽक्ष्णा यः शपन्तमसूसुचत् ॥२०॥

bhagasya netre bhagavān
pātitasya ruṣā bhuvi

ujjahāra sada-stho 'kṣṇā
yaḥ śapantam asūsucat

bhagasya—of Bhaga; *netre*—both eyes; *bhagavān*—Vīrabhadra; *pātitasya*—having been thrust; *ruṣā*—with great anger; *bhuvi*—on the ground; *ujjahāra*—plucked out; *sada-sthaḥ*—while situated in the assembly of the Viśvasṛks; *akṣṇā*—by the movement of his eyebrows; *yaḥ*—who (Bhaga); *śapantam*—(Dakṣa) who was cursing (Lord Śiva); *asūsucat*—encouraged.

TRANSLATION

Vīrabhadra immediately caught Bhaga, who had been moving his eyebrows during Bhṛgu's cursing of Lord Śiva, and out of great anger thrust him to the ground and forcibly put out his eyes.

TEXT 21

पूष्णो ह्यपातयद्दन्तान् कालिङ्गस्य यथा बलः ।
शप्यमाने गरिमणि योऽहसद्दर्शयन्दतः ॥२१॥

pūṣṇo hy apātayad dantān
kāliṅgasya yathā balaḥ
śapyamāne garimaṇi
yo 'hasad darśayan dataḥ

pūṣṇaḥ—of Pūṣā; *hi*—since; *apātayat*—extracted; *dantān*—the teeth; *kāliṅgasya*—of the King of Kaliṅga; *yathā*—as; *balaḥ*—Baladeva; *śapyamāne*—while being cursed; *garimaṇi*—Lord Śiva; *yaḥ*—who (Pūṣā); *ahasat*—smiled; *darśayan*—showing; *dataḥ*—his teeth.

TRANSLATION

Just as Baladeva knocked out the teeth of Dantavakra, the King of Kaliṅga, during the gambling match at the marriage ceremony of Aniruddha, Vīrabhadra knocked out the teeth of both Dakṣa, who had shown them while cursing Lord Śiva, and Pūṣā, who by smiling sympathetically had also shown his teeth.

PURPORT

Here a reference is made to the marriage of Aniruddha, a grandson of Lord Kṛṣṇa's. He kidnapped the daughter of Dantavakra, and thereafter he was arrested. Just as he was to be punished for the kidnapping, the soldiers from Dvārakā arrived, headed by Balarāma, and a fight ensued amongst the *kṣatriyas.* This sort of fight was very common, especially during marriage ceremonies, when everyone was in a challenging spirit. In that challenging spirit, a fight was sure to occur, and in such fights there was commonly killing and misfortune. After finishing such fighting, the parties would come to a compromise, and everything would be settled. This Dakṣa *yajña* was similar to such events. Now all of them—Dakṣa and the demigods Bhaga and Pūṣā and Bhṛgu Muni—were punished by the soldiers of Lord Śiva, but later everything would come to a peaceful end. So this spirit of fighting between one another was not exactly inimical. Because everyone was so powerful and wanted to show his strength by Vedic *mantra* or mystic power, all these fighting skills were very elaborately exhibited by the different parties at the Dakṣa *yajña.*

TEXT 22

आक्रम्योरसि दक्षस्य शितधारेण हेतिना ।
छिन्दन्नपि तदुद्धर्तुं नाशक्नोत् त्र्यम्बकस्तदा ॥२२॥

ākramyorasi dakṣasya
śita-dhāreṇa hetinā
chindann api tad uddhartuṁ
nāśaknot tryambakas tadā

ākramya—having sat; *urasi*—on the chest; *dakṣasya*—of Dakṣa; *śita-dhāreṇa*—having a sharp blade; *hetinā*—with a weapon; *chindan*—cutting; *api*—even though; *tat*—that (head); *uddhartum*—to separate; *na aśaknot*—was not able; *tri-ambakaḥ*—Vīrabhadra (who had three eyes); *tadā*—after this.

TRANSLATION

Then Vīrabhadra, the giantlike personality, sat on the chest of Dakṣa and tried to separate his head from his body with sharp weapons, but was unsuccessful.

TEXT 23

शस्त्रैरस्त्रान्वितैरेवमनिर्भिन्नत्वचं हरः ।
विस्मयं परमापन्नो दध्यौ पशुपतिश्चिरम् ॥२३॥

śastrair astrānvitair evam
anirbhinna-tvacaṁ haraḥ
vismayaṁ param āpanno
dadhyau paśupatiś ciram

śastraiḥ—with weapons; *astra-anvitaiḥ*—with hymns (*mantras*); *evam*—thus; *anirbhinna*—not being cut; *tvacam*—the skin; *haraḥ*—Vīrabhadra; *vismayam*—bewilderment; *param*—greatest; *āpannaḥ*—was struck with; *dadhyau*—thought; *paśupatiḥ*—Vīrabhadra; *ciram*—for a long time.

TRANSLATION

He tried to cut the head of Dakṣa with hymns as well as weapons, but still it was hard to cut even the surface of the skin of Dakṣa's head. Thus Vīrabhadra was exceedingly bewildered.

TEXT 24

दृष्ट्वा संज्ञपनं योगं पशूनां स पतिर्मखे ।
यजमानपशोः कस्य कायात्तेनाहरच्छिरः ॥२४॥

dṛṣṭvā saṁjñapanaṁ yogaṁ
paśūnāṁ sa patir makhe
yajamāna-paśoḥ kasya
kāyāt tenāharac chiraḥ

dṛṣṭvā—having seen; *saṁjñapanam*—for the killing of the animals in the sacrifice; *yogam*—the device; *paśūnām*—of the animals; *saḥ*—he (Vīrabhadra); *patiḥ*—the lord; *makhe*—in the sacrifice; *yajamāna-paśoḥ*—who was an animal in the form of the chief of the sacrifice; *kasya*—of Dakṣa; *kāyāt*—from the body; *tena*—by that (device); *aharat*—severed; *śiraḥ*—his head.

TRANSLATION

Then Vīrabhadra saw the wooden device in the sacrificial arena by which the animals were to have been killed. He took the opportunity of this facility to behead Dakṣa.

PURPORT

In this connection it is to be noted that the device used for killing animals in the sacrifice was not designed to facilitate eating their flesh. The killing was specifically intended to give a new life to the sacrificed animal by the power of Vedic *mantra.* The animals were sacrificed to test the strength of Vedic *mantras; yajñas* were performed as a test of the *mantra.* Even in the modern age, tests are executed on animal bodies in the physiology laboratory. Similarly, whether or not the *brāhmaṇas* were uttering the Vedic hymns correctly was tested by sacrifice in the arena. On the whole, the animals thus sacrificed were not at all the losers. Some old animals would be sacrificed, but in exchange for their old bodies they received other, new bodies. That was the test of Vedic *mantras.* Vīrabhadra, instead of sacrificing animals with the wooden device, immediately beheaded Dakṣa, to the astonishment of everyone.

TEXT 25

साधुवादस्तदा तेषां कर्म तत्तस्य पश्यताम् ।
भूतप्रेतपिशाचानामन्येषां तद्विपर्ययः ॥२५॥

sādhu-vādas tadā teṣāṁ
karma tat tasya paśyatām
bhūta-preta-piśācānāṁ
anyeṣāṁ tad-viparyayaḥ

sādhu-vādaḥ—joyful exclamation; *tadā*—at that time; *teṣām*—of those (followers of Lord Śiva); *karma*—action; *tat*—that; *tasya*—of him (Vīrabhadra); *paśyatām*—seeing; *bhūta-preta-piśācānām*—of the *bhūtas* (ghosts), *pretas* and *piśācas; anyeṣām*—of the others (in the party of Dakṣa); *tat-viparyayaḥ*—the opposite of that (an exclamation of grief).

TRANSLATION

Upon seeing the action of Vīrabhadra, the party of Lord Śiva was pleased and cried out joyfully, and all the bhūtas, ghosts and demons that had come made a tumultuous sound. On the other hand, the brāhmaṇas in charge of the sacrifice cried out in grief at the death of Dakṣa.

TEXT 26

जुहावैतच्छिरस्तस्मिन्दक्षिणाग्नावमर्षितः ।
तद्देवयजनं दग्ध्वा प्रातिष्ठद् गुह्यकालयम् ॥२६॥

juhāvaitac chiras tasmin
dakṣiṇāgnāv amarṣitaḥ
tad-deva-yajanaṁ dagdhvā
prātiṣṭhad guhyakālayam

juhāva—sacrificed as an oblation; *etat*—that; *śiraḥ*—head; *tasmin*—in that; *dakṣiṇa-agnau*—in the sacrificial fire on the southern side; *amarṣitaḥ*—Vīrabhadra, being greatly angry; *tat*—of Dakṣa; *deva-yajanam*—the arrangements for the sacrifice to the demigods; *dagdhvā*—having set fire; *prātiṣṭhat*—departed; *guhyaka-ālayam*—to the abode of the Guhyakas (Kailāsa).

TRANSLATION

Vīrabhadra then took the head and with great anger threw it into the southern side of the sacrificial fire, offering it as an oblation. In this way the followers of Lord Śiva devastated all the arrangements for sacrifice. After setting fire to the whole arena, they departed for their master's abode, Kailāsa.

Thus end the Bhaktivedanta purports of the Fourth Canto, Fifth Chapter, of the Śrīmad-Bhāgavatam, *entitled "Frustration of the Sacrifice of Dakṣa."*

CHAPTER SIX

Brahmā Satisfies Lord Śiva

TEXTS 1–2

मैत्रेय उवाच

अथ देवगणाः सर्वे रुद्रानीकैः पराजिताः ।
शूलपट्टिशनिस्त्रिंशगदापरिघमुद्गरैः ॥ १ ॥
संछिन्नभिन्नसर्वाङ्गाः सर्त्विक्सभ्या भयाकुलाः ।
स्वयम्भुवे नमस्कृत्य कार्त्स्न्येनैतन्न्यवेदयन् ॥ २ ॥

maitreya uvāca
atha deva-gaṇāḥ sarve
rudrānīkaiḥ parājitāḥ
śūla-paṭṭiśa-nistriṁśa-
gadā-parigha-mudgaraiḥ

sañchinna-bhinna-sarvāṅgāḥ
sartvik-sabhyā bhayākulāḥ
svayambhuve namaskṛtya
kārtsnyenaitan nyavedayan

maitreyaḥ uvāca—Maitreya said; *atha*—after this; *deva-gaṇāḥ*—the demigods; *sarve*—all; *rudra-anīkaiḥ*—by the soldiers of Lord Śiva; *parājitāḥ*—having been defeated; *śūla*—trident; *paṭṭiśa*—a sharp-edged spear; *nistriṁśa*—a sword; *gadā*—mace; *parigha*—an iron bludgeon; *mudgaraiḥ*—a hammerlike weapon; *sañchinna-bhinna-sarva-aṅgāḥ*—all the limbs wounded; *sa-ṛtvik-sabhyāḥ*—with all the priests and members of the sacrificial assembly; *bhaya-ākulāḥ*—with great fear; *svayambhuve*—unto Lord Brahmā; *namaskṛtya*—after offering obeisances; *kārtsnyena*—in detail; *etat*—the events of Dakṣa's sacrifice; *nyavedayan*—reported.

TRANSLATION

All the priests and other members of the sacrificial assembly and all the demigods, having been defeated by the soldiers of Lord Śiva and injured by weapons like tridents and swords, approached Lord Brahmā with great fear. After offering him obeisances, they began to speak in detail of all the events which had taken place.

TEXT 3

उपलभ्य पुरैवैतद्भगवानब्जसम्भवः ।
नारायणश्च विश्वात्मा न कस्याध्वरमीयतुः ॥ ३ ॥

upalabhya puraivaitad
bhagavān abja-sambhavaḥ
nārāyaṇaś ca viśvātmā
na kasyādhvaram īyatuḥ

upalabhya—knowing; *purā*—beforehand; *eva*—certainly; *etat*—all these events of Dakṣa's sacrifice; *bhagavān*—the possessor of all opulences; *abja-sambhavaḥ*—born from a lotus flower (Lord Brahmā); *nārāyaṇaḥ*—Nārāyaṇa; *ca*—and; *viśva-ātmā*—the Supersoul of the entire universe; *na*—not; *kasya*—of Dakṣa; *adhvaram*—to the sacrifice; *īyatuḥ*—did go.

TRANSLATION

Both Lord Brahmā and Viṣṇu had already known that such events would occur in the sacrificial arena of Dakṣa, and knowing beforehand, they did not go to the sacrifice.

PURPORT

As stated in *Bhagavad-gītā* (7.26), *vedāhaṁ samatītāni vartamānāni cārjuna.* The Lord says, "I know everything that has happened in the past and is going to happen in the future." Lord Viṣṇu is omniscient, and He therefore knew what would happen at Dakṣa's sacrificial arena. For this reason neither Nārāyaṇa nor Lord Brahmā attended the great sacrifice performed by Dakṣa.

TEXT 4

तदाकर्ण्य विभुः प्राह तेजीयसि कृतागसि ।
क्षेमाय तत्र सा भूयान्न प्रायेण बुभूषताम् ॥ ४ ॥

tad ākarṇya vibhuḥ prāha
tejīyasi kṛtāgasi
kṣemāya tatra sā bhūyān
na prāyeṇa bubhūṣatām

tat—the events related by the demigods and the others; *ākarṇya*—after hearing; *vibhuḥ*—Lord Brahmā; *prāha*—replied; *tejīyasi*—a great personality; *kṛta-āgasi*—has been offended; *kṣemāya*—for your happiness; *tatra*—in that way; *sā*—that; *bhūyāt na*—is not conducive; *prāyeṇa*—generally; *bubhūṣatām*—desire to exist.

TRANSLATION

When Lord Brahmā heard everything from the demigods and the members who had attended the sacrifice, he replied: You cannot be happy in executing a sacrifice if you blaspheme a great personality and thereby offend his lotus feet. You cannot have happiness in that way.

PURPORT

Lord Brahmā explained to the demigods that although Dakṣa wanted to enjoy the results of fruitive sacrificial activities, it is not possible to enjoy when one offends a great personality like Lord Śiva. It was good for Dakṣa to have died in the fight because if he had lived he would have committed such offenses at the lotus feet of great personalities again and again. According to Manu's law, when a person commits murder, punishment is beneficial for him because if he is not killed he might commit more and more murders and therefore be entangled in his future lives for having killed so many persons. Therefore the king's punishment of a murderer is appropriate. If those who are extremely offensive are killed by the grace of the Lord, that is good for them. In other words, Lord Brahmā explained to the demigods that it was good for Dakṣa to have been killed.

TEXT 5

अथापि यूयं कृतकिल्बिषा भवं
ये बर्हिषो भागभाजं परादुः ।
प्रसादयध्वं परिशुद्धचेतसा
क्षिप्रप्रसादं प्रगृहीताङ्घ्रिपद्मम् ॥ ५ ॥

athāpi yūyaṁ kṛta-kilbiṣā bhavaṁ
ye barhiṣo bhāga-bhājaṁ parāduḥ
prasādayadhvaṁ pariśuddha-cetasā
kṣipra-prasādaṁ pragṛhītāṅghri-padmam

atha api—still; *yūyam*—all of you; *kṛta-kilbiṣāḥ*—having committed offenses; *bhavam*—Lord Śiva; *ye*—all of you; *barhiṣaḥ*—of the sacrifice; *bhāga-bhājam*—entitled to a share; *parāduḥ*—have excluded; *prasādayadhvam*—all of you should satisfy; *pariśuddha-cetasā*—without mental reservations; *kṣipra-prasādam*—quick mercy; *pragṛhīta-aṅghri-padmam*—his lotus feet having been taken shelter of.

TRANSLATION

You have excluded Lord Śiva from taking part in the sacrificial results, and therefore you are all offenders at his lotus feet. Still, if you go without mental reservations and surrender unto him and fall down at his lotus feet, he will be very pleased.

PURPORT

Lord Śiva is also called Āśutoṣa. *Āśu* means "very soon," and *toṣa* means "to become satisfied." The demigods were advised to go to Lord Śiva and beg his pardon, and because he is very easily pleased, it was certain that their purpose would be served. Lord Brahmā knew the mind of Lord Śiva very well, and he was confident that the demigods, who were offenders at his lotus feet, could mitigate their offenses by going to him and surrendering without reservation.

TEXT 6

आशासाना जीवितमध्वरस्य
लोकः सपालः कुपिते न यस्मिन् ।

तमाशु देवं प्रियया विहीनं
क्षमापयध्वं हृदि विद्धं दुरुक्तैः ॥ ६ ॥

āśāsānā jīvitam adhvarasya
lokaḥ sa-pālaḥ kupite na yasmin
tam āśu devaṁ priyayā vihīnaṁ
kṣamāpayadhvaṁ hṛdi viddhaṁ duruktaiḥ

āśāsānāḥ—wishing to ask; *jīvitam*—for the duration; *adhvarasya*—of the sacrifice; *lokaḥ*—all the planets; *sa-pālaḥ*—with their controllers; *kupite*—when angered; *na*—not; *yasmin*—whom; *tam*—that; *āśu*—at once; *devam*—Lord Śiva; *priyayā*—of his dear wife; *vihīnam*—having been deprived; *kṣamāpayadhvam*—beg his pardon; *hṛdi*—in his heart; *viddham*—very much afflicted; *duruktaiḥ*—by unkind words.

TRANSLATION

Lord Brahmā also advised them that Lord Śiva is so powerful that by his anger all the planets and their chief controllers can be destroyed immediately. Also, he said that Lord Śiva was especially sorry because he had recently lost his dear wife and was also very much afflicted by the unkind words of Dakṣa. Under the circumstances, Lord Brahmā suggested, it would behoove them to go at once and beg his pardon.

TEXT 7

नाहं न यज्ञो न च यूयमन्ये
ये देहभाजो मुनयश्च तत्त्वम् ।
विदुः प्रमाणं बलवीर्ययोर्वा
यस्यात्मतन्त्रस्य क उपायं विधित्सेत् ॥ ७ ॥

nāhaṁ na yajño na ca yūyam anye
ye deha-bhājo munayaś ca tattvam
viduḥ pramāṇaṁ bala-vīryayor vā
yasyātma-tantrasya ka upāyaṁ vidhitset

na—not; *aham*—I; *na*—nor; *yajñaḥ*—Indra; *na*—nor; *ca*—and; *yūyam*—all of you; *anye*—others; *ye*—who; *deha-bhājaḥ*—of those who bear material bodies; *munayaḥ*—the sages; *ca*—and; *tattvam*—the truth; *viduḥ*—know; *pramāṇam*—the extent; *bala-vīryayoḥ*—of the strength and power; *vā*—or; *yasya*—of Lord Śiva; *ātma-tantrasya*—of Lord Śiva, who is self-dependent; *kaḥ*—what; *upāyam*—means; *vidhitset*—should wish to devise.

TRANSLATION

Lord Brahmā said that no one, not even himself, Indra, all the members assembled in the sacrificial arena, or all the sages, could know how powerful Lord Śiva is. Under the circumstances, who would dare to commit an offense at his lotus feet?

PURPORT

After Lord Brahmā advised the demigods to go to Lord Śiva and beg his pardon, it was suggested how he should be satisfied and how the matter should be placed before him. Brahmā also asserted that none of the conditioned souls, including himself and all the demigods, could know how to satisfy Lord Śiva. But he said, "It is known that he is very easily satisfied, so let us try to satisfy him by falling at his lotus feet."

Actually the position of the subordinate is always to surrender to the Supreme. That is the instruction of *Bhagavad-gītā*. The Lord asks everyone to give up all kinds of concocted occupations and simply surrender unto Him. That will protect the conditioned souls from all sinful reactions. Similarly, in this case Brahmā also suggested that they go and surrender unto the lotus feet of Lord Śiva, for since he is very kind and easily satisfied, this action would prove effective.

TEXT 8

स इत्थमादिश्य सुरानजस्तु तैः
समन्वितः पितृभिः सप्रजेशैः ।
ययौ स्वधिष्ण्यान्निलयं पुरद्विषः
कैलासमद्रिप्रवरं प्रियं प्रभोः ॥ ८ ॥

sa ittham ādiśya surān ajas tu taiḥ
samanvitaḥ pitṛbhiḥ sa-prajeśaiḥ
yayau sva-dhiṣṇyān nilayaṁ pura-dviṣaḥ
kailāsam adri-pravaraṁ priyaṁ prabhoḥ

saḥ—he (Brahmā); *ittham*—thus; *ādiśya*—after instructing; *surān*—the demigods; *ajaḥ*—Lord Brahmā; *tu*—then; *taiḥ*—those; *samanvitaḥ*—followed; *pitṛbhiḥ*—by the Pitās; *sa-prajeśaiḥ*—along with the lords of the living entities; *yayau*—went; *sva-dhiṣṇyāt*—from his own place; *nilayam*—the abode; *pura-dviṣaḥ*—of Lord Śiva; *kailāsam*—Kailāsa; *adri-pravaram*—the best among mountains; *priyam*—dear; *prabhoḥ*—of the lord (Śiva).

TRANSLATION

After thus instructing all the demigods, the Pitās and the lords of the living entities, Lord Brahmā took them with him and left for the abode of Lord Śiva, known as the Kailāsa Hill.

PURPORT

The abode of Lord Śiva, which is known as Kailāsa, is described in the fourteen verses which follow.

TEXT 9

जन्मौषधितपोमन्त्रयोगसिद्धैर्नरेतरैः ।
जुष्टं किंनरगन्धर्वैरप्सरोभिर्वृतं सदा ॥ ९ ॥

janmauṣadhi-tapo-mantra-
yoga-siddhair naretaraiḥ
juṣṭaṁ kinnara-gandharvair
apsarobhir vṛtaṁ sadā

janma—birth; *auṣadhi*—herbs; *tapaḥ*—austerity; *mantra*—Vedic hymns; *yoga*—mystic *yoga* practices; *siddhaiḥ*—with perfected beings; *nara-itaraiḥ*—by demigods; *juṣṭam*—enjoyed; *kinnara-gandharvaiḥ*—by Kinnaras and Gandharvas; *apsarobhiḥ*—by Apsarās; *vṛtam*—full of; *sadā*—always.

TRANSLATION

The abode known as Kailāsa is full of different herbs and vegetables, and it is sanctified by Vedic hymns and mystic yoga practice. Thus the residents of that abode are demigods by birth and have all mystic powers. Besides them there are other human beings,

who are known as Kinnaras and Gandharvas and are accompanied by their beautiful wives, who are known as Apsarās, or angels.

TEXT 10

नानामणिमयैः शृङ्गैर्नानाधातुविचित्रितैः ।
नानाद्रुमलतागुल्मैर्नानामृगगणावृतैः ॥१०॥

nānā-maṇimayaiḥ śṛṅgair
nānā-dhātu-vicitritaiḥ
nānā-druma-latā-gulmair
nānā-mṛga-gaṇāvṛtaiḥ

nānā—different kinds; *maṇi*—jewels; *mayaiḥ*—made of; *śṛṅgaiḥ*—with the peaks; *nānā-dhātu-vicitritaiḥ*—decorated with various minerals; *nānā*—various; *druma*—trees; *latā*—creepers; *gulmaiḥ*—plants; *nānā*—various; *mṛga-gaṇa*—by groups of deer; *āvṛtaiḥ*—inhabited by.

TRANSLATION

Kailāsa is full of mountains filled with all kinds of valuable jewels and minerals and surrounded by all varieties of valuable trees and plants. The top of the hill is nicely decorated by various types of deer.

TEXT 11

नानामलप्रस्रवणैर्नानाकन्दरसानुभिः ।
रमणं विहरन्तीनां रमणैः सिद्धयोषिताम् ॥११॥

nānāmala-prasravaṇair
nānā-kandara-sānubhiḥ
ramaṇaṁ viharantīnāṁ
ramaṇaiḥ siddha-yoṣitām

nānā—various; *amala*—transparent; *prasravaṇaiḥ*—with waterfalls; *nānā*—various; *kandara*—caves; *sānubhiḥ*—with summits; *ramaṇam*—giving pleasure; *viharantīnām*—sporting; *ramaṇaiḥ*—with their lovers; *siddha-yoṣitām*—of the damsels of the mystics.

TRANSLATION

There are many waterfalls, and in the mountains there are many beautiful caves in which the very beautiful wives of the mystics are found.

TEXT 12

मयूरकेकाभिरुतं मदान्धालिविमूर्च्छितम् ।
प्लावितै रक्तकण्ठानां कूजितैश्च पतत्त्रिणाम् ॥१२॥

mayūra-kekābhirutaṁ
madāndhāli-vimūrcchitam
plāvitai rakta-kaṇṭhānāṁ
kūjitaiś ca patattriṇām

mayūra—peacocks; *kekā*—with the cries; *abhirutam*—resounding; *mada*—by intoxication; *andha*—blinded; *ali*—by the bees; *vimūrcchitam*—resounded; *plāvitaiḥ*—with the singing; *rakta-kaṇṭhānām*—of the cuckoos; *kūjitaiḥ*—with the whispering; *ca*—and; *patattriṇām*—of other birds.

TRANSLATION

On Kailāsa Hill there is always the rhythmical sound of the peacocks' sweet vibrations and the bees' humming. Cuckoos are always singing, and other birds whisper amongst themselves.

TEXT 13

आह्वयन्तमिवोद्धस्तैर्द्विजान् कामदुघैर्द्रुमैः ।
व्रजन्तमिव मातङ्गैर्गृणन्तमिव निर्झरैः ॥१३॥

āhvayantam ivoddhastair
dvijān kāma-dughair drumaiḥ
vrajantam iva mātaṅgair
gṛṇantam iva nirjharaiḥ

āhvayantam—calling; *iva*—as if; *ut-hastaiḥ*—with upraised hands (branches); *dvijān*—the birds; *kāma-dughaiḥ*—yielding desires; *drumaiḥ*—with trees; *vrajantam*—moving; *iva*—as if; *mātaṅgaiḥ*—by elephants; *gṛṇantam*—resounding; *iva*—as if; *nirjharaiḥ*—by the waterfalls.

TRANSLATION

There are tall trees with straight branches that appear to call the sweet birds, and when herds of elephants pass through the hills, it appears that the Kailāsa Hill moves with them. When the waterfalls resound, it appears that Kailāsa Hill does also.

TEXTS 14–15

मन्दारैः पारिजातैश्च सरलैश्चोपशोभितम् ।
तमालैः शालतालैश्च कोविदारासनार्जुनैः ॥१४॥
चूतैः कदम्बैर्नीपैश्च नागपुन्नागचम्पकैः ।
पाटलाशोकबकुलैः कुन्दैः कुरबकैरपि ॥१५॥

mandāraiḥ pārijātaiś ca
saralaiś copaśobhitam
tamālaiḥ śāla-tālaiś ca
kovidārāsanārjunaiḥ

cūtaiḥ kadambair nīpaiś ca
nāga-punnāga-campakaiḥ
pāṭalāśoka-bakulaiḥ
kundaiḥ kurabakair api

mandāraiḥ—with *mandāras; pārijātaiḥ*—with *pārijātas; ca*—and; *saralaiḥ*—with *saralas; ca*—and; *upaśobhitam*—decorated; *tamālaiḥ*—with *tamāla* trees; *śāla-tālaiḥ*—with *śālas* and *tālas; ca*—and; *kovidāra-āsana-arjunaiḥ*—*kovidāras, āsanas* (*vijaya-sāras*) and *arjuna* trees (*kāñcanārakas*); *cūtaiḥ*—with *cūtas* (a species of mango); *kadambaiḥ*—with *kadambas; nīpaiḥ*—with *nīpas* (*dhūli-kadambas*); *ca*—and; *nāga-punnāga-campakaiḥ*—with *nāgas, punnāgas* and *campakas; pāṭala-aśoka-bakulaiḥ*—with *pāṭalas, aśokas* and *bakulas; kundaiḥ*—with *kundas; kurabakaiḥ*—with *kurabakas; api*—also.

TRANSLATION

The whole of Kailāsa Hill is decorated with various kinds of trees, of which the following names may be mentioned: mandāra, pārijāta, sarala, tamāla, tāla, kovidāra, āsana, arjuna, āmra-jāti (mango), kadamba, dhūli-kadamba, nāga, punnāga, campaka, pāṭala, aśoka, bakula, kunda and kurabaka. The entire hill is decorated with such trees, which produce flowers with fragrant aromas.

TEXT 16

स्वर्णार्णशतपत्रैश्च वररेणुकजातिभिः ।
कुब्जकैर्मल्लिकाभिश्च माधवीभिश्च मण्डितम् ॥१६॥

svarṇārṇa-śata-patraiś ca
vara-reṇuka-jātibhiḥ
kubjakair mallikābhiś ca
mādhavībhiś ca maṇḍitam

svarṇārṇa—golden colored; *śata-patraiḥ*—with lotuses; *ca*—and; *vara-reṇuka-jātibhiḥ*—with *varas, reṇukas* and *mālatīs; kubjakaiḥ*—with *kubjakas; mallikābhiḥ*—with *mallikās; ca*—and; *mādhavībhiḥ*—with *mādhavīs; ca*—and; *maṇḍitam*—decorated.

TRANSLATION

There are other trees also which decorate the hill, such as the golden lotus flower, the cinnamon tree, mālatī, kubja, mallikā and mādhavī.

TEXT 17

पनसोदुम्बराश्वत्थप्लक्षन्यग्रोधहिङ्गुभिः ।
भूर्जैरोषधिभिः पूगै राजपूगैश्च जम्बुभिः ॥१७॥

panasodumbarāśvattha-
plakṣa-nyagrodha-hiṅgubhiḥ
bhūrjair oṣadhibhiḥ pūgai
rājapūgaiś ca jambubhiḥ

panasa-udumbara-aśvattha-plakṣa-nyagrodha-hiṅgubhiḥ—with *panasas* (jackfruit trees), *udumbaras, aśvatthas, plakṣas, nyagrodhas* and trees producing asafetida; *bhūrjaiḥ*—with *bhūrjas; oṣadhibhiḥ*—with betel nut trees; *pūgaiḥ*—with *pūgas; rājapūgaiḥ*—with *rājapūgas; ca*—and; *jambubhiḥ*—with *jambus.*

TRANSLATION

Kailāsa Hill is also decorated with such trees as kata, jackfruit, julara, banyan trees, plakṣas, nyagrodhas and trees producing asafetida. Also there are trees of betel nuts and bhūrja-patra, as well as rājapūga, blackberries and similar other trees.

TEXT 18

खर्जूराम्रातकाम्राद्यैः प्रियालमधुकेङ्गुदैः ।
द्रुमजातिभिरन्यैश्च राजितं वेणुकीचकैः ॥१८॥

kharjūrāmrātakāmrādyaiḥ
priyāla-madhukeṅgudaiḥ
druma-jātibhir anyaiś ca
rājitaṁ veṇu-kīcakaiḥ

kharjūra-āmrātaka-āmra-ādyaiḥ—with *kharjūras, āmrātakas, āmras* and others; *priyāla-madhuka-iṅgudaiḥ*—with *priyālas, madhukas* and *iṅgudas; druma-jātibhiḥ*—with varieties of trees; *anyaiḥ*—other; *ca*—and; *rājitam*—decorated; *veṇu-kīcakaiḥ*—with *veṇus* (bamboos) and *kīcakas* (hollow bamboos).

TRANSLATION

There are mango trees, priyāla, madhuka and iṅguda. Besides these there are other trees, like thin bamboos, kīcaka and varieties of other bamboo trees, all decorating the tract of Kailāsa Hill.

TEXTS 19–20

कुमुदोत्पलकह्लारशतपत्रवनर्द्धिभिः ।
नलिनीषु कलं कूजत्खगवृन्दोपशोभितम् ॥१९॥

मृगैः शाखामृगैः क्रोडैर्मृगेन्द्रैर्ऋक्षशल्यकैः ।
गवयैः शरभैर्व्याघ्रै रुरुभिर्महिषादिभिः ॥२०॥

kumudotpala-kahlāra-
śatapatra-vanarddhibhiḥ
nalinīṣu kalaṁ kūjat-
khaga-vṛndopaśobhitam

mṛgaiḥ śākhāmṛgaiḥ kroḍair
mṛgendrair ṛkṣa-śalyakaiḥ
gavayaiḥ śarabhair vyāghrai
rurubhir mahiṣādibhiḥ

kumuda—kumuda; utpala—utpala; kahlāra—kahlāra; śatapatra—lotuses; *vana*—forest; *ṛddhibhiḥ*—being covered with; *nalinīṣu*—in the lakes; *kalam*—very sweetly; *kūjat*—whispering; *khaga*—of birds; *vṛnda*—groups; *upaśobhitam*—decorated with; *mṛgaiḥ*—with deer; *śākhā-mṛgaiḥ*—with monkeys; *kroḍaiḥ*—with boars; *mṛga-indraiḥ*—with lions; *ṛkṣa-śalyakaiḥ*—with *ṛkṣas* and *śalyakas; gavayaiḥ*—with forest cows; *śarabhaiḥ*—with forest asses; *vyāghraiḥ*—with tigers; *rurubhiḥ*—with small deer; *mahiṣa-ādibhiḥ*—with buffalo, etc.

TRANSLATION

There are different kinds of lotus flowers, such as kumuda, utpala and śatapatra. The forest appears to be a decorated garden, and the small lakes are full of various kinds of birds who whisper very sweetly. There are many kinds of other animals also, like deer, monkeys, boars, lions, ṛkṣas, śalyakas, forest cows, forest asses, tigers, small deer, buffalo and many other animals, who are fully enjoying their lives.

TEXT 21

कर्णान्त्रैकपदाश्वास्यैर्निर्जुष्टं वृकनाभिभिः ।
कदलीखण्डसंरुद्धनलिनीपुलिनश्रियम् ॥२१॥

karṇāntraikapadāśvāsyair
nirjuṣṭaṁ vṛka-nābhibhiḥ

kadalī-khaṇḍa-saṁruddha-
nalinī-pulina-śriyam

karṇāntra—by the *karṇāntra; ekapada*—the *ekapada; aśvāsyaiḥ*—by the *aśvāsya; nirjuṣṭam*—fully enjoyed; *vṛka-nābhibhiḥ*—by the *vṛka* and *nābhi,* or *kastūrī* deer; *kadalī*—of banana trees; *khaṇḍa*—with groups; *saṁruddha*—covered; *nalinī*—of small lakes filled with lotus flowers; *pulina*—with the sandy banks; *śriyam*—very beautiful.

TRANSLATION

There are varieties of deer, such as karṇāntra, ekapada, aśvāsya, vṛka and kastūrī, the deer which bears musk. Besides the deer there are many banana trees which decorate the small hillside lakes very nicely.

TEXT 22

पर्यस्तं नन्दया सत्याः स्नानपुण्यतरोदया ।
विलोक्य भूतेशगिरिं विबुधा विस्मयं ययुः ॥२२॥

paryastaṁ nandayā satyāḥ
snāna-puṇyatarodayā
vilokya bhūteśa-giriṁ
vibudhā vismayaṁ yayuḥ

paryastam—surrounded; *nandayā*—by the Nandā; *satyāḥ*—of Satī; *snāna*—by the bathing; *puṇya-tara*—especially flavored; *udayā*—with water; *vilokya*—after seeing; *bhūta-īśa*—of Bhūteśa (the lord of the ghosts, Lord Śiva); *girim*—the mountain; *vibudhāḥ*—the demigods; *vismayam*—wonder; *yayuḥ*—obtained.

TRANSLATION

There is a small lake named Alakanandā in which Satī used to take her bath, and that lake is especially auspicious. All the demigods, after seeing the specific beauty of Kailāsa Hill, were struck with wonder at the great opulence to be found there.

PURPORT

According to the commentary called *Śrī-Bhāgavata-candra-candrikā,* the water in which Satī used to bathe was Ganges water. In other words, the Ganges flowed through the Kailāsa-parvata. There is every possibility of accepting such a statement because Ganges water also flows from the hair of Lord Śiva. Since Ganges water rests on the head of Lord Śiva and then flows to the other parts of the universe, it is quite possible that the water in which Satī bathed, which was certainly very nicely scented, was Ganges water.

TEXT 23

ददृशुस्तत्र ते रम्यामलकां नाम वै पुरीम् ।
वनं सौगन्धिकं चापि यत्र तन्नाम पङ्कजम् ॥२३॥

dadṛśus tatra te ramyām
alakāṁ nāma vai purīm
vanaṁ saugandhikaṁ cāpi
yatra tan-nāma paṅkajam

dadṛśuḥ—saw; *tatra*—there (in Kailāsa); *te*—they (the demigods); *ramyām*—very attractive; *alakām*—Alakā; *nāma*—known as; *vai*—indeed; *purīm*—abode; *vanam*—forest; *saugandhikam*—Saugandhika; *ca*—and; *api*—even; *yatra*—in which place; *tat-nāma*—known by that name; *paṅkajam*—species of lotus flowers.

TRANSLATION

Thus the demigods saw the wonderfully beautiful region known as Alakā in the forest known as Saugandhika, which means "full of fragrance." The forest is known as Saugandhika because of its abundance of lotus flowers.

PURPORT

Sometimes Alakā is known as Alakā-purī, which is also the name of the abode of Kuvera. Kuvera's abode, however, cannot be seen from Kailāsa. Therefore the region of Alakā referred to here is different from the Alakā-purī of Kuvera. According to Vīrarāghava Ācārya, *alakā* means "uncommonly beautiful." In the region of Alakā the demigods saw, there is a type of lotus flower known as Saugandhika that distributes an especially fragrant scent.

TEXT 24

नन्दा चालकनन्दा च सरितौ बाह्यतः पुरः ।
तीर्थपादपदाम्भोजरजसातीव पावने ॥२४॥

nandā cālakanandā ca
saritau bāhyataḥ puraḥ
tīrthapāda-padāmbhoja-
rajasātīva pāvane

nandā—the Nandā; *ca*—and; *alakanandā*—the Alakanandā; *ca*—and; *saritau*—two rivers; *bāhyataḥ*—outside; *puraḥ*—from the city; *tīrtha-pāda*—of the Supreme Personality of Godhead; *pada-ambhoja*—of the lotus feet; *rajasā*—by the dust; *atīva*—exceedingly; *pāvane*—sanctified.

TRANSLATION

They also saw the two rivers named Nandā and Alakanandā. These two rivers are sanctified by the dust of the lotus feet of the Supreme Personality of Godhead, Govinda.

TEXT 25

ययोः सुरस्त्रियः क्षत्तरवरुह्य स्वधिष्ण्यतः ।
क्रीडन्ति पुंसः सिञ्चन्त्यो विगाह्य रतिकर्शिताः॥२५॥

yayoḥ sura-striyaḥ kṣattar
avaruhya sva-dhiṣṇyataḥ
krīḍanti puṁsaḥ siñcantyo
vigāhya rati-karśitāḥ

yayoḥ—in both of which (rivers); *sura-striyaḥ*—the celestial damsels along with their husbands; *kṣattaḥ*—O Vidura; *avaruhya*—descending; *sva-dhiṣṇyataḥ*—from their own airplanes; *krīḍanti*—they play; *puṁ-*

saḥ—their husbands; *siñcantyaḥ*—sprinkling with water; *vigāhya*—after entering (the water); *rati-karśitāḥ*—whose enjoyment has become diminished.

TRANSLATION

My dear Kṣattā, Vidura, the celestial damsels come down to those rivers in their airplanes with their husbands, and after sexual enjoyment, they enter the water and enjoy sprinkling their husbands with water.

PURPORT

It is understood that even the damsels of the heavenly planets are polluted by thoughts of sex enjoyment, and therefore they come in airplanes to bathe in the rivers Nandā and Alakanandā. It is significant that these rivers, Nandā and Alakanandā, are sanctified by the dust of the lotus feet of the Supreme Personality of Godhead. In other words, just as the Ganges is sacred because its water emanates from the toes of the Supreme Personality of Godhead, Nārāyaṇa, so whenever water or anything is in touch with devotional service to the Supreme Personality of Godhead, it is purified and spiritualized. The rules and regulations of devotional service are based on this principle: anything in touch with the lotus feet of the Lord is immediately freed from all material contamination.

The damsels of the heavenly planets, polluted by thoughts of sex life, come down to bathe in the sanctified rivers and enjoy sprinkling water on their husbands. Two words are very significant in this connection. *Rati-karśitāḥ* means that the damsels become morose after sex enjoyment. Although they accept sex enjoyment as a bodily demand, afterwards they are not happy.

Another significant point is that Lord Govinda, the Supreme Personality of Godhead, is described here as Tīrthapāda. *Tīrtha* means "sanctified place," and *pāda* means "the lotus feet of the Lord." People go to a sanctified place to free themselves from all sinful reactions. In other words, those who are devoted to the lotus feet of the Supreme Personality of Godhead, Kṛṣṇa, automatically become sanctified. The Lord's lotus feet are called *tīrtha-pāda* because under their protection there are hundreds and thousands of saintly persons who sanctify the sacred places of pilgrimage. Śrīla Narottama dāsa Ṭhākura, a great *ācārya* of the

Gauḍīya Vaiṣṇava-sampradāya, advises us not to travel to different places of pilgrimage. Undoubtedly it is troublesome to go from one place to another, but one who is intelligent can take shelter of the lotus feet of Govinda and thereby be automatically sanctified as the result of his pilgrimage. Anyone who is fixed in the service of the lotus feet of Govinda is called *tīrtha-pāda;* he does not need to travel on various pilgrimages, for he can enjoy all the benefits of such travel simply by engaging in the service of the lotus feet of the Lord. Such a pure devotee, who has implicit faith in the lotus feet of the Lord, can create sacred places in any part of the world where he decides to remain. *Tīrthī-kurvanti tīrthāni* (*Bhāg.* 1.13.10). The places are sanctified due to the presence of pure devotees; any place automatically becomes a place of pilgrimage if either the Lord or His pure devotee remains or resides there. In other words, such a pure devotee, who is engaged one hundred percent in the service of the Lord, can remain anywhere in the universe, and that part of the universe immediately becomes a sacred place where he can peacefully render service to the Lord as the Lord desires.

TEXT 26

ययोस्तत्स्नानविभ्रष्टनवकुङ्कुमपिञ्जरम् ।
वितृषोऽपि पिबन्त्यम्भः पाययन्तो गजा गजीः ॥२६॥

yayos tat-snāna-vibhraṣṭa-
nava-kuṅkuma-piñjaram
vitṛṣo 'pi pibanty ambhaḥ
pāyayanto gajā gajīḥ

yayoḥ—in both of which rivers; *tat-snāna*—by the bathing of them (the damsels of the heavenly planets); *vibhraṣṭa*—fallen off; *nava*—fresh; *kuṅkuma*—with *kuṅkuma* powder; *piñjaram*—yellow; *vitṛṣaḥ*—not being thirsty; *api*—even; *pibanti*—drink; *ambhaḥ*—the water; *pāyayantaḥ*—causing to drink; *gajāḥ*—the elephants; *gajīḥ*—the female elephants.

TRANSLATION

After the damsels of the heavenly planets bathe in the water, it becomes yellowish and fragrant due to the kuṅkuma from their

bodies. Thus the elephants come to bathe there with their wives, the she-elephants, and they also drink the water, although they are not thirsty.

TEXT 27

तारहेममहारत्नविमानशतसंकुलाम् ।
जुष्टां पुण्यजनस्त्रीभिर्यथा खं सतडिद्घनम् ॥२७॥

tāra-hema-mahāratna-
vimāna-śata-saṅkulām
juṣṭāṁ puṇyajana-strībhir
yathā khaṁ sataḍid-ghanam

tāra-hema—of pearls and gold; *mahā-ratna*—valuable jewels; *vimāna*—of airplanes; *śata*—with hundreds; *saṅkulām*—crowded; *juṣṭām*—occupied, enjoyed; *puṇyajana-strībhiḥ*—by the wives of the Yakṣas; *yathā*—as; *kham*—the sky; *sa-taḍit-ghanam*—with the lightning and the clouds.

TRANSLATION

The airplanes of the heavenly denizens are bedecked with pearls, gold and many valuable jewels. The heavenly denizens are compared to clouds in the sky decorated with occasional flashes of electric lightning.

PURPORT

The airplanes described in this verse are different from the airplanes of which we have experience. In the *Śrīmad-Bhāgavatam* and all the Vedic literatures, there are many descriptions of *vimāna*, which means "airplanes." On different planets there are different kinds of airplanes. On this gross planet earth, there are airplanes run by machine, but on other planets the airplanes are run not by machine but by mantric hymns. They are also used especially for enjoyment by the denizens of the heavenly planets so that they can go from one planet to another. On other planets which are called Siddhalokas, the denizens can travel from one planet to another without airplanes. The beautiful airplanes from the heavenly planets are compared here to the sky because they fly in the sky; the passengers are compared to the clouds. The beautiful damsels, the wives of the denizens of the heavenly planets, are compared to lightning. In summation, the airplanes with their passengers which came from higher planets to Kailāsa were very pleasant to look at.

TEXT 28

हित्वा यक्षेश्वरपुरीं वनं सौगन्धिकं च तत् ।
द्रुमैः कामदुघैर्हृद्यं चित्रमाल्यफलच्छदैः ॥२८॥

hitvā yakṣeśvara-purīṁ
vanaṁ saugandhikaṁ ca tat
drumaiḥ kāma-dughair hṛdyaṁ
citra-mālya-phala-cchadaiḥ

hitvā—passing over; *yakṣa-īśvara*—the lord of the Yakṣas (Kuvera); *purīm*—the abode; *vanam*—the forest; *saugandhikam*—named Saugandhika; *ca*—and; *tat*—that; *drumaiḥ*—with trees; *kāma-dughaiḥ*—yielding desires; *hṛdyam*—attractive; *citra*—variegated; *mālya*—flowers; *phala*—fruits; *chadaiḥ*—leaves.

TRANSLATION

While traveling, the demigods passed over the forest known as Saugandhika, which is full of varieties of flowers, fruits and desire trees. While passing over the forest, they also saw the regions of Yakṣeśvara.

PURPORT

Yakṣeśvara is also known as Kuvera, and he is the treasurer of the demigods. In the descriptions of him in Vedic literature, it is stated that he is fabulously rich. It appears from these verses that Kailāsa is situated near the residential quarters of Kuvera. It is also stated here that the forest was full of desire trees. In *Brahma-saṁhitā* we learn about the desire tree which is found in the spiritual world, especially in Kṛṣṇaloka, the abode of Lord Kṛṣṇa. We learn here that such desire trees are also found in Kailāsa, the residence of Lord Śiva, by the grace of Kṛṣṇa. It thus appears that Kailāsa has a special significance; it is almost like the residence of Lord Kṛṣṇa.

TEXT 29

रक्तकण्ठखगानीकस्वरमण्डितषट्पदम् ।
कलहंसकुलप्रेष्ठं खरदण्डजलाशयम् ॥२९॥

rakta-kaṇṭha-khagānīka-
svara-maṇḍita-ṣaṭpadam
kalahaṁsa-kula-preṣṭhaṁ
kharadaṇḍa-jalāśayam

rakta—reddish; *kaṇṭha*—necks; *khaga-anīka*—of many birds; *svara*—with the sweet sounds; *maṇḍita*—decorated; *ṣaṭ-padam*—bees; *kalahaṁsa-kula*—of groups of swans; *preṣṭham*—very dear; *khara-daṇḍa*—lotus flowers; *jala-āśayam*—lakes.

TRANSLATION

In that celestial forest there were many birds whose necks were colored reddish and whose sweet sounds mixed with the humming of the bees. The lakes were abundantly decorated with crying swans as well as strong-stemmed lotus flowers.

PURPORT

The beauty of the forest was intensified by the presence of various lakes. It is described herein that the lakes were decorated with lotus flowers and with swans who played and sang with the birds and the humming bees. Considering all these attributes, one can imagine how beautiful this spot was and how much the demigods passing through enjoyed the atmosphere. There are many paths and beautiful spots created by man on this planet earth, but none of them can surpass those of Kailāsa, as they are described in these verses.

TEXT 30

वनकुञ्जरसंघृष्टहरिचन्दनवायुना ।
अधि पुण्यजनस्त्रीणां मुहुरुन्मथयन्मनः ॥३०॥

vana-kuñjara-saṅghṛṣṭa-
haricandana-vāyunā
adhi puṇyajana-strīṇāṁ
muhur unmathayan manaḥ

vana-kuñjara—by wild elephants; *saṅghṛṣṭa*—rubbed against; *hari-candana*—the sandalwood trees; *vāyunā*—by the breeze; *adhi*—further; *puṇyajana-strīṇām*—of the wives of the Yakṣas; *muhuḥ*—again and again; *unmathayat*—agitating; *manaḥ*—the minds.

TRANSLATION

All these atmospheric influences unsettled the forest elephants who flocked together in the sandalwood forest, and the blowing wind agitated the minds of the damsels there for further sexual enjoyment.

PURPORT

Whenever there is a nice atmosphere in the material world, immediately there is an awakening of the sexual appetite in the minds of materialistic persons. This tendency is present everywhere within this material world, not only on this earth but in higher planetary systems as well. In complete contrast with the influence of this atmosphere on the minds of the living entities within the material world is the description of the spiritual world. The women there are hundreds and thousands of times more beautiful than the women here in this material world, and the spiritual atmosphere is also many times better. Yet despite the pleasant atmosphere, the minds of the denizens do not become agitated because in the spiritual world, the Vaikuṇṭha planets, the spiritualistic minds of the inhabitants are so much absorbed in the spiritual vibration of chanting the glories of the Lord that such enjoyment could not be surpassed by any other enjoyment, even sex, which is the culmination of all pleasure in the material world. In other words, in the Vaikuṇṭha world, in spite of its better atmosphere and facilities, there is no impetus for sex life. As stated in *Bhagavad-gītā* (2.59), *paraṁ dṛṣṭvā nivartate:* the inhabitants are so spiritually enlightened that in the presence of such spirituality, sex life is insignificant.

TEXT 31

वैदूर्यकृतसोपाना वाप्य उत्पलमालिनीः ।
प्राप्तं किम्पुरुषैर्दृष्ट्वा त आराद्ददृशुर्वटम् ॥३१॥

vaidūrya-kṛta-sopānā
vāpya utpala-mālinīḥ
prāptaṁ kimpuruṣair dṛṣṭvā
ta ārād dadṛśur vaṭam

vaidūrya-kṛta—made of *vaidūrya; sopānāḥ*—staircases; *vāpyaḥ*—lakes; *utpala*—of lotus flowers; *mālinīḥ*—containing rows; *prāptam*—inhabited; *kimpuruṣaiḥ*—by the Kimpuruṣas; *dṛṣṭvā*—after seeing; *te*—those demigods; *ārāt*—not far away; *dadṛśuḥ*—saw; *vaṭam*—a banyan tree.

TRANSLATION

They also saw that the bathing ghāṭas and their staircases were made of vaidūrya-maṇi. The water was full of lotus flowers. Passing by such lakes, the demigods reached a place where there was a great banyan tree.

TEXT 32

स योजनशतोत्सेधः पादोनविटपायतः ।
पर्यक्कृताचलच्छायो निर्नीडस्तापवर्जितः ॥३२॥

sa yojana-śatotsedhaḥ
pādona-viṭapāyataḥ
paryak-kṛtācala-cchāyo
nirnīḍas tāpa-varjitaḥ

saḥ—that banyan tree; *yojana-śata*—one hundred *yojanas* (eight hundred miles); *utsedhaḥ*—height; *pāda-ūna*—less by a quarter (six hundred miles); *viṭapa*—by the branches; *āyataḥ*—spread out; *paryak*—all around; *kṛta*—made; *acala*—unshaken; *chāyaḥ*—the shadow; *nirnīḍaḥ*—without bird nests; *tāpa-varjitaḥ*—without heat.

TRANSLATION

That banyan tree was eight hundred miles high, and its branches spread over six hundred miles around. The tree cast a fine shade which permanently cooled the temperature, yet there was no noise of birds.

PURPORT

Generally, in every tree there are bird nests, and the birds congregate in the evening and create noise. But it appears that this banyan tree was devoid of nests, and therefore it was calm, quiet and peaceful. There were no disturbances from noise or heat, and therefore this place was just suitable for meditation.

TEXT 33

तस्मिन्महायोगमये मुमुक्षुशरणे सुराः ।
ददृशुः शिवमासीनं त्यक्तामर्षमिवान्तकम् ॥३३॥

tasmin mahā-yogamaye
mumukṣu-śaraṇe surāḥ
dadṛśuḥ śivam āsīnaṁ
tyaktāmarṣam ivāntakam

tasmin—under that tree; *mahā-yoga-maye*—having many sages engaged in meditation on the Supreme; *mumukṣu*—of those who desire liberation; *śaraṇe*—the shelter; *surāḥ*—the demigods; *dadṛśuḥ*—saw; *śivam*—Lord Śiva; *āsīnam*—seated; *tyakta-amarṣam*—having given up anger; *iva*—as; *antakam*—eternal time.

TRANSLATION

The demigods saw Lord Śiva sitting under that tree, which was competent to give perfection to mystic yogīs and deliver all people. As grave as time eternal, he appeared to have given up all anger.

PURPORT

In this verse the word *mahā-yogamaye* is very significant. *Yoga* means meditation on the Supreme Personality of Godhead, and *mahā-yoga* means those who engage in the devotional service of Viṣṇu. Meditation means remembering, *smaraṇam.* There are nine different kinds of devotional service, of which *smaraṇam* is one process; the *yogī* remembers the form of Viṣṇu within his heart. Thus there were many devotees engaged in meditation on Lord Viṣṇu under the big banyan tree.

The Sanskrit word *mahā* is derived from the affix *mahat.* This affix is used when there is a great number or quantity, so *mahā-yoga* indicates that there were many great *yogīs* and devotees meditating on the form of Lord Viṣṇu. Generally such meditators are desirous of liberation from material bondage, and they are promoted to the spiritual world, to one of the Vaikuṇṭhas. Liberation means freedom from material bondage or nescience. In the material world we are suffering life after life because of our bodily identification, and liberation is freedom from that miserable condition of life.

TEXT 34

सनन्दनाद्यैर्महासिद्धैः शान्तैः संशान्तविग्रहम् ।
उपास्यमानं सख्या च भर्त्रा गुह्यकरक्षसाम् ॥३४॥

sanandanādyair mahā-siddhaiḥ
śāntaiḥ saṁśānta-vigraham
upāsyamānaṁ sakhyā ca
bhartrā guhyaka-rakṣasām

sanandana-ādyaiḥ—the four Kumāras, headed by Sanandana; *mahā-siddhaiḥ*—liberated souls; *śāntaiḥ*—saintly; *saṁśānta-vigraham*—the grave and saintly Lord Śiva; *upāsyamānam*—was being praised; *sakhyā*—by Kuvera; *ca*—and; *bhartrā*—by the master; *guhyaka-rakṣasām*—of the Guhyakas and the Rākṣasas.

TRANSLATION

Lord Śiva sat there, surrounded by saintly persons like Kuvera, the master of the Guhyakas, and the four Kumāras, who were already liberated souls. Lord Śiva was grave and saintly.

PURPORT

The personalities sitting with Lord Śiva are significant because the four Kumāras were liberated from birth. It may be remembered that after their birth these Kumāras were requested by their father to get married and beget children in order to increase the population of the newly created universe. But they refused, and at that time Lord Brahmā was angry. In that angry mood, Rudra, or Lord Śiva, was born. Thus they were intimately related. Kuvera, the treasurer of the demigods, is fabulously rich. Thus Lord Śiva's association with the Kumāras and Kuvera indicates that he has all transcendental and material opulences. Actually, he is the qualitative incarnation of the Supreme Lord; therefore his position is very exalted.

TEXT 35

विद्यातपोयोगपथमास्थितं तमधीश्वरम् ।
चरन्तं विश्वसुहृदं वात्सल्याल्लोकमङ्गलम् ॥३५॥

vidyā-tapo-yoga-patham
āsthitaṁ tam adhīśvaram
carantaṁ viśva-suhṛdaṁ
vātsalyāl loka-maṅgalam

vidyā—knowledge; *tapaḥ*—austerity; *yoga-patham*—the path of devotional service; *āsthitam*—situated; *tam*—him (Lord Śiva); *adhīśvaram*—the master of the senses; *carantam*—performing (austerity, etc.); *viśva-suhṛdam*—the friend of the whole world; *vātsalyāt*—out of full affection; *loka-maṅgalam*—auspicious for everyone.

TRANSLATION

The demigods saw Lord Śiva situated in his perfection as the master of the senses, knowledge, fruitive activities and the path of achieving perfection. He was the friend of the entire world, and by virtue of his full affection for everyone, he was very auspicious.

PURPORT

Lord Śiva is full of wisdom and *tapasya,* austerity. One who knows the modes of work is understood to be situated on the path of devotional service to the Supreme Personality of Godhead. One cannot serve the Supreme Personality of Godhead unless one has achieved full perfectional knowledge in the ways and means of performing devotional service.

Lord Śiva is described here as *adhīśvara*. *Īśvara* means "controller," and *adhīśvara* means particularly "controller of the senses." Generally our materially contaminated senses are apt to engage in sense gratificatory activities, but when a person is elevated by wisdom and austerity, the senses then become purified, and they become engaged in the service of the Supreme Personality of Godhead. Lord Śiva is the emblem of such perfection, and therefore in the scriptures it is said, *vaiṣṇavānāṁ yathā śambhuḥ:* Lord Śiva is a Vaiṣṇava. Lord Śiva, by his actions within this material world, teaches all conditioned souls how to engage in devotional service twenty-four hours a day. Therefore he is described here as *loka-maṅgala*, good fortune personified for all conditioned souls.

TEXT 36

लिङ्गं च तापसाभीष्टं भस्मदण्डजटाजिनम् ।
अङ्गेन संध्याभ्ररुचा चन्द्रलेखां च बिभ्रतम् ॥३६॥

liṅgaṁ ca tāpasābhīṣṭaṁ
bhasma-daṇḍa-jaṭājinam
aṅgena sandhyābhra-rucā
candra-lekhāṁ ca bibhratam

liṅgam—symptom; *ca*—and; *tāpasa-abhīṣṭam*—desired by Śaivite ascetics; *bhasma*—ashes; *daṇḍa*—staff; *jaṭā*—matted hair; *ajinam*—antelope skin; *aṅgena*—with his body; *sandhyā-ābhra*—reddish; *rucā*—colored; *candra-lekhām*—the crest of a half-moon; *ca*—and; *bibhratam*—bearing.

TRANSLATION

He was seated on a deerskin and was practicing all forms of austerity. Because his body was smeared with ashes, he looked like an evening cloud. On his hair was the sign of a half-moon, a symbolic representation.

PURPORT

Lord Śiva's symptoms of austerity are not exactly those of a Vaiṣṇava. Lord Śiva is certainly the number one Vaiṣṇava, but he exhibits a feature for a particular class of men who cannot follow the Vaiṣṇava principles. The Śaivites, the devotees of Lord Śiva, generally dress like Lord Śiva, and sometimes they indulge in smoking and taking intoxicants. Such practices are never accepted by the followers of Vaiṣṇava rituals.

TEXT 37

उपविष्टं दर्भमय्यां बृस्यां ब्रह्म सनातनम् ।
नारदाय प्रवोचन्तं पृच्छते शृण्वतां सताम् ॥३७॥

upaviṣṭaṁ darbhamayyāṁ
bṛsyāṁ brahma sanātanam
nāradāya pravocantaṁ
pṛcchate śṛṇvatāṁ satām

upaviṣṭam—seated; *darbha-mayyām*—made of *darbha*, straw; *bṛsyām*—on a mattress; *brahma*—the Absolute Truth; *sanātanam*—the eternal; *nāradāya*—unto Nārada; *pravocantam*—speaking; *pṛcchate*—asking; *śṛṇvatām*—listening; *satām*—of the great sages.

TRANSLATION

He was seated on a straw mattress and speaking to all present, including the great sage Nārada, to whom he specifically spoke about the Absolute Truth.

PURPORT

The lord was sitting on a mattress of straw because such a sitting place is accepted by persons who are practicing austerities to gain understanding of the Absolute Truth. In this verse it is specifically mentioned that he was speaking to the great sage Nārada, a celebrated devotee. Nārada was asking Lord Śiva about devotional service, and Śiva, being the topmost Vaiṣṇava, was instructing him. In other words, Lord Śiva and Nārada were discussing the knowledge of the *Veda*, but it is to be understood that the subject matter was devotional service. Another point in this connection is that Lord Śiva is the supreme instructor and the great sage Nārada is the supreme audience. Therefore, the supreme subject matter of Vedic knowledge is *bhakti*, or devotional service.

TEXT 38

कृत्वोरौ दक्षिणे सव्यं पादपद्मं च जानुनि ।
बाहुं प्रकोष्ठेऽक्षमालामासीनं तर्कमुद्रया ॥३८॥

kṛtvorau dakṣiṇe savyaṁ
pāda-padmaṁ ca jānuni
bāhuṁ prakoṣṭhe 'kṣa-mālām
āsīnaṁ tarka-mudrayā

kṛtvā—having placed; *ūrau*—thigh; *dakṣiṇe*—at the right; *savyam*—the left; *pāda-padmam*—lotus feet; *ca*—and; *jānuni*—on his knee; *bāhum*—hand; *prakoṣṭhe*—in the end of the right hand; *akṣa-mālām*—*rudrākṣa* beads; *āsīnam*—sitting; *tarka-mudrayā*—with the *mudrā* of argument.

TRANSLATION

His left leg was placed on his right thigh, and his left hand was placed on his left thigh. In his right hand he held rudrākṣa beads. This sitting posture is called vīrāsana. He sat in the vīrāsana posture, and his finger was in the mode of argument.

PURPORT

The sitting posture described herein is called *vīrāsana* according to the system of *aṣṭāṅga-yoga* performances. In the performance of *yoga* there are eight divisions, such as *yama* and *niyama*—controlling, following the rules and regulations, then practicing the sitting postures, etc. Besides *vīrāsana* there are other sitting postures, such as *padmāsana* and *siddhāsana.* Practice of these *āsanas* without elevating oneself to the position of realizing the Supersoul, Viṣṇu, is not the perfectional stage of *yoga.* Lord Śiva is called *yogīśvara,* the master of all *yogīs,* and Kṛṣṇa is also called *yogeśvara. Yogīśvara* indicates that no one can surpass the *yoga* practice of Lord Śiva, and *yogeśvara* indicates that no one can surpass the yogic perfection of Kṛṣṇa. Another significant word is *tarka-mudrā.* This indicates that the fingers are opened and the second finger is raised, along with the arm, to impress the audience with some subject matter. This is actually a symbolic representation.

TEXT 39

तं ब्रह्मनिर्वाणसमाधिमाश्रितं
व्युपाश्रितं गिरिशं योगकक्षाम् ।
सलोकपाला मुनयो मनूना-
माद्यं मनुं प्राञ्जलयः प्रणेमुः ॥३९॥

taṁ brahma-nirvāṇa-samādhim āśritaṁ
vyupāśritaṁ giriśaṁ yoga-kakṣām
sa-loka-pālā munayo manūnām
ādyaṁ manuṁ prāñjalayaḥ praṇemuḥ

tam—him (Lord Śiva); *brahma-nirvāṇa*—in *brahmānanda; samādhim*—in trance; *āśritam*—absorbed; *vyupāśritam*—leaning on; *giriśam*—Lord Śiva; *yoga-kakṣām*—having his left knee firmly fixed with a knotted cloth; *sa-loka-pālāḥ*—along with the demigods (headed by Indra); *munayaḥ*—the sages; *manūnām*—of all thinkers; *ādyam*—the chief; *manum*—thinker; *prāñjalayaḥ*—with folded palms; *praṇemuḥ*—offered respectful obeisances.

TRANSLATION

All the sages and demigods, headed by Indra, offered their respectful obeisances unto Lord Śiva with folded hands. Lord Śiva was dressed in saffron garments and absorbed in trance, thus appearing to be the foremost of all sages.

PURPORT

In this verse the word *brahmānanda* is significant. This *brahmānanda,* or *brahma-nirvāṇa,* is explained by Prahlāda Mahārāja. When one is completely absorbed in the *adhokṣaja,* the Supreme Personality of Godhead, who is beyond the sense perception of materialistic persons, one is situated in *brahmānanda.*

It is impossible to conceive of the existence, name, form, quality and pastimes of the Supreme Personality of Godhead because He is transcendentally situated beyond the conception of materialistic persons. Because materialists cannot imagine or conceive of the Supreme Personality of

Godhead, they may think that God is dead, but factually He is always existing in His *sac-cid-ānanda-vigraha,* His eternal form. Constant meditation concentrated on the form of the Lord is called *samādhi,* ecstasy or trance. *Samādhi* means particularly concentrated attention, so one who has achieved the qualification of always meditating on the Personality of Godhead is to be understood to be always in trance and enjoying *brahma-nirvāṇa,* or *brahmānanda.* Lord Śiva exhibited those symptoms, and therefore it is stated that he was absorbed in *brahmānanda.*

Another significant word is *yoga-kakṣām. Yoga-kakṣā* is the sitting posture in which the left thigh is fixed under one's tightly knotted saffron-colored garment. Also the words *manūnām ādyam* are significant here because they mean a philosopher, or one who is thoughtful and can think very nicely. Such a man is called *manu.* Lord Śiva is described in this verse as the chief of all thinkers. Lord Śiva, of course, does not engage in useless mental speculation, but as stated in the previous verse, he is always thoughtful regarding how to deliver the demons from their fallen condition of life. It is said that during the advent of Lord Caitanya, Sadāśiva appeared as Advaita Prabhu, and Advaita Prabhu's chief concern was to elevate the fallen conditioned souls to the platform of devotional service to Lord Kṛṣṇa. Since people were engaged in useless occupations which would continue their material existence, Lord Śiva, in the form of Lord Advaita, appealed to the Supreme Lord to appear as Lord Caitanya to deliver these illusioned souls. Actually Lord Caitanya appeared on the request of Lord Advaita. Similarly, Lord Śiva has a *sampradāya,* the Rudra-sampradāya. He is always thinking about the deliverance of the fallen souls, as exhibited by Lord Advaita Prabhu.

TEXT 40

स तूपलभ्यागतमात्मयोनिं
सुरासुरेशैरभिवन्दिताङ्घ्रिः ।
उत्थाय चक्रे शिरसाभिवन्दन-
मर्हत्तमः कस्य यथैव विष्णुः ॥४०॥

sa tūpalabhyāgatam ātma-yonim̐
surāsureśair abhivanditāṅghriḥ

utthāya cakre śirasābhivandanam
arhattamaḥ kasya yathaiva viṣṇuḥ

saḥ—Lord Śiva; *tu*—but; *upalabhya*—seeing; *āgatam*—had arrived; *ātma-yonim*—Lord Brahmā; *sura-asura-īśaiḥ*—by the best of the demigods and demons; *abhivandita-aṅghriḥ*—whose feet are worshiped; *utthāya*—standing up; *cakre*—made; *śirasā*—with his head; *abhivandanam*—respectful; *arhattamaḥ*—Vāmanadeva; *kasya*—of Kaśyapa; *yathā eva*—just as; *viṣṇuḥ*—Viṣṇu.

TRANSLATION

Lord Śiva's lotus feet were worshiped by both the demigods and demons, but still, in spite of his exalted position, as soon as he saw that Lord Brahmā was there among all the other demigods, he immediately stood up and offered him respect by bowing down and touching his lotus feet, just as Vāmanadeva offered His respectful obeisances to Kaśyapa Muni.

PURPORT

Kaśyapa Muni was in the category of the living entities, but he had a transcendental son, Vāmanadeva, who was an incarnation of Viṣṇu. Thus although Lord Viṣṇu is the Supreme Personality of Godhead, He offered His respects to Kaśyapa Muni. Similarly, when Lord Kṛṣṇa was a child He used to offer His respectful obeisances to His mother and father, Nanda and Yaśodā. Also, at the Battle of Kurukṣetra, Lord Kṛṣṇa touched the feet of Mahārāja Yudhiṣṭhira because the King was His elder. It appears, then, that the Personality of Godhead, Lord Śiva and other devotees, in spite of their being situated in exalted positions, instructed by practical example how to offer obeisances to their superiors. Lord Śiva offered his respectful obeisances to Brahmā because Brahmā was his father, just as Kaśyapa Muni was the father of Vāmana.

TEXT 41

तथापरे सिद्धगणा महर्षिभि-
र्ये वै समन्तादनु नीललोहितम् ।

नमस्कृतः प्राह शशाङ्कशेखरं
कृतप्रणामं प्रहसन्निवात्मभूः ॥४१॥

tathāpare siddha-gaṇā maharṣibhir
ye vai samantād anu nīlalohitam
namaskṛtaḥ prāha śaśāṅka-śekharaṁ
kṛta-praṇāmaṁ prahasann ivātmabhūḥ

tathā—so; *apare*—the others; *siddha-gaṇāḥ*—the Siddhas; *mahā-ṛṣibhiḥ*—along with the great sages; *ye*—who; *vai*—indeed; *samantāt*—from all sides; *anu*—after; *nīlalohitam*—Lord Śiva; *namaskṛtaḥ*—making obeisances; *prāha*—said; *śaśāṅka-śekharam*—to Lord Śiva; *kṛta-praṇāmam*—having made obeisances; *prahasan*—smiling; *iva*—as; *ātmabhūḥ*—Lord Brahmā.

TRANSLATION

All the sages who were sitting with Lord Śiva, such as Nārada and others, also offered their respectful obeisances to Lord Brahmā. After being so worshiped, Lord Brahmā, smiling, began to speak to Lord Śiva.

PURPORT

Lord Brahmā was smiling because he knew that Lord Śiva is not only easily satisfied but easily irritated as well. He was afraid that Lord Śiva might be in an angry mood because he had lost his wife and had been insulted by Dakṣa. In order to conceal this fear, he smiled and addressed Lord Śiva as follows.

TEXT 42

ब्रह्मोवाच
जाने त्वामीशं विश्वस्य जगतो योनिबीजयोः ।
शक्तेः शिवस्य च परं यत्तद्ब्रह्म निरन्तरम् ॥४२॥

brahmovāca
jāne tvām īśaṁ viśvasya
jagato yoni-bījayoḥ
śakteḥ śivasya ca paraṁ
yat tad brahma nirantaram

brahmā uvāca—Lord Brahmā said; *jāne*—I know; *tvām*—you (Lord Śiva); *īśam*—the controller; *viśvasya*—of the entire material manifestation; *jagataḥ*—of the cosmic manifestation; *yoni-bījayoḥ*—of both the mother and father; *śakteḥ*—of potency; *śivasya*—of Śiva; *ca*—and; *param*—the Supreme; *yat*—which; *tat*—that; *brahma*—without change; *nirantaram*—with no material qualities.

TRANSLATION

Lord Brahmā said: My dear Lord Śiva, I know that you are the controller of the entire material manifestation, the combination father and mother of the cosmic manifestation, and the Supreme Brahman beyond the cosmic manifestation as well. I know you in that way.

PURPORT

Although Lord Brahmā had received very respectful obeisances from Lord Śiva, he knew that Lord Śiva was in a more exalted position than himself. Lord Śiva's position is described in *Brahma-saṁhitā:* there is no difference between Lord Viṣṇu and Lord Śiva in their original positions, but still Lord Śiva is different from Lord Viṣṇu. The example is given that the milk in yogurt is not different from the original milk from which it was made.

TEXT 43

त्वमेव भगवन्नेतच्छिवशक्त्योः स्वरूपयोः ।
विश्वं सृजसि पास्यत्सि क्रीडन्नूर्णपटो यथा ॥४३॥

tvam eva bhagavann etac
chiva-śaktyoḥ svarūpayoḥ
viśvaṁ sṛjasi pāsy atsi
krīḍann ūrṇa-paṭo yathā

tvam—you; *eva*—certainly; *bhagavan*—O my lord; *etat*—this; *śiva-śaktyoḥ*—being situated in your auspicious energy; *svarūpayoḥ*—by your personal expansion; *viśvam*—this universe; *sṛjasi*—create; *pāsi*—maintain; *atsi*—annihilate; *krīḍan*—working; *ūrṇa-paṭaḥ*—spider's web; *yathā*—just like.

TRANSLATION

My dear lord, you create this cosmic manifestation, maintain it, and annihilate it by expansion of your personality, exactly as a spider creates, maintains and winds up its web.

PURPORT

In this verse the word *śiva-śakti* is significant. *Śiva* means "auspicious," and *śakti* means "energy." There are many types of energies of the Supreme Lord, and all of them are auspicious. Brahmā, Viṣṇu and Maheśvara are called *guṇa-avatāras*, or incarnations of material qualities. In the material world we compare these different incarnations from different angles of vision, but since all of them are expansions of the supreme auspicious, all of them are auspicious, although sometimes we consider one quality of nature to be higher or lower than another. The mode of ignorance, or *tamo-guṇa*, is considered very much lower than the others, but in the higher sense it is also auspicious. The example may be given herein that the government has both an educational department and criminal department. An outsider may consider the criminal department inauspicious, but from the government's point of view it is as important as the education department, and therefore the government finances both departments equally, without discrimination.

TEXT 44

त्वमेव धर्मार्थदुघाभिपत्तये
दक्षेण सूत्रेण ससर्जिथाध्वरम् ।
त्वयैव लोकेऽवसिताश्च सेतवो
यान्ब्राह्मणाः श्रद्दधते धृतव्रताः ॥४४॥

tvam eva dharmārtha-dughābhipattaye
dakṣeṇa sūtreṇa sasarjithādhvaram
tvayaiva loke 'vasitāś ca setavo
yān brāhmaṇāḥ śraddadhate dhṛta-vratāḥ

tvam—Your Lordship; *eva*—certainly; *dharma-artha-dugha*—benefit derived from religion and economic development; *abhipattaye*—for their protection; *dakṣeṇa*—by Dakṣa; *sūtreṇa*—making him the cause; *sasarjitha*—created; *adhvaram*—sacrifices; *tvayā*—by you; *eva*—certainly; *loke*—in this world; *avasitāḥ*—regulated; *ca*—and; *setavaḥ*—respect for the *varṇāśrama* institution; *yān*—which; *brāhmaṇāḥ*—the *brāhmaṇas; śraddadhate*—respect very much; *dhṛta-vratāḥ*—taking it as a vow.

TRANSLATION

My dear lord, Your Lordship has introduced the system of sacrifices through the agency of Dakṣa, and thus one may derive the benefits of religious activities and economic development. Under your regulative principles, the institution of the four varṇas and āśramas is respected. The brāhmaṇas therefore vow to follow this system strictly.

PURPORT

The Vedic system of *varṇa* and *āśrama* is never to be neglected, for these divisions are created by the Supreme Lord Himself for the upkeep of social and religious order in human society. The *brāhmaṇas*, as the intelligent class of men in society, must vow to steadily respect this regulative principle. The tendency in this age of Kali to make a classless society and not observe the principles of *varṇa* and *āśrama* is a manifestation of an impossible dream. Destruction of the social and spiritual orders will not bring fulfillment of the idea of a classless society. One should strictly observe the principles of *varṇa* and *āśrama* for the satisfaction of the creator, for it is stated in the *Bhagavad-gītā* by Lord Kṛṣṇa that the four orders of the social system—*brāhmaṇas, kṣatriyas, vaiśyas* and *śūdras*—are His creation. They should act according to the regulative principles of this institution and satisfy the Lord, just as different parts of the body all engage in the service of the whole. The whole is the Supreme Personality of Godhead in His *virāṭ-rūpa*, or universal form. The *brāhmaṇas, kṣatriyas, vaiśyas* and *śūdras* are respectively the mouth, arms, abdomen and legs of the universal form of the Lord. As long as they are engaged in the service of the complete whole, their position is secure, otherwise they fall down from their respective positions and become degraded.

TEXT 45

त्वं कर्मणां मङ्गल मङ्गलानां
कर्तुः स्वलोकं तनुषे स्वः परं वा ।
अमङ्गलानां च तमिस्रमुल्बणं
विपर्ययः केन तदेव कस्यचित् ॥४५॥

tvaṁ karmaṇāṁ maṅgala maṅgalānāṁ
kartuḥ sva-lokaṁ tanuṣe svaḥ paraṁ vā
amaṅgalānāṁ ca tamisram ulbaṇaṁ
viparyayaḥ kena tad eva kasyacit

tvam—Your Lordship; *karmaṇām*—of the prescribed duties; *maṅgala*—O most auspicious; *maṅgalānām*—of the auspicious; *kartuḥ*—of the performer; *sva-lokam*—respective higher planetary systems; *tanuṣe*—expand; *svaḥ*—heavenly planets; *param*—transcendental world; *vā*—or; *amaṅgalānām*—of the inauspicious; *ca*—and; *tamisram*—the name of a particular hell; *ulbaṇam*—ghastly; *viparyayaḥ*—the opposite; *kena*—why; *tat eva*—certainly that; *kasyacit*—for someone.

TRANSLATION

O most auspicious lord, you have ordained the heavenly planets, the spiritual Vaikuṇṭha planets and the impersonal Brahman sphere as the respective destinations of the performers of auspicious activities. Similarly, for others, who are miscreants, you have destined different kinds of hells which are horrible and ghastly. Yet sometimes it is found that their destinations are just the opposite. It is very difficult to ascertain the cause of this.

PURPORT

The Supreme Personality of Godhead is called the supreme will. It is by the supreme will that everything is happening. It is said, therefore, that not a blade of grass moves without the supreme will. Generally it is prescribed that performers of pious activities are promoted to the higher planetary systems, devotees are promoted to the Vaikuṇṭhas, or spiritual worlds, and impersonal speculators are promoted to the impersonal Brahman effulgence; but it sometimes so happens that a miscreant like Ajāmila is immediately promoted to the Vaikuṇṭhaloka simply by chanting the name of Nārāyaṇa. Although when Ajāmila uttered this vibration he intended to call his son Nārāyaṇa, Lord Nārāyaṇa took it seriously and immediately gave him promotion to Vaikuṇṭhaloka, despite his background, which was full of sinful activities. Similarly King Dakṣa was always engaged in the pious activities of performing sacrifices, yet simply because of creating a little misunderstanding with Lord Śiva, he was severely taken to task. The conclusion is, therefore, that the supreme will is the ultimate judgment; no one can argue upon this. A pure devotee therefore submits in all circumstances to the supreme will of the Lord, accepting it as all-auspicious.

tat te 'nukampāṁ susamīkṣamāṇo
bhuñjāna evātma-kṛtaṁ vipākam
hṛd-vāg-vapurbhir vidadhan namas te
jīveta yo mukti-pade sa dāya-bhāk
(*Bhāg.* 10.14.8)

The purport of this verse is that when a devotee is in a calamitous condition he takes it as a benediction of the Supreme Lord and takes responsibility himself for his past misdeeds. In such a condition, he offers still more devotional service and is not disturbed. One who lives in such a disposition of mind, engaged in devotional service, is the most eligible candidate for promotion to the spiritual world. In other words, such a devotee's claim for promotion to the spiritual world is assured in all circumstances.

TEXT 46

न वै सतां त्वच्चरणार्पितात्मनां
भूतेषु सर्वेष्वभिपश्यतां तव ।
भूतानि चात्मन्यपृथग्दिदृक्षतां
प्रायेण रोषोऽभिभवेद्यथा पशुम् ॥४६॥

na vai satāṁ tvac-caraṇārpitātmanāṁ
bhūteṣu sarveṣv abhipaśyatāṁ tava

bhūtāni cātmany apṛthag-didṛkṣatāṁ
prāyeṇa roṣo 'bhibhaved yathā paśum

na—not; *vai*—but; *satām*—of the devotees; *tvat-caraṇa-arpita-ātmanām*—of those who are completely surrendered at your lotus feet; *bhūteṣu*—among living entities; *sarveṣu*—all varieties; *abhipaśyatām*—perfectly seeing; *tava*—your; *bhūtāni*—living entities; *ca*—and; *ātmani*—in the Supreme; *apṛthak*—nondifferent; *didṛkṣatām*—those who see like that; *prāyeṇa*—almost always; *roṣaḥ*—anger; *abhibhavet*—takes place; *yathā*—exactly like; *paśum*—the animals.

TRANSLATION

My dear Lord, devotees who have fully dedicated their lives unto your lotus feet certainly observe your presence as Paramātmā in each and every being, and as such they do not differentiate between one living being and another. Such persons treat all living entities equally. They never become overwhelmed by anger like animals, who can see nothing without differentiation.

PURPORT

When the Supreme Personality of Godhead becomes angry or kills a demon, materially this may appear unfavorable, but spiritually it is a blissful blessing upon him. Therefore pure devotees do not make any distinction between the Lord's anger and His blessings. They see both with reference to the Lord's behavior with others and themselves. A devotee does not find fault with the behavior of the Lord in any circumstances.

TEXT 47

पृथग्धियः कर्मदृशो दुराशयाः
परोदयेनार्पितहृद्रुजोऽनिशम् ।
परान् दुरुक्तैर्वितुदन्त्यरुन्तुदा-
स्तान्मावधीद्दैववधान् भवद्विधः ॥४७॥

pṛthag-dhiyaḥ karma-dṛśo durāśayāḥ
parodayenārpita-hṛd-rujo 'niśam

parān duruktair vitudanty aruntudās
tān māvadhīd daiva-vadhān bhavad-vidhaḥ

pṛthak—differently; *dhiyaḥ*—those who are thinking; *karma*—fruitive activities; *dṛśaḥ*—observer; *durāśayāḥ*—mean minded; *para-udayena*—by others' flourishing condition; *arpita*—given up; *hṛt*—heart; *rujaḥ*—anger; *aniśam*—always; *parān*—others; *duruktaiḥ*—harsh words; *vitudanti*—gives pain; *aruntudāḥ*—by piercing words; *tān*—unto them; *mā*—not; *avadhīt*—kill; *daiva*—by providence; *vadhān*—already killed; *bhavat*—you; *vidhaḥ*—like.

TRANSLATION

Persons who observe everything with differentiation, who are simply attached to fruitive activities, who are mean minded, who are always pained to see the flourishing condition of others and who thus give distress to them by uttering harsh and piercing words have already been killed by providence. Thus there is no need for them to be killed again by an exalted personality like you.

PURPORT

Persons who are materialistic and always engaged in fruitive activities for material profit cannot endure seeing the flourishing life of others. Except for a few persons in Kṛṣṇa consciousness, the entire world is full of such envious persons, who are perpetually full of anxieties because they are attached to the material body and are without self-realization. Since their hearts are always filled with anxiety, it is understood that they have already been killed by providence. Thus Lord Śiva, as a self-realized Vaiṣṇava, was advised not to kill Dakṣa. A Vaiṣṇava is described as *para-duḥkha-duḥkhī* because although he is never distressed in any condition of life, he is distressed to see others in a distressed condition. Vaiṣṇavas, therefore, should not try to kill by any action of the body or mind, but should try to revive the Kṛṣṇa consciousness of others out of compassion for them. The Kṛṣṇa consciousness movement has been started to deliver the envious persons of the world from the clutches of *māyā*, and even though devotees are sometimes put into trouble, they push on the Kṛṣṇa consciousness movement in all tolerance. Lord Caitanya advises:

tṛṇād api sunīcena
taror api sahiṣṇunā
amāninā mānadena
kīrtanīyaḥ sadā hariḥ

"One can chant the holy name of the Lord in a humble state of mind, thinking himself lower than the straw in the street. One should be more tolerant than the tree, devoid of all sense of false prestige and ready to offer all respects to others. In such a state of mind one can chant the holy name of the Lord constantly." (*Śikṣāṣṭaka* 3)

A Vaiṣṇava should follow the examples of such Vaiṣṇavas as Haridāsa Ṭhākura, Nityānanda Prabhu and also Lord Jesus Christ. There is no need to kill anyone who has already been killed. But it should be noted herewith that a Vaiṣṇava should not tolerate the blaspheming of Viṣṇu or Vaiṣṇavas, although he should tolerate personal insults to himself.

TEXT 48

यस्मिन् यदा पुष्करनाभमायया
दुरन्तया स्पृष्टधियः पृथग्दृशः ।
कुर्वन्ति तत्र ह्यनुकम्पया कृपां
न साधवो दैवबलात्कृते क्रमम् ॥४८॥

yasmin yadā puṣkara-nābha-māyayā
durantayā spṛṣṭa-dhiyaḥ pṛthag-dṛśaḥ
kurvanti tatra hy anukampayā kṛpāṁ
na sādhavo daiva-balāt kṛte kramam

yasmin—in some place; *yadā*—when; *puṣkara-nābha-māyayā*—by the illusory energy of Puṣkaranābha, the Supreme Personality of Godhead; *durantayā*—insurmountable; *spṛṣṭa-dhiyaḥ*—bewildered; *pṛthak-dṛśaḥ*—the same persons who see differently; *kurvanti*—do; *tatra*—there; *hi*—certainly; *anukampayā*—out of compassion; *kṛpām*—mercy; *na*—never; *sādhavaḥ*—saintly persons; *daiva-balāt*—by providence; *kṛte*—being done; *kramam*—prowess.

TRANSLATION

My dear lord, if in some places materialists, who are already bewildered by the insurmountable illusory energy of the Supreme Godhead, sometimes commit offenses, a saintly person, with compassion, does not take this seriously. Knowing that they commit offenses because they are overpowered by the illusory energy, he does not show his prowess to counteract them.

PURPORT

It is said that the beauty of a *tapasvī*, or saintly person, is forgiveness. There are many instances in the spiritual history of the world in which many saintly persons, although unnecessarily harassed, did not take action, although they could have done so. Parīkṣit Mahārāja, for example, was unnecessarily cursed by a *brāhmaṇa* boy, and this was very much regretted by the boy's father, but Parīkṣit Mahārāja accepted the curse and agreed to die within a week as the *brāhmaṇa* boy desired. Parīkṣit Mahārāja was the emperor and was full in power both spiritually and materially, but out of compassion and out of respect for the *brāhmaṇa* community, he did not counteract the action of the *brāhmaṇa* boy but agreed to die within seven days. Because it was desired by Kṛṣṇa that Parīkṣit Mahārāja agree to the punishment so that the instruction of *Śrīmad-Bhāgavatam* would thus be revealed to the world, Parīkṣit Mahārāja was advised not to take action. A Vaiṣṇava is personally tolerant for the benefit of others. When he does not show his prowess, this does not mean that he is lacking in strength; rather, it indicates that he is tolerant for the welfare of the entire human society.

TEXT 49

भवांस्तु पुंसः परमस्य मायया
दुरन्तयास्पृष्टमतिः समस्तदृक् ।
तया हतात्मस्वनुकर्मचेतः-
स्वनुग्रहं कर्तुमिहार्हसि प्रभो ॥४९॥

bhavāṁs tu puṁsaḥ paramasya māyayā
durantayāspṛṣṭa-matiḥ samasta-dṛk

tayā hatātmasv anukarma-cetaḥsv
anugrahaṁ kartum ihārhasi prabho

bhavān—Your Lordship; *tu*—but; *puṁsaḥ*—of the person; *paramasya*—the supreme; *māyayā*—by the material energy; *durantayā*—of great potency; *aspṛṣṭa*—unaffected; *matiḥ*—intelligence; *samasta-dṛk*—seer or knower of everything; *tayā*—by the same illusory energy; *hata-ātmasu*—bewildered at heart; *anukarma-cetaḥsu*—whose hearts are attracted by fruitive activities; *anugraham*—mercy; *kartum*—to do; *iha*—in this case; *arhasi*—desire; *prabho*—O lord.

TRANSLATION

My dear lord, you are never bewildered by the formidable influence of the illusory energy of the Supreme Personality of Godhead. Therefore you are omniscient and should be merciful and compassionate toward those who are bewildered by the same illusory energy and are very much attached to fruitive activities.

PURPORT

A Vaiṣṇava is never bewildered by the influence of the external energy because he is engaged in the transcendental loving service of the Lord. The Lord states in *Bhagavad-gītā* (7.14):

daivī hy eṣā guṇamayī
mama māyā duratyayā
mām eva ye prapadyante
māyām etāṁ taranti te

"My divine energy consisting of the three modes of material nature is difficult to overcome. But those who have surrendered unto Me can easily cross beyond it." A Vaiṣṇava should take care of those who are bewildered by this *māyā* instead of becoming angry with them, because without a Vaiṣṇava's mercy they have no way to get out of the clutches of *māyā*. Those who have been condemned by *māyā* are rescued by the mercy of devotees.

vāñchā-kalpatarubhyaś ca
kṛpā-sindhubhya eva ca
patitānāṁ pāvanebhyo
vaiṣṇavebhyo namo namaḥ

"I offer my respectful obeisances unto all the Vaiṣṇava devotees of the Lord. They are just like desire trees who can fulfill the desires of everyone, and they are full of compassion for the fallen conditioned souls." Those who are under the influence of the illusory energy are attracted to fruitive activities, but a Vaiṣṇava preacher attracts their hearts to the Supreme Personality of Godhead, Śrī Kṛṣṇa.

TEXT 50

कुर्वध्वरस्योद्धरणं हतस्य भोः
त्वयासमाप्तस्य मनो प्रजापतेः ।
न यत्र भागं तव भागिनो ददुः
कुयाजिनो येन मखो निनीयते ॥५०॥

kurv adhvarasyoddharaṇaṁ hatasya bhoḥ
tvayāsamāptasya mano prajāpateḥ
na yatra bhāgaṁ tava bhāgino daduḥ
kuyājino yena makho ninīyate

kuru—just execute; *adhvarasya*—of the sacrifice; *uddharaṇam*—complete regularly; *hatasya*—killed; *bhoḥ*—O; *tvayā*—by you; *asamāptasya*—of the unfinished sacrifice; *mano*—O Lord Śiva; *prajāpateḥ*—of Mahārāja Dakṣa; *na*—not; *yatra*—where; *bhāgam*—share; *tava*—your; *bhāginaḥ*—deserving to take the share; *daduḥ*—did not give; *ku-yājinaḥ*—bad priests; *yena*—by the bestower; *makhaḥ*—sacrifice; *ninīyate*—gets the result.

TRANSLATION

My dear Lord Śiva, you are a shareholder of a portion of the sacrifice, and you are the giver of the result. The bad priests did not deliver your share, and therefore you destroyed everything,

and the sacrifice remains unfinished. Now you can do the needful and take your rightful share.

TEXT 51

जीवताद्यजमानोऽयं प्रपद्येताक्षिणी भगः ।
भृगोः श्मश्रूणि रोहन्तु पूष्णो दन्ताश्च पूर्ववत् ॥५१॥

jīvatād yajamāno 'yaṁ
prapadyetākṣiṇī bhagaḥ
bhṛgoḥ śmaśrūṇi rohantu
pūṣṇo dantāś ca pūrvavat

jīvatāt—let him be alive; *yajamānaḥ*—the performer of the sacrifice (Dakṣa); *ayam*—this; *prapadyeta*—let him get back; *akṣiṇī*—by the eyes; *bhagaḥ*—Bhagadeva; *bhṛgoḥ*—of the sage Bhṛgu; *śmaśrūṇi*—mustache; *rohantu*—may grow again; *pūṣṇaḥ*—of Pūṣādeva; *dantāḥ*—the chain of teeth; *ca*—and; *pūrva-vat*—like before.

TRANSLATION

My dear lord, by your mercy the performer of the sacrifice (King Dakṣa) may get back his life, Bhaga may get back his eyes, Bhṛgu his mustache, and Pūṣā his teeth.

TEXT 52

देवानां भग्नगात्राणामृत्विजां चायुधाश्मभिः ।
भवतानुगृहीतानामाशु मन्योऽस्त्वनातुरम् ॥५२॥

devānāṁ bhagna-gātrāṇām
ṛtvijāṁ cāyudhāśmabhiḥ
bhavatānugṛhītānām
āśu manyo 'stv anāturam

devānām—of the demigods; *bhagna-gātrāṇām*—whose limbs are badly broken; *ṛtvijām*—of the priests; *ca*—and; *āyudha-aśmabhiḥ*—by weapons and by stones; *bhavatā*—by you; *anugṛhītānām*—being favored; *āśu*—at once; *manyo*—O Lord Śiva (in an angry mood); *astu*—let there be; *anāturam*—recovery from injuries.

TRANSLATION

O Lord Śiva, may the demigods and the priests whose limbs have been broken by your soldiers recover from the injuries by your grace.

TEXT 53

एष ते रुद्र भागोऽस्तु यदुच्छिष्टोऽध्वरस्य वै ।
यज्ञस्ते रुद्रभागेन कल्पतामद्य यज्ञहन् ॥५३॥

eṣa te rudra bhāgo 'stu
yad-ucchiṣṭo 'dhvarasya vai
yajñas te rudra bhāgena
kalpatām adya yajña-han

eṣaḥ—this; *te*—your; *rudra*—O Lord Śiva; *bhāgaḥ*—portion; *astu*—let it be; *yat*—whatever; *ucchiṣṭaḥ*—is the remainder; *adhvarasya*—of the sacrifice; *vai*—indeed; *yajñaḥ*—the sacrifice; *te*—your; *rudra*—O Rudra; *bhāgena*—by the portion; *kalpatām*—may be completed; *adya*—today; *yajña-han*—O destroyer of the sacrifice.

TRANSLATION

O destroyer of the sacrifice, please take your portion of the sacrifice and let the sacrifice be completed by your grace.

PURPORT

A sacrifice is a ceremony performed to please the Supreme Personality of Godhead. In the *Śrīmad-Bhāgavatam*, First Canto, Second Chapter, it is stated that everyone should try to understand whether the Supreme Personality of Godhead is satisfied by his activity. In other words, the aim of our activities should be to satisfy the Supreme Personality of Godhead. Just as in an office it is the duty of the worker to see that the proprietor or the master is satisfied, so everyone's duty is to see whether the Supreme Personality of Godhead is satisfied by one's activity. Activities to satisfy the Supreme Godhead are prescribed in the Vedic literature, and execution of such activities is called *yajña.* In other words, acting on behalf of the Supreme Lord is called *yajña.* One should know very well that any activity besides *yajña* is the cause of material bondage. That is explained in *Bhagavad-gītā* (3.9): *yajñārthāt karmaṇo 'nyatra loko 'yaṁ karma-bandhanaḥ. Karma-bandhanaḥ* means that if we do not work for the satisfaction of the Supreme Lord, Viṣṇu, then the reaction of our work will bind us. One should not work for his own sense gratification. Everyone should work for the satisfaction of God. That is called *yajña.*

After the *yajña* was performed by Dakṣa, all the demigods expected *prasāda,* the remnants of foodstuffs offered to Viṣṇu. Lord Śiva is one of the demigods, so naturally he also expected his share of the *prasāda* from the *yajña.* But Dakṣa, out of his envy of Lord Śiva, neither invited Śiva to participate in the *yajña* nor gave him his share after the offering. But after the destruction of the *yajña* arena by the followers of Lord Śiva, Lord Brahmā pacified him and assured him that he would get his share of *prasāda.* Thus he was requested to rectify whatever destruction was caused by his followers.

In *Bhagavad-gītā* (3.11) it is said that all the demigods are satisfied when one performs *yajña.* Because the demigods expect *prasāda* from *yajñas, yajña* must be performed. Those who engage in sense gratificatory, materialistic activities must perform *yajña,* otherwise they will be implicated. Thus Dakṣa, being the father of mankind, was performing *yajña,* and Lord Śiva expected his share. But since Śiva was not invited, there was trouble. By the mediation of Lord Brahmā, however, everything was settled satisfactorily.

The performance of *yajña* is a very difficult task because all the demigods must be invited to participate in the *yajña.* In this Kali-yuga it is not possible to perform such costly sacrifices, nor is it possible to invite the demigods to participate. Therefore in this age it is recommended, *yajñaiḥ saṅkīrtana-prāyair yajanti hi sumedhasaḥ* (*Bhāg.* 11.5.32). Those who are intelligent should know that in the Kali-yuga there is no possibility of performing the Vedic sacrifices. But unless one pleases the demigods, there will be no regulated seasonal activities or rainfall. Everything is controlled by the demigods. Under the circumstances, in this age, in order to keep the balance of social peace and prosperity, all intelligent men should execute the performance of *saṅkīrtana-yajña* by chanting the holy names Hare Kṛṣṇa, Hare Kṛṣṇa, Kṛṣṇa Kṛṣṇa, Hare Hare/ Hare Rāma, Hare Rāma, Rāma Rāma, Hare Hare. One should invite people, chant Hare Kṛṣṇa, and then distribute *prasāda.* This *yajña* will satisfy all the demigods, and thus there will be peace and prosperity in the world. Another difficulty in performing the Vedic rituals is that if one fails to satisfy even one demigod out of the many hundreds of thousands of demigods, just as Dakṣa failed to satisfy Lord Śiva, there will be disaster. But in this age the performance of sacrifice has been simplified. One can chant Hare Kṛṣṇa, and by pleasing Kṛṣṇa one can satisfy all the demigods automatically.

Thus end the Bhaktivedanta purports of the Fourth Canto, Sixth Chapter, of the Śrīmad-Bhāgavatam, *entitled "Brahmā Satisfies Lord Śiva."*

CHAPTER SEVEN

The Sacrifice Performed by Dakṣa

TEXT 1

मैत्रेय उवाच

इत्यजेनानुनीतेन भवेन परितुष्यता ।
अभ्यधायि महाबाहो प्रहस्य श्रूयतामिति ॥ १ ॥

maitreya uvāca
ity ajenānunītena
bhavena parituṣyatā
abhyadhāyi mahā-bāho
prahasya śrūyatām iti

maitreyaḥ—Maitreya; *uvāca*—said; *iti*—thus; *ajena*—by Lord Brahmā; *anunītena*—pacified; *bhavena*—by Lord Śiva; *parituṣyatā*—fully satisfied; *abhyadhāyi*—said; *mahā-bāho*—O Vidura; *prahasya*—smiling; *śrūyatām*—listen; *iti*—thus.

TRANSLATION

The sage Maitreya said: O mighty-armed Vidura, Lord Śiva, being thus pacified by the words of Lord Brahmā, spoke as follows in answer to Lord Brahmā's request.

TEXT 2

महादेव उवाच

नाघं प्रजेश बालानां वर्णये नानुचिन्तये ।
देवमायाभिभूतानां दण्डस्तत्र धृतो मया ॥ २ ॥

mahādeva uvāca
nāghaṁ prajeśa bālānāṁ
varṇaye nānucintaye
deva-māyābhibhūtānāṁ
daṇḍas tatra dhṛto mayā

mahādevaḥ—Lord Śiva; *uvāca*—said; *na*—not; *agham*—offense; *prajā-īśa*—O lord of created beings; *bālānām*—of the children; *varṇaye*—I regard; *na*—not; *anucintaye*—I consider; *deva-māyā*—the external energy of the Lord; *abhibhūtānām*—of those deluded by; *daṇḍaḥ*—rod; *tatra*—there; *dhṛtaḥ*—used; *mayā*—by me.

TRANSLATION

Lord Śiva said: My dear father, Brahmā, I do not mind the offenses created by the demigods. Because these demigods are childish and less intelligent, I do not take a serious view of their offenses, and I have punished them only in order to right them.

PURPORT

There are two types of punishment. One is that which a conqueror imposes on an enemy, and the other is like that a father imposes on his son. There is a gulf of difference between these two kinds of punishment. Lord Śiva is by nature a Vaiṣṇava, a great devotee, and his name in this connection is Āśutoṣa. He is always satisfied, and therefore he did not become angry as if he were an enemy. He is not inimical to any living entity; rather, he always wishes the welfare of all. Whenever he chastises a person, it is just like a father's punishment of his son. Lord Śiva is like a father because he never takes seriously any offense by any living entities, especially the demigods.

TEXT 3

प्रजापतेर्दग्धशीर्ष्णो भवत्वजमुखं शिरः ।
मित्रस्य चक्षुषेक्षेत भागं स्वं बर्हिषो भगः ॥ ३ ॥

prajāpater dagdha-śīrṣṇo
bhavatv aja-mukhaṁ śiraḥ

mitrasya cakṣuṣekṣeta
bhāgaṁ svaṁ barhiṣo bhagaḥ

prajāpateḥ—of Prajāpati Dakṣa; *dagdha-śīrṣṇaḥ*—whose head has been burned to ashes; *bhavatu*—let there be; *aja-mukham*—with the face of a goat; *śiraḥ*—a head; *mitrasya*—of Mitra; *cakṣuṣā*—through the eyes; *īkṣeta*—may see; *bhāgam*—share; *svam*—his own; *barhiṣaḥ*—of the sacrifice; *bhagaḥ*—Bhaga.

TRANSLATION

Lord Śiva continued: Since the head of Dakṣa has already been burned to ashes, he will have the head of a goat. The demigod known as Bhaga will be able to see his share of sacrifice through the eyes of Mitra.

TEXT 4

पूषा तु यजमानस्य दद्भिर्जक्षतु पिष्टभुक् ।
देवाः प्रकृतसर्वाङ्गा ये म उच्छेषणं ददुः ॥ ४ ॥

pūṣā tu yajamānasya
dadbhir jakṣatu piṣṭa-bhuk
devāḥ prakṛta-sarvāṅgā
ye ma uccheṣaṇaṁ daduḥ

pūṣā—Pūṣā; *tu*—but; *yajamānasya*—of the performer of the sacrifice; *dadbhiḥ*—with the teeth; *jakṣatu*—chew; *piṣṭa-bhuk*—eating flour; *devāḥ*—the demigods; *prakṛta*—made; *sarva-aṅgāḥ*—complete; *ye*—who; *me*—unto me; *uccheṣaṇam*—a share of the sacrifice; *daduḥ*—gave.

TRANSLATION

The demigod Pūṣā will be able to chew only through the teeth of his disciples, and if alone, he will have to satisfy himself by eating dough made from chickpea flour. But the demigods who have agreed to give me my share of the sacrifice will recover from all their injuries.

PURPORT

The demigod Pūṣā became dependent on his disciples for chewing. Otherwise he was allowed to swallow only dough made of chickpea flour. Thus his punishment continued. He could not use his teeth for eating, since he had laughed at Lord Śiva, deriding him by showing his teeth. In other words, it was not appropriate for him to have teeth, for he had used them against Lord Śiva.

TEXT 5

बाहुभ्यामश्विनोः पूष्णो हस्ताभ्यां कृतबाहवः ।
भवन्त्वध्वर्यवश्चान्ये बस्तश्मश्रुर्भृगुर्भवेत् ॥ ५ ॥

bāhubhyām aśvinoḥ pūṣṇo
hastābhyāṁ kṛta-bāhavaḥ
bhavantv adhvaryavaś cānye
basta-śmaśrur bhṛgur bhavet

bāhubhyām—with two arms; *aśvinoḥ*—of Aśvinī-kumāra; *pūṣṇaḥ*—of Pūṣā; *hastābhyām*—with two hands; *kṛta-bāhavaḥ*—those in need of arms; *bhavantu*—they will have to; *adhvaryavaḥ*—the priests; *ca*—and; *anye*—others; *basta-śmaśruḥ*—the beard of the goat; *bhṛguḥ*—Bhṛgu; *bhavet*—he may have.

TRANSLATION

Those who have had their arms cut off will have to work with the arms of Aśvinī-kumāra, and those whose hands were cut off will have to do their work with the hands of Pūṣā. The priests will also have to act in that manner. As for Bhṛgu, he will have the beard from the goat's head.

PURPORT

Bhṛgu Muni, a great supporter of Dakṣa, was awarded the beard of the goat's head which was substituted for the head of Dakṣa. It appears from the exchange of Dakṣa's head that the modern scientific theory that the brain substance is the cause of all intelligent work is not valid. The brain substance of Dakṣa and that of a goat are different, but Dakṣa still acted like himself, even though his head was replaced by that of a goat. The conclusion is that it is the particular consciousness of an individual soul which acts. The brain substance is only an instrument which has nothing to do with real intelligence. The real intelligence, mind and consciousness are part of the particular individual soul. It will be found in the verses ahead that after Dakṣa's head was replaced by the goat's head, he was as intelligent as he had previously been. He prayed very nicely to satisfy Lord Śiva and Lord Viṣṇu, which is not possible for a goat to do. Therefore it is definitely concluded that the brain substance is not the center of intelligence; it is the consciousness of a particular soul that works intelligently. The whole movement of Kṛṣṇa consciousness is to purify the consciousness. It doesn't matter what kind of brain one has because if he simply transfers his consciousness from matter to Kṛṣṇa, his life becomes successful. It is confirmed by the Lord Himself in *Bhagavad-gītā* that anyone who takes up Kṛṣṇa consciousness achieves the highest perfection of life, regardless of whatever abominable condition of life he may have fallen into. Specifically, anyone in Kṛṣṇa consciousness goes back to Godhead, back to home, on leaving his present material body.

TEXT 6

मैत्रेय उवाच

तदा सर्वाणि भूतानि श्रुत्वा मीढुष्टमोदितम् ।
परितुष्टात्मभिस्तात साधु साध्वित्यथाब्रुवन् ॥ ६ ॥

maitreya uvāca
tadā sarvāṇi bhūtāni
śrutvā mīḍhuṣṭamoditam
rituṣṭātmabhis tāta
sādhu sādhv ity athābruvan

maitreyaḥ—the sage Maitreya; *uvāca*—said; *tadā*—at that time; *sarvāṇi*—all; *bhūtāni*—personalities; *śrutvā*—after hearing; *mīḍhuḥ-tama*—the best of the benedictors (Lord Śiva); *uditam*—spoken by; *arituṣṭa*—being satisfied; *ātmabhiḥ*—by heart and soul; *tāta*—my dear Vidura; *sādhu sādhu*—well done, well done; *iti*—thus; *atha abruvan*—as we have said.

TRANSLATION

The great sage Maitreya said: My dear Vidura, all the personalities present were very much satisfied in heart and soul upon hearing the words of Lord Śiva, who is the best among the benedictors.

PURPORT

In this verse Lord Śiva is described as *mīḍhuṣṭama*, the best of the benedictors. He is also known as Āśutoṣa, which indicates that he is very quickly satisfied and very quickly angered. It is said in *Bhagavad-gītā* that less intelligent persons go to the demigods for material benedictions. In this connection, people generally go to Lord Śiva, and because he is always quickly satisfied and gives benedictions to his devotees without consideration, he is called *mīḍhuṣṭama*, or the best of the benedictors. Materialistic persons are always anxious to get material profit, but they are not serious about spiritual profit.

Sometimes, of course, it so happens that Lord Śiva becomes the best benedictor in spiritual life. It is said that once a poor *brāhmaṇa* worshiped Lord Śiva for a benediction, and Lord Śiva advised the devotee to go to see Sanātana Gosvāmī. The devotee went to Sanātana Gosvāmī and informed him that Lord Śiva had advised him to seek out the best benediction from him (Sanātana). Sanātana had a touchstone with him, which he kept with the garbage. On the request of the poor *brāhmaṇa*, Sanātana Gosvāmī gave him the touchstone, and the *brāhmaṇa* was very happy to have it. He now could get as much gold as he desired simply by touching the touchstone to iron. But after he left Sanātana, he thought, "If a touchstone is the best benediction, why has Sanātana Gosvāmī kept it with the garbage?" He therefore returned and asked Sanātana Gosvāmī, "Sir, if this is the best benediction, why did you keep it with the garbage?" Sanātana Gosvāmī then informed him, "Actually, this is not the best benediction. But are you prepared to take the best benediction from me?" The *brāhmaṇa* said, "Yes, sir. Lord Śiva has sent me to you for the best benediction." Then Sanātana Gosvāmī asked him to throw the touchstone in the water nearby and then come back. The poor *brāhmaṇa* did so, and when he returned, Sanātana Gosvāmī initiated him with the Hare Kṛṣṇa *mantra*. Thus by the benediction of Lord Śiva the *brāhmaṇa* got the association of the best devotee of Lord Kṛṣṇa and was thus initiated in the *mahā-mantra,* Hare Kṛṣṇa, Hare Kṛṣṇa, Kṛṣṇa Kṛṣṇa, Hare Hare/ Hare Rāma, Hare Rāma, Rāma Rāma, Hare Hare.

TEXT 7

ततो मीढ्वांसमामन्त्र्य शुनासीराः सहर्षिभिः ।
भूयस्तद्देवयजनं समीढ्वद्वेधसो ययुः ॥ ७ ॥

tato mīḍhvāṁsam āmantrya
śunāsīrāḥ saharṣibhiḥ
bhūyas tad deva-yajanaṁ
sa-mīḍhvad-vedhaso yayuḥ

tataḥ—thereafter; *mīḍhvāṁsam*—Lord Śiva; *āmantrya*—inviting; *śunāsīrāḥ*—the demigods headed by King Indra; *saha ṛṣibhiḥ*—with all the great sages, headed by Bhṛgu; *bhūyaḥ*—again; *tat*—that; *deva-yajanam*—place where the demigods are worshiped; *sa-mīḍhvat*—with Lord Śiva; *vedhasaḥ*—with Lord Brahmā; *yayuḥ*—went.

TRANSLATION

Thereafter, Bhṛgu, the chief of the great sages, invited Lord Śiva to come to the sacrificial arena. Thus the demigods, accompanied by the sages, Lord Śiva, and Lord Brahmā, all went to the place where the great sacrifice was being performed.

PURPORT

The whole sacrifice arranged by King Dakṣa had been disturbed by Lord Śiva. Therefore all the demigods present there, along with Lord Brahmā and the great sages, specifically requested Lord Śiva to come and revive the sacrificial fire. There is a common phrase, *śiva-hīna-yajña:* "Any sacrifice without the presence of Lord Śiva is baffled." Lord Viṣṇu is Yajñeśvara, the Supreme Personality in the matter of sacrifice, yet in each *yajña* it is necessary for all the demigods, headed by Lord Brahmā and Lord Śiva, to be present.

TEXT 8

विधाय कार्त्स्न्येन च तद्यदाह भगवान् भवः ।
संदधुः कस्य कायेन सवनीयपशोः शिरः ॥ ८ ॥

vidhāya kārtsnyena ca tad
yad āha bhagavān bhavaḥ
sandadhuḥ kasya kāyena
savanīya-paśoḥ śiraḥ

vidhāya—executing; *kārtsnyena*—all in all; *ca*—also; *tat*—that; *yat*—which; *āha*—was said; *bhagavān*—the Lord; *bhavaḥ*—Śiva; *sandadhuḥ*—executed; *kasya*—of the living (Dakṣa); *kāyena*—with the body; *savanīya*—meant for sacrifice; *paśoḥ*—of the animal; *śiraḥ*—head.

TRANSLATION

After everything was executed exactly as directed by Lord Śiva, Dakṣa's body was joined to the head of the animal meant to be killed in the sacrifice.

PURPORT

This time, all the demigods and great sages were very careful not to irritate Lord Śiva. Therefore whatever he asked was done. It is specifically said here that Dakṣa's body was joined to the head of an animal (a goat).

TEXT 9

संधीयमाने शिरसि दक्षो रुद्राभिवीक्षितः ।
सद्यः सुप्त इवोत्तस्थौ ददृशे चाग्रतो मृडम् ॥ ९ ॥

sandhīyamāne śirasi
dakṣo rudrābhivīkṣitaḥ
sadyaḥ supta ivottasthau
dadṛśe cāgrato mṛḍam

sandhīyamāne—being executed; *śirasi*—by the head; *dakṣaḥ*—King Dakṣa; *rudra-abhivīkṣitaḥ*—having been seen by Rudra (Lord Śiva);

sadyaḥ—immediately; *supte*—sleeping; *iva*—like; *uttasthau*—awakened; *dadṛśe*—saw; *ca*—also; *agrataḥ*—in front; *mṛḍam*—Lord Śiva.

TRANSLATION

When the animal's head was fixed on the body of King Dakṣa, Dakṣa was immediately brought to consciousness, and as he awakened from sleep, the King saw Lord Śiva standing before him.

PURPORT

The example given here is that Dakṣa got up as if he were awakened from deep sleep. In Sanskrit this is called *supta ivottasthau.* The meaning is that after a man awakens from sleep, he immediately remembers all the duties which he must execute. Dakṣa was killed, and his head was taken away and burned to ashes. His body was lying dead, but by the grace of Lord Śiva, as soon as the head of a goat was joined to the body, Dakṣa came back to consciousness again. This indicates that consciousness is also individual. Dakṣa actually took another body when he took on the head of a goat, but because consciousness is individual, his consciousness remained the same although his bodily condition changed. Thus bodily construction has nothing to do with the development of consciousness. Consciousness is carried with the transmigration of the soul. There are many instances of this in Vedic history, such as the case of Mahārāja Bharata. After quitting his body as a king, Mahārāja Bharata was transferred to the body of a deer, but he retained the same consciousness. He knew that although formerly he was King Bharata, he had been transferred to the body of a deer because of his absorption in thinking of a deer at the time of his death. In spite of his having the body of a deer, however, his consciousness was as good as it was in the body of King Bharata. The arrangement by the Lord is so nice that if a person's consciousness is turned into Kṛṣṇa consciousness, there is no doubt that in his next life he will be a great devotee of Kṛṣṇa, even if he is offered a different type of body.

TEXT 10

तदा वृषध्वजद्वेषकलिलात्मा प्रजापतिः ।
शिवावलोकादभवच्छरद्ध्रद इवामलः ॥१०॥

tadā vṛṣadhvaja-dveṣa-
kalilātmā prajāpatiḥ
śivāvalokād abhavac
charad-dhrada ivāmalaḥ

tadā—at that time; *vṛṣa-dhvaja*—Lord Śiva, who rides on a bull; *dveṣa*—envy; *kalila-ātmā*—polluted heart; *prajāpatiḥ*—King Dakṣa; *śiva*—Lord Śiva; *avalokāt*—by seeing him; *abhavat*—became; *śarat*—in the autumn; *hradaḥ*—lake; *iva*—like; *amalaḥ*—cleansed.

TRANSLATION

At that time, when Dakṣa saw Lord Śiva, who rides upon a bull, his heart, which was polluted by envy of Lord Śiva, was immediately cleansed, just as the water in a lake is cleansed by autumn rains.

PURPORT

Here is an example of why Lord Śiva is called auspicious. If anyone sees Lord Śiva with devotion and reverence, his heart is immediately cleansed. King Dakṣa was polluted by envy of Lord Śiva, and yet by seeing him with a little love and devotion, his heart immediately became cleansed. In the rainy season, the reservoirs of water become dirty and muddy, but as soon as the autumn rain comes, all the water immediately becomes clear and transparent. Similarly, although Dakṣa's heart was impure because of his having slandered Lord Śiva, for which he was severely punished, Dakṣa now came to consciousness, and just by seeing Lord Śiva with veneration and respect, he became immediately purified.

TEXT 11

भवस्तवाय कृतधीर्नाशक्नोदनुरागतः ।
औत्कण्ठ्याद्बाष्पकलया सम्परेतां सुतां स्मरन् ॥ ११ ॥

bhava-stavāya kṛta-dhīr
nāśaknod anurāgataḥ
autkaṇṭhyād bāṣpa-kalayā
samparetāṁ sutāṁ smaran

bhava-stavāya—for praying to Lord Śiva; *kṛta-dhīḥ*—although decided; *na*—never; *aśaknot*—was able; *anurāgataḥ*—by feeling; *autkaṇṭhyāt*—because of eagerness; *bāṣpa-kalayā*—with tears in the eyes; *samparetām*—dead; *sutām*—daughter; *smaran*—remembering.

TRANSLATION

King Dakṣa wanted to offer prayers to Lord Śiva, but as he remembered the ill-fated death of his daughter Satī, his eyes filled with tears, and in bereavement his voice choked up, and he could not say anything.

TEXT 12

कृच्छ्रात्संस्तभ्य च मनः प्रेमविह्वलितः सुधीः ।
शशंस निर्व्यलीकेन भावेनेशं प्रजापतिः ॥१२॥

kṛcchrāt saṁstabhya ca manaḥ
prema-vihvalitaḥ sudhīḥ
śaśaṁsa nirvyalīkena
bhāveneśaṁ prajāpatiḥ

kṛcchrāt—with great endeavor; *saṁstabhya*—pacifying; *ca*—also; *manaḥ*—mind; *prema-vihvalitaḥ*—bewildered by love and affection; *su-dhīḥ*—one who has come to his real senses; *śaśaṁsa*—praised; *nirvyalīkena*—without duplicity, or with great love; *bhāvena*—in feeling; *īśam*—to Lord Śiva; *prajāpatiḥ*—King Dakṣa.

TRANSLATION

At this time, King Dakṣa, afflicted by love and affection, was very much awakened to his real senses. With great endeavor, he pacified his mind, checked his feelings, and with pure consciousness began to offer prayers to Lord Śiva.

TEXT 13

दक्ष उवाच

भूयाननुग्रह अहो भवता कृतो मे
दण्डस्त्वया मयि भृतो यदपि प्रलब्धः ।

न ब्रह्मबन्धुषु च वां भगवन्नवज्ञा
तुभ्यं हरेश्च कुत एव धृतव्रतेषु ॥१३॥

dakṣa uvāca
bhūyān anugraha aho bhavatā kṛto me
daṇḍas tvayā mayi bhṛto yad api pralabdhaḥ
na brahma-bandhuṣu ca vāṁ bhagavann avajñā
tubhyaṁ hareś ca kuta eva dhṛta-vrateṣu

dakṣaḥ—King Dakṣa; *uvāca*—said; *bhūyān*—very great; *anugrahaḥ*—favor; *aho*—alas; *bhavatā*—by you; *kṛtaḥ*—done; *me*—upon me; *daṇḍaḥ*—punishment; *tvayā*—by you; *mayi*—unto me; *bhṛtaḥ*—done; *yat api*—although; *pralabdhaḥ*—defeated; *na*—neither; *brahma-bandhuṣu*—unto an unqualified *brāhmaṇa; ca*—also; *vām*—both of you; *bhagavan*—my lord; *avajñā*—negligence; *tubhyam*—of you; *hareḥ ca*—of Lord Viṣṇu; *kutaḥ*—where; *eva*—certainly; *dhṛta-vrateṣu*—one who is engaged in the performance of sacrifice.

TRANSLATION

King Dakṣa said: My dear Lord Śiva, I committed a great offense against you, but you are so kind that instead of withdrawing your mercy, you have done me a great favor by punishing me. You and Lord Viṣṇu never neglect even useless, unqualified brāhmaṇas. Why, then, should you neglect me, who am engaged in performing sacrifices?

PURPORT

Although Dakṣa felt defeated, he knew that his punishment was simply the great mercy of Lord Śiva. He remembered that Lord Śiva and Lord Viṣṇu are never neglectful of the *brāhmaṇas*, even though the *brāhmaṇas* are sometimes unqualified. According to Vedic civilization, a descendant of a *brāhmaṇa* family should never be heavily punished. This was exemplified in Arjuna's treatment of Aśvatthāmā. Aśvatthāmā was the son of a great *brāhmaṇa*, Droṇācārya, and in spite of his having committed the great offense of killing all the sleeping sons of the Pāṇḍavas, for which he was condemned even by Lord Kṛṣṇa, Arjuna excused him by not killing him because he happened to be the son of a *brāhmaṇa.* The word *brahma-bandhuṣu* used here is significant. *Brahma-bandhu* means a person who is born of a *brāhmaṇa* father but whose activities are not up to the standard of the *brāhmaṇas.* Such a person is not a *brāhmaṇa* but a *brahma-bandhu.* Dakṣa proved himself to be a *brahma-bandhu.* He was born of a great *brāhmaṇa* father, Lord Brahmā, but his treatment of Lord Śiva was not exactly brahminical; therefore he admitted that he was not a perfect *brāhmaṇa.* Lord Śiva and Lord Viṣṇu, however, are affectionate even to an imperfect *brāhmaṇa.* Lord Śiva punished Dakṣa not as one does his enemy; rather, he punished Dakṣa just to bring him to his senses, so that he would know that he had done wrong. Dakṣa could understand this, and he acknowledged the great mercy of Lord Kṛṣṇa and Lord Śiva towards the fallen *brāhmaṇas,* including even himself. Although he was fallen, his vow was to execute the sacrifice, as is the duty of *brāhmaṇas,* and thus he began his prayers to Lord Śiva.

TEXT 14

विद्यातपोव्रतधरान् मुखतः स्म विप्रान्
ब्रह्मात्मतत्त्वमवितुं प्रथमं त्वमस्राक् ।
तद्ब्राह्मणान् परम सर्वविपत्सु पासि
पालः पशूनिव विभो प्रगृहीतदण्डः ॥१४॥

vidyā-tapo-vrata-dharān mukhataḥ sma viprān
brahmātma-tattvam avituṁ prathamaṁ tvam asrāk
tad brāhmaṇān parama sarva-vipatsu pāsi
pālaḥ paśūn iva vibho pragṛhīta-daṇḍaḥ

vidyā—learning; *tapaḥ*—austerities; *vrata*—vows; *dharān*—the followers; *mukhataḥ*—from the mouth; *sma*—was; *viprān*—the *brāhmaṇas; brahmā*—Lord Brahmā; *ātma-tattvam*—self-realization; *avitum*—to disseminate; *prathamam*—first; *tvam*—you; *asrāk*—created; *tat*—therefore; *brāhmaṇān*—the *brāhmaṇas; parama*—O great one; *sarva*—all; *vipatsu*—in dangers; *pāsi*—you protect; *pālaḥ*—like the protector; *paśūn*—the animals; *iva*—like; *vibho*—O great one; *pragṛhīta*—taking in hand; *daṇḍaḥ*—a stick.

TRANSLATION

My dear great and powerful Lord Śiva, you were created first from the mouth of Lord Brahmā in order to protect the brāhmaṇas in pursuing education, austerities, vows and self-realization. As protector of the brāhmaṇas, you always protect the regulative principles they follow, just as a cowherd boy keeps a stick in his hand to give protection to the cows.

PURPORT

The specific function of a human being in society, irrespective of his social status, is to practice control of the mind and senses by observing the regulative principles enjoined in the Vedic *śāstras*. Lord Śiva is called *paśupati* because he protects the living entities in their developed consciousness so that they may follow the Vedic system of *varṇa* and *āśrama*. The word *paśu* refers to the animal as well as to the human entity. It is stated here that Lord Śiva is always interested in protecting the animals and the animalistic living entities, who are not very advanced in the spiritual sense. It is also stated that the *brāhmaṇas* are produced from the mouth of the Supreme Lord. We should always remember that Lord Śiva is being addressed as the representative of the Supreme Lord, Viṣṇu. In the Vedic literature it is described that the *brāhmaṇas* are born from the mouth of the universal form of Viṣṇu, the *kṣatriyas* are born from His arms, the *vaiśyas* from His abdomen or waist, and the *śūdras* from His legs. In the formation of a body, the head is the principal factor. The *brāhmaṇas* are born from the mouth of the Supreme Personality of Godhead in order to accept charity for worship of Viṣṇu and to spread Vedic knowledge. Lord Śiva is known as *paśupati*, the protector of the *brāhmaṇas* and other living entities. He protects them from the attacks of non-*brāhmaṇas*, or uncultured persons who are against the self-realization process.

Another feature of this word is that persons who are simply attached to the ritualistic portion of the *Vedas* and do not understand the situation of the Supreme Personality of Godhead are not any more advanced than animals. In the beginning of *Śrīmad-Bhāgavatam* it is confirmed that even though one performs the rituals of the *Vedas*, if he does not develop a sense of Kṛṣṇa consciousness, then all his labor in performing Vedic rituals is considered to be simply a waste of time. Lord Śiva's aim in destroying the Dakṣa *yajña* was to punish Dakṣa because by neglecting him (Lord Śiva), Dakṣa was committing a great offense. Lord Śiva's punishment was just like that of a cowherd boy, who keeps a stick to frighten his animals. It is commonly said that to give protection to animals, a stick is needed because animals cannot reason and argue. Their reasoning and argument is *argumentum ad baculum;* unless there is a rod, they do not obey. Force is required for the animalistic class of men, whereas those who are advanced are convinced by reasons, arguments and scriptural authority. Persons who are simply attached to Vedic rituals, without further advancement of devotional service, or Kṛṣṇa consciousness, are almost like animals, and Lord Śiva is in charge of giving them protection and sometimes punishing them, as he punished Dakṣa.

TEXT 15

योऽसौ मयाविदिततत्त्वदृशा सभायां
क्षिप्तो दुरुक्तिविशिखैर्विगणय्य तन्माम् ।
अर्वाक् पतन्तमर्हत्तमनिन्दयापाद्
दृष्ट्यार्द्रया स भगवान् स्वकृतेन तुष्येत् ॥१५॥

yo 'sau mayāvidita-tattva-dṛśā sabhāyāṁ
kṣipto durukti-viśikhair vigaṇayya tan mām
arvāk patantam arhattama-nindayāpād
dṛṣṭyārdrayā sa bhagavān sva-kṛtena tuṣyet

yaḥ—who; *asau*—that; *mayā*—by me; *avidita-tattva*—without knowing the actual fact; *dṛśā*—by experience; *sabhāyām*—in the assembly; *kṣiptaḥ*—was abused; *durukti*—unkind words; *viśikhaiḥ*—by the arrows of; *vigaṇayya*—taking no notice of; *tat*—that; *mām*—me; *arvāk*—downwards; *patantam*—gliding down to hell; *arhat-tama*—the most respectable; *nindayā*—by defamation; *apāt*—saved; *dṛṣṭyā*—seeing; *ārdrayā*—out of compassion; *saḥ*—that; *bhagavān*—Your Lordship; *sva-kṛtena*—by your own mercy; *tuṣyet*—be satisfied.

TRANSLATION

I did not know your full glories. For this reason, I threw arrows of sharp words at you in the open assembly, although you did not

take them into account. I was going down to hell because of my disobedience to you, who are the most respectable personality, but you took compassion upon me and saved me by awarding punishment. I request that you be pleased by your own mercy, since I cannot satisfy you by my words.

PURPORT

As usual, a devotee in an adverse condition of life accepts such a condition to be the mercy of the Lord. Factually, the insulting words used by Dakṣa against Lord Śiva were enough to have him thrown perpetually into a hellish life. But Lord Śiva, being kind toward him, awarded him punishment to neutralize the offense. King Dakṣa realized this and, feeling obliged for Lord Śiva's magnanimous behavior, wanted to show his gratitude. Sometimes a father punishes his child, and when the child is grown up and comes to his senses, he understands that the father's punishment was not actually punishment but mercy. Similarly, Dakṣa appreciated that the punishment offered to him by Lord Śiva was a manifestation of Lord Śiva's mercy. That is the symptom of a person making progress on the path of Kṛṣṇa consciousness. It is said that a devotee in Kṛṣṇa consciousness never takes any miserable condition of life to be condemnation by the Supreme Personality of Godhead. He accepts the miserable condition to be the grace of the Lord. He thinks, "I would have been punished or put into a more dangerous condition of life due to my past misdeeds, but the Lord has protected me. Thus I have received only a little punishment as token execution of the law of *karma.*" Thinking of His grace in that way, a devotee always surrenders to the Supreme Personality of Godhead more and more seriously and is not disturbed by such so-called punishment.

TEXT 16

मैत्रेय उवाच

क्षमाप्यैवं स मीढ्वांसं ब्रह्मणा चानुमन्त्रितः ।
कर्म सन्तानयामास सोपाध्यायर्त्विगादिभिः ॥१६॥

maitreya uvāca
kṣamāpyaivaṁ sa mīḍhvāṁsaṁ

brahmaṇā cānumantritaḥ
karma santānayām āsa
sopādhyāyartvig-ādibhiḥ

maitreyaḥ—the sage Maitreya; *uvāca*—said; *kṣamā*—forgiveness; *āpya*—receiving; *evam*—thus; *saḥ*—King Dakṣa; *mīḍhvāṁsam*—unto Lord Śiva; *brahmaṇā*—along with Lord Brahmā; *ca*—also; *anumantritaḥ*—being permitted; *karma*—the sacrifice; *santānayām āsa*—began again; *sa*—along with; *upādhyāya*—learned sages; *ṛtvik*—the priests; *ādibhiḥ*—and others.

TRANSLATION

The great sage Maitreya said: Thus being pardoned by Lord Śiva, King Dakṣa, with the permission of Lord Brahmā, again began the performance of the yajña, along with the great learned sages, the priests and others.

TEXT 17

वैष्णवं यज्ञसन्तत्यै त्रिकपालं द्विजोत्तमाः ।
पुरोडाशं निरवपन् वीरसंसर्गशुद्धये ॥१७॥

vaiṣṇavaṁ yajña-santatyai
tri-kapālaṁ dvijottamāḥ
puroḍāśaṁ niravapan
vīra-saṁsarga-śuddhaye

vaiṣṇavam—meant for Lord Viṣṇu or His devotees; *yajña*—sacrifice; *santatyai*—for performances; *tri-kapālam*—three kinds of offerings; *dvija-uttamāḥ*—the best of the *brāhmaṇas; puroḍāśam*—the oblation called *puroḍāśa; niravapan*—offered; *vīra*—Vīrabhadra and other followers of Lord Śiva; *saṁsarga*—contamination (*doṣa*) due to his touching; *śuddhaye*—for purification.

TRANSLATION

Thereafter, in order to resume the activities of sacrifice, the brāhmaṇas first arranged to purify the sacrificial arena of the contamination caused by the touch of Vīrabhadra and the other

ghostly followers of Lord Śiva. Then they arranged to offer into the fire the oblations known as puroḍāśa.

PURPORT

Lord Śiva's followers and devotees, headed by Vīrabhadra, are known as *vīras*, and they are ghostly demons. Not only did they pollute the entire sacrificial arena by their very presence, but they disturbed the whole situation by passing stool and urine. Therefore, the infection they had created was to be first purified by the method of offering *puroḍāśa* oblations. A *viṣṇu-yajña*, or an offering to Lord Viṣṇu, cannot be performed uncleanly. To offer anything in an unclean state is called a *sevāparādha.* The worship of the Viṣṇu Deity in the temple is also *viṣṇu-yajña.* In all Viṣṇu temples, therefore, the priest who takes care of the *arcanā-vidhi* must be very clean. Everything should be always kept neat and clean, and the foodstuffs should be prepared in a neat and clean manner. All these regulative principles are described in *The Nectar of Devotion.* There are thirty-two kinds of offenses in discharging *arcanā* service. It is required, therefore, that one be extremely careful not to be unclean. Generally, whenever any ritualistic ceremony is begun, the holy name of Lord Viṣṇu is first chanted in order to purify the situation. Whether one is in a pure or impure condition, internally or externally, if one chants or even remembers the holy name of the Supreme Personality of Godhead Viṣṇu, one immediately becomes purified. The *yajña* arena was desecrated by the presence of Lord Śiva's followers, headed by Vīrabhadra, and therefore the entire arena had to be sanctified. Although Lord Śiva was present and he is all-auspicious, it was still necessary to sanctify the place because his followers had broken into the arena and committed so many obnoxious acts. That sanctification was possible only by chanting the holy name of Viṣṇu, Trikapāla, which can sanctify the three worlds. In other words, it is admitted herein that the followers of Lord Śiva are generally unclean. They are not even very hygienic; they do not take baths regularly, they wear long hair, and they smoke *gāñjā.* Persons of such irregular habits are counted amongst the ghosts. Since they were present in the sacrificial arena, the atmosphere became polluted, and it had to be sanctified by *trikapāla* oblations, which indicated the invocation of Viṣṇu's favor.

TEXT 18

अध्वर्युणात्तहविषा यजमानो विशाम्पते ।
धिया विशुद्धया दध्यौ तथा प्रादुरभूद्धरिः ॥१८॥

adhvaryuṇātta-haviṣā
yajamāno viśāmpate
dhiyā viśuddhayā dadhyau
tathā prādurabhūd dhariḥ

adhvaryuṇā—with the *Yajur Veda; ātta*—taking; *haviṣā*—with clarified butter; *yajamānaḥ*—King Dakṣa; *viśām-pate*—O Vidura; *dhiyā*—in meditation; *viśuddhayā*—sanctified; *dadhyau*—offered; *tathā*—immediately; *prāduḥ*—manifest; *abhūt*—became; *hariḥ*—Hari, the Lord.

TRANSLATION

The great sage Maitreya said to Vidura: My dear Vidura, as soon as King Dakṣa offered the clarified butter with Yajur Veda mantras in sanctified meditation, Lord Viṣṇu appeared there in His original form as Nārāyaṇa.

PURPORT

Lord Viṣṇu is all-pervading. Any devotee who, in sanctified meditation, following the regulative principles, chants the required *mantras* in service and in a devotional mood can see Viṣṇu. It is said in the *Brahma-saṁhitā* that a devotee whose eyes are anointed with the ointment of love of Godhead can see the Supreme Personality of Godhead always within his heart. Lord Śyāmasundara is so kind to His devotee.

TEXT 19

तदा स्वप्रभया तेषां द्योतयन्त्या दिशो दश ।
मुष्णंस्तेज उपानीतस्तार्क्ष्येण स्तोत्रवाजिना ॥१९॥

tadā sva-prabhayā teṣāṁ
dyotayantyā diśo daśa

muṣṇaṁs teja upānītas
tārkṣyeṇa stotra-vājinā

tadā—at that time; *sva-prabhayā*—by His own effulgence; *teṣām*—all of them; *dyotayantyā*—by brightness; *diśaḥ*—directions; *daśa*—ten; *muṣṇan*—diminishing; *tejaḥ*—effulgence; *upānītaḥ*—brought; *tārkṣyeṇa*—by Garuḍa; *stotra-vājinā*—whose wings are called Bṛhat and Rathantara.

TRANSLATION

Lord Nārāyaṇa was seated on the shoulder of Stotra, or Garuḍa, who had big wings. As soon as the Lord appeared, all directions were illuminated, diminishing the luster of Brahmā and the others present.

PURPORT

A description of Nārāyaṇa is given in the following two *ślokas.*

TEXT 20

श्यामो हिरण्यरशनोऽर्ककिरीटजुष्टो
नीलालकभ्रमरमण्डितकुण्डलास्यः ।
शङ्खाब्जचक्रशरचापगदासिचर्म-
व्यग्रैर्हिरण्मयभुजैरिव कर्णिकारः ॥२०॥

śyāmo hiraṇya-raśano 'rka-kirīṭa-juṣṭo
nīlālaka-bhramara-maṇḍita-kuṇḍalāsyaḥ
śaṅkhābja-cakra-śara-cāpa-gadāsi-carma-
vyagrair hiraṇmaya-bhujair iva karṇikāraḥ

śyāmaḥ—blackish; *hiraṇya-raśanaḥ*—a garment like gold; *arka-kirīṭa-juṣṭaḥ*—with a helmet as dazzling as the sun; *nīla-alaka*—bluish curls; *bhramara*—big black bees; *maṇḍita-kuṇḍala-āsyaḥ*—having a face decorated with earrings; *śaṅkha*—conchshell; *abja*—lotus flower; *cakra*—wheel; *śara*—arrows; *cāpa*—bow; *gadā*—club; *asi*—sword; *carma*—shield; *vyagraiḥ*—filled with; *hiraṇmaya*—golden (bracelets and bangles); *bhujaiḥ*—with hands; *iva*—as; *karṇikāraḥ*—flower tree.

TRANSLATION

His complexion was blackish, His garment yellow like gold, and His helmet as dazzling as the sun. His hair was bluish, the color of black bees, and His face was decorated with earrings. His eight hands held a conchshell, wheel, club, lotus flower, arrow, bow, shield and sword, and they were decorated with golden ornaments such as bangles and bracelets. His whole body resembled a blossoming tree beautifully decorated with various kinds of flowers.

PURPORT

The face of Lord Viṣṇu as described in this verse appears like a lotus flower with bees humming over it. All of the ornaments on the body of Lord Viṣṇu resemble molten gold of the reddish-gold color of the morning sunrise. The Lord appears, just as the morning sun rises, to protect the whole universal creation. His arms display different weapons, and His eight hands are compared to the eight petals of a lotus flower. All the weapons mentioned are for the protection of His devotees.

Generally in the four hands of Viṣṇu there are a wheel, club, conchshell and lotus flower. These four symbols are seen in the four hands of Viṣṇu in different arrangements. The club and the wheel are the Lord's symbols of punishment for the demons and miscreants, and the lotus flower and conchshell are used to bless the devotees. There are always two classes of men, the devotees and the demons. As confirmed in *Bhagavad-gītā* (*paritrāṇāya sādhūnām*), the Lord is always ready for the protection of the devotees and annihilation of the demons. There are demons and devotees in this material world, but in the spiritual world there is no such distinction. In other words, Lord Viṣṇu is the proprietor of both the material and spiritual worlds. In the material world almost everyone is of the demoniac nature, but there are also devotees, who appear to be in the material world although they are always situated in the spiritual world. A devotee's position is always transcendental, and he is always protected by Lord Viṣṇu.

TEXT 21

वक्षस्यधिश्रितवधूर्वनमाल्युदार-
हासावलोककलया रमयंश्च विश्वम् ।

पार्श्वभ्रमद्व्यजनचामरराजहंसः
श्वेतातपत्रशशिनोपरि रज्यमानः ॥२१॥

vakṣasy adhiśrita-vadhūr vana-mäly udāra-
hāsāvaloka-kalayā ramayaṁś ca viśvam
pārśva-bhramad-vyajana-cāmara-rāja-haṁsaḥ
śvetātapatra-śaśinopari rajyamānaḥ

vakṣasi—on the chest; *adhiśrita*—situated; *vadhūḥ*—a woman (the goddess of fortune, Lakṣmī); *vana-mālī*—garlanded with forest flowers; *udāra*—beautiful; *hāsa*—smiling; *avaloka*—glance; *kalayā*—with a small part; *ramayan*—pleasing; *ca*—and; *viśvam*—the whole world; *pārśva*—side; *bhramat*—moving back and forth; *vyajana-cāmara*—white yak-tail hair for fanning; *rāja-haṁsaḥ*—swan; *śveta-ātapatra-śaśinā*—with a white canopy like the moon; *upari*—above; *rajyamānaḥ*—looking beautiful.

TRANSLATION

Lord Viṣṇu looked extraordinarily beautiful because the goddess of fortune and a garland were situated on His chest. His face was beautifully decorated with a smiling attitude which can captivate the entire world, especially the devotees. Fans of white hair appeared on both sides of the Lord like white swans, and the white canopy overhead looked like the moon.

PURPORT

The smiling face of Lord Viṣṇu is pleasing to the whole world. Not only devotees but even nondevotees are attracted by such a smile. This verse nicely describes how the sun, moon, eight-petaled lotus flower and humming black bees were represented by the fans of hair, the overhead canopy, the moving earrings on both sides of His face, and His blackish hair. All together, accompanied by the conchshell, wheel, club, lotus flower, bow, arrows, shield and sword in His hands, these presented a grand and beautiful audience for Lord Viṣṇu which captivated all the demigods there, including Dakṣa and Lord Brahmā.

TEXT 22

तमुपागतमालक्ष्य सर्वे सुरगणादयः ।
प्रणेमुः सहसोत्थाय ब्रह्मेन्द्रत्र्यक्षनायकाः ॥२२॥

tam upāgatam ālakṣya
sarve sura-gaṇādayaḥ
praṇemuḥ sahasotthāya
brahmendra-tryakṣa-nāyakāḥ

tam—Him; *upāgatam*—arrived; *ālakṣya*—after seeing; *sarve*—all; *sura-gaṇa-ādayaḥ*—the demigods and others; *praṇemuḥ*—obeisances; *sahasā*—immediately; *utthāya*—after standing up; *brahma*—Lord Brahmā; *indra*—Lord Indra; *tri-akṣa*—Lord Śiva (who has three eyes); *nāyakāḥ*—led by.

TRANSLATION

As soon as Lord Viṣṇu was visible, all the demigods—Lord Brahmā and Lord Śiva, the Gandharvas and all present there—immediately offered their respectful obeisances by falling down straight before Him.

PURPORT

It appears that Lord Viṣṇu is the Supreme Lord even of Lord Śiva and Lord Brahmā, what to speak of the demigods, Gandharvas and ordinary living entities. It is stated in a prayer, *yaṁ brahmā varuṇendra-rudra-marutāḥ:* all the demigods worship Lord Viṣṇu. Similarly, *dhyānāvasthita-tad-gatena manasā paśyanti yaṁ yoginaḥ: yogīs* concentrate their minds on the form of Lord Viṣṇu. Thus Lord Viṣṇu is worshipable by all demigods, all Gandharvas and even Lord Śiva and Lord Brahmā. *Tad viṣṇoḥ paramaṁ padaṁ sadā paśyanti sūrayaḥ:* Viṣṇu is therefore the Supreme Personality of Godhead. Even though Lord Śiva was previously referred to in prayers by Lord Brahmā as the Supreme, when Lord Viṣṇu appeared, Śiva also fell prostrated before Him to offer respectful obeisances.

TEXT 23

तत्तेजसा हतरुचः सन्नजिह्वाः ससाध्वसाः ।
मूर्ध्ना धृताञ्जलिपुटा उपतस्थुरधोक्षजम् ॥२३॥

tat-tejasā hata-rucaḥ
sanna-jihvāḥ sa-sādhvasāḥ
mūrdhnā dhṛtāñjali-puṭā
upatasthur adhokṣajam

tat-tejasā—by the glaring effulgence of His body; *hata-rucaḥ*—having faded lusters; *sanna-jihvāḥ*—having silent tongues; *sa-sādhvasāḥ*—having fear of Him; *mūrdhnā*—with the head; *dhṛta-añjali-puṭāḥ*—with hands touched to the head; *upatasthuḥ*—prayed; *adhokṣajam*—to Adhokṣaja, the Supreme Personality of Godhead.

TRANSLATION

In the presence of the glaring effulgence of the bodily luster of Nārāyaṇa, everyone else's luster faded away, and everyone stopped speaking. Fearful with awe and veneration, all present touched their hands to their heads and prepared to offer their prayers to the Supreme Personality of Godhead, Adhokṣaja.

TEXT 24

अप्यर्वाग्वृत्तयो यस्य महि त्वात्मभुवादयः ।
यथामति गृणन्ति स्म कृतानुग्रहविग्रहम् ॥२४॥

apy arvāg-vṛttayo yasya
mahi tv ātmabhuv-ādayaḥ
yathā-mati gṛṇanti sma
kṛtānugraha-vigraham

api—still; *arvāk-vṛttayaḥ*—beyond the mental activities; *yasya*—whose; *mahi*—glory; *tu*—but; *ātmabhū-ādayaḥ*—Brahmā, etc.; *yathā-mati*—according to their different capacities; *gṛṇanti sma*—offered prayers; *kṛta-anugraha*—manifested by His grace; *vigraham*—transcendental form.

TRANSLATION

Although the mental scope of even demigods like Brahmā was unable to comprehend the unlimited glories of the Supreme Lord, they were all able to perceive the transcendental form of the Supreme Personality of Godhead by His grace. Only by such grace could they offer their respectful prayers according to their different capacities.

PURPORT

The Supreme Lord, the Personality of Godhead, is always unlimited, and His glories cannot be completely enumerated by anyone, even by a personality like Lord Brahmā. It is said that Ananta, a direct incarnation of the Lord, has unlimited mouths, and with each mouth He has been trying to describe the glories of the Lord for an unlimited span of time, yet the glories of the Lord remain unlimited, and He therefore never finishes. It is not possible for any ordinary living entity to understand or to glorify the unlimited Personality of Godhead, but one can offer prayers or service to the Lord according to one's particular capacity. This capacity is increased by the service spirit. *Sevonmukhe hi jihvādau* means that the service of the Lord begins with the tongue. This refers to chanting. By chanting Hare Kṛṣṇa, one begins the service of the Lord. Another function of the tongue is to taste and accept the Lord's *prasāda.* We have to begin our service to the Unlimited with the tongue and become perfect in chanting, and accepting the Lord's *prasāda.* To accept the Lord's *prasāda* means to control the entire set of senses. The tongue is considered to be the most uncontrollable sense because it hankers for so many unwholesome eatables, thereby forcing the living entity into the dungeon of material conditional life. As the living entity transmigrates from one form of life to another, he has to eat so many abominable foodstuffs that finally there is no limit. The tongue should be engaged in chanting and in eating the Lord's *prasāda* so that the other senses will be controlled. Chanting is the medicine, and *prasāda* is the diet. With these processes one can begin his service, and as the service increases, the Lord reveals more and more to the devotee. But there is no limit to His glories, and there is no limit to engaging oneself in the service of the Lord.

TEXT 25

दक्षो गृहीतार्हणसादनोत्तमं
यज्ञेश्वरं विश्वसृजां परं गुरुम् ।
सुनन्दनन्दाद्यनुगैर्वृतं मुदा
गृणन् प्रपेदे प्रयतः कृताञ्जलिः॥२५॥

dakṣo gṛhītārhaṇa-sādanottamaṁ
yajñeśvaraṁ viśva-sṛjāṁ paraṁ gurum
sunanda-nandādy-anugair vṛtaṁ mudā
gṛṇan prapede prayataḥ kṛtāñjaliḥ

dakṣaḥ—Dakṣa; *gṛhīta*—accepted; *arhaṇa*—rightful; *sādana-uttamam*—sacrificial vessel; *yajña-īśvaram*—unto the master of all sacrifices; *viśva-sṛjām*—of all the Prajāpatis; *param*—the supreme; *gurum*—preceptor; *sunanda-nanda-ādi-anugaiḥ*—by associates like Sunanda and Nanda; *vṛtam*—surrounded; *mudā*—with great pleasure; *gṛṇan*—offering respectful prayers; *prapede*—took shelter; *prayataḥ*—having a subdued mind; *kṛta-añjaliḥ*—with folded hands.

TRANSLATION

When Lord Viṣṇu accepted the oblations offered in the sacrifice, Dakṣa, the Prajāpati, began with great pleasure to offer respectful prayers unto Him. The Supreme Personality of Godhead is actually the master of all sacrifices and preceptor of all the Prajāpatis, and He is served even by such personalities as Nanda and Sunanda.

TEXT 26

दक्ष उवाच

शुद्धं स्वधाम्न्युपरताखिलबुद्ध्यवस्थं
चिन्मात्रमेकमभयं प्रतिषिध्य मायाम् ।

तिष्ठंस्तयैव पुरुषत्वमुपेत्य तस्या-
मास्ते भवानपरिशुद्ध इवात्मतन्त्रः ॥२६॥

dakṣa uvāca
śuddhaṁ sva-dhāmny uparatākhila-buddhy-avasthaṁ
cin-mātram ekam abhayaṁ pratiṣidhya māyām
tiṣṭhaṁs tayaiva puruṣatvam upetya tasyām
āste bhavān apariśuddha ivātma-tantraḥ

dakṣaḥ—Dakṣa; *uvāca*—said; *śuddham*—pure; *sva-dhāmni*—in Your own abode; *uparata-akhila*—completely turned back; *buddhi-avastham*—position of mental speculation; *cit-mātram*—completely spiritual; *ekam*—one without a second; *abhayam*—fearless; *pratiṣidhya*—controlling; *māyām*—material energy; *tiṣṭhan*—being situated; *tayā*—with her (Māyā); *eva*—certainly; *puruṣatvam*—overseer; *upetya*—entering into; *tasyām*—in her; *āste*—is present; *bhavān*—Your Lordship; *apariśuddhaḥ*—impure; *iva*—as if; *ātma-tantraḥ*—self-sufficient.

TRANSLATION

Dakṣa addressed the Supreme Personality of Godhead: My dear Lord, You are transcendental to all speculative positions. You are completely spiritual, devoid of all fear, and You are always in control of the material energy. Even though You appear in the material energy, You are situated transcendentally. You are always free from material contamination because You are completely self-sufficient.

TEXT 27

ऋत्विज ऊचुः
तत्त्वं न ते वयमनञ्जन रुद्रशापात्
कर्मण्यवग्रहधियो भगवन्विदामः ।
धर्मोपलक्षणमिदं त्रिवृदध्वराख्यं
ज्ञातं यदर्थमधिदैवमदोव्यवस्थाः ॥२७॥

ṛtvija ūcuḥ
tattvaṁ na te vayam anañjana rudra-śāpāt
karmaṇy avagraha-dhiyo bhagavan vidāmaḥ

dharmopalakṣaṇam idaṁ trivṛd adhvarākhyaṁ
jñātaṁ yad-artham adhidaivam ado vyavasthāḥ

ṛtvijaḥ—the priests; *ūcuḥ*—began to say; *tattvam*—truth; *na*—not; *te*—of Your Lordship; *vayam*—all of us; *anañjana*—without material contamination; *rudra*—Lord Śiva; *śāpāt*—by his curse; *karmaṇi*—in fruitive activities; *avagraha*—being too much attached; *dhiyaḥ*—of such intelligence; *bhagavan*—O Lord; *vidāmaḥ*—know; *dharma*—religion; *upalakṣaṇam*—symbolized; *idam*—this; *tri-vṛt*—the three departments of knowledge of the *Vedas; adhvara*—sacrifice; *ākhyam*—of the name; *jñātam*—known to us; *yat*—that; *artham*—for the matter of; *adhidaivam*—for worshiping the demigods; *adaḥ*—this; *vyavasthāḥ*—arrangement.

TRANSLATION

The priests addressed the Lord, saying: O Lord, transcendental to material contamination, by the curse offered by Lord Śiva's men we have become attached to fruitive activities, and thus we are now fallen and therefore do not know anything about You. On the contrary, we are now involved in the injunctions of the three departments of the Vedic knowledge under the plea of executing rituals in the name of yajña. We know that You have made arrangements for distributing the respective shares of the demigods.

PURPORT

The *Vedas* are known as *traiguṇya-viṣayā vedāḥ* (Bg. 2.45). Those who are serious students of the *Vedas* are very much attached to the ritualistic ceremonies mentioned in the *Vedas*, and therefore these *veda-vādīs* cannot understand that the ultimate goal of the *Vedas* is to understand Lord Kṛṣṇa, or Viṣṇu. Those who have transcended the qualitative Vedic attractions, however, can understand Kṛṣṇa, who is never contaminated by the material qualities. Therefore Lord Viṣṇu is addressed here as *anañjana* (free from material contamination). In *Bhagavad-gītā* (2.42) the crude Vedic scholars have been deprecated by Kṛṣṇa as follows:

yām imāṁ puṣpitāṁ vācaṁ
pravadanty avipaścitaḥ

veda-vāda-ratāḥ pārtha
nānyad astīti vādinaḥ

"Men of small knowledge are very much attached to the flowery words of the *Vedas*, and they say that there is nothing more than this."

TEXT 28

सदस्या ऊचुः
उत्पत्त्यध्वन्यशरण उरुक्लेशदुर्गेऽन्तकोग्र-
व्यालान्विष्टे विषयमृगतृष्यात्मगेहोरुभारः ।
द्वन्द्वश्वभ्रे खलमृगभये शोकदावेऽज्ञसार्थः
पादौकस्ते शरणद कदा याति कामोपसृष्टः ॥२८॥

sadasyā ūcuḥ
utpatty-adhvany aśaraṇa uru-kleśa-durge 'ntakogra-
vyālānviṣṭe viṣaya-mṛga-tṛṣy ātma-gehoru-bhāraḥ
dvandva-śvabhre khala-mṛga-bhaye śoka-dāve 'jña-sārthaḥ
pādaukas te śaraṇada kadā yāti kāmopasṛṣṭaḥ

sadasyāḥ—the members of the assembly; *ūcuḥ*—said; *utpatti*—repeated birth and death; *adhvani*—on the path of; *aśaraṇe*—not having a place to take shelter; *uru*—great; *kleśa*—troublesome; *durge*—in the formidable fort; *antaka*—termination; *ugra*—ferocious; *vyāla*—snakes; *anviṣṭe*—being infested with; *viṣaya*—material happiness; *mṛga-tṛṣi*—mirage; *ātma*—body; *geha*—home; *uru*—heavy; *bhāraḥ*—burden; *dvandva*—dual; *śvabhre*—holes, ditches of so-called happiness and distress; *khala*—ferocious; *mṛga*—animals; *bhaye*—being afraid of; *śoka-dāve*—the forest fire of lamentation; *ajña-sa-arthaḥ*—for the interest of the rascals; *pāda-okaḥ*—shelter of Your lotus feet; *te*—unto You; *śaraṇa-da*—giving shelter; *kadā*—when; *yāti*—went; *kāma-upasṛṣṭaḥ*—being afflicted by all sorts of desires.

TRANSLATION

The members of the assembly addressed the Lord: O exclusive shelter for all who are situated in troubled life, in this formidable

fort of conditional existence the time element, like a snake, is always looking for an opportunity to strike. This world is full of ditches of so-called distress and happiness, and there are many ferocious animals always ready to attack. The fire of lamentation is always blazing, and the mirage of false happiness is always alluring, but one has no shelter from them. Thus foolish persons live in the cycle of birth and death, always overburdened in discharging their so-called duties, and we do not know when they will accept the shelter of Your lotus feet.

PURPORT

Persons who are not in Kṛṣṇa consciousness are living a very precarious life, as described in this verse, but all these circumstantial conditions are due to forgetfulness of Kṛṣṇa. The Kṛṣṇa consciousness movement is meant to give relief to all these bewildered and distressed persons; therefore it is the greatest relief work for all human society, and the workers thereof are the greatest well-wishers, for they follow in the footsteps of Lord Caitanya, who is the greatest friend to all living entities.

TEXT 29

रुद्र उवाच

तव वरद वराङ्घ्रावाशिषेहाखिलार्थे
ह्यपि मुनिभिरसक्तैरादरेणार्हणीये ।
यदि रचितधियं माविद्यलोकोऽपविद्धं
जपति न गणये तत्त्वत्परानुग्रहेण ॥२९॥

rudra uvāca
tava varada varāṅghrāv āśiṣehākhilārthe
hy api munibhir asaktair ādareṇārhaṇīye
yadi racita-dhiyaṁ māvidya-loko 'paviddhaṁ
japati na gaṇaye tat tvat-parānugraheṇa

rudraḥ uvāca—Lord Śiva said; *tava*—Your; *vara-da*—O supreme benefactor; *vara-aṅghrau*—precious lotus feet; *āśiṣā*—by desire; *iha*—in the material world; *akhila-arthe*—for fulfillment; *hi api*—certainly;

munibhiḥ—by the sages; *asaktaiḥ*—liberated; *ādareṇa*—with care; *arhaṇīye*—worshipable; *yadi*—if; *racita-dhiyam*—mind fixed; *mā*—me; *avidya-lokaḥ*—the ignorant persons; *apaviddham*—unpurified activity; *japati*—utters; *na gaṇaye*—do not value; *tat*—it; *tvat-para-anugraheṇa*—by compassion like Yours.

TRANSLATION

Lord Śiva said: My dear Lord, my mind and consciousness are always fixed on Your lotus feet, which, as the source of all benediction and the fulfillment of all desires, are worshiped by all liberated great sages because Your lotus feet are worthy of worship. With my mind fixed on Your lotus feet, I am no longer disturbed by persons who blaspheme me, claiming that my activities are not purified. I do not mind their accusations, and I excuse them out of compassion, just as You exhibit compassion toward all living entities.

PURPORT

Lord Śiva expresses herein his regret at having been angry and having disturbed the sacrificial activities of Dakṣa. King Dakṣa had insulted him in many ways, and thus he had become angry and had frustrated the entire sacrificial ceremony. Later, when he was pleased, the *yajña* performances were reinstituted, and therefore he regretted his activities. Now he says that because his mind is fixed on the lotus feet of the Supreme Lord, Viṣṇu, he is no longer disturbed by the ordinary critics of his way of life. From this statement by Lord Śiva it is understood that as long as one is on the material platform one is affected by the three modes of material nature. As soon as one is in Kṛṣṇa consciousness, however, one is no longer affected by such material activities. One should therefore always be fixed in Kṛṣṇa consciousness, busy in the transcendental loving service of the Lord. It is guaranteed that such a devotee will never be affected by the actions and reactions of the three modes of material nature. This fact is also corroborated in *Bhagavad-gītā:* anyone who is fixed in the transcendental service of the Lord has surpassed all the material qualities and is situated in the status of Brahman realization, in which one is not afflicted by hankering for material objects. The recommendation of the *Śrīmad-Bhāgavatam* is that one should always be

Kṛṣṇa conscious and should never forget his transcendental relationship with the Lord. This program has to be followed strictly by everyone. From the statement of Lord Śiva it is understood that he was always in Kṛṣṇa consciousness, and thus he remained free from material affliction. The only remedy, therefore, is to continue Kṛṣṇa consciousness rigidly, in order to get out of the contamination of the material modes.

TEXT 30

भृगुरुवाच

यन्मायया गहनयापहृतात्मबोधा
ब्रह्मादयस्तनुभृतस्तमसि स्वपन्तः ।
नात्मन्श्रितं तव विदन्त्यधुनापि तत्त्वं
सोऽयं प्रसीदतु भवान् प्रणतात्मबन्धुः ॥३०॥

bhṛgur uvāca
yan māyayā gahanayāpahṛtātma-bodhā
brahmādayas tanu-bhṛtas tamasi svapantaḥ
nātman-śritaṁ tava vidanty adhunāpi tattvaṁ
so 'yaṁ prasīdatu bhavān praṇatātma-bandhuḥ

bhṛguḥ uvāca—Śrī Bhṛgu said; *yat*—who; *māyayā*—by illusory energy; *gahanayā*—insurmountable; *apahṛta*—stolen; *ātma-bodhāḥ*—knowledge of the constitutional position; *brahma-ādayaḥ*—Lord Brahmā, etc.; *tanu-bhṛtaḥ*—embodied living entities; *tamasi*—in the darkness of illusion; *svapantaḥ*—lying down; *na*—not; *ātman*—in the living entity; *śritam*—situated in; *tava*—Your; *vidanti*—understand; *adhunā*—now; *api*—certainly; *tattvam*—absolute position; *saḥ*—You; *ayam*—this; *prasīdatu*—be kind; *bhavān*—Your Lordship; *praṇata-ātma*—surrendered soul; *bandhuḥ*—friend.

TRANSLATION

Śrī Bhṛgu said: My dear Lord, all living entities, beginning from the highest, namely Lord Brahmā, down to the ordinary ant, are under the influence of the insurmountable spell of illusory energy, and thus they are ignorant of their constitutional position.

Everyone believes in the concept of the body, and all are thus submerged in the darkness of illusion. They are actually unable to understand how You live in every living entity as the Supersoul, nor can they understand Your absolute position. But You are the eternal friend and protector of all surrendered souls. Therefore, please be kind toward us and forgive all our offenses.

PURPORT

Bhṛgu Muni was conscious of the scandalous behavior exhibited by each and every one of them, including Brahmā and Lord Śiva, in the sacrificial ceremony of Dakṣa. By mentioning Brahmā, the chief of all living entities within this material world, he wanted to state that everyone, including also Brahmā and Lord Śiva, is under the concept of the body and under the spell of material energy—all but Viṣṇu. That is the version of Bhṛgu. As long as one is under the concept of the body as self, it is very difficult to understand the Supersoul or the Supreme Personality of Godhead. Conscious that he was not greater than Brahmā, Bhṛgu included himself in the list of offenders. Ignorant personalities, or conditioned souls, have no choice but to accept their precarious condition under material nature. The only remedy is to surrender to Viṣṇu and always pray to be excused. One should depend only on the causeless mercy of the Lord for deliverance and not even slightly on one's own strength. That is the perfect position of a Kṛṣṇa conscious person. The Lord is everyone's friend, but He is especially friendly to the surrendered soul. The simple process, therefore, is that a conditioned soul should remain surrendered to the Lord, and the Lord will give him all protection to keep him out of the clutches of material contamination.

TEXT 31

ब्रह्मोवाच

नैतत्स्वरूपं भवतोऽसौ पदार्थ-
भेदग्रहैः पुरुषो यावदीक्षेत् ।
ज्ञानस्य चार्थस्य गुणस्य चाश्रयो
मायामयाद् व्यतिरिक्तो मतस्त्वम् ॥३१॥

brahmovāca
naitat svarūpaṁ bhavato 'sau padārtha-
bheda-grahaiḥ puruṣo yāvad īkṣet
jñānasya cārthasya guṇasya cāśrayo
māyāmayād vyatirikto matas tvam

brahmā uvāca—Lord Brahmā said; *na*—not; *etat*—this; *svarūpam*—eternal form; *bhavataḥ*—Your; *asau*—that other; *pada-artha*—knowledge; *bheda*—different; *grahaiḥ*—by the acquiring; *puruṣaḥ*—person; *yāvat*—as long as; *īkṣet*—wants to see; *jñānasya*—of knowledge; *ca*—also; *arthasya*—of the objective; *guṇasya*—of the instruments of knowledge; *ca*—also; *āśrayaḥ*—the basis; *māyā-mayāt*—from being made of material energy; *vyatiriktaḥ*—distinct; *mataḥ*—regarded; *tvam*—You.

TRANSLATION

Lord Brahmā said: My dear Lord, Your personality and eternal form cannot be understood by any person who is trying to know You through the different processes of acquiring knowledge. Your position is always transcendental to the material creation, whereas the empiric attempt to understand You is material, as are its objectives and instruments.

PURPORT

It is said that the transcendental name, qualities, activities, paraphernalia, etc., of the Supreme Personality of Godhead cannot be understood with our material senses. The attempt of the empiric philosophers to understand the Absolute Truth by speculation is always futile because their process of understanding, their objective and the instruments by which they try to understand the Absolute Truth are all material. The Lord is *aprākṛta*, beyond the creation of the material world. This fact is also accepted by the great impersonalist Śaṅkarācārya: *nārāyaṇaḥ paro 'vyaktād aṇḍam avyakta-sambhavam. Avyakta*, or the original material cause, is beyond this material manifestation and is the cause of the material world. Because Nārāyaṇa, the Supreme Personality of Godhead, is beyond the material world, one cannot speculate upon Him by any material method. One has to understand the Supreme Personality of Godhead simply by the transcendental method of Kṛṣṇa consciousness. This is confirmed in *Bhagavad-gītā* (18.55). *Bhaktyā mām abhijānāti:* only by devotional service can one understand the transcendental form of the Lord. The difference between the impersonalists and the personalists is that the impersonalists, limited by their speculative processes, cannot even approach the Supreme Personality of Godhead, whereas the devotees please the Supreme Personality of Godhead through His transcendental loving service. *Sevonmukhe hi:* due to the service attitude of the devotee, the Lord is revealed to him. The Supreme Lord cannot be understood by materialistic persons even though He is present before them. In *Bhagavad-gītā,* Lord Kṛṣṇa therefore condemns such materialists as *mūḍhas. Mūḍha* means "rascal." It is said in the *Gītā,* "Only rascals think of Lord Kṛṣṇa as an ordinary person. They do not know what Lord Kṛṣṇa's position is or what His transcendental potencies are." Unaware of His transcendental potencies, the impersonalists deride the person of Lord Kṛṣṇa, whereas the devotees, by dint of their service attitude, can understand Him as the Personality of Godhead. In the Tenth Chapter of *Bhagavad-gītā,* Arjuna also confirmed that it is very difficult to understand the personality of the Lord.

TEXT 32

इन्द्र उवाच
इदमप्यच्युत विश्वभावनं
वपुरानन्दकरं मनोदृशाम् ।
सुरविद्विट्क्षपणैरुदायुधै-
र्भुजदण्डैरुपपन्नमष्टभिः ॥३२॥

indra uvāca
idam apy acyuta viśva-bhāvanaṁ
vapur ānanda-karaṁ mano-dṛśām
sura-vidviṭ-kṣapaṇair udāyudhair
bhuja-daṇḍair upapannam aṣṭabhiḥ

indraḥ uvāca—King Indra said; *idam*—this; *api*—certainly; *acyuta*—O infallible one; *viśva-bhāvanam*—for the welfare of the universe; *vapuḥ*—transcendental form; *ānanda-karam*—a cause of pleasure; *manaḥ-dṛśām*—to the mind and the eye; *sura-vidviṭ*—envious of Your devotees; *kṣapaṇaiḥ*—by punishment; *ud-āyudhaiḥ*—with uplifted weapons; *bhuja-daṇḍaiḥ*—with arms; *upapannam*—possessed of; *aṣṭabhiḥ*—with eight.

TRANSLATION

King Indra said: My dear Lord, Your transcendental form with eight hands and weapons in each of them appears for the welfare of the entire universe, and it is very pleasing to the mind and eyes. In such a form, Your Lordship is always prepared to punish the demons, who are envious of Your devotees.

PURPORT

It is generally understood from revealed scriptures that Lord Viṣṇu appears with four hands, but in this particular sacrificial arena Lord Viṣṇu arrived with eight hands. King Indra said, "Even though we are accustomed to see Your four-handed Viṣṇu form, this appearance with eight hands is as real as the four-handed form." As Lord Brahmā had said, to realize the transcendental form of the Lord is beyond the power of the senses. In reply to that statement by Brahmā, King Indra said that even though the transcendental form of the Lord is not perceivable by the material senses, His activities and His transcendental form can be understood. The Lord's uncommon features, uncommon activities and uncommon beauty can be perceived even by an ordinary man. For example, when Lord Kṛṣṇa appeared just like a six- or seven-year-old boy in Vṛndāvana, He was approached by the residents there. There were torrents of rain, and the Lord saved the residents of Vṛndāvana by lifting Govardhana Hill and resting it on the little finger of His left hand for seven days. This uncommon feature of the Lord should convince even materialistic persons who want to speculate to the limit of their material senses. The activities of the Lord are pleasing to experimental vision also, but impersonalists will not believe in His identity because they study the personality of the Lord by comparing their personality to His. Because men in this material world cannot lift a hill, they do not believe that the Lord can lift one. They accept the statements of *Śrīmad-Bhāgavatam* to be allegorical, and they try to interpret them in their own way. But factually the Lord lifted the hill in the presence of all the inhabitants of

Vṛndāvana, as corroborated by great *ācāryas* and authors like Vyāsadeva and Nārada. Everything about the Lord—His activities, pastimes and uncommon features—should be accepted as is, and in this way, even in our present condition, we can understand the Lord. In the instance herein, King Indra confirmed: "Your presence with eight hands is as good as Your presence with four hands." There is no doubt about it.

TEXT 33

पत्न्य ऊचुः

यज्ञोऽयं तव यजनाय केन सृष्टो
विध्वस्तः पशुपतिनाद्य दक्षकोपात् ।
तं नस्त्वं शवशयनाभशान्तमेधं
यज्ञात्मन्नलिनरुचा दृशा पुनीहि ॥३३॥

patnya ūcuḥ
yajño 'yaṁ tava yajanāya kena sṛṣṭo
vidhvastaḥ paśupatinādya dakṣa-kopāt
taṁ nas tvaṁ śava-śayanābha-śānta-medhaṁ
yajñātman nalina-rucā dṛśā punīhi

patnyaḥ ūcuḥ—the wives of the executors of the sacrifice said; *yajñaḥ*—the sacrifice; *ayam*—this; *tava*—Your; *yajanāya*—worshiping; *kena*—by Brahmā; *sṛṣṭaḥ*—arranged; *vidhvastaḥ*—devastated; *paśupatinā*—by Lord Śiva; *adya*—today; *dakṣa-kopāt*—from anger at Dakṣa; *tam*—it; *naḥ*—our; *tvam*—You; *śava-śayana*—dead bodies; *ābha*—like; *śānta-medham*—the still sacrificial animals; *yajña-ātman*—O Lord of sacrifice; *nalina*—lotus; *rucā*—beautiful; *dṛśā*—by the vision of Your eyes; *punīhi*—sanctify.

TRANSLATION

The wives of the performers of the sacrifice said: My dear Lord, this sacrifice was arranged under the instruction of Brahmā, but unfortunately Lord Śiva, being angry at Dakṣa, devastated the entire scene, and because of his anger the animals meant for sacrifice are lying dead. Therefore the preparations of the yajña have been

lost. Now, by the glance of Your lotus eyes, the sanctity of this sacrificial arena may be again invoked.

PURPORT

Animals were offered in sacrifice in order to give them renewed life; that was the purpose of having animals there. Offering an animal in sacrifice and giving him renewed life was the evidence of the strength of chanting *mantras.* Unfortunately, when Dakṣa's sacrifice was devastated by Lord Śiva, some of the animals were killed. (One was killed just to replace the head of Dakṣa.) Their bodies were lying about, and the sacrificial arena was turned into a crematorium. Thus the real purpose of *yajña* was lost.

Lord Viṣṇu, being the ultimate objective of such sacrificial ceremonies, was requested by the wives of the priests to glance over the *yajña* arena with His causeless mercy so that the routine work of the *yajña* might be continued. The purport here is that animals should not be unnecessarily killed. They were used to prove the strength of the *mantras* and were to have been rejuvenated by the use of the *mantras.* They should not have been killed, as they were by Lord Śiva to replace the head of Dakṣa with an animal's head. It was pleasing to see an animal sacrificed and rejuvenated, and that pleasing atmosphere had been lost. The wives of the priests requested that the animals be brought back to life by the glance of Lord Viṣṇu to make a pleasing *yajña.*

TEXT 34

ऋषय ऊचुः
अनन्वितं ते भगवन् विचेष्टितं
यदात्मना चरसि हि कर्म नाज्यसे ।
विभूतये यत उपसेदुरीश्वरीं
न मन्यते स्वयमनुवर्ततीं भवान् ॥३४॥

ṛṣaya ūcuḥ
ananvitaṁ te bhagavan viceṣṭitaṁ
yad ātmanā carasi hi karma nājyase

vibhūtaye yata upasedur īśvarīṁ
na manyate svayam anuvartatīṁ bhavān

ṛṣayaḥ—the sages; *ūcuḥ*—prayed; *ananvitam*—wonderful; *te*—Your; *bhagavan*—O possessor of all opulences; *viceṣṭitam*—activities; *yat*—which; *ātmanā*—by Your potencies; *carasi*—You execute; *hi*—certainly; *karma*—to such activities; *na ajyase*—You are not attached; *vibhūtaye*—for her mercy; *yataḥ*—from whom; *upaseduḥ*—worshiped; *īśvarīm*—Lakṣmī, the goddess of fortune; *na manyate*—are not attached; *svayam*—Yourself; *anuvartatīm*—to Your obedient servant (Lakṣmī); *bhavān*—Your Lordship.

TRANSLATION

The sages prayed: Dear Lord, Your activities are most wonderful, and although You do everything by Your different potencies, You are not at all attached to such activities. You are not even attached to the goddess of fortune, who is worshiped by the great demigods like Brahmā, who pray to achieve her mercy.

PURPORT

In *Bhagavad-gītā* it is said that the Lord has no desire to achieve any result from His wonderful activities, nor has He any need to perform them. But still, in order to give an example to people in general, He sometimes acts, and those activities are very wonderful. He is not attached to anything. *Na māṁ karmāṇi limpanti:* although He acts very wonderfully, He is not at all attached to anything (Bg. 4.14). He is self-sufficient. The example is given here that the goddess of fortune, Lakṣmī, is always engaged in the service of the Lord, but still He is not attached to her. Even great demigods like Brahmā worship the goddess of fortune in order to win her favor, but although the Lord is worshiped by many hundreds and thousands of goddesses of fortune, He is not at all attached to any one of them. This distinction concerning the exalted transcendental position of the Lord is specifically mentioned by the great sages; He is not like the ordinary living entity, who is attached to the results of pious activities.

TEXT 35

सिद्धा ऊचुः
अयं त्वत्कथामृष्टपीयूषनद्यां
मनोवारणः क्लेशदावाग्निदग्धः ।
तृषार्तोऽवगाढो न सस्मार दावं
न निष्क्रामति ब्रह्मसम्पन्नवन्नः ॥३५॥

siddhā ūcuḥ
ayaṁ tvat-kathā-mṛṣṭa-pīyūṣa-nadyāṁ
mano-vāraṇaḥ kleśa-dāvāgni-dagdhaḥ
tṛṣārto 'vagāḍho na sasmāra dāvaṁ
na niṣkrāmati brahma-sampannavan naḥ

siddhāḥ—the Siddhas; *ūcuḥ*—prayed; *ayam*—this; *tvat-kathā*—Your pastimes; *mṛṣṭa*—pure; *pīyūṣa*—of nectar; *nadyām*—in the river; *manaḥ*—of the mind; *vāraṇaḥ*—the elephant; *kleśa*—sufferings; *dāva-agni*—by the forest fire; *dagdhaḥ*—burned; *tṛṣā*—thirst; *ārtaḥ*—afflicted; *avagāḍhaḥ*—being immersed; *na sasmāra*—does not remember; *dāvam*—the forest fire or the miseries; *na niṣkrāmati*—not come out; *brahma*—the Absolute; *sampanna-vat*—like having merged; *naḥ*—our.

TRANSLATION

The Siddhas prayed: Like an elephant that has suffered in a forest fire but can forget all its troubles by entering a river, our minds, O Lord, always merge in the nectarean river of Your transcendental pastimes, and they desire never to leave such transcendental bliss, which is as good as the pleasure of merging in the Absolute.

PURPORT

This statement is from the Siddhas, the inhabitants of Siddhaloka, where the eight kinds of material perfection are complete. The residents of Siddhaloka have full control in the eight kinds of yogic perfection, but from their statement it appears that they are pure devotees. They always merge in the nectarean river of hearing of the pastimes of the Lord. Hearing of the pastimes of the Lord is called *kṛṣṇa-kathā*. Similarly, there is a statement by Prahlāda Mahārāja that those who are always merged in the ocean of the nectar of describing the Lord's pastimes are liberated and have no fear of the material condition of life. The Siddhas say that the mind of an ordinary person is full of anxieties. The example is given of the elephant who has suffered in a forest fire and who enters into a river for relief. If persons who are suffering in the forest fire of this material existence will only enter into the nectarean river of the description of the pastimes of the Lord, they will forget all the troubles of the miserable material existence. The Siddhas do not care for fruitive activities, such as performing sacrifices and achieving the good results. They simply merge in the transcendental discussions of the pastimes of the Lord. That makes them completely happy, without care for pious or impious activities. For those who are always in Kṛṣṇa consciousness there is no need to perform any kind of pious or impious sacrifices or activities. Kṛṣṇa consciousness is itself complete, for it includes all the processes praised in the Vedic scriptures.

TEXT 36

यजमान्युवाच
स्वागतं ते प्रसीदेश तुभ्यं नमः
श्रीनिवास श्रिया कान्तया त्राहि नः ।
त्वामृतेऽधीश नाङ्गैर्मखः शोभते
शीर्षहीनः कबन्धो यथा पुरुषः ॥३६॥

yajamāny uvāca
svāgataṁ te prasīdeśa tubhyaṁ namaḥ
śrīnivāsa śriyā kāntayā trāhi naḥ
tvām ṛte 'dhīśa nāṅgair makhaḥ śobhate
śīrṣa-hīnaḥ ka-bandho yathā puruṣaḥ

yajamānī—the wife of Dakṣa; *uvāca*—prayed; *su-āgatam*—auspicious appearance; *te*—Your; *prasīda*—become pleased; *īśa*—my dear Lord; *tubhyam*—unto You; *namaḥ*—respectful obeisances; *śrīnivāsa*—O abode of the goddess of fortune; *śriyā*—with Lakṣmī; *kāntayā*—Your wife; *trāhi*—protect; *naḥ*—us; *tvām*—You; *ṛte*—without; *adhīśa*—O supreme controller; *na*—not; *aṅgaiḥ*—with bodily limbs;

makhaḥ—the sacrificial arena; *śobhate*—is beautiful; *śīrṣa-hīnaḥ*—without the head; *ka-bandhaḥ*—possessed of only a body; *yathā*—as; *puruṣaḥ*—a person.

TRANSLATION

The wife of Dakṣa prayed as follows: My dear Lord, it is very fortunate that You have appeared in this arena of sacrifice. I offer my respectful obeisances unto You, and I request that You be pleased on this occasion. The sacrificial arena is not beautiful without You, just as a body is not beautiful without the head.

PURPORT

Another name of Lord Viṣṇu is Yajñeśvara. In *Bhagavad-gītā* it is said that all activities should be performed as *viṣṇu-yajña*, for the pleasure of Lord Viṣṇu. Unless we please Him, whatever we do is the cause of our bondage in the material world. This is confirmed herein by the wife of Dakṣa: "Without Your presence, the grandeur of this sacrificial ceremony is useless, just as a body without the head, however decorated it may be, is useless." The comparison is equally applicable to the social body. Material civilization is very proud of being advanced, but it is actually the useless trunk of a body without a head. Without Kṛṣṇa consciousness, without an understanding of Viṣṇu, the Supreme Personality of Godhead, any advancement in a civilization, no matter how sophisticated, is of no value. There is a statement in the *Hari-bhakti-sudhodaya* (3.11):

bhagavad-bhakti-hīnasya
jātiḥ śāstraṁ japas tapaḥ
aprāṇasyaiva dehasya
maṇḍanaṁ loka-rañjanam

The purport is that sometimes when a friend or relative dies, especially among lower class men, the dead body is decorated. Dressed and ornamented, the body is taken in procession. That sort of decoration of the dead body has no actual value because the life force is already gone. Similarly, any aristocracy, any social prestige or any advancement of material civilization without Kṛṣṇa consciousness is as good as the decoration of a dead body. The name of the wife of Dakṣa was Prasūti, and she was the daughter of Svāyambhuva Manu. Her sister, Devahūti, was married to Kardama Muni, and Kapiladeva, the Personality of Godhead, became her son. Prasūti, then, was the aunt of Lord Viṣṇu. She was asking the favor of Lord Viṣṇu in an affectionate mode; since she was His aunt, she sought some special favor. Also significant in this verse is that the Lord is praised with the goddess of fortune. Wherever Lord Viṣṇu is worshiped, naturally there is the favor of the goddess of fortune. Lord Viṣṇu is addressed as *amṛta*, transcendental. The demigods, including Brahmā and Lord Śiva, were produced after the creation, but Lord Viṣṇu existed before the creation. He is addressed, therefore, as *amṛta*. Lord Viṣṇu is worshiped with His internal energy by the Vaiṣṇavas. Prasūti, the wife of Dakṣa, implored the Lord to turn the priests into Vaiṣṇavas instead of simply fruitive workers performing sacrifices for some material benefits.

TEXT 37

लोकपाला ऊचुः

दृष्टः किं नो दृग्भिरसद्ग्रहैस्त्वं
प्रत्यग्द्रष्टा दृश्यते येन विश्वम् ।
माया ह्येषा भवदीया हि भूमन्
यस्त्वं षष्ठः पञ्चभिर्भासि भूतैः ॥३७॥

lokapālā ūcuḥ
dṛṣṭaḥ kiṁ no dṛgbhir asad-grahais tvaṁ
pratyag-draṣṭā dṛśyate yena viśvam
māyā hy eṣā bhavadīyā hi bhūman
yas tvaṁ ṣaṣṭhaḥ pañcabhir bhāsi bhūtaiḥ

loka-pālāḥ—the governors of the different planets; *ūcuḥ*—said; *dṛṣṭaḥ*—seen; *kim*—whether; *naḥ*—by us; *dṛgbhiḥ*—by the material senses; *asat-grahaiḥ*—revealing the cosmic manifestation; *tvam*—You; *pratyak-draṣṭā*—inner witness; *dṛśyate*—is seen; *yena*—by whom; *viśvam*—the universe; *māyā*—material world; *hi*—because; *eṣā*—this; *bhavadīyā*—Your; *hi*—certainly; *bhūman*—O possessor of the universe; *yaḥ*—because; *tvam*—You; *ṣaṣṭhaḥ*—the sixth; *pañcabhiḥ*—with the five; *bhāsi*—appear; *bhūtaiḥ*—with the elements.

TRANSLATION

The governors of various planets spoke as follows: Dear Lord, we believe only in our direct perception, but under the circumstances we do not know whether we have actually seen You with our material senses. By our material senses we can simply perceive the cosmic manifestation, but You are beyond the five elements. You are the sixth. We see You, therefore, as a creation of the material world.

PURPORT

The governors of the various planets are certainly materially opulent and very puffed up. Such persons are unable to understand the transcendental, eternal form of the Lord. In the *Brahma-saṁhitā* it is stated that only persons who have anointed their eyes with love of Godhead can see the Personality of Godhead in every step of their activities. Also, in the prayers of Kuntī (*Bhāg.* 1.8.26) it is stated that only those who are *akiñcana-gocaram*, who are not materially puffed up, can see the Supreme Personality of Godhead; others are bewildered and cannot even think of the Absolute Truth.

TEXT 38

योगेश्वरा ऊचुः

प्रेयान्न तेऽन्योऽस्त्यमुतस्त्वयि प्रभो
विश्वात्मनीक्षेन्न पृथग्य आत्मनः ।
अथापि भक्त्येशतयोपधावता-
मनन्यवृत्त्यानुगृहाण वत्सल ॥३८॥

yogeśvarā ūcuḥ
preyān na te 'nyo 'sty amutas tvayi prabho
viśvātmanīkṣen na pṛthag ya ātmanaḥ
athāpi bhaktyeśa tayopadhāvatām
ananya-vṛttyānugṛhāṇa vatsala

yoga-īśvarāḥ—the great mystics; *ūcuḥ*—said; *preyān*—very dear; *na*—not; *te*—of You; *anyaḥ*—another; *asti*—there is; *amutaḥ*—from that; *tvayi*—in You; *prabho*—dear Lord; *viśva-ātmani*—in the Supersoul of all living entities; *īkṣet*—see; *na*—not; *pṛthak*—different; *yaḥ*—who; *ātmanaḥ*—the living entities; *atha api*—so much more; *bhaktyā*—with devotion; *īśa*—O Lord; *tayā*—with it; *upadhāvatām*—of those who worship; *ananya-vṛttyā*—unfailing; *anugṛhāṇa*—favor; *vatsala*—O favorable Lord.

TRANSLATION

The great mystics said: Dear Lord, persons who see You as nondifferent from themselves, knowing that You are the Supersoul of all living entities, are certainly very, very dear to You. You are very favorable toward those who engage in devotional service, accepting You as the Lord and themselves as the servants. By Your mercy, You are always inclined in their favor.

PURPORT

It is indicated in this verse that the monists and the great mystics know the Supreme Personality of Godhead as one. This oneness is not the misunderstanding that a living entity is equal in every respect to the Supreme Personality of Godhead. This monism is based on pure knowledge as described and confirmed in *Bhagavad-gītā* (7.17): *priyo hi jñānino 'tyartham ahaṁ sa ca mama priyaḥ.* The Lord says that those who are advanced in transcendental knowledge and know the science of Kṛṣṇa consciousness are very dear to Him, and He also is very dear to them. Those who are actually in perfect knowledge of the science of God know that the living entities are superior energy of the Supreme Lord. This is stated in *Bhagavad-gītā,* Seventh Chapter: the material energy is inferior, and the living entities are superior energy. Energy and the energetic are nondifferent; therefore, energies possess the same quality as the energetic. Persons who are in full knowledge of the Personality of Godhead, analyzing His different energies and knowing their own constitutional position, are certainly very, very dear to the Lord. Persons, however, who may not even be conversant with knowledge of the Supreme Personality but who always think of the Lord with love and faith, feeling that He is great and that they are His parts and parcels, ever His servitors, are even more favored by Him. The particular significance of this verse is that the Lord is addressed as *vatsala. Vatsala* means "always favorably disposed." The Lord's name is *bhakta-vatsala.* The Lord is famous as *bhakta-vatsala,* which means that He is always favorably inclined to the devotees, whereas He is never addressed anywhere in the Vedic literature as *jñāni-vatsala.*

TEXT 39

जगदुद्भवस्थितिलयेषु दैवतो
बहुभिद्यमानगुणयात्ममायया ।
रचितात्मभेदमतये स्वसंस्थया
विनिवर्तितभ्रमगुणात्मने नमः ॥३९॥

jagad-udbhava-sthiti-layeṣu daivato
bahu-bhidyamāna-guṇayātma-māyayā
racitātma-bheda-mataye sva-saṁsthayā
vinivartita-bhrama-guṇātmane namaḥ

jagat—the material world; *udbhava*—creation; *sthiti*—maintenance; *layeṣu*—in annihilation; *daivataḥ*—destiny; *bahu*—many; *bhidyamāna*—being variegated; *guṇayā*—by material qualities; *ātma-māyayā*—by His material energy; *racita*—produced; *ātma*—in the living entities; *bheda-mataye*—who produced different inclinations; *sva-saṁsthayā*—by His internal potency; *vinivartita*—caused to stop; *bhrama*—interaction; *guṇa*—of material modes; *ātmane*—unto Him in His personal form; *namaḥ*—obeisances.

TRANSLATION

We offer our respectful obeisances unto the Supreme, who has created varieties of manifestations and put them under the spell of the three qualities of the material world in order to create, maintain and annihilate them. He Himself is not under the control of the external energy; in His personal feature He is completely devoid of the variegated manifestation of material qualities, and He is under no illusion of false identification.

PURPORT

Two situations are described in this verse. One is the creation, maintenance and annihilation of the material world, and the other is the Lord's own establishment. There is also quality in the Lord's own establishment, the kingdom of God. It is stated here that Goloka is His personal situation. There is also quality in Goloka, but that quality is not divided into creation, maintenance and annihilation. In the external energy, the interaction of the three qualities makes it possible for things to be created, maintained and annihilated. But in the spiritual world, or the kingdom of God, there is no such exhibition, since everything is eternal, sentient and blissful. There is a class of philosophers who misunderstand the appearance of the Personality of Godhead within this material world. They are under the impression that when the Supreme Personality of Godhead appears, He is under the spell of the three qualities, like all the other living entities who appear within this material world. That is their misunderstanding; as it is clearly stated here (*sva-saṁsthayā*), by His internal potency He is transcendental to all these material qualities. Similarly, in *Bhagavad-gītā* the Lord says, "I appear by My internal potency." Both the internal and external potencies are under the control of the Supreme, so He does not come under the control of either of these potencies. Rather, everything is under His control. In order to manifest His transcendental name, form, quality, pastimes and paraphernalia, He brings into action His internal energy. On account of the variegatedness of the external potency, there are manifestations of many qualitative demigods, beginning with Brahmā and Lord Śiva, and people are attracted to these demigods according to their own material quality. But when one is transcendental or surpasses the material qualities, he is simply fixed in the worship of the Supreme Personality. This fact is explained in *Bhagavad-gītā:* anyone engaged in the service of the Lord is already transcendental to the variegatedness and interaction of the three material qualities. The summary is that the conditioned souls are being pulled by the action and reaction of the material qualities, which create a differentiation of energies. But in the spiritual world the worshipable one is the Supreme Lord and no one else.

TEXT 40

ब्रह्मोवाच

नमस्ते श्रितसत्त्वाय धर्मादीनां च सूतये ।
निर्गुणाय च यत्काष्ठां नाहं वेदापरेऽपि च ॥४०॥

brahmovāca
namas te śrita-sattvāya
dharmādīnāṁ ca sūtaye
nirguṇāya ca yat-kāṣṭhāṁ
nāhaṁ vedāpare 'pi ca

brahma—the personified *Vedas; uvāca*—said; *namaḥ*—respectful obeisances; *te*—unto You; *śrita-sattvāya*—the shelter of the quality of goodness; *dharma-ādīnām*—of all religion, austerity and penance; *ca*—and; *sūtaye*—the source; *nirguṇāya*—transcendental to material qualities; *ca*—and; *yat*—of whom (of the Supreme Lord); *kāṣṭhām*—the situation; *na*—not; *aham*—I; *veda*—know; *apare*—others; *api*—certainly; *ca*—and.

TRANSLATION

The personified Vedas said: We offer our respectful obeisances unto You, the Lord, the shelter of the quality of goodness and therefore the source of all religion, austerity and penance, for You are transcendental to all material qualities and no one knows You or Your actual situation.

PURPORT

In the material world there is the trinity of the three material qualities. Lord Viṣṇu has accepted the superintendence of the quality of goodness, which is the source of religion, knowledge, austerity, renunciation, opulence, etc. Because of this, actual peace, prosperity, knowledge and religion can be attained when the living entities are under the control of the quality of goodness in the material world. As soon as they are subjected to the control of the other two qualities, namely passion and ignorance, their precarious conditional life becomes intolerable. But Lord Viṣṇu, in His original position, is always *nirguṇa*, which means transcendental to these material qualities. *Guṇa* means "quality," and *nir* means "negation." This does not indicate, however, that He has no qualities; He has transcendental qualities by which He appears and manifests His pastimes. The positive transcendental qualitative manifestation is unknown to the students of the *Vedas* as well as to the great stalwart demigods like Brahmā and Śiva. Actually, the transcendental qualities are manifested only to the devotees. As confirmed in *Bhagavad-gītā*, simply by discharging devotional service one can understand the transcendental position of the Supreme Lord. Those who are in the mode of goodness can partially enter into the transcendental understanding, but it is advised in *Bhagavad-gītā* that one has to surpass this. The Vedic principles are based on the three qualities of the material modes. One has to transcend the three qualities, and then one can be situated in pure and simple spiritual life.

TEXT 41

अग्निरुवाच
यत्तेजसाहं सुसमिद्धतेजा
हव्यं वहे स्वध्वर आज्यसिक्तम् ।
तं यज्ञियं पञ्चविधं च पञ्चभिः
स्विष्टं यजुर्भिः प्रणतोऽस्मि यज्ञम् ॥४१॥

agnir uvāca
yat-tejasāhaṁ susamiddha-tejā
havyaṁ vahe svadhvara ājya-siktam
taṁ yajñiyaṁ pañca-vidhaṁ ca pañcabhiḥ
sviṣṭaṁ yajurbhiḥ praṇato 'smi yajñam

agniḥ—the fire-god; *uvāca*—said; *yat-tejasā*—by whose effulgence; *aham*—I; *su-samiddha-tejāḥ*—as luminous as blazing fire; *havyam*—offerings; *vahe*—I am accepting; *su-adhvare*—in the sacrifice; *ājya-siktam*—mixed with butter; *tam*—that; *yajñiyam*—the protector of the sacrifice; *pañca-vidham*—five; *ca*—and; *pañcabhiḥ*—by five; *su-iṣṭam*—worshiped; *yajurbhiḥ*—Vedic hymns; *praṇataḥ*—offer respectful obeisances; *asmi*—I; *yajñam*—to Yajña (Viṣṇu).

TRANSLATION

The fire-god said: My dear Lord, I offer my respectful obeisances unto You because by Your favor I am as luminous as blazing fire and I accept the offerings mixed with butter and offered in sacrifice. The five kinds of offerings according to the Yajur Veda are all Your different energies, and You are worshiped by five

kinds of Vedic hymns. Sacrifice means Your Supreme Personality of Godhead.

PURPORT

In *Bhagavad-gītā* it is clearly said that *yajña* should be performed for Lord Viṣṇu. Lord Viṣṇu has one thousand popular, transcendental names, out of which one name is Yajña. It is clearly said that everything should be done for the satisfaction of Yajña, or Viṣṇu. All other actions a person may take are only causes for his bondage. Everyone has to perform *yajña* according to the Vedic hymns. As stated in the *Upaniṣads*, fire, the altar, the auspicious full moon, the period of four months called *cāturmāsya*, the sacrificial animal, and the beverage called *soma* are necessary requisites, as are the specific hymns mentioned in the *Vedas* and composed of four letters. One hymn is as follows: *āśrāvayeti catur-akṣaraṁ astu śrauṣaḍ iti catur-akṣaraṁ yajeti dvābhyāṁ ye yajāmahaḥ.* These *mantras*, chanted according to the *śruti* and *smṛti* literatures, are only to please Lord Viṣṇu. For the deliverance of those who are materially conditioned and attached to material enjoyment, performing *yajña* and following the rules and regulations of the four divisions of society and of spiritual life are recommended. It is said in the *Viṣṇu Purāṇa* that by offering sacrifice to Viṣṇu one can gradually be liberated. The whole target of life, therefore, is to please Lord Viṣṇu. That is *yajña.* Any person who is in Kṛṣṇa consciousness has dedicated his life for the satisfaction of Kṛṣṇa, the origin of all Viṣṇu forms, and by offering worship and *prasāda* daily, he becomes the best performer of *yajña.* In the *Śrīmad-Bhāgavatam* it is clearly stated that in this age of Kali the only successful performance of *yajña*, or sacrifice, is *yajñaiḥ saṅkīrtana-prāyaiḥ:* the best type of sacrifice is simply to chant Hare Kṛṣṇa, Hare Kṛṣṇa, Kṛṣṇa Kṛṣṇa, Hare Hare/ Hare Rāma, Hare Rāma, Rāma Rāma, Hare Hare. This *yajña* is offered before the form of Lord Caitanya, as other *yajñas* are offered before the form of Lord Viṣṇu. These recommendations are found in the Eleventh Canto of the *Śrīmad-Bhāgavatam.* Moreover, this *yajña* performance confirms that Lord Caitanya Mahāprabhu is Viṣṇu Himself. As Lord Viṣṇu appeared at the Dakṣa *yajña* long, long ago, Lord Caitanya has appeared in this age to accept our *saṅkīrtana-yajña.*

TEXT 42

देवा ऊचुः
पुरा कल्पापाये स्वकृतमुदरीकृत्य विकृतं
त्वमेवाद्यस्तस्मिन् सलिल उरगेन्द्राधिशयने ।
पुमान् शेषे सिद्धैर्हृदि विमृशिताध्यात्मपदविः
स एवाद्याक्ष्णोर्यः पथि चरसि भृत्यानवसि नः॥४२॥

devā ūcuḥ
purā kalpāpāye sva-kṛtam udarī-kṛtya vikṛtaṁ
tvam evādyas tasmin salila uragendrādhiśayane
pumān śeṣe siddhair hṛdi vimṛśitādhyātma-padaviḥ
sa evādyākṣṇor yaḥ pathi carasi bhṛtyān avasi naḥ

devāḥ—the demigods; *ūcuḥ*—said; *purā*—formerly; *kalpa-apāye*—at the devastation of the *kalpa; sva-kṛtam*—self-produced; *udarī-kṛtya*—having drawn within Your abdomen; *vikṛtam*—effect; *tvam*—You; *eva*—certainly; *ādyaḥ*—original; *tasmin*—in that; *salile*—water; *uraga-indra*—on Śeṣa; *adhiśayane*—on the bed; *pumān*—personality; *śeṣe*—taking rest; *siddhaiḥ*—by the liberated souls (like Sanaka, etc.); *hṛdi*—in the heart; *vimṛśita*—meditated on; *adhyātma-padaviḥ*—the path of philosophical speculation; *saḥ*—He; *eva*—certainly; *adya*—now; *akṣṇoḥ*—of both eyes; *yaḥ*—who; *pathi*—on the path; *carasi*—You move; *bhṛtyān*—servants; *avasi*—protect; *naḥ*—us.

TRANSLATION

The demigods said: Dear Lord, formerly, when there was a devastation, You conserved all the different energies of material manifestation. At that time, all the inhabitants of the higher planets, represented by such liberated souls as Sanaka, were meditating on You by philosophical speculation. You are therefore the original person, and You rest in the water of devastation on the bed of the Śeṣa snake. Now, today, You are visible to us, who are all Your servants. Please give us protection.

PURPORT

The devastation indicated in this verse is the partial devastation of the lower planets within the universe when Lord Brahmā goes to sleep. The higher planetary systems, beginning with Maharloka, Janaloka and Tapoloka, are not inundated at the time of this devastation. The Lord is the creator, as indicated in this verse, because the energies of creation are manifested through His body, and after annihilation, He conserves all the energy within His abdomen.

Another significant point in this verse is that the demigods said, "We are all Your servants (*bhṛtyān*). Give us Your protection." The demigods depend on the protection of Viṣṇu; they are not independent. *Bhagavad-gītā*, therefore, condemns the worship of demigods because there is no need of it and clearly states that only those who have lost their sense go asking favors of the demigods. Generally, if anyone has material desires to be fulfilled, he can ask Viṣṇu instead of going to the demigods. Those who worship demigods are not very intelligent. Besides that, the demigods say, "We are Your eternal servants." So those who are servants, or devotees of the Lord, are not very much concerned with fruitive activities, the performance of the prescribed *yajñas*, or mental speculation. They simply serve the Supreme Personality of Godhead sincerely, with love and faith, performing everything with that loving service, and the Lord gives such devotees direct protection. In *Bhagavad-gītā* Lord Kṛṣṇa says, "Simply surrender unto Me, and I will give you protection from all the reactions of sinful activities." This material world is so created that one has to act sinfully, knowingly or unknowingly, and unless his life is dedicated to Viṣṇu, he has to suffer all the reactions of sinful activities. But one who surrenders and dedicates his life for the service of the Lord has direct protection from the Lord. He has no fear of suffering from sinful activities, nor does he desire, willingly or unwillingly, to do anything which is sinful.

TEXT 43

गन्धर्वा ऊचुः

अंशांशास्ते देव मरीच्यादय एते
ब्रह्मेन्द्राद्या देवगणा रुद्रपुरोगाः ।

क्रीडाभाण्डं विश्वमिदं यस्य विभूमन्
तस्मै नित्यं नाथ नमस्ते करवाम ॥४३॥

gandharvā ūcuḥ
aṁśāṁśās te deva marīcy-ādaya ete
brahmendrādyā deva-gaṇā rudra-purogāḥ
krīḍā-bhāṇḍaṁ viśvam idaṁ yasya vibhūman
tasmai nityaṁ nātha namas te karavāma

gandharvāḥ—the Gandharvas; *ūcuḥ*—said; *aṁśa-aṁśāḥ*—parts and parcels of Your body; *te*—Your; *deva*—dear Lord; *marīci-ādayaḥ*—Marīci and the great sages; *ete*—these; *brahma-indra-ādyāḥ*—headed by Brahmā and Indra; *deva-gaṇāḥ*—the demigods; *rudra-purogāḥ*—having Lord Śiva as the chief; *krīḍā-bhāṇḍam*—a plaything; *viśvam*—the whole creation; *idam*—this; *yasya*—of whom; *vibhūman*—the Supreme Almighty Great; *tasmai*—unto Him; *nityam*—always; *nātha*—O Lord; *namaḥ*—respectful obeisances; *te*—unto You; *karavāma*—we offer.

TRANSLATION

The Gandharvas said: Dear Lord, all the demigods, including Lord Śiva, Lord Brahmā, Indra and Marīci and the great sages, are all only differentiated parts and parcels of Your body. You are the Supreme Almighty Great; the whole creation is just like a plaything for You. We always accept You as the Supreme Personality of Godhead, and we offer our respectful obeisances unto You.

PURPORT

In the *Brahma-saṁhitā* it is said that Kṛṣṇa is the Supreme Personality of Godhead. There may be many gods, from Brahmā, Lord Śiva, Indra and Candra down to the rulers of the lower planetary systems, the presidents, ministers, chairmen and kings. In fact, anyone can think that he is God. That is the false, puffed-up conviction of material life. Actually Viṣṇu is the Supreme Lord, but there is even one above Viṣṇu, for Viṣṇu is also the plenary portion of a part of Kṛṣṇa. In this verse this is referred to by the word *aṁśāṁśāḥ*, which refers to part and parcel of a part and parcel. There are similar verses in the *Caitanya-caritāmṛta* which indicate that the Supreme Lord's parts and parcels again expand into other parts and parcels. As described in *Śrīmad-Bhāgavatam*, there are many manifestations of Viṣṇu and many manifestations of living entities. Viṣṇu manifestations are called *svāṁśa*, partial manifestations, and the living entities are called *vibhinnāṁśa*. The demigods like Brahmā and Indra have been promoted to such exalted positions by pious activities and austerities, but actually Viṣṇu, or Kṛṣṇa, is the master of everyone. In the *Caitanya-caritāmṛta* it is said, *ekale īśvara kṛṣṇa, āra saba bhṛtya*. This means that Kṛṣṇa alone is the Supreme Personality of Godhead, and all others, even the *viṣṇu-tattva* and certainly the living entities, are His servitors. Baladeva is the immediate expansion of Kṛṣṇa. He also engages in the service of Kṛṣṇa, and certainly the ordinary living entities are serving. Everyone is created, constitutionally, for serving Kṛṣṇa. Here the Gandharvas acknowledge that although the demigods may represent themselves as the Supreme, actually they are not supreme. Real supremacy belongs to Kṛṣṇa. *Kṛṣṇas tu bhagavān svayam* is the statement of *Śrīmad-Bhāgavatam:* "Kṛṣṇa is the only Supreme Lord." Worship of Kṛṣṇa alone, therefore, includes worship of all the parts and parcels, just as watering the root of a tree also waters all the branches, twigs, leaves and flowers.

TEXT 44

विद्याधरा ऊचुः

त्वन्माययार्थमभिपद्य कलेवरेऽस्मिन्
कृत्वा ममाहमिति दुर्मतिरुत्पथैः स्वैः ।
क्षिप्तोऽप्यसद्विषयलालस आत्ममोहं
युष्मत्कथामृतनिषेवक उद्व्युदस्येत् ॥४४॥

vidyādharā ūcuḥ
tvan-māyayārtham abhipadya kalevare 'smin
kṛtvā mamāham iti durmatir utpathaiḥ svaiḥ
kṣipto 'py asad-viṣaya-lālasa ātma-mohaṁ
yuṣmat-kathāmṛta-niṣevaka udvyudasyet

vidyādharāḥ—the Vidyādharas; *ūcuḥ*—said; *tvat-māyayā*—by Your external potency; *artham*—the human body; *abhipadya*—after obtaining; *kalevare*—in the body; *asmin*—in this; *kṛtvā*—having misidentified; *mama*—mine; *aham*—I; *iti*—thus; *durmatiḥ*—the ignorant person; *utpathaiḥ*—by wrong roads; *svaiḥ*—by one's own belongings; *kṣiptaḥ*—distracted; *api*—even; *asat*—temporary; *viṣaya-lālasaḥ*—having his happiness in sense objects; *ātma-moham*—the illusion of the body as the self; *yuṣmat*—Your; *kathā*—topics; *amṛta*—nectar; *niṣevakaḥ*—relishing; *ut*—from a long distance; *vyudasyet*—can be delivered.

TRANSLATION

The Vidyādharas said: Dear Lord, this human form of body is meant for attaining the highest perfectional objective, but, impelled by Your external energy, the living entity misidentifies himself with his body and with the material energy, and therefore, influenced by māyā, he wants to become happy by material enjoyment. He is misled and always attracted by temporary, illusory happiness. But Your transcendental activities are so powerful that if one engages in the hearing and chanting of such topics, he can be delivered from illusion.

PURPORT

The human form of life is called *arthada* because the body can very nicely help the embodied soul to achieve the highest perfection. Prahlāda Mahārāja said that even though temporary, the body can give us the highest perfectional achievement. In the process of evolution from the lower to the higher grade of living, the human form of life is a great boon. But *māyā* is so strong that in spite of achieving this great boon of the human form of life, we are influenced by temporary material happiness, and we forget our goal of life. We are attracted by things which will cease to exist. The beginning of such attraction is the temporary body. In this horrible condition of life there is only one way of liberation—to engage in the activities of transcendental chanting and hearing of the holy name of the Supreme Lord: Hare Kṛṣṇa, Hare Kṛṣṇa, Kṛṣṇa Kṛṣṇa, Hare Hare/ Hare Rāma, Hare Rāma, Rāma Rāma, Hare Hare. The words *yuṣmat-kathāmṛta-niṣevakaḥ* mean "those who engage in relishing the nectar of the topics of Your Lordship." There are two narrative books which especially concern the words and activities of Kṛṣṇa. *Bhagavad-gītā* is the instruction given by Kṛṣṇa, and *Śrīmad-Bhāgavatam* is the book containing topics exclusively about Kṛṣṇa and His devotees. These two books are the special nectar of the words of Kṛṣṇa. For those who engage in the preaching of these two Vedic literatures it is very easy to get out of the illusory conditional life imposed upon us by *māyā*. The illusion is that the conditioned soul does not try to understand his spiritual identity. He is more interested in his external body, which is only a flash and which will be finished as soon as the time is designated. The whole atmosphere will change when the living entity has to transmigrate from one body to another. Under the spell of *māyā*, he will again be satisfied in a different atmosphere. This spell of *māyā* is called *āvaraṇātmikā śakti* because it is so strong that the living entity is satisfied in any abominable condition. Even if he is born as a worm living within the intestine or abdomen in the midst of urine and stool, still he is satisfied. This is the covering influence of *māyā*. But the human form of life is a chance to understand, and if one misses this opportunity, he is most unfortunate. The way to get out of illusory *māyā* is to engage in the topics of Kṛṣṇa. Lord Caitanya advocated a process whereby everyone may remain in his present position without change but simply hear from the proper authoritative sources about Kṛṣṇa. Lord Caitanya advised everyone to spread the word of Kṛṣṇa. He advised, "All of you become spiritual masters. Your duty is simply to talk to whomever you meet of Kṛṣṇa or of the instructions given by Kṛṣṇa." The International Society for Krishna Consciousness is operating for this purpose. We do not ask anyone to first change his position and then come to us. Instead, we invite everyone to come with us and simply chant Hare Kṛṣṇa, Hare Kṛṣṇa, Kṛṣṇa Kṛṣṇa, Hare Hare/ Hare Rāma, Hare Rāma, Rāma Rāma, Hare Hare, because we know that if one simply chants and hears the topics of Kṛṣṇa, one's life will change; he will see a new light, and his life will be successful.

TEXT 45

ब्राह्मणा ऊचुः

त्वं क्रतुस्त्वं हविस्त्वं हुताशः स्वयं
त्वं हि मन्त्रः समिद्दर्भपात्राणि च ।
त्वं सदस्यर्त्विजो दम्पती देवता
अग्निहोत्रं स्वधा सोम आज्यं पशुः ॥४५॥

brāhmaṇā ūcuḥ
tvaṁ kratus tvaṁ havis tvaṁ hutāśaḥ svayaṁ
tvaṁ hi mantraḥ samid-darbha-pātrāṇi ca
tvaṁ sadasyartvijo dampatī devatā
agnihotraṁ svadhā soma ājyaṁ paśuḥ

brāhmaṇāḥ—the *brāhmaṇas; ūcuḥ*—said; *tvam*—You; *kratuḥ*—sacrifice; *tvam*—You; *haviḥ*—offering of clarified butter; *tvam*—You; *huta-āśaḥ*—fire; *svayam*—personified; *tvam*—You; *hi*—for; *mantraḥ*—the Vedic hymns; *samit-darbha-pātrāṇi*—the fuel, the *kuśa* grass and the sacrificial pots; *ca*—and; *tvam*—You; *sadasya*—the members of the assembly; *ṛtvijaḥ*—the priests; *dampatī*—the chief person of the sacrifice and his wife; *devatā*—demigods; *agni-hotram*—the sacred fire ceremony; *svadhā*—the offering to the forefathers; *somaḥ*—the *soma* plant; *ājyam*—the clarified butter; *paśuḥ*—the sacrificial animal.

TRANSLATION

The brāhmaṇas said: Dear Lord, You are sacrifice personified. You are the offering of clarified butter, You are the fire, You are the chanting of Vedic hymns by which the sacrifice is conducted, You are the fuel, You are the flame, You are the kuśa grass, and You are the sacrificial pots. You are the priests who perform the yajña, You are the demigods headed by Indra, and You are the sacrificial animal. Everything that is sacrificed is You or Your energy.

PURPORT

In this statement Lord Viṣṇu's all-pervasiveness is partially explained. It is said in the *Viṣṇu Purāṇa* that as a fire situated in one place emanates its heat and illumination everywhere, so whatever we see within the material or spiritual worlds is nothing but a manifestation of different energies emanating from the Supreme Personality of Godhead. The *brāhmaṇas'* statement is that Lord Viṣṇu is everything—the fire, the offering, the clarified butter, the utensils, the place of sacrifice and the *kuśa.* He is everything. It is confirmed herein that the performance of *saṅkīrtana-yajña* in this age is as good as all other *yajñas* in all other ages. If one performs *saṅkīrtana-yajña* by chanting Hare Kṛṣṇa, Hare Kṛṣṇa, Kṛṣṇa Kṛṣṇa, Hare Hare/ Hare Rāma, Hare Rāma, Rāma Rāma,

Hare Hare, there is no need to arrange elaborate paraphernalia for the prescribed sacrificial ceremonies recommended in the *Vedas.* In the chant of the holy names, Hare and Kṛṣṇa, *Hare* means the energy of Kṛṣṇa, and *Kṛṣṇa* is the *viṣṇu-tattva.* Combined together they are everything. In this age, persons are harassed by the influence of Kali-yuga and cannot arrange for all the requisite paraphernalia for performing sacrifice as recommended in the *Vedas.* But if one simply chants Hare Kṛṣṇa, it is to be understood that he is performing all kinds of *yajña* because there is nothing within our vision except Hare (the energy of Kṛṣṇa) and Kṛṣṇa. There is no difference between Kṛṣṇa and His energies. Thus since everything is a manifestation of His energy, it is to be understood that everything is Kṛṣṇa. One simply has to accept everything in Kṛṣṇa consciousness, and he is a liberated person. One should not misunderstand that because everything is Kṛṣṇa, Kṛṣṇa has no personal identity. Kṛṣṇa is so full that in spite of keeping Himself separate from everything by His energy, He is everything. This is confirmed in *Bhagavad-gītā,* Ninth Chapter. He is spread throughout the creation as everything, but still He is not everything. The philosophy recommended by Lord Caitanya is that He is simultaneously one and different.

TEXT 46

त्वं पुरा गां रसाया महासूकरो
दंष्ट्रया पद्मिनीं वारणेन्द्रो यथा ।
स्तूयमानो नदल्लीलया योगिभि-
र्व्युज्जहर्थ त्रयीगात्र यज्ञक्रतुः ॥४६॥

tvaṁ purā gāṁ rasāyā mahā-sūkaro
daṁṣṭrayā padminīṁ vāraṇendro yathā
stūyamāno nadal līlayā yogibhir
vyujjahartha trayī-gātra yajña-kratuḥ

tvam—You; *purā*—in the past; *gām*—the earth; *rasāyāḥ*—from within the water; *mahā-sūkaraḥ*—the great boar incarnation; *daṁṣṭrayā*—with Your tusk; *padminīm*—a lotus; *vāraṇa-indraḥ*—an elephant; *yathā*—as; *stūyamānaḥ*—being offered prayers; *nadan*—

vibrating; *līlayā*—very easily; *yogibhiḥ*—by great sages like Sanaka, etc.; *vyujjahartha*—picked up; *trayī-gātra*—O personified Vedic knowledge; *yajña-kratuḥ*—having the form of sacrifice.

TRANSLATION

Dear Lord, O personified Vedic knowledge, in the past millennium, long, long ago, when You appeared as the great boar incarnation, You picked up the world from the water, as an elephant picks up a lotus flower from a lake. When You vibrated transcendental sound in that gigantic form of a boar, the sound was accepted as a sacrificial hymn, and great sages like Sanaka meditated upon it and offered prayers for Your glorification.

PURPORT

A significant word used in this verse is *trayī-gātra*, which means that the transcendental form of the Lord is the *Vedas*. Anyone who engages in the worship of the Deity, or the form of the Lord in the temple, is understood to be studying all the *Vedas* twenty-four hours a day. Simply by decorating the Deities of the Lord, Rādhā and Kṛṣṇa, in the temple, one very minutely studies the injunctions of the *Vedas*. Even a neophyte devotee who simply engages in the worship of the Deity is understood to be in direct touch with the purport of Vedic knowledge. As confirmed in *Bhagavad-gītā* (15.15), *vedaiś ca sarvair aham eva vedyaḥ:* the purport of the *Vedas* is to understand Him, Kṛṣṇa. One who worships and serves Kṛṣṇa directly has understood the truths of the *Vedas*.

TEXT 47

स प्रसीद त्वमस्माकमाकाङ्क्षतां
दर्शनं ते परिभ्रष्टसत्कर्मणाम् ।
कीर्त्यमाने नृभिर्नाम्नि यज्ञेश ते
यज्ञविघ्नाः क्षयं यान्ति तस्मै नमः ॥४७॥

sa prasīda tvam asmākam ākāṅkṣatāṁ
darśanaṁ te paribhraṣṭa-sat-karmaṇām

kīrtyamāne nṛbhir nāmni yajñeśa te
yajña-vighnāḥ kṣayaṁ yānti tasmai namaḥ

saḥ—that same person; *prasīda*—be pleased; *tvam*—You; *asmākam*—upon us; *ākāṅkṣatām*—awaiting; *darśanam*—audience; *te*—Your; *paribhraṣṭa*—fallen down; *sat-karmaṇām*—of whom the performance of sacrifice; *kīrtyamāne*—being chanted; *nṛbhiḥ*—by persons; *nāmni*—Your holy name; *yajña-īśa*—O Lord of sacrifice; *te*—Your; *yajña-vighnāḥ*—obstacles; *kṣayam*—destruction; *yānti*—attain; *tasmai*—unto You; *namaḥ*—respectful obeisances.

TRANSLATION

Dear Lord, we were awaiting Your audience because we have been unable to perform the yajñas according to the Vedic rituals. We pray unto You, therefore, to be pleased with us. Simply by chanting Your holy name, one can surpass all obstacles. We offer our respectful obeisances unto You in Your presence.

PURPORT

The *brāhmaṇa* priests were very hopeful that their sacrifice would be carried out without obstacles now that Lord Viṣṇu was present. It is significant in this verse that the *brāhmaṇas* say, "Simply by chanting Your holy name we can surpass the obstacles, but now You are personally present." The performance of *yajña* by Dakṣa was obstructed by the disciples and followers of Lord Śiva. The *brāhmaṇas* indirectly criticized the followers of Lord Śiva, but because the *brāhmaṇas* were always protected by Lord Viṣṇu, Śiva's followers could not do any harm to their prosecution of the sacrificial process. There is a saying that when Kṛṣṇa protects someone, no one can do him harm, and when Kṛṣṇa wants to kill someone, no one can protect him. The vivid example was Rāvaṇa. Rāvaṇa was a great devotee of Lord Śiva, but when Lord Rāmacandra wanted to kill him, Lord Śiva could not protect him. If some demigod, even Lord Śiva or Lord Brahmā, wants to do harm to a devotee, Kṛṣṇa protects the devotee. But when Kṛṣṇa wants to kill someone, such as Rāvaṇa or Hiraṇyakaśipu, no demigod can protect him.

TEXT 48

मैत्रेय उवाच

इति दक्षः कविर्यज्ञं भद्र रुद्राभिमर्शितम् ।
कीर्त्यमाने हृषीकेशे संनिन्ये यज्ञभावने ॥४८॥

maitreya uvāca
iti dakṣaḥ kavir yajñaṁ
bhadra rudrābhimarśitam
kīrtyamāne hṛṣīkeśe
sanninye yajña-bhāvane

maitreyaḥ—Maitreya; *uvāca*—said; *iti*—thus; *dakṣaḥ*—Dakṣa; *kaviḥ*—being purified in consciousness; *yajñam*—the sacrifice; *bhadra*—O Vidura; *rudra-abhimarśitam*—devastated by Vīrabhadra; *kīrtyamāne*—being glorified; *hṛṣīkeśe*—Hṛṣīkeśa (Lord Viṣṇu); *sanninye*—arranged for restarting; *yajña-bhāvane*—the protector of sacrifice.

TRANSLATION

Śrī Maitreya said: After Lord Viṣṇu was glorified by all present, Dakṣa, his consciousness purified, arranged to begin again the yajña which had been devastated by the followers of Lord Śiva.

TEXT 49

भगवान् स्वेन भागेन सर्वात्मा सर्वभागभुक् ।
दक्षं बभाष आभाष्य प्रीयमाण इवानघ ॥४९॥

bhagavān svena bhāgena
sarvātmā sarva-bhāga-bhuk
dakṣaṁ babhāṣa ābhāṣya
prīyamāṇa ivānagha

bhagavān—Lord Viṣṇu; *svena*—with His own; *bhāgena*—with the share; *sarva-ātmā*—the Supersoul of all living entities; *sarva-bhāga-bhuk*—the enjoyer of the results of all sacrifices; *dakṣam*—Dakṣa;

babhāṣe—said; *ābhāṣya*—addressing; *prīyamāṇaḥ*—being satisfied; *iva*—as; *anagha*—O sinless Vidura.

TRANSLATION

Maitreya continued: My dear sinless Vidura, Lord Viṣṇu is actually the enjoyer of the results of all sacrifices. Yet because of His being the Supersoul of all living entities, He was satisfied simply with His share of the sacrificial offerings. He therefore addressed Dakṣa in a pleasing attitude.

PURPORT

In *Bhagavad-gītā* (5.29) it is said, *bhoktāraṁ yajña-tapasām:* Lord Viṣṇu, or Kṛṣṇa, is the supreme enjoyer of all the results of sacrifices, austerities and penances; in whatever one may engage, the ultimate goal is Viṣṇu. If a person does not know that, he is misled. As the Supreme Personality of Godhead, Viṣṇu has nothing to demand from anyone. He is self-satisfied, self-sufficient, but He accepts the offerings of *yajña* because of His friendly attitude toward all living entities. When His share of the sacrificial results was offered to Him, He appeared very pleased. It is said in *Bhagavad-gītā* (9.26), *patraṁ puṣpaṁ phalaṁ toyaṁ yo me bhaktyā prayacchati:* if any devotee offers Him even a small leaf, or a flower or water, if it is offered with love and affection, the Lord accepts it and is pleased. Although He is self-sufficient and does not need anything from anyone, He accepts such offerings because, as Supersoul, He has such a friendly attitude toward all living entities. Another point here is that He does not encroach upon another's share. In the *yajña* there is a share for the demigods, Lord Śiva, and Lord Brahmā, and a share for Lord Viṣṇu. He is satisfied with His own share and does not encroach upon others'. Indirectly, He indicated that He was not satisfied with Dakṣa's trying to deny Lord Śiva his share. Maitreya addressed Vidura as sinless because Vidura was a pure Vaiṣṇava and never committed any offense to any demigod. Although Vaiṣṇavas accept Lord Viṣṇu as the Supreme, they are not prone to offend demigods. They give the demigods proper respect. Vaiṣṇavas accept Lord Śiva as the best Vaiṣṇava. For a Vaiṣṇava there is no possibility of offending any demigods, and the demigods are also pleased with the Vaiṣṇava because they are faultless devotees of Lord Viṣṇu.

TEXT 50

श्रीभगवानुवाच
अहं ब्रह्मा च शर्वश्च जगतः कारणं परम् ।
आत्मेश्वर उपद्रष्टा स्वयंदृगविशेषणः ॥५०॥

śrī-bhagavān uvāca
ahaṁ brahmā ca śarvaś ca
jagataḥ kāraṇaṁ param
ātmeśvara upadraṣṭā
svayan-dṛg aviśeṣaṇaḥ

śrī-bhagavān—Lord Viṣṇu; *uvāca*—said; *aham*—I; *brahmā*—Brahmā; *ca*—and; *śarvaḥ*—Lord Śiva; *ca*—and; *jagataḥ*—of the material manifestation; *kāraṇam*—cause; *param*—supreme; *ātma-īśvaraḥ*—the Supersoul; *upadraṣṭā*—the witness; *svayam-dṛk*—self-sufficient; *aviśeṣaṇaḥ*—there is no difference.

TRANSLATION

Lord Viṣṇu replied: Brahmā, Lord Śiva and I are the supreme cause of the material manifestation. I am the Supersoul, the self-sufficient witness. But impersonally there is no difference between Brahmā, Lord Śiva and Me.

PURPORT

Lord Brahmā was born out of the transcendental body of Lord Viṣṇu, and Lord Śiva was born out of the body of Brahmā. Lord Viṣṇu, therefore, is the supreme cause. In the *Vedas* also it is stated that in the beginning there was only Viṣṇu, Nārāyaṇa; there was no Brahmā or Śiva. Similarly, Śaṅkarācārya confirmed this: *nārāyaṇaḥ paraḥ*. Nārāyaṇa, or Lord Viṣṇu, is the origin, and Brahmā and Śiva are manifested after creation. Lord Viṣṇu is also *ātmeśvara*, the Supersoul in everyone. Under His direction, everything is prompted from within. For example, in the beginning of the *Śrīmad-Bhāgavatam* it is stated, *tene brahma hṛdā:* He first educated Lord Brahmā from within.

In *Bhagavad-gītā* (10.2) Lord Kṛṣṇa states, *aham ādir hi devānām:* Lord Viṣṇu, or Kṛṣṇa, is the origin of all demigods, including Lord

Brahmā and Lord Śiva. In another place in *Bhagavad-gītā* (10.8) Kṛṣṇa states, *ahaṁ sarvasya prabhavaḥ:* "Everything is generated from Me." This includes all the demigods. Similarly, in the *Vedānta-sūtra: janmādy asya yataḥ*. And in the *Upaniṣads* is the statement *yato vā imāni bhūtāni jāyante*. Everything is generated from Lord Viṣṇu, everything is maintained by Him, and everything is annihilated by His energy. Therefore, by their actions and reactions, the energies which come from Him create the cosmic manifestations and also dissolve the whole creation. Thus the Lord is the cause and also the effect. Whatever effect we see is the interaction of His energy, and because the energy is generated from Him, He is both cause and effect. Simultaneously, everything is different and the same. It is said that everything is Brahman: *sarvaṁ khalv idaṁ brahma*. In the highest vision, nothing is beyond Brahman, and therefore Lord Brahmā and Lord Śiva are certainly nondifferent from Him.

TEXT 51

आत्ममायां समाविश्य सोऽहं गुणमयीं द्विज ।
सृजन् रक्षन् हरन् विश्वं दध्रे संज्ञां क्रियोचिताम् ॥५१॥

ātma-māyāṁ samāviśya
so 'haṁ guṇamayīṁ dvija
sṛjan rakṣan haran viśvaṁ
dadhre saṁjñāṁ kriyocitām

ātma-māyām—My energy; *samāviśya*—having entered; *saḥ*—Myself; *aham*—I; *guṇa-mayīm*—composed of the modes of material nature; *dvi-ja*—O twice-born Dakṣa; *sṛjan*—creating; *rakṣan*—maintaining; *haran*—annihilating; *viśvam*—the cosmic manifestation; *dadhre*—I cause to be born; *saṁjñām*—a name; *kriyā-ucitām*—according to the activity.

TRANSLATION

The Lord continued: My dear Dakṣa Dvija, I am the original Personality of Godhead, but in order to create, maintain and annihilate this cosmic manifestation, I act through My material energy, and according to the different grades of activity, My representations are differently named.

PURPORT

As explained in *Bhagavad-gītā* (7.5), *jīva-bhūtāṁ mahā-bāho:* the whole world is energy released from the supreme source, the Personality of Godhead, who, it is further stated in *Bhagavad-gītā*, acts in superior energies and inferior energies. The superior energy is the living entity, who is part and parcel of the Supreme Lord. As parts and parcels, the living entities are not different from the Supreme Lord; the energy emanated from Him is not different from Him. But in the actual activity of this material world, the living entity is under the different qualities of material energy and in different forms. There are 8,400,000 life forms. The same living entity acts under the influence of the different qualities of material nature. The entities have different bodies, but originally, in the beginning of creation, Lord Viṣṇu is alone. For the purpose of creation, Brahmā is manifested, and for annihilation there is Lord Śiva. As far as the spiritual entrance into the material world is concerned, all beings are part and parcel of the Supreme Lord, but under the covering of different material qualities they have different names. Lord Brahmā and Lord Śiva are qualitative incarnations of Viṣṇu, as *guṇa-avatāras*, and Viṣṇu with them accepts control of the quality of goodness; therefore He is also a qualitative incarnation like Lord Śiva and Lord Brahmā. Actually the different names exist for different directions, otherwise the origin is one only.

TEXT 52

तस्मिन् ब्रह्मण्यद्वितीये केवले परमात्मनि ।
ब्रह्मरुद्रौ च भूतानि भेदेनाज्ञोऽनुपश्यति ॥५२॥

tasmin brahmaṇy advitīye
kevale paramātmani
brahma-rudrau ca bhūtāni
bhedenājño 'nupaśyati

tasmin—Him; *brahmaṇi*—the Supreme Brahman; *advitīye*—without a second; *kevale*—being one; *parama-ātmani*—the Supersoul; *brahma-rudrau*—both Brahmā and Śiva; *ca*—and; *bhūtāni*—the living entities; *bhedena*—with separation; *ajñaḥ*—one who is not properly conversant; *anupaśyati*—thinks.

TRANSLATION

The Lord continued: One who is not in proper knowledge thinks that demigods like Brahmā and Śiva are independent, or he even thinks that the living entities are independent.

PURPORT

The living entities, including Brahmā, are not independently separated, but are counted within the marginal potency of the Supreme Lord. The Supreme Lord, being the Supersoul in every living entity, including Lord Brahmā and Lord Śiva, is directing everyone in the activities of the material modes of nature. No one can act independently of the sanction of the Lord, and therefore, indirectly, no one is different from the Supreme Person—certainly not Brahmā and Rudra, who are incarnations of the material nature's modes of passion and ignorance.

TEXT 53

यथा पुमान्न स्वाङ्गेषु शिरःपाण्यादिषु क्वचित् ।
पारक्यबुद्धिं कुरुते एवं भूतेषु मत्परः ॥५३॥

yathā pumān na svāṅgeṣu
śiraḥ-pāṇy-ādiṣu kvacit
pārakya-buddhiṁ kurute
evaṁ bhūteṣu mat-paraḥ

yathā—as; *pumān*—a person; *na*—not; *sva-aṅgeṣu*—in his own body; *śiraḥ-pāṇi-ādiṣu*—between the head and the hands and other parts of the body; *kvacit*—sometimes; *pārakya-buddhim*—differentiation; *kurute*—make; *evam*—thus; *bhūteṣu*—among living entities; *mat-paraḥ*—My devotee.

TRANSLATION

A person with average intelligence does not think the head and other parts of the body to be separate. Similarly, My devotee does not differentiate Viṣṇu, the all-pervading Personality of Godhead, from any thing or any living entity.

PURPORT

Whenever there is disease in any part of the body, the whole body takes care of the ailing part. Similarly, a devotee's oneness is manifested in His compassion for all conditioned souls. *Bhagavad-gītā* (5.18) says, *paṇḍitāḥ sama-darśinaḥ:* those who are learned see everyone's conditional life equally. Devotees are compassionate to every conditioned soul, and therefore they are known as *apārakya-buddhi.* Because devotees are learned and know that every living entity is part and parcel of the Supreme Lord, they preach Kṛṣṇa consciousness to everyone so that everyone may be happy. If a particular part of the body is diseased, the whole attention of the body goes to that part. Similarly, devotees care for any person who is forgetful of Kṛṣṇa and therefore in material consciousness. The equal vision of the devotee is that he works to get all living entities back home, back to Godhead.

TEXT 54

त्रयाणामेकभावानां यो न पश्यति वै भिदाम् ।
सर्वभूतात्मनां ब्रह्मन् स शान्तिमधिगच्छति ॥५४॥

trayāṇām eka-bhāvānāṁ
yo na paśyati vai bhidām
sarva-bhūtātmanāṁ brahman
sa śāntim adhigacchati

trayāṇām—of the three; *eka-bhāvānām*—having one nature; *yaḥ*—who; *na paśyati*—does not see; *vai*—certainly; *bhidām*—separateness; *sarva-bhūta-ātmanām*—of the Supersoul of all living entities; *brahman*—O Dakṣa; *saḥ*—he; *śāntim*—peace; *adhigacchati*—realizes.

TRANSLATION

The Lord continued: One who does not consider Brahmā, Viṣṇu, Śiva or the living entities in general to be separate from the Supreme, and who knows Brahman, actually realizes peace; others do not.

PURPORT

Two words are very significant in this verse. *Trayāṇām* indicates "three," namely Lord Brahmā, Lord Śiva and Lord Viṣṇu. *Bhidām* means "different." They are three, and therefore they are separate, but at the same time they are one. This is the philosophy of simultaneous oneness and difference, which is called *acintya-bhedābheda-tattva.* The example given in the *Brahma-saṁhitā* is that milk and yogurt are simultaneously one and different; both are milk, but the yogurt has become changed. In order to achieve real peace, one should see everything and every living entity, including Lord Brahmā and Lord Śiva, as non-different from the Supreme Personality of Godhead. No one is independent. Every one of us is an expansion of the Supreme Personality of Godhead. This accounts for unity in diversity. There are diverse manifestations, but, at the same time, they are one in Viṣṇu. Everything is an expansion of Viṣṇu's energy.

TEXT 55

मैत्रेय उवाच

एवं भगवतादिष्टः प्रजापतिपतिर्हरिम् ।
अर्चित्वा क्रतुना स्वेन देवानुभयतोऽयजत् ॥५५॥

maitreya uvāca
evaṁ bhagavatādiṣṭaḥ
prajāpati-patir harim
arcitvā kratunā svena
devān ubhayato 'yajat

maitreyaḥ—Maitreya; *uvāca*—said; *evam*—thus; *bhagavatā*—by the Supreme Personality of Godhead; *ādiṣṭaḥ*—having been instructed; *prajāpati-patiḥ*—the head of all the Prajāpatis; *harim*—Hari; *arcitvā*—after worshiping; *kratunā*—with the sacrificial ceremonies; *svena*—his own; *devān*—the demigods; *ubhayataḥ*—separately; *ayajat*—worshiped.

TRANSLATION

The sage Maitreya said: Thus Dakṣa, the head of all Prajāpatis, having been nicely instructed by the Supreme Personality of God-

head, worshiped Lord Viṣṇu. After worshiping Him by performing the prescribed sacrificial ceremonies, Dakṣa separately worshiped Lord Brahmā and Lord Śiva.

PURPORT

Lord Viṣṇu should be offered everything, and His *prasāda* should be distributed to all the demigods. This practice is still followed in the temple of Jagannātha at Purī. There are many temples of demigods around the main temple of Jagannātha, and the *prasāda* which is offered first to Jagannātha is distributed to all the demigods. The deity of Bhagālin is worshiped with the *prasāda* of Viṣṇu, and also, in the famous Lord Śiva temple of Bhuvaneśvara, the *prasāda* of Lord Viṣṇu or Lord Jagannātha is offered to the deity of Lord Śiva. This is the Vaiṣṇava principle. The Vaiṣṇava does not deride even ordinary living entities, including the small ant; everyone is offered proper respect according to his position. The offering, however, is in relation to the center, the Supreme Personality of Godhead, Kṛṣṇa, or Viṣṇu. The devotee who is highly elevated sees the relationship to Kṛṣṇa in everything; he does not see anything as being independent of Kṛṣṇa. That is his vision of oneness.

TEXT 56

रुद्रं च स्वेन भागेन ह्युपाधावत्समाहितः ।
कर्मणोदवसानेन सोमपानितरानपि ।
उदवस्य सहर्त्विग्भिः सस्नाववभृथं ततः ॥५६॥

rudraṁ ca svena bhāgena
hy upādhāvat samāhitaḥ
karmaṇodavasānena
somapān itarān api
udavasya sahartvigbhiḥ
sasnāv avabhṛthaṁ tataḥ

rudram—Lord Śiva; *ca*—and; *svena*—with his own; *bhāgena*—share; *hi*—since; *upādhāvat*—he worshiped; *samāhitaḥ*—with concentrated mind; *karmaṇā*—by the performance; *udavasānena*—by the act of finishing; *soma-pān*—demigods; *itarān*—other; *api*—even;

udavasya—after finishing; *saha*—along with; *ṛtvigbhiḥ*—with the priests; *sasnau*—bathed; *avabhṛtham*—the *avabhṛtha* bath; *tataḥ*—then.

TRANSLATION

With all respect, Dakṣa worshiped Lord Śiva with his share of the remnants of the yajña. After finishing the ritualistic sacrificial activities, he satisfied all the other demigods and the other people assembled there. Then, after finishing all these duties with the priests, he took a bath and was fully satisfied.

PURPORT

Lord Rudra, Śiva, was properly worshiped with his share of the remnants of the *yajña.* Yajña is Viṣṇu, and whatever *prasāda* is offered to Viṣṇu is offered to everyone, even to Lord Śiva. Śrīdhara Svāmī also comments in this connection, *svena bhāgena:* the remnants of the *yajña* are offered to all the demigods and others.

TEXT 57

तस्मा अप्यनुभावेन स्वेनैवावाप्तराधसे ।
धर्म एव मतिं दत्त्वा त्रिदशास्ते दिवं ययुः ॥५७॥

tasmā apy anubhāvena
svenaivāvāpta-rādhase
dharma eva matiṁ dattvā
tridaśās te divaṁ yayuḥ

tasmai—unto him (Dakṣa); *api*—even; *anubhāvena*—by worshiping the Supreme Lord; *svena*—by his own; *eva*—certainly; *avāpta-rādhase*—having attained perfection; *dharme*—in religion; *eva*—certainly; *matim*—intelligence; *dattvā*—having given; *tridaśāḥ*—demigods; *te*—those; *divam*—to the heavenly planets; *yayuḥ*—went.

TRANSLATION

Thus worshiping the Supreme Lord Viṣṇu by the ritualistic performance of sacrifice, Dakṣa was completely situated on the

religious path. Moreover, all the demigods who had assembled at the sacrifice blessed him that he might increase his piety, and then they left.

PURPORT

Although Dakṣa was considerably advanced in religious principles, he awaited the blessings of the demigods. Thus the great sacrifice conducted by Dakṣa ended in harmony and peace.

TEXT 58

एवं दाक्षायणी हित्वा सती पूर्वकलेवरम् ।
जज्ञे हिमवतः क्षेत्रे मेनायामिति शुश्रुम ॥५८॥

evaṁ dākṣāyaṇī hitvā
satī pūrva-kalevaram
jajñe himavataḥ kṣetre
menāyām iti śuśruma

evam—thus; *dākṣāyaṇī*—the daughter of Dakṣa; *hitvā*—after giving up; *satī*—Satī; *pūrva-kalevaram*—her former body; *jajñe*—was born; *himavataḥ*—of the Himalayas; *kṣetre*—in the wife; *menāyām*—in Menā; *iti*—thus; *śuśruma*—I have heard.

TRANSLATION

Maitreya said: I have heard that after giving up the body she had received from Dakṣa, Dākṣāyaṇī (his daughter) took her birth in the kingdom of the Himalayas. She was born as the daughter of Menā. I heard this from authoritative sources.

PURPORT

Menā is also known as Menakā and is the wife of the king of the Himalayas.

TEXT 59

तमेव दयितं भूय आवृङ्क्ते पतिमम्बिका ।
अनन्यभावैकगतिं शक्तिः सुप्तेव पूरुषम् ॥५९॥

tam eva dayitaṁ bhūya
āvṛṅkte patim ambikā
ananya-bhāvaika-gatiṁ
śaktiḥ supteva pūruṣam

tam—him (Lord Śiva); *eva*—certainly; *dayitam*—beloved; *bhūyaḥ*—again; *āvṛṅkte*—accepted; *patim*—as her husband; *ambikā*—Ambikā, or Satī; *ananya-bhāvā*—without attachment for others; *eka-gatim*—the one goal; *śaktiḥ*—the feminine (marginal and external) energies; *suptā*—lying dormant; *iva*—as; *pūruṣam*—the masculine (Lord Śiva, as representative of the Supreme Lord).

TRANSLATION

Ambikā [goddess Durgā], who was known as Dākṣāyiṇī [Satī], again accepted Lord Śiva as her husband, just as different energies of the Supreme Personality of Godhead act during the course of a new creation.

PURPORT

According to a verse of the Vedic *mantras, parāsya śaktir vividhaiva śrūyate:* the Supreme Personality of Godhead has different varieties of energies. *Śakti* is feminine, and the Lord is *puruṣa,* masculine. It is the duty of the female to serve under the supreme *puruṣa.* As stated in *Bhagavad-gītā,* all living entities are marginal energies of the Supreme Lord. Therefore it is the duty of all living entities to serve this Supreme Person. Durgā is the representation in the material world of both the marginal and external energies, and Lord Śiva is the representation of the Supreme Person. The connection of Lord Śiva and Ambikā, or Durgā, is eternal. Satī could not accept any husband but Lord Śiva. How Lord Śiva remarried Durgā as Himavatī, the daughter of the Himalayas, and how Kārttikeya was born, is a great story in itself.

TEXT 60

एतद्भगवतः शम्भोः कर्म दक्षाध्वरद्रुहः ।
श्रुतं भागवताच्छिष्यादुद्धवान्मे बृहस्पतेः ॥६०॥

etad bhagavataḥ śambhoḥ
karma dakṣādhvara-druhaḥ
śrutaṁ bhāgavatāc chiṣyād
uddhavān me bṛhaspateḥ

etat—this; *bhagavataḥ*—of the possessor of all opulences; *śambhoḥ*—of Śambhu (Lord Śiva); *karma*—story; *dakṣa-adhvara-druhaḥ*—who devastated the sacrifice of Dakṣa; *śrutam*—was heard; *bhāgavatāt*—from a great devotee; *śiṣyāt*—from the disciple; *uddhavāt*—from Uddhava; *me*—by me; *bṛhaspateḥ*—of Bṛhaspati.

TRANSLATION

Maitreya said: My dear Vidura, I heard this story of the Dakṣa yajña, which was devastated by Lord Śiva, from Uddhava, a great devotee and a disciple of Bṛhaspati.

TEXT 61

इदं पवित्रं परमीशचेष्टितं
यशस्यमायुष्यमघौघमर्षणम् ।
यो नित्यदाकर्ण्य नरोऽनुकीर्तयेद्
धुनोत्यघं कौरव भक्तिभावतः ॥६१॥

idaṁ pavitraṁ param īśa-ceṣṭitaṁ
yaśasyam āyuṣyam aghaugha-marṣaṇam
yo nityadākarṇya naro 'nukīrtayed
dhunoty aghaṁ kaurava bhakti-bhāvataḥ

idam—this; *pavitram*—pure; *param*—supreme; *īśa-ceṣṭitam*—pastime of the Supreme Lord; *yaśasyam*—fame; *āyuṣyam*—long duration of life; *agha-ogha-marṣaṇam*—destroying sins; *yaḥ*—who; *nityadā*—always; *ākarṇya*—after hearing; *naraḥ*—a person; *anukīrtayet*—should narrate; *dhunoti*—clears off; *agham*—material contamination; *kaurava*—O descendant of Kuru; *bhakti-bhāvataḥ*—with faith and devotion.

TRANSLATION

The great sage Maitreya concluded: If one hears and again narrates, with faith and devotion, this story of the Dakṣa yajña as it was conducted by the Supreme Personality of Godhead, Viṣṇu, then certainly one is cleared of all contamination of material existence, O son of Kuru.

Thus end the Bhaktivedanta purports of the Fourth Canto, Seventh Chapter, of the Śrīmad-Bhāgavatam, *entitled "The Sacrifice Performed by Dakṣa."*

CHAPTER EIGHT

Dhruva Mahārāja Leaves Home for the Forest

TEXT 1

मैत्रेय उवाच
सनकाद्या नारदश्च ऋभुर्हंसोऽरुणिर्यतिः ।
नैते गृहान् ब्रह्मसुता ह्यावसन्नूर्ध्वरेतसः ॥ १ ॥

maitreya uvāca
sanakādyā nāradaś ca
ṛbhur haṁso 'ruṇir yatiḥ
naite gṛhān brahma-sutā
hy āvasann ūrdhva-retasaḥ

maitreyaḥ uvāca—Maitreya said; *sanaka-ādyāḥ*—those headed by Sanaka; *nāradaḥ*—Nārada; *ca*—and; *ṛbhuḥ*—Ṛbhu; *haṁsaḥ*—Haṁsa; *aruṇiḥ*—Aruṇi; *yatiḥ*—Yati; *na*—not; *ete*—all these; *gṛhān*—at home; *brahma-sutāḥ*—sons of Brahmā; *hi*—certainly; *āvasan*—did live; *ūrdhva-retasaḥ*—unadulterated celibates.

TRANSLATION

The great sage Maitreya said: The four great Kumāra sages headed by Sanaka, as well as Nārada, Ṛbhu, Haṁsa, Aruṇi and Yati, all sons of Brahmā, did not live at home, but became ūrdhva-retā, or naiṣṭhika-brahmacārīs, unadulterated celibates.

PURPORT

The system of *brahmacarya* has been current since the birth of Brahmā. A section of the population, especially male, did not marry at all. Instead of allowing their semen to be driven downwards, they used to lift the semen up to the brain. They are called *ūrdhva-retasaḥ*, those who lift up. Semen is so important that if, by the yogic process, one can lift the semen up to the brain, he can perform wonderful work—one's memory is enabled to act very swiftly, and the duration of life is increased. *Yogīs* can thus perform all kinds of austerity with steadiness and be elevated to the highest perfectional stage, even to the spiritual world. Vivid examples of *brahmacārīs* who accepted this principle of life are the four sages Sanaka, Sanandana, Sanātana and Sanat-kumāra, as well as Nārada and others.

Another significant phrase here is *naite gṛhān hy āvasan*, "they did not live at home." *Gṛha* means "home" as well as "wife." In fact, "home" means wife; "home" does not mean a room or a house. One who lives with a wife lives at home, otherwise a *sannyāsī* or *brahmacārī*, even though he may live in a room or in a house, does not live at home. That they did not live at home means that they did not accept a wife, and so there was no question of their discharging semen. Semen is meant to be discharged when one has a home, a wife and the intention to beget children, otherwise there is no injunction for discharging semen. These principles were followed from the beginning of creation, and such *brahmacārīs* never created progeny. This narration has dealt with the descendants of Lord Brahmā from Manu's daughter Prasūti. Prasūti's daughter was Dākṣāyaṇī, or Satī, in relation to whom the story of the Dakṣa *yajña* was narrated. Maitreya is now explaining about the progeny of the sons of Brahmā. Out of the many sons of Brahmā, the *brahmacārī* sons headed by Sanaka and Nārada did not marry at all, and therefore there is no question of narrating the history of their descendants.

TEXT 2

मृषाधर्मस्य भार्यासीद्दम्भं मायां च शत्रुहन् ।
असूत मिथुनं तत्तु निर्ऋतिर्जगृहेऽप्रजः ॥ २ ॥

mṛṣādharmasya bhāryāsīd
dambhaṁ māyāṁ ca śatru-han
asūta mithunaṁ tat tu
nirṛtir jagṛhe 'prajaḥ

mṛṣā—Mṛṣā; *adharmasya*—of Irreligion; *bhāryā*—wife; *āsīt*—was; *dambham*—Bluffing; *māyām*—Cheating; *ca*—and; *śatru-han*—O slayer of enemies; *asūta*—produced; *mithunam*—combination; *tat*—that; *tu*—but; *nirṛtiḥ*—Nirṛti; *jagṛhe*—took; *aprajaḥ*—being childless.

TRANSLATION

Another son of Lord Brahmā was Irreligion, whose wife's name was Falsity. From their combination were born two demons named Dambha, or Bluffing, and Māyā, or Cheating. These two demons were taken by a demon named Nirṛti, who had no children.

PURPORT

It is understood herein that Adharma, Irreligion, was also a son of Brahmā, and he married his sister Mṛṣā. This is the beginning of sex life between brother and sister. This unnatural combination of sex life can be possible in human society only where there is Adharma, or Irreligion. It is understood that in the beginning of creation Brahmā created not only saintly sons like Sanaka, Sanātana and Nārada but also demonic offspring like Nirṛti, Adharma, Dambha and Falsity. Everything was created by Brahmā in the beginning. Regarding Nārada, it is understood that because his previous life was very pious and his association very good, he was born as Nārada. Others were also born in their own capacities, according to their backgrounds. The law of *karma* continues birth after birth, and when there is a new creation, the same *karma* comes back with the living entities. They are born in different capacities according to *karma* even though their father is originally Brahmā, who is the exalted qualitative incarnation of the Supreme Personality of Godhead.

TEXT 3

तयोः समभवल्लोभो निकृतिश्च महामते ।
ताभ्यां क्रोधश्च हिंसा च यदुरुक्तिः स्वसा कलिः ॥३॥

tayoḥ samabhaval lobho
nikṛtiś ca mahā-mate
tābhyāṁ krodhaś ca hiṁsā ca
yad duruktiḥ svasā kaliḥ

tayoḥ—those two; *samabhavat*—were born; *lobhaḥ*—Greed; *nikṛtiḥ*—Cunning; *ca*—and; *mahā-mate*—O great soul; *tābhyām*—from both of them; *krodhaḥ*—Anger; *ca*—and; *hiṁsā*—Envy; *ca*—and; *yat*—from both of whom; *duruktiḥ*—Harsh Speech; *svasā*—sister; *kaliḥ*—Kali.

TRANSLATION

Maitreya told Vidura: O great soul, from Dambha and Māyā were born Greed and Nikṛti, or Cunning. From their combination came children named Krodha (Anger) and Hiṁsā (Envy), and from their combination were born Kali and his sister Durukti (Harsh Speech).

TEXT 4

दुरुक्तौ कलिराधत्त भयं मृत्युं च सत्तम ।
तयोश्च मिथुनं जज्ञे यातना निरयस्तथा ॥ ४ ॥

duruktau kalir ādhatta
bhayaṁ mṛtyuṁ ca sattama
tayoś ca mithunaṁ jajñe
yātanā nirayas tathā

duruktau—in Durukti; *kaliḥ*—Kali; *ādhatta*—produced; *bhayam*—Fearfulness; *mṛtyum*—Death; *ca*—and; *sat-tama*—O greatest of all good men; *tayoḥ*—of those two; *ca*—and; *mithunam*—by combination; *jajñe*—were produced; *yātanā*—Excessive Pain; *nirayaḥ*—Hell; *tathā*—as well.

TRANSLATION

O greatest of all good men, by the combination of Kali and Harsh Speech were born children named Mṛtyu (Death) and Bhīti (Fear). From the combination of Mṛtyu and Bhīti came children named Yātanā (Excessive Pain) and Niraya (Hell).

TEXT 5

संग्रहेण मयाख्यातः प्रतिसर्गस्तवानघ ।
त्रिःश्रुत्वैतत्पुमान् पुण्यं विधुनोत्यात्मनो मलम् ॥५॥

saṅgraheṇa mayākhyātaḥ
pratisargas tavānagha
triḥ śrutvaitat pumān puṇyaṁ
vidhunoty ātmano malam

saṅgraheṇa—in summary; *mayā*—by me; *ākhyātaḥ*—is explained; *pratisargaḥ*—cause of devastation; *tava*—your; *anagha*—O pure one; *triḥ*—three times; *śrutvā*—having heard; *etat*—this description; *pumān*—one who; *puṇyam*—piety; *vidhunoti*—washes off; *ātmanaḥ*—of the soul; *malam*—contamination.

TRANSLATION

My dear Vidura, I have summarily explained the causes of devastation. One who hears this description three times attains piety and washes the sinful contamination from his soul.

PURPORT

The creation takes place on the basis of goodness, but devastation takes place because of irreligion. That is the way of material creation and devastation. Here it is stated that the cause of devastation is Adharma, or Irreligion. The descendants of Irreligion and Falsity, born one after another, are Bluffing, Cheating, Greed, Cunning, Anger, Envy, Quarrel, Harsh Speech, Death, Fear, Severe Pain and Hell. All these descendants are described as signs of devastation. If a person is pious and hears about these causes of devastation, he will feel hatred for all these, and that will cause his advancement in a life of piety. Piety refers to the process of cleansing the heart. As recommended by Lord Caitanya, one has to cleanse the dust from the mirror of the mind, and then advancement on the path of liberation begins. Here also the same process is recommended. *Malam* means "contamination." We should learn to despise all the causes of devastation, beginning from irreligion and cheating, and then we shall be able to make advancement in a life of piety. The possibility of our attaining Kṛṣṇa consciousness will be easier, and we shall not be subjected to repeated devastation. The present life is repeated birth and death, but if we seek the path of liberation, we may be saved from repeated suffering.

TEXT 6

अथातः कीर्तये वंशं पुण्यकीर्तेः कुरूद्वह ।
स्वायम्भुवस्यापि मनोर्हरेरंशांशजन्मनः ॥ ६ ॥

athātaḥ kīrtaye vaṁśaṁ
puṇya-kīrteḥ kurūdvaha
svāyambhuvasyāpi manor
harer aṁśāṁśa-janmanaḥ

atha—now; *ataḥ*—hereafter; *kīrtaye*—I shall describe; *vaṁśam*—dynasty; *puṇya-kīrteḥ*—celebrated for virtuous activities; *kuru-ud-vaha*—O best of the Kurus; *svāyambhuvasya*—of Svāyambhuva; *api*—even; *manoḥ*—of the Manu; *hareḥ*—of the Personality of Godhead; *aṁśa*—plenary expansion; *aṁśa*—part of; *janmanaḥ*—born of.

TRANSLATION

Maitreya continued: O best of the Kuru dynasty, I shall now describe before you the descendants of Svāyambhuva Manu, who was born of a part of a plenary expansion of the Supreme Personality of Godhead.

PURPORT

Lord Brahmā is a powerful expansion of the Supreme Personality of Godhead. Although Brahmā is *jīva-tattva*, he is empowered by the Lord, and therefore he is considered a plenary expansion of the Supreme Godhead. Sometimes it happens that when there is no suitable living being to be empowered to act as Brahmā, the Supreme Lord Himself appears as Brahmā. Brahmā is the plenary expansion of the Supreme Personality of Godhead, and Svāyambhuva Manu was the direct son of Brahmā. The great sage Maitreya is now going to explain about the descendants of this Manu, all of whom are widely celebrated for their pious activities. Before speaking of these pious descendants, Maitreya has already described the descendants of impious activities, representing anger, envy, unpalatable speech, quarrel, fear and death. Purposely, therefore, he is next relating the history of the life of Dhruva Mahārāja, the most pious king within this universe.

TEXT 7

प्रियव्रतोत्तानपादौ शतरूपापतेः सुतौ ।
वासुदेवस्य कलया रक्षायां जगतः स्थितौ ॥ ७ ॥

priyavratottānapādau
śatarūpā-pateḥ sutau
vāsudevasya kalayā
rakṣāyāṁ jagataḥ sthitau

priyavrata—Priyavrata; *uttānapādau*—Uttānapāda; *śatarūpā-pateḥ*—of Queen Śatarūpā and her husband, Manu; *sutau*—the two sons; *vāsudevasya*—of the Supreme Personality of Godhead; *kalayā*—by plenary expansion; *rakṣāyām*—for the protection; *jagataḥ*—of the world; *sthitau*—for the maintenance.

TRANSLATION

Svāyambhuva Manu had two sons by his wife, Śatarūpā, and the names of the sons were Uttānapāda and Priyavrata. Because both of them were descendants of a plenary expansion of Vāsudeva, the Supreme Personality of Godhead, they were very competent to rule the universe to maintain and protect the citizens.

PURPORT

It is said that these two kings, Uttānapāda and Priyavrata, were specifically empowered by the Supreme Personality of Godhead, unlike the great King Ṛṣabha, who was the Supreme Personality of Godhead Himself.

TEXT 8

जाये उत्तानपादस्य सुनीतिः सुरुचिस्तयोः ।
सुरुचिः प्रेयसी पत्युर्नेतरा यत्सुतो ध्रुवः ॥ ८ ॥

jāye uttānapādasya
sunītiḥ surucis tayoḥ
suruciḥ preyasī patyur
netarā yat-suto dhruvaḥ

jāye—of the two wives; *uttānapādasya*—of King Uttānapāda; *sunītiḥ*—Sunīti; *suruciḥ*—Suruci; *tayoḥ*—of both of them; *suruciḥ*—Suruci; *preyasī*—very dear; *patyuḥ*—of the husband; *na itarā*—not the other; *yat*—whose; *sutaḥ*—son; *dhruvaḥ*—Dhruva.

TRANSLATION

King Uttānapāda had two queens, named Sunīti and Suruci. Suruci was much more dear to the King; Sunīti, who had a son named Dhruva, was not his favorite.

PURPORT

The great sage Maitreya wanted to describe the pious activities of the kings. Priyavrata was the first son of Svāyambhuva Manu, and Uttānapāda was the second, but the great sage Maitreya immediately began to speak of Dhruva Mahārāja, the son of Uttānapāda, because Maitreya was very eager to describe pious activities. The incidents in the life of Dhruva Mahārāja are very attractive for devotees. From his pious actions, one can learn how one can detach himself from material possessions and how one can enhance one's devotional service by severe austerities and penances. By hearing the activities of pious Dhruva, one can enhance one's faith in God and can directly connect with the Supreme Personality of Godhead, and thus one can very soon be elevated to the transcendental platform of devotional service. The example of Dhruva Mahārāja's austerities can immediately generate a feeling of devotional service in the hearts of the hearers.

TEXT 9

एकदा सुरुचेः पुत्रमङ्कमारोप्य लालयन् ।
उत्तमं नारुरुक्षन्तं ध्रुवं राजाभ्यनन्दत ॥ ९ ॥

ekadā suruceḥ putram
aṅkam āropya lālayan
uttamaṁ nāruruksantaṁ
dhruvaṁ rājābhyanandata

ekadā—once upon a time; *suruceḥ*—of Queen Suruci; *putram*—the son; *aṅkam*—on the lap; *āropya*—placing; *lālayan*—while patting; *ut-*

tamam—Uttama; *na*—did not; *āruruksantam*—trying to get on; *dhruvam*—Dhruva; *rājā*—the King; *abhyanandata*—welcome.

TRANSLATION

Once upon a time, King Uttānapāda was patting the son of Suruci, Uttama, placing him on his lap. Dhruva Mahārāja was also trying to get on the King's lap, but the King did not very much welcome him.

TEXT 10

तथा चिकीर्षमाणं तं सपत्न्यास्तनयं ध्रुवम् ।
सुरुचिः शृण्वतो राज्ञः सेर्ष्यमाहातिगर्विता ॥१०॥

tathā cikīrṣamāṇaṁ taṁ
sapatnyās tanayaṁ dhruvam
suruciḥ śṛṇvato rājñaḥ
serṣyam āhātigarvitā

tathā—thus; *cikīrṣamāṇam*—the child Dhruva, who was trying to get up; *tam*—unto him; *sa-patnyāḥ*—of her co-wife (Sunīti); *tanayam*—son; *dhruvam*—Dhruva; *suruciḥ*—Queen Suruci; *śṛṇvataḥ*—while hearing; *rājñaḥ*—of the King; *sa-īrṣyam*—with envy; *āha*—said; *atigarvitā*—being too proud.

TRANSLATION

While the child, Dhruva Mahārāja, was trying to get on the lap of his father, Suruci, his stepmother, became very envious of the child, and with great pride she began to speak so as to be heard by the King himself.

PURPORT

The King, of course, was equally affectionate toward both his sons, Uttama and Dhruva, so he had a natural inclination to take Dhruva, as well as Uttama, on his lap. But because of his favoritism towards his queen Suruci, he could not welcome Dhruva Mahārāja, despite his feelings. King Uttānapāda's feeling was understood by Suruci, and therefore with great pride she began to speak about the King's affection for her. This is the nature of woman. If a woman understands that her husband regards her as a favorite and is especially affectionate to her, she takes undue advantage. These symptoms are visible even in such an elevated society as the family of Svāyambhuva Manu. Therefore it is concluded that the feminine nature of woman is present everywhere.

TEXT 11

न वत्स नृपतेर्धिष्ण्यं भवानारोढुमर्हति ।
न गृहीतो मया यत्त्वं कुक्षावपि नृपात्मजः ॥११॥

na vatsa nṛpater dhiṣṇyaṁ
bhavān āroḍhum arhati
na gṛhīto mayā yat tvaṁ
kukṣāv api nṛpātmajaḥ

na—not; *vatsa*—my dear child; *nṛpateḥ*—of the King; *dhiṣṇyam*—seat; *bhavān*—yourself; *āroḍhum*—to get on; *arhati*—deserve; *na*—not; *gṛhītaḥ*—taken; *mayā*—by me; *yat*—because; *tvam*—you; *kukṣau*—in the womb; *api*—although; *nṛpa-ātmajaḥ*—son of the King.

TRANSLATION

Queen Suruci told Dhruva Mahārāja: My dear child, you do not deserve to sit on the throne or on the lap of the King. Surely you are also the son of the King, but because you did not take your birth from my womb, you are not qualified to sit on your father's lap.

PURPORT

Queen Suruci very proudly informed Dhruva Mahārāja that to be the King's son was not the qualification for sitting on the lap or throne of the King. Rather, this privilege was dependent on one's having taken birth from her womb. In other words, she indirectly informed Dhruva Mahārāja that although he happened to be born of the King, he was considered an illegitimate son because of his birth from the womb of the other queen.

TEXT 12

बालोऽसि बत नात्मानमन्यस्त्रीगर्भसम्भृतम् ।
नूनं वेद भवान् यस्य दुर्लभेऽर्थे मनोरथः ॥१२॥

bālo 'si bata nātmānam
anya-strī-garbha-sambhṛtam
nūnaṁ veda bhavān yasya
durlabhe 'rthe manorathaḥ

bālaḥ—child; *asi*—you are; *bata*—however; *na*—not; *ātmānam*—my own; *anya*—other; *strī*—woman; *garbha*—womb; *sambhṛtam*—born by; *nūnam*—however; *veda*—just try to know; *bhavān*—yourself; *yasya*—of which; *durlabhe*—unapproachable; *arthe*—matter; *manaḥ-rathaḥ*—desirous.

TRANSLATION

My dear child, you are unaware that you were born not of my womb but of another woman. Therefore you should know that your attempt is doomed to failure. You are trying to fulfill a desire which is impossible to fulfill.

PURPORT

The small child, Dhruva Mahārāja, was naturally affectionate toward his father, and he did not know that there was a distinction between his two mothers. This distinction was pointed out by Queen Suruci, who informed him that since he was a child he did not understand the distinction between the two queens. This is another statement of Queen Suruci's pride.

TEXT 13

तपसाराध्य पुरुषं तस्यैवानुग्रहेण मे ।
गर्भे त्वं साधयात्मानं यदीच्छसि नृपासनम् ॥१३॥

tapasārādhya puruṣaṁ
tasyaivānugraheṇa me

garbhe tvaṁ sādhayātmānaṁ
yadīcchasi nṛpāsanam

tapasā—by austerities; *ārādhya*—having satisfied; *puruṣam*—the Supreme Personality of Godhead; *tasya*—by His; *eva*—only; *anugraheṇa*—by the mercy of; *me*—my; *garbhe*—in the womb; *tvam*—you; *sādhaya*—place; *ātmānam*—yourself; *yadi*—if; *icchasi*—you desire; *nṛpa-āsanam*—on the throne of the King.

TRANSLATION

If you at all desire to rise to the throne of the King, then you have to undergo severe austerities. First of all you must satisfy the Supreme Personality of Godhead, Nārāyaṇa, and then, when you are favored by Him because of such worship, you shall have to take your next birth from my womb.

PURPORT

Suruci was so envious of Dhruva Mahārāja that she indirectly asked him to change his body. According to her, first of all he had to die, then take his next body in her womb, and only then would it be possible for Dhruva Mahārāja to ascend the throne of his father.

TEXT 14

मैत्रेय उवाच

मातुः सपत्न्याः स दुरुक्तिविद्धः
श्वसन् रुषा दण्डहतो यथाहिः ।
हित्वा मिषन्तं पितरं सन्नवाचं
जगाम मातुः प्ररुदन् सकाशम् ॥१४॥

maitreya uvāca
mātuḥ sapatnyāḥ sa durukti-viddhaḥ
śvasan ruṣā daṇḍa-hato yathāhiḥ
hitvā miṣantaṁ pitaraṁ sanna-vācaṁ
jagāma mātuḥ prarudan sakāśam

maitreyaḥ uvāca—the great sage Maitreya said; *mātuḥ*—of his mother; *sa-patnyāḥ*—of the co-wife; *saḥ*—he; *durukti*—harsh words; *viddhaḥ*—being pierced by; *śvasan*—breathing very heavily; *ruṣā*—out of anger; *daṇḍa-hataḥ*—struck by a stick; *yathā*—as much as; *ahiḥ*—a snake; *hitvā*—giving up; *miṣantam*—simply looking over; *pitaram*—his father; *sanna-vācam*—silently; *jagāma*—went; *mātuḥ*—to his mother; *prarudan*—weeping; *sakāśam*—near.

TRANSLATION

The sage Maitreya continued: My dear Vidura, as a snake, when struck by a stick, breathes very heavily, Dhruva Mahārāja, having been struck by the strong words of his stepmother, began to breathe very heavily because of great anger. When he saw that his father was silent and did not protest, he immediately left the palace and went to his mother.

TEXT 15

तं निःश्वसन्तं स्फुरिताधरोष्ठं
सुनीतिरुत्सङ्ग उदूह्य बालम् ।
निशम्य तत्पौरमुखान्नितान्तं
सा विव्यथे यद्गदितं सपत्न्या ॥१५॥

taṁ niḥśvasantaṁ sphuritādharoṣṭhaṁ
sunītir utsaṅga udūhya bālam
niśamya tat-paura-mukhān nitāntaṁ
sā vivyathe yad gaditaṁ sapatnyā

tam—him; *niḥśvasantam*—heavily breathing; *sphurita*—trembling; *adhara-oṣṭham*—upper and lower lips; *sunītiḥ*—Queen Sunīti; *utsaṅge*—on her lap; *udūhya*—lifting; *bālam*—her son; *niśamya*—after hearing; *tat-paura-mukhāt*—from the mouths of other inhabitants; *nitāntam*—all descriptions; *sā*—she; *vivyathe*—became aggrieved; *yat*—that which; *gaditam*—spoken; *sa-patnyā*—by her co-wife.

TRANSLATION

When Dhruva Mahārāja reached his mother, his lips were trembling in anger, and he was crying very grievously. Queen Sunīti

immediately lifted her son onto her lap, while the palace residents who had heard all the harsh words of Suruci related everything in detail. Thus Sunīti also became greatly aggrieved.

TEXT 16

सोत्सृज्य धैर्यं विललाप शोक-
दावाग्निना दावलतेव बाला ।
वाक्यं सपत्न्याः स्मरती सरोज-
श्रिया दृशा बाष्पकलामुवाह ॥१६॥

sotsṛjya dhairyaṁ vilalāpa śoka-
dāvāgninā dāva-lateva bālā
vākyaṁ sapatnyāḥ smaratī saroja-
śriyā dṛśā bāṣpa-kalām uvāha

sā—she; *utsṛjya*—giving up; *dhairyam*—patience; *vilalāpa*—lamented; *śoka-dāva-agninā*—by the fire of grief; *dāva-latā iva*—like burnt leaves; *bālā*—the woman; *vākyam*—words; *sa-patnyāḥ*—spoken by her co-wife; *smaratī*—remember; *saroja-śriyā*—a face as beautiful as a lotus; *dṛśā*—by looking; *bāṣpa-kalām*—weeping; *uvāha*—said.

TRANSLATION

This incident was unbearable to Sunīti's patience. She began to burn as if in a forest fire, and in her grief she became just like a burnt leaf and so lamented. As she remembered the words of her co-wife, her bright, lotuslike face filled with tears, and thus she spoke.

PURPORT

When a man is aggrieved, he feels exactly like a burnt leaf in a forest fire. Sunīti's position was like that. Although her face was as beautiful as a lotus flower, it dried up because of the burning fire caused by the harsh words of her co-wife.

TEXT 17

दीर्घं श्वसन्ती वृजिनस्य पार-
मपश्यती बालकमाह बाला ।

मामङ्गलं तात परेषु मंस्था
भुङ्क्ते जनो यत्परदुःखदस्तत् ॥१७॥

dīrghaṁ śvasantī vṛjinasya pāram
apaśyatī bālakam āha bālā
māmaṅgalaṁ tāta pareṣu maṁsthā
bhuṅkte jano yat para-duḥkhadas tat

dīrgham—heavy; *śvasantī*—breathing; *vṛjinasya*—of the danger; *pāram*—limitation; *apaśyatī*—without finding; *bālakam*—to her son; *āha*—said; *bālā*—the lady; *mā*—let there not be; *amaṅgalam*—ill fortune; *tāta*—my dear son; *pareṣu*—unto others; *maṁsthāḥ*—desire; *bhuṅkte*—suffered; *janaḥ*—person; *yat*—that which; *para-duḥkha-daḥ*—who is apt to inflict pains upon others; *tat*—that.

TRANSLATION

She also was breathing very heavily, and she did not know the factual remedy for the painful situation. Not finding any remedy, she said to her son: My dear son, don't wish for anything inauspicious for others. Anyone who inflicts pains upon others suffers himself from that pain.

TEXT 18

सत्यं सुरुच्याभिहितं भवान्मे
यद् दुर्भगाया उदरे गृहीतः ।
स्तन्येन वृद्धश्च विलज्जते यां
भार्येति वा वोढुमिडस्पतिर्माम् ॥१८॥

satyaṁ surucyābhihitaṁ bhavān me
yad durbhagāyā udare gṛhītaḥ
stanyena vṛddhaś ca vilajjate yāṁ
bhāryeti vā voḍhum iḍaspatir mām

satyam—truth; *surucyā*—by Queen Suruci; *abhihitam*—narrated; *bhavān*—unto you; *me*—of me; *yat*—because; *durbhagāyāḥ*—of the unfortunate; *udare*—in the womb; *gṛhītaḥ*—taken birth; *stanyena*—

fed by the breast milk; *vṛddhaḥ ca*—grown up; *vilajjate*—becomes ashamed; *yām*—unto one; *bhāryā*—wife; *iti*—thus; *vā*—or; *voḍhum*—to accept; *iḍaḥ-patiḥ*—the King; *mām*—me.

TRANSLATION

Sunīti said: My dear boy, whatever has been spoken by Suruci is so, because the King, your father, does not consider me his wife or even his maidservant. He feels ashamed to accept me. Therefore it is a fact that you have taken birth from the womb of an unfortunate woman, and by being fed from her breast you have grown up.

TEXT 19

आतिष्ठ तत्तात विमत्सरस्त्व-
मुक्तं समात्रापि यदव्यलीकम् ।
आराधयाधोक्षजपादपद्मं
यदीच्छसेऽध्यासनमुत्तमो यथा ॥१९॥

ātiṣṭha tat tāta vimatsaras tvam
uktaṁ samātrāpi yad avyalīkam
ārādhayādhokṣaja-pāda-padmaṁ
yadīcchase 'dhyāsanam uttamo yathā

ātiṣṭha—just execute; *tat*—that; *tāta*—my dear son; *vimatsaraḥ*—without being envious; *tvam*—unto you; *uktam*—said; *samātrā api*—by your stepmother; *yat*—whatever; *avyalīkam*—they are all factual; *ārādhaya*—just begin worshiping; *adhokṣaja*—the Transcendence; *pāda-padmam*—lotus feet; *yadi*—if; *icchase*—desire; *adhyāsanam*—to be seated along with; *uttamaḥ*—your stepbrother; *yathā*—as much as.

TRANSLATION

My dear boy, whatever has been spoken by Suruci, your stepmother, although very harsh to hear, is factual. Therefore, if you desire at all to sit on the same throne as your stepbrother, Uttama, then give up your envious attitude and immediately try to execute the instructions of your stepmother. Without further delay, you

must engage yourself in worshiping the lotus feet of the Supreme Personality of Godhead.

PURPORT

The harsh words used by Suruci to her stepson were true because unless one is favored by the Supreme Personality of Godhead one cannot achieve any success in life. Man proposes, God disposes. Sunīti, the mother of Dhruva Mahārāja, agreed with her co-wife's advice that Dhruva engage himself in the worship of the Supreme Personality of Godhead. Indirectly, the words of Suruci were a benediction for Dhruva Mahārāja, for because of the influence of his stepmother's words, he became a great devotee.

TEXT 20

यस्याङ्घ्रिपद्मं परिचर्य विश्व-
विभावनायात्तगुणाभिपत्तेः ।
अजोऽध्यतिष्ठत्खलु पारमेष्ठ्यं
पदं जितात्मश्वसनाभिवन्द्यम् ॥२०॥

yasyāṅghri-padmaṁ paricarya viśva-
vibhāvanāyātta-guṇābhipatteḥ
ajo 'dhyatiṣṭhat khalu pārameṣṭhyaṁ
padaṁ jitātma-śvasanābhivandyam

yasya—whose; *aṅghri*—leg; *padmam*—lotus feet; *paricarya*—worshiping; *viśva*—universe; *vibhāvanāya*—for creating; *ātta*—received; *guṇa-abhipatteḥ*—for acquiring the required qualifications; *ajaḥ*—the unborn (Lord Brahmā); *adhyatiṣṭhat*—became situated; *khalu*—undoubtedly; *pārameṣṭhyam*—the supreme position within the universe; *padam*—position; *jita-ātma*—one who has conquered his mind; *śvasana*—by controlling the life air; *abhivandyam*—worshipable.

TRANSLATION

Sunīti continued: The Supreme Personality of Godhead is so great that simply by worshiping His lotus feet, your great-grandfather, Lord Brahmā, acquired the necessary qualifications

to create this universe. Although he is unborn and is the chief of all living creatures, he is situated in that exalted post because of the mercy of the Supreme Personality of Godhead, whom even great yogīs worship by controlling the mind and regulating the life air [prāṇa].

PURPORT

Sunīti cited the example of Lord Brahmā, who was Dhruva Mahārāja's great-grandfather. Although Lord Brahmā is also a living being, by his penance and austerity he acquired the exalted position of creator of this universe by the mercy of the Supreme Lord. To become successful in any attempt, one not only has to undergo severe penances and austerities, but also must be dependent on the mercy of the Supreme Personality of Godhead. This indication had been given to Dhruva Mahārāja by his stepmother and was now confirmed by his own mother, Sunīti.

TEXT 21

तथा मनुर्वो भगवान् पितामहो
यमेकमत्या पुरुदक्षिणैर्मखैः ।
इष्ट्वाभिपेदे दुरवापमन्यतो
भौमं सुखं दिव्यमथापवर्ग्यम् ॥२१॥

tathā manur vo bhagavān pitāmaho
yam eka-matyā puru-dakṣiṇair makhaiḥ
iṣṭvābhipede duravāpam anyato
bhaumaṁ sukhaṁ divyam athāpavargyam

tathā—similarly; *manuḥ*—Svāyambhuva Manu; *vaḥ*—your; *bhagavān*—worshipable; *pitāmahaḥ*—grandfather; *yam*—unto whom; *eka-matyā*—with unflinching devotion; *puru*—great; *dakṣiṇaiḥ*—charity; *makhaiḥ*—by executing sacrifices; *iṣṭvā*—worshiping; *abhipede*—achieved; *duravāpam*—difficult to achieve; *anyataḥ*—by any other means; *bhaumam*—material; *sukham*—happiness; *divyam*—celestial; *atha*—thereafter; *āpavargyam*—liberation.

TRANSLATION

Sunīti informed her son: Your grandfather Svāyambhuva Manu executed great sacrifices with distribution of charity, and thereby, with unflinching faith and devotion, he worshiped and satisfied the Supreme Personality of Godhead. By acting in that way, he achieved the greatest success in material happiness and afterwards achieved liberation, which is impossible to obtain by worshiping the demigods.

PURPORT

The success of one's life is measured by one's material happiness in this life and liberation in the next. Such success can be achieved only by the grace of the Supreme Personality of Godhead. The words *eka-matyā* mean concentrating one's mind on the Lord without deviation. This process of undeviating worship of the Supreme Lord is also expressed in *Bhagavad-gītā* as *ananya-bhāk.* "That which is impossible to obtain from any other source" is also mentioned here. "Other source" refers to worship of the demigods. It is especially stressed here that the opulence of Manu was due to his undeviating faithfulness in the transcendental service of the Lord. One who diverts his mind to worshiping many demigods to obtain material happiness is considered bereft of intelligence. If anyone wants even material happiness, he can worship the Supreme Lord without deviation, and persons who are desirous of liberation can also worship the Supreme Lord and achieve their goal of life.

TEXT 22

तमेव वत्साश्रय भृत्यवत्सलं
मुमुक्षुभिर्मृग्यपदाब्जपद्धतिम् ।
अनन्यभावे निजधर्मभाविते
मनस्यवस्थाप्य भजस्व पूरुषम् ॥२२॥

tam eva vatsāśraya bhṛtya-vatsalaṁ
mumukṣubhir mṛgya-padābja-paddhatim
ananya-bhāve nija-dharma-bhāvite
manasy avasthāpya bhajasva pūruṣam

tam—Him; *eva*—also; *vatsa*—my dear boy; *āśraya*—take shelter; *bhṛtya-vatsalam*—of the Supreme Personality of Godhead, who is very kind to His devotees; *mumukṣubhiḥ*—also by persons desiring liberation; *mṛgya*—to be sought; *pada-abja*—lotus feet; *paddhatim*—system; *ananya-bhāve*—in an unflinching situation; *nija-dharma-bhāvite*—being situated in one's original constitutional position; *manasi*—unto the mind; *avasthāpya*—placing; *bhajasva*—go on executing devotional service; *pūruṣam*—the Supreme Person.

TRANSLATION

My dear boy, you also should take shelter of the Supreme Personality of Godhead, who is very kind to His devotees. Persons seeking liberation from the cycle of birth and death always take shelter of the lotus feet of the Lord in devotional service. Becoming purified by executing your allotted occupation, just situate the Supreme Personality of Godhead in your heart, and without deviating for a moment, engage always in His service.

PURPORT

The system of *bhakti-yoga* described by Queen Sunīti to her son is the standard way of God realization. Everyone can continue in his constitutional occupational duties and at the same time keep the Supreme Personality of Godhead within his heart. This was also instructed by the Lord Himself to Arjuna in *Bhagavad-gītā:* "Go on fighting, but keep Me within your mind." That should be the motto of every honest person seeking perfection in Kṛṣṇa consciousness. In this connection, Queen Sunīti advised her son that the Supreme Personality of Godhead is known as *bhṛtya-vatsala,* which indicates that He is very kind to His devotees. She said, "You came to me crying, having been insulted by your stepmother, but I am unable to do any good for you. But Kṛṣṇa is so kind to His devotees that if you go to Him, then the combined kindness of millions of mothers like me will be surpassed by His affectionate and tender dealings. When everyone else fails to mitigate one's misery, Kṛṣṇa is able to help the devotee." Queen Sunīti also stressed that the process of approaching the Supreme Personality of Godhead is not easy, but is sought after by great sages who are very advanced in spiritual realization. Queen Sunīti also indicated by her instruction that Dhruva Mahārāja was only a small child, five years old, and it was not possible for him to purify himself by the way of *karma-kāṇḍa*. But by the process of *bhakti-yoga*, even a child less than five years old, or anyone of any age, can be purified. That is the special significance of *bhakti-yoga*. Therefore she advised him not to accept worship of the demigods or any other process, but simply to take to the Supreme Personality of Godhead, and the result would be all perfection. As soon as one places the Supreme Personality of Godhead within one's heart, everything becomes easy and successful.

TEXT 23

नान्यं ततः पद्मपलाशलोचनाद्
दुःखच्छिदं ते मृगयामि कंचन ।
यो मृग्यते हस्तगृहीतपद्मया
श्रियेतरैरङ्ग विमृग्यमाणया ॥२३॥

nānyaṁ tataḥ padma-palāśa-locanād
duḥkha-cchidaṁ te mṛgayāmi kañcana
yo mṛgyate hasta-gṛhīta-padmayā
śriyetarair aṅga vimṛgyamāṇayā

na anyam—no others; *tataḥ*—therefore; *padma-palāśa-locanāt*—from the lotus-eyed Supreme Personality of Godhead; *duḥkha-chidam*—one who can mitigate others' difficulties; *te*—your; *mṛgayāmi*—I am searching after; *kañcana*—anyone else; *yaḥ*—who; *mṛgyate*—searches; *hasta-gṛhīta-padmayā*—taking a lotus flower in the hand; *śriyā*—the goddess of fortune; *itaraiḥ*—by others; *aṅga*—my dear boy; *vi-mṛgyamāṇayā*—one who is worshiped.

TRANSLATION

My dear Dhruva, as far as I am concerned, I do not find anyone who can mitigate your distress but the Supreme Personality of Godhead, whose eyes are like lotus petals. Many demigods such as Lord Brahmā seek the pleasure of the goddess of fortune, but the goddess of fortune herself, with a lotus flower in her hand, is always ready to render service to the Supreme Lord.

PURPORT

Sunīti pointed out herewith that the benediction received from the Supreme Personality of Godhead and that received from the demigods are not on an equal level. Foolish persons say that no matter whom one worships one will get the same result, but actually that is not a fact. In *Bhagavad-gītā* it is also said that benedictions received from the demigods are all temporary and are meant for the less intelligent. In other words, because the demigods are all materialistically conditioned souls, although they are situated in very exalted positions, their benedictions cannot be permanent. Permanent benediction is spiritual benediction, since a spirit soul is eternal. It is also said in *Bhagavad-gītā* that only persons who have lost their intelligence go to worship the demigods. Therefore Sunīti told her son that he should not seek the mercy of the demigods, but should directly approach the Supreme Personality of Godhead to mitigate his misery.

Material opulences are controlled by the Supreme Personality of Godhead through His different potencies and specifically the goddess of fortune. Therefore, those who are after material opulences seek the pleasure or mercy of the goddess of fortune. Even the highly placed demigods worship the goddess of fortune, but the goddess of fortune, Mahā-Lakṣmī herself, is always seeking the pleasure of the Supreme Personality of Godhead. Anyone, therefore, who takes to the worship of the Supreme Lord automatically receives the blessings of the goddess of fortune. At this stage of his life, Dhruva Mahārāja was seeking material opulences, and his mother advised rightly that even for material opulences it is better to worship not the demigods but the Supreme Lord.

Although a pure devotee does not seek benedictions from the Supreme Lord for material advancement, it is stated in *Bhagavad-gītā* that pious persons go to the Lord even for material benedictions. A person who goes to the Supreme Personality of Godhead for material gain is gradually purified in association with the Supreme Lord. Thus he becomes free from all material desires and is elevated to the platform of spiritual life. Unless one is raised to the spiritual platform, it is not possible for him to completely transcend all material contamination.

Sunīti, the mother of Dhruva, was a farseeing woman, and therefore she advised her son to worship the Supreme Lord and no one else. The

Lord is described herein as lotus eyed (*padma-palāśa-locanāt*). When a person is fatigued, if he sees a lotus flower all his fatigue can be immediately reduced to nil. Similarly, when an aggrieved person sees the lotus face of the Supreme Personality of Godhead, immediately all his grief is reduced. A lotus flower is also an insignia in the hand of Lord Viṣṇu as well as in the hand of the goddess of fortune. The worshipers of the goddess of fortune and Lord Viṣṇu together are certainly very opulent in all respects, even in material life. The Lord is sometimes described as *śiva-viriñci-nutam*, which means that Lord Śiva and Lord Brahmā also offer their respectful obeisances unto the lotus feet of the Supreme Personality of Godhead, Nārāyaṇa.

TEXT 24

मैत्रेय उवाच

एवं संजल्पितं मातुराकर्ण्यार्थागमं वचः ।
संनियम्यात्मनात्मानं निश्चक्राम पितुः पुरात् ॥२४॥

maitreya uvāca
evaṁ sañjalpitaṁ mātur
ākarṇyārthāgamaṁ vacaḥ
sanniyamyātmanātmānaṁ
niścakrāma pituḥ purāt

maitreyaḥ uvāca—the great sage Maitreya said; *evam*—thus; *sañjalpitam*—spoken together; *mātuḥ*—from the mother; *ākarṇya*—hearing; *artha-āgamam*—purposeful; *vacaḥ*—words; *sanniyamya*—controlling; *ātmanā*—by the mind; *ātmānam*—own self; *niścakrāma*—got out; *pituḥ*—of the father; *purāt*—from the house.

TRANSLATION

The great sage Maitreya continued: The instruction of Dhruva Mahārāja's mother, Sunīti, was actually meant for fulfilling his desired objective. Therefore, after deliberate consideration and with intelligence and fixed determination, he left his father's house.

PURPORT

Both the mother and the son were lamenting Dhruva Mahārāja's having been insulted by his stepmother and his father's not having taken any step on this issue. But mere lamentation is useless—one should find out the means to mitigate one's lamentation. Thus both mother and son decided to take shelter of the lotus feet of the Lord because that is the only solution to all material problems. It is indicated in this connection that Dhruva Mahārāja left his father's capital city to go to a secluded place to search out the Supreme Personality of Godhead. It is the instruction of Prahlāda Mahārāja also that if one is seeking peace of mind he should free himself from all contamination of family life and take shelter of the Supreme Godhead by going to the forest. To the Gauḍīya Vaiṣṇava this forest is the forest of Vṛndā, or Vṛndāvana. If one takes shelter of Vṛndāvana under Vṛndāvaneśvarī, Śrīmatī Rādhārāṇī, certainly all the problems of his life are solved very easily.

TEXT 25

नारदस्तदुपाकर्ण्य ज्ञात्वा तस्य चिकीर्षितम् ।
स्पृष्ट्वा मूर्धन्यघघ्नेन पाणिना प्राह विस्मितः ॥२५॥

nāradas tad upākarṇya
jñātvā tasya cikīrṣitam
spṛṣṭvā mūrdhany agha-ghnena
pāṇinā prāha vismitaḥ

nāradaḥ—the great sage Nārada; *tat*—that; *upākarṇya*—overhearing; *jñātvā*—and knowing; *tasya*—his (Dhruva Mahārāja's); *cikīrṣitam*—activities; *spṛṣṭvā*—by touching; *mūrdhani*—on the head; *agha-ghnena*—which can drive away all sinful activities; *pāṇinā*—by the hand; *prāha*—said; *vismitaḥ*—being surprised.

TRANSLATION

The great sage Nārada overheard this news, and understanding all the activities of Dhruva Mahārāja, he was struck with wonder. He approached Dhruva, and touching the boy's head with his all-virtuous hand, he spoke as follows.

PURPORT

When Dhruva Mahārāja was talking with his mother, Sunīti, of all the incidents that had taken place in the palace, Nārada was not present. Thus the question may be raised how Nārada overheard all these topics. The answer is that Nārada is *trikāla-jña;* he is so powerful that he can understand the past, future and present of everyone's heart, just like the Supersoul, the Supreme Personality of Godhead. Therefore, after understanding the strong determination of Dhruva Mahārāja, Nārada came to help him. It may be explained in this way: The Supreme Personality of Godhead is present in everyone's heart, and as soon as He understands that a living entity is serious about entering devotional service, He sends His representative. In this way Nārada was sent to Dhruva Mahārāja. This is explained in the *Caitanya-caritāmṛta. Guru-kṛṣṇa-prasāde pāya bhakti-latā-bīja:* by the grace of the spiritual master and Kṛṣṇa, one can enter into devotional service. Because of Dhruva Mahārāja's determination, Kṛṣṇa, the Supersoul, immediately sent His representative, Nārada, to initiate him.

TEXT 26

अहो तेजः क्षत्रियाणां मानभङ्गममृष्यताम् ।
बालोऽप्ययं हृदा धत्ते यत्समातुरसद्वचः ॥२६॥

aho tejaḥ kṣatriyāṇāṁ
māna-bhaṅgam amṛṣyatām
bālo 'py ayaṁ hṛdā dhatte
yat samātur asad-vacaḥ

aho—how surprising it is; *tejaḥ*—power; *kṣatriyāṇām*—of the *kṣatriyas; māna-bhaṅgam*—hurting the prestige; *amṛṣyatām*—unable to tolerate; *bālaḥ*—only a child; *api*—although; *ayam*—this; *hṛdā*—at heart; *dhatte*—has taken; *yat*—that which; *sa-mātuḥ*—of the stepmother; *asat*—unpalatable; *vacaḥ*—words.

TRANSLATION

How wonderful are the powerful kṣatriyas. They cannot tolerate even a slight infringement upon their prestige. Just imagine! This

boy is only a small child, yet harsh words from his stepmother proved unbearable to him.

PURPORT

The qualifications of the *kṣatriyas* are described in *Bhagavad-gītā.* Two important qualifications are to have a sense of prestige and not to flee from battle. It appears that the *kṣatriya* blood within the body of Dhruva Mahārāja was naturally very active. If the brahminical, *kṣatriya* or *vaiśya* culture is maintained in a family, naturally the sons and grandsons inherit the spirit of the particular class. Therefore, according to the Vedic system, the *saṁskāra,* or the reformatory system, is maintained very rigidly. If one fails to observe the reformatory measures current in the family, one is immediately degraded to a lower standard of life.

TEXT 27

नारद उवाच

नाधुनाप्यवमानं ते सम्मानं वापि पुत्रक ।
लक्षयामः कुमारस्य सक्तस्य क्रीडनादिषु ॥२७॥

nārada uvāca
nādhunāpy avamānaṁ te
sammānaṁ vāpi putraka
lakṣayāmaḥ kumārasya
saktasya krīḍanādiṣu

nāradaḥ uvāca—the great sage Nārada said; *na*—not; *adhunā*—just now; *api*—although; *avamānam*—insult; *te*—unto you; *sammānam*—offering respects; *vā*—or; *api*—certainly; *putraka*—my dear boy; *lakṣayāmaḥ*—I can see; *kumārasya*—of boys like you; *saktasya*—being attached; *krīḍana-ādiṣu*—to sports and frivolities.

TRANSLATION

The great sage Nārada told Dhruva: My dear boy, you are only a little boy whose attachment is to sports and other frivolities. Why are you so affected by words insulting your honor?

PURPORT

Ordinarily if a child is rebuked as a rascal or fool, he smiles and does not take such insulting words very seriously. Similarly, if words of honor are offered, he does not appreciate them. But in the case of Dhruva Mahārāja, the *kṣatriya* spirit was so strong that he could not tolerate a slight insult from his stepmother which injured his *kṣatriya* prestige.

TEXT 28

विकल्पे विद्यमानेऽपि न ह्यसंतोषहेतवः ।
पुंसो मोहमृते भिन्ना यल्लोके निजकर्मभिः ॥२८॥

vikalpe vidyamāne 'pi
na hy asantoṣa-hetavaḥ
puṁso moham ṛte bhinnā
yal loke nija-karmabhiḥ

vikalpe—alternation; *vidyamāne api*—although there is; *na*—not; *hi*—certainly; *asantoṣa*—dissatisfaction; *hetavaḥ*—causes; *puṁsaḥ*—of the persons; *moham ṛte*—without being illusioned; *bhinnāḥ*—separated; *yat loke*—within this world; *nija-karmabhiḥ*—by his own work.

TRANSLATION

My dear Dhruva, if you feel that your sense of honor has been insulted, you still have no cause for dissatisfaction. This kind of dissatisfaction is another feature of the illusory energy; every living entity is controlled by his previous actions, and therefore there are different varieties of life for enjoying or suffering.

PURPORT

In the *Vedas* it is said that the living entity is always uncontaminated and unaffected by material association. The living entity gets different types of material bodies because of his previous fruitive actions. If, however, one understands the philosophy that as a living spirit soul he has an affinity for neither suffering nor enjoyment, then he is considered to be a liberated person. It is confirmed in *Bhagavad-gītā* (18.54), *brahma-bhūtaḥ prasannātmā:* when one is actually situated on the transcendental platform, he has nothing for which to lament and nothing for which to hanker. Nārada Ṛṣi first of all wanted to impress upon Dhruva Mahārāja that he was only a child; he should not have been affected by words of insult or honor. And if he were so developed as to understand honor and insult, then this understanding should have been applied in his own life; he should have known that honor and dishonor are both destined only by one's previous actions; therefore one should not be sorry or happy under any circumstances.

TEXT 29

परितुष्येत्ततस्तात तावन्मात्रेण पूरुषः ।
दैवोपसादितं यावद्वीक्ष्येश्वरगतिं बुधः ॥२९॥

parituṣyet tatas tāta
tāvan-mātreṇa pūruṣaḥ
daivopasāditaṁ yāvad
vīkṣyeśvara-gatiṁ budhaḥ

parituṣyet—one should be satisfied; *tataḥ*—therefore; *tāta*—my dear boy; *tāvat*—up to such; *mātreṇa*—quality; *pūruṣaḥ*—a person; *daiva*—destiny; *upasāditam*—offered by; *yāvat*—as; *vīkṣya*—seeing; *īśvara-gatim*—the process of the Supreme; *budhaḥ*—one who is intelligent.

TRANSLATION

The process of the Supreme Personality of Godhead is very wonderful. One who is intelligent should accept that process and be satisfied with whatever comes, favorable or unfavorable, by His supreme will.

PURPORT

The great sage Nārada instructed Dhruva Mahārāja that one should be satisfied in all circumstances. Everyone who is intelligent should know that because of our concept of bodily existence, we are subjected to suffering and enjoyment. One who is in the transcendental position, beyond the concept of bodily life, is considered to be intelligent. One who is a devotee especially accepts all reverses as gifts of the Supreme Lord.

When a devotee is put into distress, he accepts this as God's mercy and offers Him repeated obeisances with his body, mind and intellect. An intelligent person, therefore, should be always satisfied, depending on the mercy of the Lord.

TEXT 30

अथ मात्रोपदिष्टेन योगेनावरुरुत्ससि ।
यत्प्रसादं स वै पुंसां दुराराध्यो मतो मम ॥३०॥

atha mātropadiṣṭena
yogenāvarurutsasi
yat-prasādaṁ sa vai puṁsāṁ
durārādhyo mato mama

atha—therefore; *mātrā*—by your mother; *upadiṣṭena*—being instructed; *yogena*—by mystic meditation; *avarurutsasi*—want to elevate yourself; *yat-prasādam*—whose mercy; *saḥ*—that; *vai*—certainly; *puṁsām*—of the living entities; *durārādhyaḥ*—very difficult to perform; *mataḥ*—opinion; *mama*—my.

TRANSLATION

Now you have decided to undertake the mystic process of meditation under the instruction of your mother, just to achieve the mercy of the Lord, but in my opinion such austerities are not possible for any ordinary man. It is very difficult to satisfy the Supreme Personality of Godhead.

PURPORT

The process of *bhakti-yoga* is simultaneously very difficult and very easy to perform. Śrī Nārada Muni, the supreme spiritual master, is testing Dhruva Mahārāja to see how determined he is to prosecute devotional service. This is the process of accepting a disciple. The great sage Nārada has come to Dhruva under the direction of the Supreme Personality of Godhead just to initiate him, yet he is testing Dhruva's determination to execute the process. It is a fact, however, that for a sincere person devotional service is very easy. But for one who is not determined and sincere, this process is very difficult.

TEXT 31

मुनयः पदवीं यस्य निःसङ्गेनोरुजन्मभिः ।
न विदुर्मृगयन्तोऽपि तीव्रयोगसमाधिना ॥३१॥

munayaḥ padavīṁ yasya
niḥsaṅgenoru-janmabhiḥ
na vidur mṛgayanto 'pi
tīvra-yoga-samādhinā

munayaḥ—great sages; *padavīm*—path; *yasya*—whose; *niḥsaṅgena*—by detachment; *uru-janmabhiḥ*—after many births; *na*—never; *viduḥ*—understood; *mṛgayantaḥ*—searching for; *api*—certainly; *tīvra-yoga*—severe austerities; *samādhinā*—by trance.

TRANSLATION

Nārada Muni continued: After trying this process for many, many births and remaining unattached to material contamination, placing themselves continually in trance and executing many types of austerities, many mystic yogīs were unable to find the end of the path of God realization.

TEXT 32

अतो निवर्ततामेष निर्बन्धस्तव निष्फलः ।
यतिष्यति भवान् काले श्रेयसां समुपस्थिते ॥३२॥

ato nivartatām eṣa
nirbandhas tava niṣphalaḥ
yatiṣyati bhavān kāle
śreyasāṁ samupasthite

ataḥ—hereafter; *nivartatām*—just stop yourself; *eṣaḥ*—this; *nirbandhaḥ*—determination; *tava*—your; *niṣphalaḥ*—without any result; *yatiṣyati*—in the future you should try; *bhavān*—yourself; *kāle*—in due course of time; *śreyasām*—opportunities; *samupasthite*—being present.

TRANSLATION

For this reason, my dear boy, you should not endeavor for this; it will not be successful. It is better that you go home. When you are grown up, by the mercy of the Lord you will get a chance for these mystic performances. At that time you may execute this function.

PURPORT

Generally, a thoroughly trained person takes to spiritual perfection at the end of his life. According to the Vedic system, therefore, life is divided into four stages. In the beginning, one becomes a *brahmacārī*, a student who studies Vedic knowledge under the authoritative guidance of a spiritual master. He then becomes a householder and executes household duties according to the Vedic process. Then the householder becomes a *vānaprastha*, and gradually, when he is mature, he renounces household life and *vānaprastha* life also and takes to *sannyāsa*, completely devoting himself to devotional service.

Generally, people think that childhood is meant for enjoying life by engaging oneself in sports and play, youth is meant for enjoying the company of young girls, and when one becomes old, at the time of death, then he may try to execute devotional service or a mystic *yoga* process. But this conclusion is not for devotees who are actually serious. The great sage Nārada is instructing Dhruva Mahārāja just to test him. Actually, the direct order is that from any point of life one should begin rendering devotional service. But it is the duty of the spiritual master to test the disciple to see how seriously he desires to execute devotional service. Then he may be initiated.

TEXT 33

यस्य यद् दैवविहितं स तेन सुखदुःखयोः ।
आत्मानं तोषयन्देही तमसः पारमृच्छति ॥३३॥

yasya yad daiva-vihitaṁ
sa tena sukha-duḥkhayoḥ
ātmānaṁ toṣayan dehī
tamasaḥ pāram ṛcchati

yasya—anyone; *yat*—that which; *daiva*—by destiny; *vihitam*—destined; *saḥ*—such a person; *tena*—by that; *sukha-duḥkhayoḥ*—happiness or distress; *ātmānam*—one's self; *toṣayan*—being satisfied; *dehī*—an embodied soul; *tamasaḥ*—of the darkness; *pāram*—to the other side; *ṛcchati*—crosses.

TRANSLATION

One should try to keep himself satisfied in any condition of life—whether distress or happiness—which is offered by the supreme will. A person who endures in this way is able to cross over the darkness of nescience very easily.

PURPORT

Material existence consists of pious and impious fruitive activities. As long as one is engaged in any kind of activity other than devotional service, it will result in the happiness and distress of this material world. When we enjoy life in so-called material happiness, it is to be understood that we are diminishing the resultant actions of our pious activities. And when we are put into suffering, it is to be understood that we are diminishing the resultant actions of our impious activities. Instead of being attached to the circumstantial happiness and distress resulting from pious or impious activities, if we want to get out of the clutches of this nescience, then whatever position we are put in by the will of the Lord we should accept. Thus if we simply surrender unto the Supreme Personality of Godhead, we shall get out of the clutches of this material existence.

TEXT 34

गुणाधिकान्मुदं लिप्सेदनुक्रोशं गुणाधमात् ।
मैत्रीं समानादन्विच्छेन्न तापैरभिभूयते ॥३४॥

guṇādhikān mudaṁ lipsed
anukrośaṁ guṇādhamāt
maitrīṁ samānād anvicchen
na tāpair abhibhūyate

guṇa-adhikāt—one who is more qualified; *mudam*—pleasure; *lipset*—one should feel; *anukrośam*—compassion; *guṇa-adhamāt*—one who is less qualified; *maitrīm*—friendship; *samānāt*—with an equal; *anvicchet*—one should desire; *na*—not; *tāpaiḥ*—by tribulation; *abhibhūyate*—becomes affected.

TRANSLATION

Every man should act like this: when he meets a person more qualified than himself, he should be very pleased; when he meets someone less qualified than himself, he should be compassionate toward him; and when he meets someone equal to himself, he should make friendship with him. In this way one is never affected by the threefold miseries of this material world.

PURPORT

Generally when we find someone more qualified than ourselves, we become envious of him; when we find someone less qualified, we deride him; and when we find someone equal we become very proud of our activities. These are the causes of all material tribulations. The great sage Nārada therefore advised that a devotee should act perfectly. Instead of being envious of a more qualified man, one should be jolly to receive him. Instead of being oppressive to a less qualified man, one should be compassionate toward him just to raise him to the proper standard. And when one meets an equal, instead of being proud of one's own activities before him, one should treat him as a friend. One should also have compassion for the people in general, who are suffering due to forgetfulness of Kṛṣṇa. These important functions will make one happy within this material world.

TEXT 35

ध्रुव उवाच
सोऽयं शमो भगवता सुखदुःखहतात्मनाम् ।
दर्शितः कृपया पुंसां दुर्दर्शोऽस्मद्विधैस्तु यः ॥३५॥

dhruva uvāca
so 'yaṁ śamo bhagavatā
sukha-duḥkha-hatātmanām

darśitaḥ kṛpayā puṁsāṁ
durdarśo 'smad-vidhais tu yaḥ

dhruvaḥ uvāca—Dhruva Mahārāja said; *saḥ*—that; *ayam*—this; *śamaḥ*—equilibrium of mind; *bhagavatā*—by Your Lordship; *sukha-duḥkha*—happiness and miseries; *hata-ātmanām*—those who are affected; *darśitaḥ*—shown; *kṛpayā*—by mercy; *puṁsām*—of the people; *durdarśaḥ*—very difficult to perceive; *asmat-vidhaiḥ*—by persons like us; *tu*—but; *yaḥ*—whatever you have said.

TRANSLATION

Dhruva Mahārāja said: My dear Lord Nāradajī, for a person whose heart is disturbed by the material conditions of happiness and distress, whatever you have so kindly explained for attainment of peace of mind is certainly a very good instruction. But as far as I am concerned, I am covered by ignorance, and this kind of philosophy does not touch my heart.

PURPORT

There are various classes of men. One class is called *akāmīs*, referring to those who have no material desire. Desire must exist, either material or spiritual. Material desire arises when one wants to satisfy one's personal senses. One who is ready to sacrifice anything to satisfy the Supreme Personality of Godhead can be said to have spiritual desire. Dhruva did not accept the instruction given by the great saint Nārada because he thought himself unfit for such instruction, which prohibited all material desires. It is not a fact, however, that those who have material desires are prohibited from worshiping the Supreme Personality of Godhead. This is the essential instruction from the life of Dhruva. He frankly admitted that his heart was full of material desires. He was very much affected by the cruel words of his stepmother, whereas those who are spiritually advanced do not care about anyone's condemnation or adoration.

In *Bhagavad-gītā* it is said that persons who are actually advanced in spiritual life do not care for the dual behavior of this material world. But Dhruva Mahārāja frankly admitted that he was not beyond the affliction of material distress and happiness. He was confident that the instruction given by Nārada was valuable, yet he could not accept it. The question raised here is whether or not a person afflicted by material desires is fit to worship the Supreme Personality of Godhead. The answer is that everyone is fit to worship Him. Even if one has many material desires to fulfill, he should take to Kṛṣṇa consciousness and worship the Supreme Lord Kṛṣṇa, who is so merciful that He fulfills everyone's desires. Through this narration it will become very clear that no one is barred from worshiping the Supreme Personality of Godhead, even if one has many material desires.

TEXT 36

अथापि मेऽविनीतस्य क्षात्त्रं घोरमुपेयुषः ।
सुरुच्या दुर्वचोबाणैर्न भिन्ने श्रयते हृदि ॥३६॥

athāpi me 'vinītasya
kṣāttraṁ ghoram upeyuṣaḥ
surucyā durvaco-bāṇair
na bhinne śrayate hṛdi

atha api—therefore; *me*—my; *avinītasya*—not very submissive; *kṣāttram*—the spirit of a *kṣatriya; ghoram*—intolerant; *upeyuṣaḥ*—achieved; *surucyāḥ*—of Queen Suruci; *durvacaḥ*—harsh words; *bāṇaiḥ*—by the arrows; *na*—not; *bhinne*—being pierced; *śrayate*—remain in; *hṛdi*—the heart.

TRANSLATION

My dear lord, I am very impudent for not accepting your instructions, but this is not my fault. It is due to my having been born in a kṣatriya family. My stepmother, Suruci, has pierced my heart with her harsh words. Therefore your valuable instruction does not stand in my heart.

PURPORT

It is said that the heart or mind is just like an earthen pot; once broken, it cannot be repaired by any means. Dhruva Mahārāja gave this example to Nārada Muni. He said that his heart, having been pierced by the arrows of his stepmother's harsh words, felt so broken that nothing seemed valuable but his desire to counteract her insult. His stepmother had said that because he was born from the womb of Sunīti, a neglected queen of Mahārāja Uttānapāda, Dhruva Mahārāja was not fit to sit either on the throne or on his father's lap. In other words, according to his stepmother, he could not be declared king. Dhruva Mahārāja's determination, therefore, was to become king of a planet exalted even beyond that possessed by Lord Brahmā, the greatest of all the demigods.

Dhruva Mahārāja indirectly informed the great sage Nārada that there are four kinds of human spirit—the brahminical spirit, the *kṣatriya* spirit, the *vaiśya* spirit and the *śūdra* spirit. The spirit of one caste is not applicable to the members of another. The philosophical spirit enunciated by Nārada Muni might have been suitable for a *brāhmaṇa* spirit, but it was not suitable for a *kṣatriya.* Dhruva frankly admitted that he was lacking in brahminical humility and was therefore unable to accept the philosophy of Nārada Muni.

The statements of Dhruva Mahārāja indicate that unless a child is trained according to his tendency, there is no possibility of his developing his particular spirit. It was the duty of the spiritual master or teacher to observe the psychological movement of a particular boy and thus train him in a particular occupational duty. Dhruva Mahārāja, having already been trained in the *kṣatriya* spirit, would not accept the brahminical philosophy. In America we have practical experience of this incompatibility of the brahminical and *kṣatriya* temperaments. The American boys, who have simply been trained as *śūdras,* are not at all fit to fight in battle. Therefore, when they are called to join the military, they refuse because they do not have *kṣatriya* spirit. This is a cause of great dissatisfaction in society.

That the boys do not have the *kṣatriya* spirit does not mean that they are trained in brahminical qualities; they are trained as *śūdras,* and thus in frustration they are becoming hippies. However, as soon as they enter the Kṛṣṇa consciousness movement being started in America, they are trained to meet the brahminical qualifications, even though they have fallen to the lowest conditions as *śūdras.* In other words, since the Kṛṣṇa consciousness movement is open for everyone, people in general can attain the brahminical qualifications. This is the greatest need at the present moment, for now there are actually no *brāhmaṇas* or *kṣatriyas* but only some *vaiśyas* and, for the most part, *śūdras.* The classification of society into *brāhmaṇas*, *kṣatriyas*, *vaiśyas* and *śūdras* is very scientific. In the human social body, the *brāhmaṇas* are considered the head, the *kṣatriyas* are the arms, the *vaiśyas* are the belly, and the *śūdras* are the legs. At the present moment the body has legs and a belly, but there are no arms or head, and therefore society is topsy-turvy. It is necessary to reestablish the brahminical qualifications in order to raise the fallen human society to the highest standard of spiritual consciousness.

TEXT 37

पदं त्रिभुवनोत्कृष्टं जिगीषोः साधु वर्त्म मे ।
ब्रूह्यस्मत्पितृभिर्ब्रह्मन्नन्यैरप्यनधिष्ठितम् ॥३७॥

padaṁ tri-bhuvanotkṛṣṭaṁ
jigīṣoḥ sādhu vartma me
brūhy asmat-pitṛbhir brahmann
anyair apy anadhiṣṭhitam

padam—position; *tri-bhuvana*—the three worlds; *utkṛṣṭam*—the best; *jigīṣoḥ*—desirous; *sādhu*—honest; *vartma*—way; *me*—unto me; *brūhi*—please tell; *asmat*—our; *pitṛbhiḥ*—by the forefathers, the father and grandfather; *brahman*—O great *brāhmaṇa; anyaiḥ*—by others; *api*—even; *anadhiṣṭhitam*—not acquired.

TRANSLATION

O learned brāhmaṇa, I want to occupy a position more exalted than any yet achieved within the three worlds by anyone, even by my fathers and grandfathers. If you will oblige, kindly advise me of an honest path to follow by which I can achieve the goal of my life.

PURPORT

When Dhruva Mahārāja refused to accept the brahminical instruction of Nārada Muni, naturally the next question would be what sort of instruction he wanted. So even before Nārada Muni asked, Dhruva Mahārāja expressed his heartfelt desire. His father, of course, was the emperor of the entire world, and his grandfather, Lord Brahmā, was the creator of the universe. Dhruva Mahārāja expressed his desire to possess a kingdom better than those of his father and grandfather. He frankly stated that he wanted a kingdom which had no competitor within the three worlds, namely the higher, middle and lower planetary systems. The greatest personality within this universe is Lord Brahmā, and Dhruva Mahārāja wanted a position even greater than his. He wanted to take advantage of Nārada Muni's presence because he knew very well that if Nārada Muni, the greatest devotee of Lord Kṛṣṇa, could bless him or show him the path, then certainly he would be able to occupy a more exalted position than any person within the three worlds. Thus he wanted help from Nāradajī to achieve that position. Dhruva Mahārāja wanted a position greater than that of Brahmā. This was practically an impossible proposition, but by pleasing the Supreme Personality of Godhead a devotee can achieve even the impossible.

One particular point mentioned here is that Dhruva Mahārāja wanted to occupy an exalted position not by hook or by crook, but by honest means. This indicates that if Kṛṣṇa offered him such a position, then he would accept it. That is the nature of a devotee. He may desire material gain, but he accepts it only if Kṛṣṇa offers it. Dhruva Mahārāja was sorry to refuse the instruction of Nārada Muni; therefore he requested him to be merciful to him by showing a path by which he could fulfill his mind's desires.

TEXT 38

नूनं भवान् भगवतो योऽङ्गजः परमेष्ठिनः ।
वितुदन्नटते वीणां हिताय जगतोऽर्कवत् ॥३८॥

nūnaṁ bhavān bhagavato
yo 'ṅgajaḥ parameṣṭhinaḥ
vitudann aṭate vīṇāṁ
hitāya jagato 'rkavat

nūnam—certainly; *bhavān*—Your Honor; *bhagavataḥ*—of the Lord; *yaḥ*—that which; *aṅga-jaḥ*—born from the body; *parameṣṭhinaḥ*—Lord Brahmā; *vitudan*—by playing on; *aṭate*—travel all over; *vīṇām*—a musical instrument; *hitāya*—for the welfare; *jagataḥ*—of the world; *arka-vat*—like the sun.

TRANSLATION

My dear lord, you are a worthy son of Lord Brahmā, and you travel, playing on your musical instrument, the vīṇā, for the welfare of the entire universe. You are like the sun, which rotates in the universe for the benefit of all living beings.

PURPORT

Dhruva Mahārāja, although a young child, expressed his hope that he might be offered the benediction of a kingdom which would exceed in opulence those of his father and grandfather. He also expressed his gladness that he had met such an exalted person as Nārada, whose only concern was to illuminate the world, like the sun, which rotates all over the universe only for the purpose of benefiting the inhabitants of all planets. Nārada Muni travels all over the universe for the sole purpose of performing the best welfare activity for the entire universe by teaching everyone how to become a devotee of the Supreme Personality of Godhead. Thus Dhruva Mahārāja felt fully assured that Nārada Muni could fulfill his desire, even though the desire was very extraordinary.

The example of the sun is very significant. The sun is so kind that he distributes his sunshine everywhere, without consideration. Dhruva Mahārāja requested Nārada Muni to be merciful to him. He pointed out that Nārada travels all over the universe just for the purpose of doing good to all conditioned souls. He requested that Nārada Muni show his mercy by awarding him the benefit of his particular desire. Dhruva Mahārāja was strongly determined to fulfill his desire, and it was for that purpose that he had left his home and palace.

TEXT 39

मैत्रेय उवाच
इत्युदाहृतमाकर्ण्य भगवान्नारदस्तदा ।
प्रीतः प्रत्याह तं बालं सद्वाक्यमनुकम्पया ॥३९॥

maitreya uvāca
ity udāhṛtam ākarṇya
bhagavān nāradas tadā

prītaḥ pratyāha taṁ bālaṁ
sad-vākyam anukampayā

maitreyaḥ uvāca—the sage Maitreya continued; *iti*—thus; *udāhṛtam*—being spoken; *ākarṇya*—hearing; *bhagavān nāradaḥ*—the great personality Nārada; *tadā*—thereupon; *prītaḥ*—being pleased; *pratyāha*—replied; *tam*—him; *bālam*—the boy; *sat-vākyam*—good advice; *anukampayā*—being compassionate.

TRANSLATION

The sage Maitreya continued: The great personality Nārada Muni, upon hearing the words of Dhruva Mahārāja, became very compassionate toward him, and in order to show him his causeless mercy, he gave him the following expert advice.

PURPORT

Since the great sage Nārada is the foremost spiritual master, naturally his only activity is to bestow the greatest benefit upon whomever he meets. Dhruva Mahārāja, however, was a child, and so his demand was also that of a playful child. Still, the great sage became compassionate toward him, and for his welfare he spoke the following verses.

TEXT 40

नारद उवाच
जनन्याभिहितः पन्थाः स वै निःश्रेयसस्य ते ।
भगवान् वासुदेवस्तं भज तं प्रवणात्मना ॥४०॥

nārada uvāca
jananyābhihitaḥ panthāḥ
sa vai niḥśreyasasya te
bhagavān vāsudevas taṁ
bhaja taṁ pravaṇātmanā

nāradaḥ uvāca—the great sage Nārada said; *jananyā*—by your mother; *abhihitaḥ*—stated; *panthāḥ*—the path; *saḥ*—that; *vai*—certainly; *niḥśreyasasya*—the ultimate goal of life; *te*—for you; *bhagavān*—the Supreme Personality of Godhead; *vāsudevaḥ*—Kṛṣṇa;

tam—unto Him; *bhaja*—render your service; *tam*—by Him; *pravaṇa-ātmanā*—fully absorbing your mind.

TRANSLATION

The great sage Nārada told Dhruva Mahārāja: The instruction given by your mother, Sunīti, to follow the path of devotional service to the Supreme Personality of Godhead, is just suitable for you. You should therefore completely absorb yourself in the devotional service of the Lord.

PURPORT

Dhruva Mahārāja's demand was to achieve an abode even greater than Lord Brahmā's. Within this universe, Lord Brahmā is supposed to be in the most exalted position, for he is the chief of all demigods, but Dhruva Mahārāja wanted a realm beyond his. Therefore his desire was not to be fulfilled by worshiping any demigod. As described in *Bhagavad-gītā*, the benedictions offered by the demigods are all temporary. Therefore Nārada Muni asked Dhruva Mahārāja to follow the path recommended by his mother—to worship Kṛṣṇa, Vāsudeva. When Kṛṣṇa offers anything, it is beyond the expectation of the devotee. Both Sunīti and Nārada Muni knew that the demand of Dhruva Mahārāja was impossible for any demigod to fulfill, and therefore both of them recommended following the process of devotional service to Lord Kṛṣṇa.

Nārada Muni is referred to here as *bhagavān* because he can bless any person just as the Supreme Personality of Godhead can. He was very pleased with Dhruva Mahārāja, and he could have at once personally given whatever he wanted, but that is not the duty of the spiritual master. His duty is to engage the disciple in proper devotional service as prescribed in the *śāstras*. Kṛṣṇa was similarly present before Arjuna, and even though He could have given him all facilities for victory over the opposing party without a fight, He did not do so; instead He asked Arjuna to fight. In the same way, Nārada Muni asked Dhruva Mahārāja to undergo devotional discipline in order to achieve the desired result.

TEXT 41

धर्मार्थकाममोक्षाख्यं य इच्छेच्छ्रेय आत्मनः ।
एकं ह्येव हरेस्तत्र कारणं पादसेवनम् ॥४१॥

dharmārtha-kāma-mokṣākhyaṁ
ya icchec chreya ātmanaḥ
ekaṁ hy eva hares tatra
kāraṇaṁ pāda-sevanam

dharma-artha-kāma-mokṣa—the four principles religiosity, economic development, sense gratification and liberation; *ākhyam*—by the name; *yaḥ*—who; *icchet*—may desire; *śreyaḥ*—the goal of life; *ātmanaḥ*—of the self; *ekam hi eva*—only the one; *hareḥ*—of the Supreme Personality of Godhead; *tatra*—in that; *kāraṇam*—the cause; *pāda-sevanam*—worshiping the lotus feet.

TRANSLATION

Any person who desires the fruits of the four principles religiosity, economic development, sense gratification and, at the end, liberation, should engage himself in the devotional service of the Supreme Personality of Godhead, for worship of His lotus feet yields the fulfillment of all of these.

PURPORT

In *Bhagavad-gītā* it is said that only with the sanction of the Supreme Personality of Godhead can the demigods offer benedictions. Therefore, whenever any sacrifice is offered to a demigod, the Supreme Lord in the form of *nārāyaṇa-śilā*, or *śālagrāma-śilā*, is put forward to observe the sacrifice. Actually, the demigods cannot give any benediction without the sanction of the Supreme Lord. Nārada Muni, therefore, advised that even for religiosity, economic development, sense gratification or liberation, one should approach the Supreme Personality of Godhead, offer prayers and ask for the fulfillment of one's desire at the lotus feet of the Lord. That is real intelligence. An intelligent person never goes to demigods to pray for anything. He goes directly to the Supreme Personality of Godhead, who is the cause of all benediction.

As Lord Śrī Kṛṣṇa has said in *Bhagavad-gītā*, performance of ritualistic ceremonies is not actually religion. The real path of religion is to surrender at the lotus feet of the Lord. For one who is actually surrendered to the lotus feet of the Lord, there is no question of any separate endeavor for economic development. A devotee engaged in service to the

Lord is not disappointed in the satisfaction of his senses. If he wants to satisfy his senses, Kṛṣṇa fulfills that desire. As far as liberation is concerned, any devotee fully engaged in the service of the Lord is already liberated; therefore there is no separate necessity for his liberation.

Nārada Muni therefore advised Dhruva Mahārāja to take shelter of Vāsudeva, Lord Kṛṣṇa, and engage himself in the way that his mother had advised, for that would help him fulfill his desire. In this verse Nārada Muni has especially stressed the devotional service of the Lord as the only way. In other words, even if one is full of material desires, he can continue his devotional service to the Lord, and all his desires will be fulfilled.

TEXT 42

तत्तात गच्छ भद्रं ते यमुनायास्तटं शुचि ।
पुण्यं मधुवनं यत्र सांनिध्यं नित्यदा हरेः ॥४२॥

tat tāta gaccha bhadraṁ te
yamunāyās taṭaṁ śuci
puṇyaṁ madhuvanaṁ yatra
sānnidhyaṁ nityadā hareḥ

tat—that; *tāta*—my dear son; *gaccha*—go; *bhadram*—good fortune; *te*—for you; *yamunāyāḥ*—of the Yamunā; *taṭam*—bank; *śuci*—being purified; *puṇyam*—the holy; *madhu-vanam*—of the name Madhuvana; *yatra*—where; *sānnidhyam*—being nearer; *nityadā*—always; *hareḥ*—of the Supreme Personality of Godhead.

TRANSLATION

My dear boy, I therefore wish all good fortune for you. You should go to the bank of the Yamunā, where there is a virtuous forest named Madhuvana, and there be purified. Just by going there, one draws nearer to the Supreme Personality of Godhead, who always lives there.

PURPORT

Both Nārada Muni and Sunīti, the mother of Dhruva Mahārāja, advised Dhruva Mahārāja to worship the Supreme Personality of Godhead. Now, Nārada Muni is especially giving him directions how this worship of the Supreme Person can very quickly fructify. He recommends that Dhruva Mahārāja go to the bank of the Yamunā, where there is a forest of the name Madhuvana, and begin his meditation and worship there.

Places of pilgrimage yield a special advantage for a devotee in quickly advancing his spiritual life. Lord Kṛṣṇa lives everywhere, but still it is very easy to approach Him in holy places of pilgrimage because these places are inhabited by great sages. Lord Śrī Kṛṣṇa says that He lives wherever His devotees are chanting the glories of His transcendental activities. There are many places of pilgrimage in India, and especially prominent are Badarī-nārāyaṇa, Dvārakā, Rāmeśvara and Jagannātha Purī. These sacred places are called the four *dhāmas. Dhāma* refers to a place where one can immediately contact the Supreme Lord. To go to Badarī-nārāyaṇa one has to pass through Hardwar on the path to the Supreme Personality of Godhead. Similarly, there are other holy places of pilgrimage, such as Prayāga (Allahabad) and Mathurā, and the topmost of them all is Vṛndāvana. Unless one is very advanced in spiritual life, it is recommended that he live in such holy places and execute devotional service there. But an advanced devotee like Nārada Muni who is engaged in preaching work can serve the Supreme Lord anywhere. Sometimes he even goes to the hellish planets. Hellish conditions do not affect Nārada Muni because he is engaged in greatly responsible activities in devotional service. According to the statement of Nārada Muni, Madhuvana, which is still existing in the Vṛndāvana area, in the district of Mathurā, is a most sacred place. Many saintly persons still live there and engage in the devotional service of the Lord.

There are twelve forests in the area of Vṛndāvana, and Madhuvana is one of them. Pilgrims from all parts of India assemble together and visit all twelve of these forests. There are five forests on the eastern bank of the Yamunā: Bhadravana, Bilvavana, Lauhavana, Bhāṇḍīravana and Mahāvana. On the western side of the bank there are seven: Madhuvana, Tālavana, Kumudavana, Bahulāvana, Kāmyavana, Khadiravana and Vṛndāvana. In those twelve forests there are different *ghāṭas*, or bathing places. They are listed as follows: (1) Avimukta, (2) Adhirūḍha, (3) Guhya-tīrtha, (4) Prayāga-tīrtha, (5) Kanakhala, (6) Tinduka-tīrtha, (7) Sūrya-tīrtha, (8) Vaṭasvāmī, (9) Dhruva-ghāṭa (Dhruva-ghāṭa, where there are many nice trees of fruits and flowers, is famous because Dhruva Mahārāja meditated and underwent severe penances and austerities there in an elevated spot), (10) Ṛṣi-tīrtha, (11) Mokṣa-tīrtha, (12) Budha-tīrtha, (13) Gokarṇa, (14) Kṛṣṇagaṅgā, (15) Vaikuṇṭha, (16) Asi-kuṇḍa, (17) Catuḥ-sāmudrika-kūpa, (18) Akrūra-tīrtha (when Kṛṣṇa and Balarāma were going to Mathurā in the chariot driven by Akrūra, all of them took baths in this *ghāṭa*), (19) Yājñika-vipra-sthāna, (20) Kubjā-kūpa, (21) Raṅga-sthala, (22) Mañcha-sthala, (23) Mallayuddha-sthāna, and (24) Daśāśvamedha.

TEXT 43

स्नात्वानुसवनं तस्मिन् कालिन्द्याः सलिले शिवे ।
कृत्वोचितानि निवसन्नात्मनः कल्पितासनः ॥४३॥

snātvānusavanaṁ tasmin
kālindyāḥ salile śive
kṛtvocitāni nivasann
ātmanaḥ kalpitāsanaḥ

snātvā—after taking bath; *anusavanam*—three times; *tasmin*—in that; *kālindyāḥ*—in the River Kālindī (the Yamunā); *salile*—in the water; *śive*—which is very auspicious; *kṛtvā*—performing; *ucitāni*—suitable; *nivasan*—sitting; *ātmanaḥ*—of the self; *kalpita-āsanaḥ*—having prepared a sitting place.

TRANSLATION

Nārada Muni instructed: My dear boy, in the waters of the Yamunā River, which is known as Kālindī, you should take three baths daily because the water is very auspicious, sacred and clear. After bathing, you should perform the necessary regulative principles for aṣṭāṅga-yoga and then sit down on your āsana [sitting place] in a calm and quiet position.

PURPORT

It appears from this statement that Dhruva Mahārāja had already been instructed how to practice the eightfold *yoga* system, which is known as *aṣṭāṅga-yoga.* This system is explained in our *Bhagavad-gītā As It Is,* in the chapter entitled, "*Sāṅkhya-yoga,*" pages 319–322. It is understood that in *aṣṭāṅga-yoga* one practices settling the mind and then concentrating it on the form of Lord Viṣṇu, as will be described in the following verses. It is clearly stated here that *aṣṭāṅga-yoga* is not a bodily gymnastic exercise, but a practice to concentrate the mind on the form of Viṣṇu. Before sitting on his *āsana*, which is also described in *Bhagavad-gītā*, one has to cleanse himself very nicely in clear or sacred water thrice daily. The water of the Yamunā is naturally very clear and pure, and thus if anyone bathes there three times, undoubtedly he will be very greatly purified externally. Nārada Muni, therefore, instructed Dhruva Mahārāja to go to the bank of the Yamunā and thus become externally purified. This is part of the gradual process of practicing mystic *yoga*.

TEXT 44

प्राणायामेन त्रिवृता प्राणेन्द्रियमनोमलम् ।
शनैर्व्युदस्याभिध्यायेन्मनसा गुरुणा गुरुम् ॥४४॥

prāṇāyāmena tri-vṛtā
prāṇendriya-mano-malam
śanair vyudasyābhidhyāyen
manasā guruṇā gurum

prāṇāyāmena—by breathing exercises; *tri-vṛtā*—by the three recommended ways; *prāṇa-indriya*—the life air and the senses; *manaḥ*—mind; *malam*—impurity; *śanaiḥ*—gradually; *vyudasya*—giving up; *abhidhyāyet*—meditate upon; *manasā*—by the mind; *guruṇā*—undisturbed; *gurum*—the supreme spiritual master, Kṛṣṇa.

TRANSLATION

After sitting on your seat, practice the three kinds of breathing exercises, and thus gradually control the life air, the mind and the senses. Completely free yourself from all material contamination, and with great patience begin to meditate on the Supreme Personality of Godhead.

PURPORT

In this verse the entire *yoga* system is described in summary, and special stress is given to the breathing exercises for stopping the disturbing mind. The mind, by nature, is always oscillating, for it is very fickle, but the breathing exercise is meant to control it. This process of controlling the mind might have been very possible in those days millions of years ago when Dhruva Mahārāja took to it, but at the present moment the mind has to be fixed directly on the lotus feet of the Lord by the chanting process. By chanting the Hare Kṛṣṇa *mantra* one immediately concentrates on the sound vibration and thinks of the lotus feet of the Lord, and very quickly one is elevated to the position of *samādhi*, or trance. If one goes on chanting the holy names of the Lord, which are not different from the Supreme Personality of Godhead, naturally his mind becomes absorbed in thought of the Lord.

It is here recommended to Dhruva Mahārāja that he meditate on the supreme *guru*, or supreme spiritual master. The supreme spiritual master is Kṛṣṇa, who is therefore known as *caitya-guru*. This refers to the Supersoul, who is sitting in everyone's heart. He helps from within as stated in *Bhagavad-gītā*, and He sends the spiritual master, who helps from without. The spiritual master is the external manifestation of the *caitya-guru*, or the spiritual master sitting in everyone's heart.

The process by which we give up our thoughts of material things is called *pratyāhāra*, which entails being freed from all material thoughts and engagements. The word *abhidhyāyet*, which is used in this verse, indicates that unless one's mind is fixed, one cannot meditate. The conclusion, therefore, is that meditation means thinking of the Lord within. Whether one comes to that stage by the *aṣṭāṅga-yoga* system or by the method recommended in the *śāstras* especially for this present age—to constantly chant the holy name of the Lord—the goal is to meditate on the Supreme Personality of Godhead.

TEXT 45

प्रसादाभिमुखं शश्वत्प्रसन्नवदनेक्षणम् ।
सुनासं सुभ्रुवं चारुकपोलं सुरसुन्दरम् ॥४५॥

prasādābhimukhaṁ śaśvat
prasanna-vadanekṣaṇam
sunāsaṁ subhruvaṁ cāru-
kapolaṁ sura-sundaram

prasāda-abhimukham—always prepared to offer causeless mercy; *śaśvat*—always; *prasanna*—pleasing; *vadana*—mouth; *īkṣaṇam*—vision; *su-nāsam*—very nicely constructed nose; *su-bhruvam*—very nicely decorated eyebrows; *cāru*—beautiful; *kapolam*—forehead; *sura*—the demigods; *sundaram*—good looking.

TRANSLATION

[The form of the Lord is described herein.] The Lord's face is perpetually very beautiful and pleasing in attitude. To the devotees who see Him, He appears never to be displeased, and He is always prepared to award benedictions to them. His eyes, His nicely decorated eyebrows, His raised nose and His broad forehead are all very beautiful. He is more beautiful than all the demigods.

PURPORT

This verse clearly explains how one has to meditate on the form of the Lord. Impersonal meditation is a bogus invention of modern days. In none of the Vedic literatures is impersonal meditation recommended. In *Bhagavad-gītā*, when meditation is recommended, the word *mat-paraḥ*, which means "pertaining to Me," is used. Any Viṣṇu form pertains to Lord Kṛṣṇa because Lord Kṛṣṇa is the original Viṣṇu form. Sometimes someone tries to meditate upon the impersonal Brahman, which is described in *Bhagavad-gītā* as *avyakta*, meaning "unmanifested" or "impersonal." But it is remarked by the Lord Himself that those who are attached to this impersonal feature of the Lord suffer a very troublesome task because no one can concentrate on the impersonal feature. One has to concentrate on the form of the Lord, which is described here in connection with Dhruva Mahārāja's meditation. As will be apparent from later descriptions, Dhruva Mahārāja perfected this kind of meditation, and his *yoga* was successful.

TEXT 46

तरुणं रमणीयाङ्गमरुणोष्ठेक्षणाधरम् ।
प्रणताश्रयणं नृम्णं शरण्यं करुणार्णवम् ॥४६॥

taruṇaṁ ramaṇīyāṅgam
aruṇoṣṭhekṣaṇādharam

praṇatāśrayaṇaṁ nṛmṇaṁ
śaraṇyaṁ karuṇārṇavam

taruṇam—youthful; *ramaṇīya*—attractive; *aṅgam*—all parts of the body; *aruṇa-oṣṭha*—lips pinkish like the rising sun; *īkṣaṇa-adharam*—eyes of the same nature; *praṇata*—one who is surrendered; *āśrayaṇam*—shelter of the surrendered; *nṛmṇam*—transcendentally pleasing in all respects; *śaraṇyam*—the person unto whom it is just worthy to surrender; *karuṇā*—merciful like; *arṇavam*—the ocean.

TRANSLATION

Nārada Muni continued: The Lord's form is always youthful. Every limb and every part of His body is properly formed, free from defect. His eyes and lips are pinkish like the rising sun. He is always prepared to give shelter to the surrendered soul, and anyone so fortunate as to look upon Him feels all satisfaction. The Lord is always worthy to be the master of the surrendered soul, for He is the ocean of mercy.

PURPORT

Everyone has to surrender to someone superior. That is always the nature of our living condition. At the present moment we are trying to surrender to someone—either to society or to our nation, family, state or government. The surrendering process already exists, but it is never perfect because the person or institution unto whom we surrender is imperfect, and our surrender, having so many ulterior motives, is also imperfect. As such, in the material world no one is worthy to accept anyone's surrender, nor does anyone fully surrender to anyone else unless obliged to do so. But here the surrendering process is voluntary, and the Lord is worthy to accept the surrender. This surrender by the living entity occurs automatically as soon as he sees the beautiful youthful nature of the Lord.

The description given by Nārada Muni is not imaginary. The form of the Lord is understood by the *paramparā* system. Māyāvādī philosophers say that we have to imagine the form of the Lord, but here Nārada Muni does not say that. Rather, he gives the description of the Lord from authoritative sources. He is himself an authority, and he is able to go to

Vaikuṇṭhaloka and see the Lord personally; therefore his description of the bodily features of the Lord is not imagination. Sometimes we give instructions to our students about the bodily features of the Lord, and they paint Him. Their paintings are not imaginary. The description is given through disciplic succession, just like that given by Nārada Muni, who sees the Lord and describes His bodily features. Therefore, such descriptions should be accepted, and if they are painted, that is not imaginative painting.

TEXT 47

श्रीवत्साङ्कं घनश्यामं पुरुषं वनमालिनम् ।
शङ्खचक्रगदापद्मैरभिव्यक्तचतुर्भुजम् ॥४७॥

śrīvatsāṅkaṁ ghana-śyāmaṁ
puruṣaṁ vana-mālinam
śaṅkha-cakra-gadā-padmair
abhivyakta-caturbhujam

śrīvatsa-aṅkam—the mark of Śrīvatsa on the chest of the Lord; *ghana-śyāmam*—deeply bluish; *puruṣam*—the Supreme Person; *vana-mālinam*—with a garland of flowers; *śaṅkha*—conchshell; *cakra*—wheel; *gadā*—club; *padmaiḥ*—lotus flower; *abhivyakta*—manifested; *catuḥ-bhujam*—four handed.

TRANSLATION

The Lord is further described as having the mark of Śrīvatsa, or the sitting place of the goddess of fortune, and His bodily hue is deep bluish. The Lord is a person, He wears a garland of flowers, and He is eternally manifest with four hands, which hold [beginning from the lower left hand] a conchshell, wheel, club and lotus flower.

PURPORT

Here in this verse the word *puruṣam* is very significant. The Lord is never female. He is always male (*puruṣa*). Therefore the impersonalist who imagines the Lord's form as that of a woman is mistaken. The Lord appears in female form if necessary, but His perpetual form is *puruṣa* because He is originally male. The feminine feature of the Lord is displayed by goddesses of fortune—Lakṣmī, Rādhārāṇī, Sītā, etc. All these goddesses of fortune are servitors of the Lord; they are not the Supreme, as falsely imagined by the impersonalist. Lord Kṛṣṇa in His Nārāyaṇa feature is always four handed. On the Battlefield of Kurukṣetra, when Arjuna wanted to see His universal form, He showed this feature of four-handed Nārāyaṇa. Some devotees are of the opinion that Kṛṣṇa is an incarnation of Nārāyaṇa, but the *Bhāgavata* school says that Nārāyaṇa is a manifestation of Kṛṣṇa.

TEXT 48

किरीटिनं कुण्डलिनं केयूरवलयान्वितम् ।
कौस्तुभाभरणग्रीवं पीतकौशेयवाससम् ॥४८॥

kirīṭinaṁ kuṇḍalinaṁ
keyūra-valayānvitam
kaustubhābharaṇa-grīvaṁ
pīta-kauśeya-vāsasam

kirīṭinam—the Lord is decorated with a jeweled helmet; *kuṇḍalinam*—with pearl earrings; *keyūra*—jeweled necklace; *valaya-anvitam*—with jeweled bracelets; *kaustubha-ābharaṇa-grīvam*—His neck is decorated by the Kaustubha jewel; *pīta-kauśeya-vāsasam*—and He is dressed with yellow silk garments.

TRANSLATION

The entire body of the Supreme Personality of Godhead, Vāsudeva, is decorated. He wears a valuable jeweled helmet, necklaces and bracelets, His neck is adorned with the Kaustubha jewel, and He is dressed in yellow silk garments.

TEXT 49

काञ्चीकलापपर्यस्तं लसत्काञ्चननूपुरम् ।
दर्शनीयतमं शान्तं मनोनयनवर्धनम् ॥४९॥

kāñcī-kalāpa-paryastaṁ
lasat-kāñcana-nūpuram

darśanīyatamaṁ śāntaṁ
mano-nayana-vardhanam

kāñcī-kalāpa—small bells; *paryastam*—surrounding the waist; *lasat-kāñcana-nūpuram*—His legs are decorated with golden ankle bells; *darśanīya-tamam*—the superexcellent feature; *śāntam*—peaceful, calm and quiet; *manaḥ-nayana-vardhanam*—very pleasing to the eyes and the mind.

TRANSLATION

The Lord is decorated with small golden bells around His waist, and His lotus feet are decorated with golden ankle bells. All His bodily features are very attractive and pleasing to the eyes. He is always peaceful, calm and quiet and very pleasing to the eyes and the mind.

TEXT 50

पद्भ्यां नखमणिश्रेण्या विलसद्भ्यां समर्चताम् ।
हृत्पद्मकर्णिकाधिष्ण्यमाक्रम्यात्मन्यवस्थितम् ॥५०॥

padbhyāṁ nakha-maṇi-śreṇyā
vilasadbhyāṁ samarcatām
hṛt-padma-karṇikā-dhiṣṇyam
ākramyātmany avasthitam

padbhyām—by His lotus feet; *nakha-maṇi-śreṇyā*—by the light of the jewellike nails on the toes; *vilasadbhyām*—glittering lotus feet; *samarcatām*—persons who are engaged in worshiping them; *hṛt-padma-karṇikā*—the whorl of the lotus flower of the heart; *dhiṣṇyam*—situated; *ākramya*—seizing; *ātmani*—in the heart; *avasthitam*—situated.

TRANSLATION

Real yogīs meditate upon the transcendental form of the Lord as He stands on the whorl of the lotus of their hearts, the jewellike nails of His lotus feet glittering.

TEXT 51

स्मयमानमभिध्यायेत्सानुरागावलोकनम् ।
नियतेनैकभूतेन मनसा वरदर्षभम् ॥५१॥

smayamānam abhidhyāyet
sānurāgāvalokanam
niyatenaika-bhūtena
manasā varadarṣabham

smayamānam—the Lord's smiling; *abhidhyāyet*—one should meditate upon Him; *sa-anurāga-avalokanam*—one who is looking toward the devotees with great affection; *niyatena*—in this way, regularly; *eka-bhūtena*—with great attention; *manasā*—with the mind; *vara-darṣabham*—one should meditate upon the greatest bestower of benedictions.

TRANSLATION

The Lord is always smiling, and the devotee should constantly see the Lord in this form, as He looks very mercifully toward the devotee. In this way the meditator should look toward the Supreme Personality of Godhead, the bestower of all benedictions.

PURPORT

The word *niyatena* is very significant in this connection, for it indicates that one should execute the meditation practice as stated above. One should not manufacture a way of meditation on the Supreme Personality of Godhead, but should follow the authorized *śāstras* and personalities. By this prescribed method one can practice concentration upon the Lord until one is so fixed that he remains in trance, thinking always of the form of the Lord. The word used here is *eka-bhūtena*, which means "with great attention and concentration." If one concentrates on the descriptions of the bodily features of the Lord, one will never fall down.

TEXT 52

एवं भगवतो रूपं सुभद्रं ध्यायतो मनः ।
निर्वृत्या परया तूर्णं सम्पन्नं न निवर्तते ॥५२॥

evaṁ bhagavato rūpaṁ
subhadraṁ dhyāyato manaḥ
nirvṛtyā parayā tūrṇaṁ
sampannaṁ na nivartate

evam—thus; *bhagavataḥ*—of the Supreme Personality of Godhead; *rūpam*—form; *su-bhadram*—very auspicious; *dhyāyataḥ*—meditating; *manaḥ*—the mind; *nirvṛtyā*—being freed from all material contamination; *parayā*—transcendental; *tūrṇam*—very soon; *sampannam*—being enriched; *na*—never; *nivartate*—come down.

TRANSLATION

One who meditates in this way, concentrating his mind upon the always auspicious form of the Lord, is very soon freed from all material contamination, and he does not come down from meditation upon the Lord.

PURPORT

This fixed meditation is called *samādhi,* or trance. A person constantly engaged in the transcendental loving service of the Lord cannot be deviated from meditating on the form of the Lord, as described herein. The *arcana-mārga,* or the devotional path prescribed in the *Pāñcarātra* system of devotional service for worshiping the Deity in the temple, makes the devotee think constantly of the Lord; that is *samādhi,* or trance. One who practices in this way cannot deviate from the service of the Lord, and that makes him perfect in the mission of human life.

TEXT 53

जपश्च परमो गुह्यः श्रूयतां मे नृपात्मज ।
यं सप्तरात्रं प्रपठन् पुमान् पश्यति खेचरान् ॥५३॥

japaś ca paramo guhyaḥ
śrūyatāṁ me nṛpātmaja
yaṁ sapta-rātraṁ prapaṭhan
pumān paśyati khecarān

japaḥ ca—the chanting *mantra* in this connection; *paramaḥ*—very, very; *guhyaḥ*—confidential; *śrūyatām*—please hear; *me*—from me; *nṛpa-ātmaja*—O son of the King; *yam*—which; *sapta-rātram*—seven nights; *prapaṭhan*—chanting; *pumān*—a person; *paśyati*—can see; *khe-carān*—human beings who travel in space.

TRANSLATION

O son of the King, now I shall speak unto you the mantra which is to be chanted with this process of meditation. One who carefully chants this mantra for seven nights can see the perfect human beings flying in the sky.

PURPORT

Within this universe there is a planet called Siddhaloka. The inhabitants of Siddhaloka are by nature perfect in the *yoga* achievements, which are of eight varieties: one can become smaller than the smallest, lighter than the lightest, or bigger than the biggest; one can immediately get whatever he likes, one can even create a planet, etc. These are some of the yogic perfections. By virtue of the *laghimā-siddhi*, or purificatory process to become lighter than the lightest, the inhabitants of Siddhaloka can fly in the sky without airplanes or airships. It is hinted herein by Nārada Muni to Dhruva Mahārāja that by meditating upon the transcendental form of the Lord and at the same time chanting the *mantra* one becomes so perfect within seven days that he can see the human beings who fly in the sky. Nārada Muni uses the word *japaḥ*, which indicates that the *mantra* to be chanted is very confidential. One may ask, "If it is confidential, why is it mentioned in the writing of *Śrīmad-Bhāgavatam*?" It is confidential in this sense: one may receive a published *mantra* anywhere, but unless it is accepted through the chain of disciplic succession, the *mantra* does not act. It is said by authoritative sources that any *mantra* chanted without having been received from the disciplic succession has no efficacy.

Another point established in this verse is that meditation should be carried on with the chanting of a *mantra*. Chanting of the Hare Kṛṣṇa *mantra* is the easiest process of meditation in this age. As soon as one chants the Hare Kṛṣṇa *mantra*, he sees the forms of Kṛṣṇa, Rāma and

Their energies, and that is the perfect stage of trance. One should not artificially try to see the form of the Lord while chanting Hare Kṛṣṇa, but when the chanting is performed offenselessly the Lord will automatically reveal Himself to the view of the chanter. The chanter, therefore, has to concentrate on hearing the vibration, and without extra endeavor on his part, the Lord will automatically appear.

TEXT 54

ॐ नमो भगवते वासुदेवाय ।
मन्त्रेणानेन देवस्य कुर्याद् द्रव्यमयीं बुधः ।
सपर्यां विविधैर्द्रव्यैर्देशकालविभागवित् ॥५४॥

oṁ namo bhagavate vāsudevāya
mantreṇānena devasya
kuryād dravyamayīṁ budhaḥ
saparyāṁ vividhair dravyair
deśa-kāla-vibhāgavit

oṁ—O my Lord; *namaḥ*—I offer my respectful obeisances; *bhagavate*—unto the Supreme Personality of Godhead; *vāsudevāya*—unto the Supreme Lord, Vāsudeva; *mantreṇa*—by this hymn, or *mantra; anena*—this; *devasya*—of the Lord; *kuryāt*—one should do; *dravyamayīm*—physical; *budhaḥ*—one who is learned; *saparyām*—worship by the prescribed method; *vividhaiḥ*—with varieties; *dravyaiḥ*—paraphernalia; *deśa*—according to country; *kāla*—time; *vibhāga-vit*—one who knows the divisions.

TRANSLATION

Oṁ namo bhagavate vāsudevāya. This is the twelve-syllable mantra for worshiping Lord Kṛṣṇa. One should install the physical forms of the Lord, and with the chanting of the mantra one should offer flowers and fruits and other varieties of foodstuffs exactly according to the rules and regulations prescribed by authorities. But this should be done in consideration of place, time, and attendant conveniences and inconveniences.

PURPORT

Oṁ namo bhagavate vāsudevāya is known as the *dvādaśākṣara-mantra.* This *mantra* is chanted by Vaiṣṇava devotees, and it begins with *praṇava,* or *oṁkāra.* There is an injunction that those who are not *brāhmaṇas* cannot pronounce the *praṇava mantra.* But Dhruva Mahārāja was born a *kṣatriya.* He at once admitted before Nārada Muni that as a *kṣatriya* he was unable to accept Nārada's instruction of renunciation and mental equilibrium, which are the concern of a *brāhmaṇa.* Still, although not a *brāhmaṇa* but a *kṣatriya,* Dhruva was allowed, on the authority of Nārada, to pronounce the *praṇava oṁkāra.* This is very significant. Especially in India, the caste *brāhmaṇas* object greatly when persons from other castes, who are not born in *brāhmaṇa* families, recite this *praṇava mantra.* But here is tacit proof that if a person accepts the Vaiṣṇava *mantra* or Vaiṣṇava way of worshiping the Deity, he is allowed to chant the *praṇava mantra.* In *Bhagavad-gītā* the Lord personally accepts that anyone, even one of a low species, can be elevated to the highest position and go back home, back to Godhead, simply if he worships properly.

The prescribed rules, as stated here by Nārada Muni, are that one should accept the *mantra* through a bona fide spiritual master and hear the *mantra* in the right ear. Not only should one chant or murmur the *mantra,* but in front of him he must have the Deity, or physical form of the Lord. Of course, when the Lord appears it is no longer a physical form. For example, when an iron rod is made red-hot in a fire, it is no longer iron; it is fire. Similarly, when we make a form of the Lord—whether of wood or stone or metal or jewels or paint, or even a form within the mind—it is a bona fide, spiritual, transcendental form of the Lord. Not only must one receive the *mantra* from the bona fide spiritual master like Nārada Muni or his representative in the disciplic succession, but one must chant the *mantra.* And not only must one chant, but he should also offer whatever foodstuff is available in his part of the world, according to time and convenience.

The method of worship—chanting the *mantra* and preparing the forms of the Lord—is not stereotyped, nor is it exactly the same everywhere. It is specifically mentioned in this verse that one should take consideration of the time, place and available conveniences. Our Kṛṣṇa consciousness movement is going on throughout the entire world, and we also install Deities in different centers. Sometimes our Indian friends, puffed up with concocted notions, criticize, "This has not been done. That has not been done." But they forget this instruction of Nārada Muni to one of the greatest Vaiṣṇavas, Dhruva Mahārāja. One has to consider the particular time, country and conveniences. What is convenient in India may not be convenient in the Western countries. Those who are not actually in the line of *ācāryas*, or who personally have no knowledge of how to act in the role of *ācārya*, unnecessarily criticize the activities of the ISKCON movement in countries outside of India. The fact is that such critics cannot do anything personally to spread Kṛṣṇa consciousness. If someone does go and preach, taking all risks and allowing all considerations for time and place, it might be that there are changes in the manner of worship, but that is not at all faulty according to *śāstra*. Śrīmad Vīrarāghava Ācārya, an *ācārya* in the disciplic succession of the Rāmānuja-sampradāya, has remarked in his commentary that *caṇḍālas*, or conditioned souls who are born in lower than *śūdra* families, can also be initiated according to circumstances. The formalities may be slightly changed here and there to make them Vaiṣṇavas.

Lord Caitanya Mahāprabhu recommends that His name should be heard in every nook and corner of the world. How is this possible unless one preaches everywhere? The cult of Lord Caitanya Mahāprabhu is *bhāgavata-dharma*, and He especially recommends *kṛṣṇa-kathā*, or the cult of *Bhagavad-gītā* and *Śrīmad-Bhāgavatam*. He recommends that every Indian, considering this task to be *para-upakāra*, or welfare activity, take the Lord's message to other residents of the world. "Other residents of the world" does not refer only to those who are exactly like the Indian *brāhmaṇas* and *kṣatriyas*, or like the caste *brāhmaṇas*, who claim to be *brāhmaṇas* because they were born in the families of *brāhmaṇas*. The principle that only Indians and Hindus should be brought into the Vaiṣṇava cult is a mistaken idea. There should be propaganda to bring everyone to the Vaiṣṇava cult. The Kṛṣṇa consciousness movement is meant for this purpose. There is no bar to propagating the Kṛṣṇa consciousness movement even among people who are born in *caṇḍāla*, *mleccha* or *yavana* families. Even in India, this point has been enunciated by Śrīla Sanātana Gosvāmī in his book *Hari-bhakti-vilāsa*, which is *smṛti* and is the authorized Vedic guide for Vaiṣṇavas in their daily behavior. Sanātana Gosvāmī says that as bell metal can turn to gold when mixed with mercury in a chemical process, so, by the bona fide *dīkṣā*, or initiation method, anyone can become a Vaiṣṇava. One should take initiation from a bona fide spiritual master coming in the disciplic succession, who is authorized by his predecessor spiritual master. This is called *dīkṣā-vidhāna.* Lord Kṛṣṇa states in *Bhagavad-gītā*, *vyapāśritya:* one should accept a spiritual master. By this process the entire world can be converted to Kṛṣṇa consciousness.

TEXT 55

सलिलैः शुचिभिर्माल्यैर्वन्यैर्मूलफलादिभिः ।
शस्ताङ्कुरांशुकैश्चार्चेत्तुलस्या प्रियया प्रभुम् ॥५५॥

salilaiḥ śucibhir mālyair
vanyair mūla-phalādibhiḥ
śastāṅkurāṁśukaiś cārcet
tulasyā priyayā prabhum

salilaiḥ—by use of water; *śucibhiḥ*—being purified; *mālyaiḥ*—by garlands; *vanyaiḥ*—of forest flowers; *mūla*—roots; *phala-ādibhiḥ*—by different kinds of vegetables and fruits; *śasta*—the newly grown grass; *aṅkura*—buds; *aṁśukaiḥ*—by the skin of trees, such as the *bhūrja;* *ca*—and; *arcet*—should worship; *tulasyā*—by the *tulasī* leaves; *priyayā*—which are very dear to the Lord; *prabhum*—the Lord.

TRANSLATION

One should worship the Lord by offering pure water, pure flower garlands, fruits, flowers and vegetables, which are available in the forest, or by collecting newly grown grasses, small buds of flowers or even the skins of trees, and if possible, by offering tulasī leaves, which are very dear to the Supreme Personality of Godhead.

PURPORT

It is specifically mentioned herein that *tulasī* leaves are very dear to the Supreme Personality of Godhead, and devotees should take particular care to have *tulasī* leaves in every temple and center of worship. In the Western countries, while engaged in propagating the Kṛṣṇa consciousness movement, we were brought great unhappiness because we could not find *tulasī* leaves. We are very much obliged, therefore, to our disciple Śrīmatī Govinda dāsī because she has taken much care to grow *tulasī* plants from seeds, and she has been successful by the grace of Kṛṣṇa. Now *tulasī* plants are growing in almost every center of our movement.

Tulasī leaves are very important in the method of worshiping the Supreme Personality of Godhead. In this verse the word *salilaiḥ* means "by the water." Of course, Dhruva Mahārāja was worshiping on the bank of the Yamunā. The Yamunā and the Ganges are sacred, and sometimes devotees in India insist that the Deity must be worshiped with water of the Ganges or Yamunā. But here we understand *deśa-kāla* to mean "according to time and country." In the Western countries there is no River Yamunā or Ganges—water from such sacred rivers is not available. Does this mean that the *arcā* worship should for that reason be stopped? No. *Salilaiḥ* refers to any water—whatever is available—but it must be very clear and collected purely. That water can be used. The other paraphernalia, such as flower garlands, fruits and vegetables, should be collected according to the country and according to their availability. *Tulasī* leaves are very important for satisfying the Lord, so as far as possible an arrangement should be made for growing *tulasī* leaves. Dhruva Mahārāja was advised to worship the Lord with the fruits and flowers available in the forest. In the *Bhagavad-gītā* Kṛṣṇa frankly says that He accepts vegetables, fruits, flowers, etc. One should not offer Lord Vāsudeva anything other than what is prescribed herein by the great authority Nārada Muni. One cannot offer to the Deity according to one's whims; since these fruits and vegetables are available anywhere in the universe, we should observe this small point very attentively.

TEXT 56

लब्ध्वा द्रव्यमयीमर्चां क्षित्यम्ब्वादिषु वार्चयेत् ।
आभृतात्मा मुनिः शान्तो यतवाङ्मितवन्यभुक् ॥५६॥

labdhvā dravyamayīm arcāṁ
kṣity-ambv-ādiṣu vārcayet

ābhṛtātmā muniḥ śānto
yata-vāṅ mita-vanya-bhuk

labdhvā—by getting; *dravya-mayīm*—made of physical elements; *arcām*—worshipable Deity; *kṣiti*—earth; *ambu*—water; *ādiṣu*—beginning with; *vā*—or; *arcayet*—worship; *ābhṛta-ātmā*—one who is fully self-controlled; *muniḥ*—a great personality; *śāntaḥ*—peacefully; *yata-vāk*—controlling the force of talking; *mita*—frugal; *vanya-bhuk*—eating whatever is available in the forest.

TRANSLATION

It is possible to worship a form of the Lord made of physical elements such as earth, water, pulp, wood and metal. In the forest one can make a form with no more than earth and water and worship Him according to the above principles. A devotee who has full control over his self should be very sober and peaceful and must be satisfied simply with eating whatever fruits and vegetables are available in the forest.

PURPORT

It is essential for a devotee to worship the form of the Lord and not only meditate upon the form of the Lord within his mind with the chanting of the *mantra* given by the spiritual master. The worship of the form must be present. The impersonalist takes unnecessary trouble to meditate upon or worship something impersonal, and the path is very precarious. We are not advised to follow the impersonalist way of meditating on or worshiping the Lord. Dhruva Mahārāja was advised to worship a form made of earth and water because in the jungle, if it is not possible to have a form made of metal, wood or stone, the best process is to take earth mixed with water and make a form of the Lord and worship Him. The devotee should not be anxious about cooking food; whatever is available in the forest or in the city among the fruit and vegetable groups should be offered to the Deity, and the devotee should be satisfied eating that. He should not be anxious to have very palatable dishes. Of course, wherever it is possible, one should offer the Deities the best foodstuffs, prepared within the category of fruits and vegetables, cooked or uncooked. The important factor is that the devotee should be regulated (*mita-bhuk*); that is one of the good qualifications of a devotee. He should not hanker to satisfy the tongue with a particular kind of foodstuff. He should be satisfied to eat whatever *prasāda* is available by the grace of the Lord.

TEXT 57

स्वेच्छावतारचरितैरचिन्त्यनिजमायया ।
करिष्यत्युत्तमश्लोकस्तद् ध्यायेद्धृदयङ्गमम् ॥५७॥

svecchāvatāra-caritair
acintya-nija-māyayā
kariṣyaty uttamaślokas
tad dhyāyed dhṛdayaṅ-gamam

sva-icchā—by His own supreme will; *avatāra*—incarnation; *caritaiḥ*—activities; *acintya*—inconceivable; *nija-māyayā*—by His own potency; *kariṣyati*—performs; *uttama-ślokaḥ*—the Supreme Personality of Godhead; *tat*—that; *dhyāyet*—one should meditate; *hṛdayam-gamam*—very attractive.

TRANSLATION

My dear Dhruva, besides worshiping the Deity and chanting the mantra three times a day, you should meditate upon the transcendental activities of the Supreme Personality of Godhead in His different incarnations, as exhibited by His supreme will and personal potencies.

PURPORT

Devotional service comprises nine prescribed practices—hearing, chanting, remembering, worshiping, serving, offering everything to the Deity, etc. Here Dhruva Mahārāja is advised not only to meditate on the form of the Lord, but to think of His transcendental pastimes in His different incarnations. Māyāvādī philosophers take the incarnation of the Lord to be in the same category as the ordinary living entity. This is a great mistake. The incarnation of the Supreme Personality of Godhead is not forced to act by the material laws of nature. The word *svecchā* is used here to indicate that He appears out of His supreme will. The conditioned soul is forced to accept a particular type of body according to his *karma* given by the laws of material nature under the direction of the Supreme Lord. But when the Lord appears, He is not forced by the dictation of material nature; He appears as He likes by His own internal potency. That is the difference. The conditioned soul accepts a particular type of body, such as the body of a hog, by his work and by the superior authority of material nature. But when Lord Kṛṣṇa appears in the incarnation of a boar, He is not the same kind of hog as an ordinary animal. Kṛṣṇa appears as Varāha-avatāra in an expansive feature which cannot be compared to an ordinary hog's. His appearance and disappearance are inconceivable to us. In the *Bhagavad-gītā* it is clearly said that He appears by His own internal potency for the protection of the devotees and the annihilation of the nondevotees. A devotee should always consider that Kṛṣṇa does not appear as an ordinary human being or ordinary beast; His appearance as Varāha-mūrti or a horse or tortoise is an exhibition of His internal potency. In the *Brahma-saṁhitā* it is said, *ānanda-cinmaya-rasa-pratibhāvitābhiḥ:* one should not mistake the appearance of the Lord as a human being or a beast to be the same as the birth of an ordinary conditioned soul, who is forced to appear by the laws of nature, whether as an animal, as a human being or as a demigod. This kind of thinking is offensive. Lord Caitanya Mahāprabhu has condemned the Māyāvādīs as offensive to the Supreme Personality of Godhead because of their thinking that the Lord and the conditioned living entities are one and the same.

Nārada advises Dhruva to meditate on the pastimes of the Lord, which is as good as the meditation of concentrating one's mind on the form of the Lord. As meditation on any form of the Lord is valuable, so is chanting of different names of the Lord, such as Hari, Govinda and Nārāyaṇa. But in this age we are especially advised to chant the Hare Kṛṣṇa *mantra* as enunciated in the *śāstra:* Hare Kṛṣṇa, Hare Kṛṣṇa, Kṛṣṇa Kṛṣṇa, Hare Hare/ Hare Rāma, Hare Rāma, Rāma Rāma, Hare Hare.

TEXT 58

परिचर्या भगवतो यावत्यः पूर्वसेविताः ।
ता मन्त्रहृदयेनैव प्रयुञ्ज्यान्मन्त्रमूर्तये ॥५८॥

paricaryā bhagavato
yāvatyaḥ pūrva-sevitāḥ
tā mantra-hṛdayenaiva
prayuñjyān mantra-mūrtaye

paricaryāḥ—service; *bhagavataḥ*—of the Personality of Godhead; *yāvatyaḥ*—as they are prescribed (as above mentioned); *pūrva-sevitāḥ*—recommended or done by previous *ācāryas; tāḥ*—that; *mantra*—hymns; *hṛdayena*—within the heart; *eva*—certainly; *prayuñjyāt*—one should worship; *mantra-mūrtaye*—who is nondifferent from the *mantra.*

TRANSLATION

One should follow in the footsteps of previous devotees regarding how to worship the Supreme Lord with the prescribed paraphernalia, or one should offer worship within the heart by reciting the mantra to the Personality of Godhead, who is nondifferent from the mantra.

PURPORT

It is recommended here that even if one cannot arrange to worship the forms of the Lord with all recommended paraphernalia, one can simply think about the form of the Lord and mentally offer everything recommended in the *śāstras*, including flowers, *candana* pulp, conchshell, umbrella, fan and *cāmara*. One can meditate upon offering and chant the twelve-syllable *mantra, oṁ namo bhagavate vāsudevāya.* Since the *mantra* and the Supreme Personality of Godhead are nondifferent, one can worship the form of the Lord with the *mantra* in the absence of physical paraphernalia. The story of the *brāhmaṇa* who worshiped the Lord within his mind, as related in *Bhakti-rasāmṛta-sindhu*, or *The Nectar of Devotion*, should be consulted in this connection. If paraphernalia is not present physically, one can think of the items and offer them to the Deity by chanting the *mantra*. Such are the liberal and potent facilities in the process of devotional service.

TEXTS 59–60

एवं कायेन मनसा वचसा च मनोगतम् ।
परिचर्यमाणो भगवान् भक्तिमत्परिचर्यया ॥५९॥

पुंसाममायिनां सम्यग्भजतां भाववर्धनः ।
श्रेयो दिशत्यभिमतं यद्धर्मादिषु देहिनाम् ॥६०॥

evaṁ kāyena manasā
vacasā ca mano-gatam
paricaryamāṇo bhagavān
bhaktimat-paricaryayā

puṁsām amāyināṁ samyag
bhajatāṁ bhāva-vardhanaḥ
śreyo diśaty abhimataṁ
yad dharmādiṣu dehinām

evam—thus; *kāyena*—by the body; *manasā*—by the mind; *vacasā*—by the words; *ca*—also; *manaḥ-gatam*—simply by thinking of the Lord; *paricaryamāṇaḥ*—engaged in the devotional service; *bhagavān*—the Supreme Personality of Godhead; *bhakti-mat*—according to the regulative principles of devotional service; *paricaryayā*—by worshiping the Lord; *puṁsām*—of the devotee; *amāyinām*—who is sincere and serious; *samyak*—perfectly; *bhajatām*—engaged in devotional service; *bhāva-vardhanaḥ*—the Lord, who increases the ecstasy of the devotee; *śreyaḥ*—ultimate goal; *diśati*—bestows; *abhimatam*—desire; *yat*—as they are; *dharma-ādiṣu*—regarding spiritual life and economic development; *dehinām*—of the conditioned souls.

TRANSLATION

Anyone who thus engages in the devotional service of the Lord, seriously and sincerely, with his mind, words and body, and who is fixed in the activities of the prescribed devotional methods, is blessed by the Lord according to his desire. If a devotee desires material religiosity, economic development, sense gratification or liberation from the material world, he is awarded these results.

PURPORT

Devotional service is so potent that one who renders devotional service can receive whatever he likes as a benediction from the Supreme Personality of Godhead. The conditioned souls are very much attached to the material world, and thus by performing religious rites they want the material benefits known as *dharma* and *artha.*

TEXT 61

विरक्तश्चेन्द्रियरतौ भक्तियोगेन भूयसा ।
तं निरन्तरभावेन भजेताद्धा विमुक्तये ॥६१॥

viraktaś cendriya-ratau
bhakti-yogena bhūyasā
taṁ nirantara-bhāvena
bhajetāddhā vimuktaye

viraktaḥ ca—completely renounced order of life; *indriya-ratau*—in the matter of sense gratification; *bhakti-yogena*—by the process of devotional service; *bhūyasā*—with great seriousness; *tam*—unto Him (the Supreme); *nirantara*—constantly, twenty-four hours daily; *bhāvena*—in the topmost stage of ecstasy; *bhajeta*—must worship; *addhā*—directly; *vimuktaye*—for liberation.

TRANSLATION

If one is very serious about liberation, he must stick to the process of transcendental loving service, engaging twenty-four hours a day in the highest stage of ecstasy, and he must certainly be aloof from all activities of sense gratification.

PURPORT

There are different stages of perfection according to different persons' objectives. Generally people are *karmīs,* for they engage in activities of sense gratification. Above the *karmīs* are the *jñānīs,* who are trying to become liberated from material entanglement. *Yogīs* are still more advanced because they meditate on the lotus feet of the Supreme Personality of Godhead. And above all these are the devotees, who simply engage in the transcendental loving service of the Lord; they are situated seriously on the topmost platform of ecstasy.

Here Dhruva Mahārāja is advised that if he has no desire for sense gratification, then he should directly engage himself in the transcendental loving service of the Lord. The path of *apavarga,* or liberation, begins from the stage called *mokṣa.* In this verse the word *vimuktaye,* "for liberation," is especially mentioned. If one wants to be happy within this material world, he may aspire to go to the different material planetary systems where there is a higher standard of sense gratification, but real *mokṣa,* or liberation, is performed without any such desire. This is explained in the *Bhakti-rasāmṛta-sindhu* by the term *anyābhilāṣitā-śūnyam,* "without desire for material sense gratification." For persons who are still inclined to enjoy material life in different stages or on different planets, the stage of liberation in *bhakti-yoga* is not recommended. Only persons who are completely free from the contamination of sense gratification can execute *bhakti-yoga,* or the process of devotional service, very purely. The activities on the path of *apavarga* up to the stages of *dharma, artha* and *kāma* are meant for sense gratification, but when one comes to the stage of *mokṣa,* the impersonalist liberation, the practitioner wants to merge into the existence of the Supreme. But that is also sense gratification. When one goes above the stage of liberation, however, he at once becomes one of the associates of the Lord to render transcendental loving service. That is technically called *vimukti.* For this specific *vimukti* liberation, Nārada Muni recommends that one directly engage himself in devotional service.

TEXT 62

इत्युक्तस्तं परिक्रम्य प्रणम्य च नृपार्भकः ।
ययौ मधुवनं पुण्यं हरेश्चरणचर्चितम् ॥६२॥

ity uktas taṁ parikramya
praṇamya ca nṛpārbhakaḥ
yayau madhuvanaṁ puṇyaṁ
hareś caraṇa-carcitam

iti—thus; *uktaḥ*—being spoken; *tam*—him (Nārada Muni); *parikramya*—by circumambulating; *praṇamya*—by offering obeisances; *ca*—also; *nṛpa-arbhakaḥ*—the boy of the King; *yayau*—went to; *madhuvanam*—a forest in Vṛndāvana known as Madhuvana; *puṇyam*—which is auspicious and pious; *hareḥ*—of the Lord; *caraṇa-carcitam*—imprinted by the lotus feet of Lord Kṛṣṇa.

TRANSLATION

When Dhruva Mahārāja, the son of the King, was thus advised by the great sage Nārada, he circumambulated Nāraḍa, his spiritual master, and offered him respectful obeisances. Then he started for Madhuvana, which is always imprinted with the lotus footprints of Lord Kṛṣṇa and which is therefore especially auspicious.

TEXT 63

तपोवनं गते तस्मिन्प्रविष्टोऽन्तःपुरं मुनिः ।
अर्हितार्हणको राज्ञा सुखासीन उवाच तम् ॥६३॥

tapo-vanaṁ gate tasmin
praviṣṭo 'ntaḥ-puraṁ muniḥ
arhitārhaṇako rājñā
sukhāsīna uvāca tam

tapaḥ-vanam—the forest path where Dhruva Mahārāja executed his austerity; *gate*—having thus approached; *tasmin*—there; *praviṣṭaḥ*—having entered; *antaḥ-puram*—within the private house; *muniḥ*—the great sage Nārada; *arhita*—being worshiped; *arhaṇakaḥ*—by respectful behavior; *rājñā*—by the King; *sukha-āsīnaḥ*—when he comfortably sat on his seat; *uvāca*—said; *tam*—unto him (the King).

TRANSLATION

After Dhruva entered Madhuvana Forest to execute devotional service, the great sage Nārada thought it wise to go to the King to see how he was faring within the palace. When Nārada Muni approached, the King received him properly, offering him due obeisances. After being seated comfortably, Nārada began to speak.

TEXT 64

नारद उवाच

राजन् किं ध्यायसे दीर्घं मुखेन परिशुष्यता ।
किं वा न रिष्यते कामो धर्मो वार्थेन संयुतः ॥६४॥

nārada uvāca
rājan kiṁ dhyāyase dīrghaṁ
mukhena pariśuṣyatā
kiṁ vā na riṣyate kāmo
dharmo vārthena saṁyutaḥ

nāradaḥ uvāca—the great sage Nārada Muni said; *rājan*—my dear King; *kim*—what; *dhyāyase*—thinking of; *dīrgham*—very deeply; *mukhena*—with your face; *pariśuṣyatā*—as if drying up; *kim vā*—whether; *na*—not; *riṣyate*—been lost; *kāmaḥ*—sense gratification; *dharmaḥ*—religious rituals; *vā*—or; *arthena*—with economic development; *saṁyutaḥ*—along with.

TRANSLATION

The great sage Nārada inquired: My dear King, your face appears to be withering up, and you look like you have been thinking of something for a very long time. Why is that? Have you been hampered in following your path of religious rites, economic development and sense gratification?

PURPORT

The four stages of advancement of human civilization are religiosity, economic development, sense gratification and, for some, the stage of liberation. Nārada Muni did not inquire from the King about his liberation, but only regarding the state management, which is meant for advancement of the three principles religiosity, economic development and sense gratification. Since those who engage in such activities are not interested in liberation, Nārada did not inquire from the King about this. Liberation is meant for persons who have lost all interest in religious ritualistic ceremonies, economic development and sense gratification.

TEXT 65

राजोवाच
सुतो मे बालको ब्रह्मन् स्त्रैणेनाकरुणात्मना ।
निर्वासितः पञ्चवर्षः सह मात्रा महान्कविः ॥६५॥

rājovāca
suto me bālako brahman
straiṇenākaruṇātmanā
nirvāsitaḥ pañca-varṣaḥ
saha mātrā mahān kaviḥ

rājā uvāca—the King replied; *sutaḥ*—son; *me*—my; *bālakaḥ*—tender boy; *brahman*—my dear *brāhmaṇa; straiṇena*—one who is too addicted to his wife; *akaruṇā-ātmanā*—one who is very hard of heart and without mercy; *nirvāsitaḥ*—is banished; *pañca-varṣaḥ*—although the boy is five years old; *saha*—with; *mātrā*—mother; *mahān*—great personality; *kaviḥ*—devotee.

TRANSLATION

The King replied: O best of the brāhmaṇas, I am very much addicted to my wife, and I am so fallen that I have abandoned all merciful behavior, even to my son, who is only five years old. I have banished him and his mother, even though he is a great soul and a great devotee.

PURPORT

In this verse there are some specific words which are to be understood very carefully. The King said that since he was very much addicted to his wife, he had lost all his mercy. That is the result of becoming too affectionate toward women. The King had two wives; the first wife was Sunīti, and the second was Suruci. He was too attached to the second wife, however, so he could not behave well with Dhruva Mahārāja. That was the cause of Dhruva's leaving home to perform austerities. Although as a father the King was affectionate toward his son, he minimized his affection for Dhruva Mahārāja because he was too much addicted to the second wife. Now he was repenting that both Dhruva Mahārāja and his mother, Sunīti, were practically banished. Dhruva Mahārāja went to the forest, and since his mother was being neglected by the King, she was therefore almost banished also. The King repented having banished his boy, for Dhruva was only five years old and a father should not banish his wife and children or neglect their maintenance. Repentant over his neglect of both Sunīti and her son, he was morose, and his face appeared withered. According to *Manu-smṛti*, one should never desert his wife and children. In a case where the wife and children are disobedient and do not follow the principles of home life, they are sometimes given up. But in the case of Dhruva Mahārāja this was not applicable because Dhruva was very mannerly and obedient. Moreover, he was a great devotee. Such a person is never to be neglected, yet the King was obliged to banish him. Now he was very sorry.

TEXT 66

अप्यनाथं वने ब्रह्मन्मास्मादन्त्यर्भकं वृकाः ।
श्रान्तं शयानं क्षुधितं परिम्लानमुखाम्बुजम् ॥६६॥

apy anāthaṁ vane brahman
mā smādanty arbhakaṁ vṛkāḥ
śrāntaṁ śayānaṁ kṣudhitaṁ
parimlāna-mukhāmbujam

api—certainly; *anātham*—without being protected by anyone; *vane*—in the forest; *brahman*—my dear *brāhmaṇa; mā*—whether or not; *sma*—did not; *adanti*—devour; *arbhakam*—the helpless boy; *vṛkāḥ*—wolves; *śrāntam*—being fatigued; *śayānam*—lying down; *kṣudhitam*—being hungry; *parimlāna*—emaciated; *mukha-ambujam*—his face, which is just like a lotus flower.

TRANSLATION

My dear brāhmaṇa, the face of my son was just like a lotus flower. I am thinking of his precarious condition. He is unprotected, and he might be very hungry. He might have lain down somewhere in the forest, and the wolves might have attacked him to eat his body.

TEXT 67

अहो मे बत दौरात्म्यं स्त्रीजितस्योपधारय ।
योऽङ्कं प्रेम्णारुरुक्षन्तं नाभ्यनन्दमसत्तमः ॥६७॥

aho me bata daurātmyaṁ
strī-jitasyopadhāraya

yo 'ṅkaṁ premṇāruruksantaṁ
nābhyanandam asattamaḥ

aho—alas; *me*—my; *bata*—certainly; *daurātmyam*—cruelty; *strī-jitasya*—conquered by a woman; *upadhāraya*—just think of me in this regard; *yaḥ*—who; *aṅkam*—lap; *premṇā*—out of love; *āruruksan-tam*—trying to rise onto it; *na*—not; *abhyanandam*—received properly; *asat-tamaḥ*—the most cruel.

TRANSLATION

Alas, just see how I was conquered by my wife! Just imagine my cruelty! Out of love and affection the boy was trying to get up on my lap, but I did not receive him, nor did I even pat him for a moment. Just imagine how hardhearted I am.

TEXT 68

नारद उवाच
मा मा शुचः स्वतनयं देवगुप्तं विशाम्पते ।
तत्प्रभावमविज्ञाय प्रावृङ्क्ते यद्यशो जगत् ॥६८॥

nārada uvāca
mā mā śucaḥ sva-tanayaṁ
deva-guptaṁ viśāmpate
tat-prabhāvam avijñāya
prāvṛṅkte yad-yaśo jagat

nāradaḥ uvāca—the great sage Nārada said; *mā*—do not; *mā*—do not; *śucaḥ*—be aggrieved; *sva-tanayam*—of your own son; *deva-gup-tam*—he is well protected by the Lord; *viśām-pate*—O master of human society; *tat*—his; *prabhāvam*—influence; *avijñāya*—without knowing; *prāvṛṅkte*—widespread; *yat*—whose; *yaśaḥ*—reputation; *jagat*—all over the world.

TRANSLATION

The great sage Nārada replied: My dear King, please do not be aggrieved about your son. He is well protected by the Supreme

Personality of Godhead. Although you have no actual information of his influence, his reputation is already spread all over the world.

PURPORT

Sometimes when we hear that great sages and devotees go to the forest and engage themselves in devotional service or meditation, we become surprised: how can one live in the forest and not be taken care of by anyone? But the answer, given by a great authority, Nārada Muni, is that such persons are well protected by the Supreme Personality of Godhead. *Śaraṇāgati*, or surrender, means acceptance or firm belief that wherever the surrendered soul lives he is always protected by the Supreme Personality of Godhead; he is never alone or unprotected. Dhruva Mahārāja's affectionate father thought his young boy, only five years old, to be in a very precarious position in the jungle, but Nārada Muni assured him, "You do not have sufficient information about the influence of your son." Anyone who engages in devotional service, anywhere within this universe, is never unprotected.

TEXT 69

सुदुष्करं कर्म कृत्वा लोकपालैरपि प्रभुः ।
ऐष्यत्यचिरतो राजन् यशो विपुलयंस्तव ॥६९॥

suduṣkaraṁ karma kṛtvā
loka-pālair api prabhuḥ
aiṣyaty acirato rājan
yaśo vipulayaṁs tava

su-duṣkaram—impossible to perform; *karma*—work; *kṛtvā*—after performing; *loka-pālaiḥ*—by great personalities; *api*—even; *prabhuḥ*—quite competent; *aiṣyati*—will come back; *acirataḥ*—without delay; *rājan*—my dear King; *yaśaḥ*—reputation; *vipulayan*—causing to become great; *tava*—your.

TRANSLATION

My dear King, your son is very competent. He will perform activities which would be impossible even for great kings and sages.

Very soon he will complete his task and come back home. You should know that he will also spread your reputation all over the world.

PURPORT

Here in this verse Nārada Muni has described Dhruva Mahārāja as *prabhu.* This word is applicable to the Supreme Personality of Godhead. Sometimes the spiritual master is addressed as Prabhupāda. *Prabhu* means "the Supreme Personality of Godhead," and *pāda* means "post." According to Vaiṣṇava philosophy, the spiritual master occupies the post of the Supreme Personality of Godhead, or in other words he is the bona fide representative of the Supreme Lord. Dhruva Mahārāja is also described here as *prabhu* because he is an *ācārya* of the Vaiṣṇava school. Another meaning of *prabhu* is "master of the senses," just like the word *svāmī.* Another significant word is *suduṣkaram,* "very difficult to perform." What was the task that Dhruva Mahārāja undertook? The most difficult task in life is to satisfy the Supreme Personality of Godhead, and Dhruva Mahārāja would be able to do that. We must remember that Dhruva Mahārāja was not fickle; he was determined to execute his service and then come back. Every devotee, therefore, should be determined that in this life he will be able to satisfy the Supreme Personality of Godhead and by that process go back home, back to Godhead. That is the perfection of the highest mission of life.

TEXT 70

मैत्रेय उवाच
इति देवर्षिणा प्रोक्तं विश्रुत्य जगतीपतिः ।
राजलक्ष्मीमनादृत्य पुत्रमेवान्वचिन्तयत् ॥७०॥

maitreya uvāca
iti devarṣiṇā proktaṁ
viśrutya jagatī-patiḥ
rāja-lakṣmīm anādṛtya
putram evānvacintayat

maitreyaḥ uvāca—the great sage Maitreya said; *iti*—thus; *devarṣiṇā*—by the great sage Nārada; *proktam*—spoken; *viśrutya*—hearing; *jagatī-patiḥ*—the King; *rāja-lakṣmīm*—the opulence of his big kingdom; *anādṛtya*—without taking care of; *putram*—his son; *eva*—certainly; *anvacintayat*—began to think of him.

TRANSLATION

The great Maitreya continued: The King, Uttānapāda, after being advised by Nārada Muni, practically gave up all duties in relation with his kingdom, which was very vast and wide, opulent like the goddess of fortune, and he simply began to think of his son Dhruva.

TEXT 71

तत्राभिषिक्तः प्रयतस्तामुपोष्य विभावरीम् ।
समाहितः पर्यचरदृष्यादेशेन पूरुषम् ॥७१॥

tatrābhiṣiktaḥ prayatas
tām upoṣya vibhāvarīm
samāhitaḥ paryacarad
ṛṣy-ādeśena pūruṣam

tatra—thereupon; *abhiṣiktaḥ*—after taking a bath; *prayataḥ*—with great attention; *tām*—that; *upoṣya*—fasting; *vibhāvarīm*—night; *samāhitaḥ*—perfect attention; *paryacarat*—worshiped; *ṛṣi*—by the great sage Nārada; *ādeśena*—as advised; *pūruṣam*—the Supreme Personality of Godhead.

TRANSLATION

Elsewhere, Dhruva Mahārāja, having arrived at Madhuvana, took his bath in the River Yamunā and observed fasting in the night with great care and attention. After that, as advised by the great sage Nārada, he engaged himself in worshiping the Supreme Personality of Godhead.

PURPORT

The significance of this particular verse is that Dhruva Mahārāja acted exactly according to the advice of his spiritual master, the great sage Nārada. Śrīla Viśvanātha Cakravartī also advises that if we want to be successful in our attempt to go back to Godhead, we must very seriously act according to the instruction of the spiritual master. That is the way of perfection. There need be no anxiety over attaining perfection because if one follows the instruction given by the spiritual master he is sure to attain perfection. Our only concern should be how to execute the order of the spiritual master. A spiritual master is expert in giving special instructions to each of his disciples, and if the disciple executes the order of the spiritual master, that is the way of his perfection.

TEXT 72

त्रिरात्रान्ते त्रिरात्रान्ते कपित्थबदराशनः ।
आत्मवृत्त्यनुसारेण मासं निन्येऽर्चयन्हरिम् ॥७२॥

tri-rātrānte tri-rātrānte
kapittha-badarāśanaḥ
ātma-vṛtty-anusāreṇa
māsaṁ ninye 'rcayan harim

tri—three; *rātra-ante*—at the end of night; *tri*—three; *rātra-ante*—at the end of night; *kapittha-badara*—fruits and berries; *aśanaḥ*—eating; *ātma-vṛtti*—just to preserve the body; *anusāreṇa*—as it was necessary, minimum; *māsam*—one month; *ninye*—passed away; *arcayan*—worshiping; *harim*—the Supreme Personality of Godhead.

TRANSLATION

For the first month Dhruva Mahārāja ate only fruits and berries on every third day, only to keep his body and soul together, and in this way he progressed in his worship of the Supreme Personality of Godhead.

PURPORT

Kapittha is a flower which is known in Indian vernacular as *kayeta.* We do not find an English equivalent for the name of this flower, but its fruit is generally not accepted by human beings; it is eaten by monkeys in the forest. Dhruva Mahārāja, however, accepted such fruits, not for luxurious feasting but just to keep his body and soul together. The body needs food, but a devotee should not accept foodstuff to satisfy the tongue in sense gratification. It is recommended in *Bhagavad-gītā* that one should accept as much food as necessary to keep the body fit, but one should not eat for luxury. Dhruva Mahārāja is an *ācārya*, and by undergoing severe austerities and penances he teaches us how one should execute devotional service. We must carefully know the process of Dhruva Mahārāja's service; how severely he passed his days will be shown in later verses. We should always remember that to become a bona fide devotee of the Lord is not an easy task, but in this age, by the mercy of Lord Caitanya, it has been made very easy. But if we do not follow even the liberal instructions of Lord Caitanya, how can we expect to discharge our regular duties in devotional service? It is not possible in this age to follow Dhruva Mahārāja in his austerity, but the principles must be followed; we should not disregard the regulative principles given by our spiritual master, for they make it easier for the conditioned soul. As far as our ISKCON movement is concerned, we simply ask that one observe the four prohibitive rules, chant sixteen rounds and, instead of indulging in luxurious eating for the tongue, simply accept *prasāda* offered to the Lord. This does not mean that with our fasting the Lord should also fast. The Lord should be given foodstuff which is as nice as possible. But we should not make it a point to satisfy our own tongues. As far as possible we should accept simple foodstuff, just to keep the body and soul together to execute devotional service.

It is our duty to remember always that in comparison to Dhruva Mahārāja we are insignificant. We cannot do anything like what Dhruva Mahārāja did for self-realization because we are absolutely incompetent to execute such service. But by Lord Caitanya's mercy we have been given all concessions possible for this age, so at least we should always remember that neglect of our prescribed duties in devotional service will not make us successful in the mission we have undertaken. It is our duty to follow in the footsteps of Dhruva Mahārāja, for he was very determined. We should also be determined to finish our duties in executing devotional service in this life; we should not wait for another life to finish our job.

TEXT 73

द्वितीयं च तथा मासं षष्ठे षष्ठेऽर्भको दिने ।
तृणपर्णादिभिः शीर्णैः कृतान्नोऽभ्यर्चयन्विभुम् ॥७३॥

dvitīyaṁ ca tathā māsaṁ
ṣaṣṭhe ṣaṣṭhe 'rbhako dine
tṛṇa-parṇādibhiḥ śīrṇaiḥ
kṛtānno 'bhyarcayan vibhum

dvitīyam—the next month; *ca*—also; *tathā*—as mentioned above; *māsam*—month; *ṣaṣṭhe ṣaṣṭhe*—every sixth day; *arbhakaḥ*—the innocent boy; *dine*—on days; *tṛṇa-parṇa-ādibhiḥ*—by grasses and leaves; *śīrṇaiḥ*—which were dry; *kṛta-annaḥ*—made for his food; *abhyarcayan*—and thus continued his method of worship; *vibhum*—for the Supreme Personality of Godhead.

TRANSLATION

In the second month Dhruva Mahārāja ate only every six days, and for his eatables he took dry grass and leaves. Thus he continued his worship.

TEXT 74

तृतीयं चानयन्मासं नवमे नवमेऽहनि ।
अब्भक्ष उत्तमश्लोकमुपाधावत्समाधिना ॥७४॥

tṛtīyaṁ cānayan māsaṁ
navame navame 'hani
ab-bhakṣa uttamaślokam
upādhāvat samādhinā

tṛtīyam—the third month; *ca*—also; *ānayan*—passing; *māsam*—one month; *navame navame*—on each ninth; *ahani*—on the day; *ap-bhakṣaḥ*—drinking water only; *uttama-ślokam*—the Supreme Personality of Godhead, who is worshiped by selected verses; *upādhāvat*—worshiped; *samādhinā*—in trance.

TRANSLATION

In the third month he drank water only every nine days. Thus he remained completely in trance and worshiped the Supreme Personality of Godhead, who is adored by selected verses.

TEXT 75

चतुर्थमपि वै मासं द्वादशे द्वादशेऽहनि ।
वायुभक्षो जितश्वासो ध्यायन्देवमधारयत् ॥७५॥

caturtham api vai māsaṁ
dvādaśe dvādaśe 'hani
vāyu-bhakṣo jita-śvāso
dhyāyan devam adhārayat

caturtham—fourth; *api*—also; *vai*—in that way; *māsam*—the month; *dvādaśe dvādaśe*—on the twelfth; *ahani*—day; *vāyu*—air; *bhakṣaḥ*—eating; *jita-śvāsaḥ*—controlling the breathing process; *dhyāyan*—meditating; *devam*—the Supreme Lord; *adhārayat*—worshiped.

TRANSLATION

In the fourth month Dhruva Mahārāja became a complete master of the breathing exercise, and thus he inhaled air only every twelfth day. In this way he became completely fixed in his position and worshiped the Supreme Personality of Godhead.

TEXT 76

पञ्चमे मास्यनुप्राप्ते जितश्वासो नृपात्मजः ।
ध्यायन् ब्रह्म पदैकेन तस्थौ स्थाणुरिवाचलः ॥७६॥

pañcame māsy anuprāpte
jita-śvāso nṛpātmajaḥ
dhyāyan brahma padaikena
tasthau sthāṇur ivācalaḥ

pañcame—in the fifth; *māsi*—in the month; *anuprāpte*—being situated; *jita-śvāsaḥ*—and still controlling the breathing; *nṛpa-ātmajaḥ*—the son of the King; *dhyāyan*—meditating; *brahma*—the Supreme Personality of Godhead; *padā ekena*—with one leg; *tasthau*—stood; *sthāṇuḥ*—just like a column; *iva*—like; *acalaḥ*—without movement.

TRANSLATION

By the fifth month, Mahārāja Dhruva, the son of the King, had controlled his breathing so perfectly that he was able to stand on only one leg, just as a column stands, without motion, and concentrate his mind fully on the Parabrahman.

TEXT 77

सर्वतो मन आकृष्य हृदि भूतेन्द्रियाशयम् ।
ध्यायन्भगवतो रूपं नाद्राक्षीत्किंचनापरम् ॥७७॥

sarvato mana ākṛṣya
hṛdi bhūtendriyāśayam
dhyāyan bhagavato rūpaṁ
nādrākṣīt kiñcanāparam

sarvataḥ—in all respects; *manaḥ*—mind; *ākṛṣya*—concentrating; *hṛdi*—in the heart; *bhūta-indriya-āśayam*—resting place of the senses and the objects of the senses; *dhyāyan*—meditating; *bhagavataḥ*—of the Supreme Personality of Godhead; *rūpam*—form; *na adrākṣīt*—did not see; *kiñcana*—anything; *aparam*—else.

TRANSLATION

He completely controlled his senses and their objects, and in this way he fixed his mind, without diversion to anything else, upon the form of the Supreme Personality of Godhead.

PURPORT

The yogic principles of meditation are clearly explained here. One has to fix one's mind upon the form of the Supreme Personality of Godhead without diversion to any other objective. It is not that one can meditate or concentrate on an impersonal objective. To try to do so is simply a waste of time, for it is unnecessarily troublesome, as explained in *Bhagavad-gītā.*

TEXT 78

आधारं महदादीनां प्रधानपुरुषेश्वरम् ।
ब्रह्म धारयमाणस्य त्रयो लोकाश्चकम्पिरे ॥७८॥

ādhāraṁ mahad-ādīnāṁ
pradhāna-puruṣeśvaram
brahma dhārayamāṇasya
trayo lokāś cakampire

ādhāram—repose; *mahat-ādīnām*—of the material sum total known as the *mahat-tattva; pradhāna*—the chief; *puruṣa-īśvaram*—master of all living entities; *brahma*—the Supreme Brahman, the Personality of Godhead; *dhārayamāṇasya*—having taken into the heart; *trayaḥ*—the three planetary systems; *lokāḥ*—all the planets; *cakampire*—began to tremble.

TRANSLATION

When Dhruva Mahārāja thus captured the Supreme Personality of Godhead, who is the refuge of the total material creation and who is the master of all living entities, the three worlds began to tremble.

PURPORT

In this verse the particular word *brahma* is very significant. *Brahman* refers to one who not only is the greatest, but has the potency to expand to an unlimited extent. How was it possible for Dhruva Mahārāja to capture Brahman within his heart? This question has been very nicely answered by Jīva Gosvāmī. He says that the Supreme Personality of Godhead is the origin of Brahman, for since He comprises everything material and spiritual, there cannot be anything greater than He. In the *Bhagavad-gītā* also the Supreme Godhead says, "I am the resting place of Brahman." Many persons, especially the Māyāvādī philosophers, consider Brahman the biggest, all-expanding substance, but according to this verse and other Vedic literatures, such as *Bhagavad-gītā*, the resting place of Brahman is the Supreme Personality of Godhead, just as the resting place of the sunshine is the sun globe. Śrīla Jīva Gosvāmī, therefore, says that since the transcendental form of the Lord is the seed of all greatness, He is the Supreme Brahman. Since the Supreme Brahman was situated in the heart of Dhruva Mahārāja, he became heavier than the heaviest, and therefore everything trembled in all three worlds and in the spiritual world.

The *mahat-tattva*, or the sum total of the material creation, is to be understood to be the ultimate end of all universes, including all the living entities therein. Brahman is the resort of the *mahat-tattva*, which includes all material and spiritual entities. It is described in this connection that the Supreme Brahman, the Personality of Godhead, is the master of both *pradhāna* and *puruṣa*. *Pradhāna* means subtle matter, such as ether. *Puruṣa* means the spiritual spark living entities who are entangled in that subtle material existence. These may also be described as *parā prakṛti* and *aparā prakṛti*, as stated in *Bhagavad-gītā*. Kṛṣṇa, being the controller of both the *prakṛtis*, is thus the master of *pradhāna* and *puruṣa*. In the Vedic hymns also the Supreme Brahman is described as *antaḥ-praviṣṭaḥ śāstā*. This indicates that the Supreme Personality of Godhead is controlling everything and entering into everything. The *Brahma-saṁhitā* (5.35) further confirms this. *Aṇḍāntara-stha-paramāṇu-cayāntara-stham:* He has entered not only the universes, but even the atom. In *Bhagavad-gītā* (10.42) Kṛṣṇa also says, *viṣṭabhyāham idaṁ kṛtsnam*. The Supreme Personality of Godhead controls everything by entering into everything. By associating constantly with the Supreme Personality in his heart, Dhruva Mahārāja naturally became equal to the greatest, Brahman, by His association, and thus became the heaviest, and the entire universe trembled. In conclusion, a person who always concentrates on the transcendental form of Kṛṣṇa within his heart can very easily strike the whole world with wonder at his activities. This is the perfection of *yoga* performance, as confirmed in *Bhagavad-gītā* (6.47). *Yoginām api sarveṣām:* of all *yogīs*, the *bhakti-yogī*, who thinks of Kṛṣṇa always within his heart and engages in His loving transcendental service, is the topmost. Ordinary *yogīs* can exhibit wonderful material activities, known as *aṣṭa-siddhi*, eight kinds of yogic perfection, but a pure devotee of the Lord can surpass these perfections by performing activities which can make the whole universe tremble.

TEXT 79

यदैकपादेन स पार्थिवार्भक-
स्तस्थौ तदङ्गुष्ठनिपीडिता मही ।
ननाम तत्रार्धमिभेन्द्रधिष्ठिता
तरीव सव्येतरतः पदे पदे ॥७९॥

yadaika-pādena sa pārthivārbhakas
tasthau tad-aṅguṣṭha-nipīḍitā mahī
nanāma tatrārdham ibhendra-dhiṣṭhitā
tarīva savyetarataḥ pade pade

yadā—when; *eka*—with one; *pādena*—leg; *saḥ*—Dhruva Mahārāja; *pārthiva*—the King's; *arbhakaḥ*—child; *tasthau*—remained standing; *tat-aṅguṣṭha*—his big toe; *nipīḍitā*—being pressed; *mahī*—the earth; *nanāma*—bent down; *tatra*—then; *ardham*—half; *ibha-indra*—the king of elephants; *dhiṣṭhitā*—being situated; *tarī iva*—like a boat; *savya-itarataḥ*—right and left; *pade pade*—in every step.

TRANSLATION

As Dhruva Mahārāja, the King's son, kept himself steadily standing on one leg, the pressure of his big toe pushed down half the earth, just as an elephant being carried on a boat rocks the boat left and right with his every step.

PURPORT

The most significant expression in this verse is *pārthivārbhakaḥ*, son of the King. When Dhruva Mahārāja was at home, although he was a king's son, he was prevented from getting on the lap of his father. But when he became advanced in self-realization, or devotional service, by the pressure of his toe he could push down the whole earth. That is the difference between ordinary consciousness and Kṛṣṇa consciousness. In ordinary consciousness a king's son may be refused something even by his father, but when the same person becomes fully Kṛṣṇa conscious within his heart, he can push down the earth with the pressure of his toe.

One cannot argue, "How is it that Dhruva Mahārāja, who was prevented from getting up on the lap of his father, could press down the whole earth?" This argument is not very much appreciated by the learned, for it is an example of *nagna-mātṛkā* logic. By this logic one would think that because his mother in her childhood was naked, she should remain naked even when she is grown up. The stepmother of Dhruva Mahārāja might have been thinking in a similar way: since she had refused to allow him to get up on the lap of his father, how could Dhruva perform such wonderful activities as pressing down the whole earth? She must have been very surprised when she learned that Dhruva Mahārāja, by concentrating constantly on the Supreme Personality of Godhead within his heart, could press down the entire earth, like an elephant who presses down the boat on which it is loaded.

TEXT 80

तस्मिन्नभिध्यायति विश्वमात्मनो
द्वारं निरुध्यासुमनन्यया धिया ।
लोका निरुच्छ्वासनिपीडिता भृशं
सलोकपालाः शरणं ययुर्हरिम् ॥८०॥

tasminn abhidhyāyati viśvam ātmano
dvāraṁ nirudhyāsum ananyayā dhiyā
lokā nirucchvāsa-nipīḍitā bhṛśaṁ
sa-loka-pālāḥ śaraṇaṁ yayur harim

tasmin—Dhruva Mahārāja; *abhidhyāyati*—when meditating with full concentration; *viśvam ātmanaḥ*—the total body of the universe; *dvāram*—the holes; *nirudhya*—closed; *asum*—the life air; *ananyayā*—without being diverted; *dhiyā*—meditation; *lokāḥ*—all the planets; *nirucchvāsa*—having stopped breathing; *nipīḍitāḥ*—thus being suffocated; *bhṛśam*—very soon; *sa-loka-pālāḥ*—all the great demigods from different planets; *śaraṇam*—shelter; *yayuḥ*—took; *harim*—of the Supreme Personality of Godhead.

TRANSLATION

When Dhruva Mahārāja became practically one in heaviness with Lord Viṣṇu, the total consciousness, due to his fully concentrating, and closing all the holes of his body, the total universal breathing became choked up, and all the great demigods in all the planetary systems felt suffocated and thus took shelter of the Supreme Personality of Godhead.

PURPORT

When hundreds of persons are sitting in an airplane, although they remain individual units, they each share in the total force of the airplane, which runs at thousands of miles per hour; similarly, when unit energy is identified with the service of the total energy, the unit energy becomes as powerful as the total energy. As explained in the previous verse, Dhruva Mahārāja, because of his spiritual advancement, became almost the total heaviness, and thus he pressed down the whole earth. Moreover, by such spiritual power his unit body became the total body of the universe. Thus when he closed the holes of his unit body to firmly concentrate his mind on the Supreme Personality of Godhead, all the units of the universe—namely all the living entities, including the big demigods—felt the pressure of suffocation, as if their breathing were being choked. Therefore they all took shelter of the Supreme Personality of Godhead because they were perplexed as to what had happened.

This example of Dhruva Mahārāja's closing the holes of his personal body and thereby closing the breathing holes of the total universe clearly indicates that a devotee, by his personal devotional service, can influence all the people of the whole world to become devotees of the Lord. If there is only one pure devotee in pure Kṛṣṇa consciousness, he can change the total consciousness of the world into Kṛṣṇa consciousness. This is not very difficult to understand if we study the behavior of Dhruva Mahārāja.

TEXT 81

देवा ऊचुः

नैवं विदामो भगवन् प्राणरोधं
चराचरस्याखिलसत्त्वधाम्नः ।

विधेहि तन्नो वृजिनाद्विमोक्षं
प्राप्ता वयं त्वां शरणं शरण्यम् ॥८१॥

devā ūcuḥ
naivaṁ vidāmo bhagavan prāṇa-rodhaṁ
carācarasyākhila-sattva-dhāmnaḥ
vidhehi tan no vṛjinād vimokṣaṁ
prāptā vayaṁ tvāṁ śaraṇaṁ śaraṇyam

devāḥ ūcuḥ—all the demigods said; *na*—not; *evam*—thus; *vidāmaḥ*—we can understand; *bhagavan*—O Personality of Godhead; *prāṇa-rodham*—how we feel our breathing choked; *cara*—moving; *acarasya*—not moving; *akhila*—universal; *sattva*—existence; *dhāmnaḥ*—the reservoir of; *vidhehi*—kindly do the needful; *tat*—therefore; *naḥ*—our; *vṛjināt*—from the danger; *vimokṣam*—liberation; *prāptāḥ*—approaching; *vayam*—all of us; *tvām*—unto You; *śaraṇam*—shelter; *śaraṇyam*—worthy to be taken shelter of.

TRANSLATION

The demigods said: Dear Lord, You are the refuge of all moving and nonmoving living entities. We feel all living entities to be suffocating, their breathing processes choked up. We have never experienced such a thing. Since You are the ultimate shelter of all surrendered souls, we have therefore approached You; kindly save us from this danger.

PURPORT

Dhruva Mahārāja's influence, attained by executing devotional service unto the Lord, was felt even by the demigods, who had never before experienced such a situation. Because of Dhruva Mahārāja's controlling his breathing, the entire universal breathing process was choked. It is by the will of the Supreme Personality of Godhead that material entities cannot breathe whereas spiritual entities are able to breathe; material entities are products of the Lord's external energy, whereas spiritual entities are products of the Lord's internal energy. The demigods approached the Supreme Personality of Godhead, who is the controller of both kinds of entities, in order to know why their breathing was choked. The Supreme Lord is the ultimate goal for the solution to all problems within this material world. In the spiritual world there are no problems, but the material world is always problematic. Since the Supreme Personality of Godhead is the master of both the material and spiritual worlds, it is better to approach Him in all problematic situations. Those who are devotees, therefore, have no problems in this material world. *Viśvaṁ pūrṇa-sukhāyate* (*Caitanya-candrāmṛta*): devotees are free from all problems because they are fully surrendered unto the Supreme Personality of Godhead. For a devotee, everything in the world is very pleasing because he knows how to use everything in the transcendental loving service of the Lord.

TEXT 82

श्रीभगवानुवाच

मा भैष्ट बालं तपसो दुरत्यया-
न्निवर्तयिष्ये प्रतियात स्वधाम ।
यतो हि वः प्राणनिरोध आसी-
दौत्तानपादिर्मयि संगतात्मा ॥८२॥

śrī-bhagavān uvāca
mā bhaiṣṭa bālaṁ tapaso duratyayān
nivartayiṣye pratiyāta sva-dhāma
yato hi vaḥ prāṇa-nirodha āsīd
auttānapādir mayi saṅgatātmā

śrī-bhagavān uvāca—the Supreme Personality of Godhead replied; *mā bhaiṣṭa*—do not be afraid; *bālam*—the boy Dhruva; *tapasaḥ*—by his severe austerity; *duratyayāt*—strongly determined; *nivartayiṣye*—I shall ask him to stop this; *pratiyāta*—you can return; *sva-dhāma*—your own respective homes; *yataḥ*—from whom; *hi*—certainly; *vaḥ*—your; *prāṇa-nirodhaḥ*—choking the life air; *āsīt*—happened; *auttānapādiḥ*—on account of the son of King Uttānapāda; *mayi*—unto Me; *saṅgata-ātmā*—fully absorbed in thought of Me.

TRANSLATION

The Supreme Personality of Godhead replied: My dear demigods, do not be perturbed by this. It is due to the severe austerity and full determination of the son of King Uttānapāda, who is now fully absorbed in thought of Me. He has obstructed the universal breathing process. You can safely return to your respective homes. I shall stop this boy in his severe acts of austerities, and you will be saved from this situation.

PURPORT

Here one word, *saṅgatātmā,* is misinterpreted by the Māyāvādī philosophers, who say that the self of Dhruva Mahārāja became one with the Supreme Self, the Personality of Godhead. The Māyāvādī philosophers want to prove by this word that the Supersoul and the individual soul become united in this way and that after such unification the individual soul has no separate existence. But here it is clearly said by the Supreme Lord that Dhruva Mahārāja was so absorbed in meditation on the thought of the Supreme Personality of Godhead that He Himself, the universal consciousness, was attracted to Dhruva. In order to please the demigods, He wanted to go Himself to Dhruva Mahārāja to stop him from this severe austerity. The Māyāvādī philosophers' conclusion that the Supersoul and the individual soul become united is not supported by this statement. Rather, the Supersoul, the Personality of Godhead, wanted to stop Dhruva Mahārāja from this severe austerity.

By pleasing the Supreme Personality of Godhead, one pleases everyone, just as by watering the root of a tree one satisfies every branch, twig and leaf of the tree. If one can attract the Supreme Personality of Godhead, one naturally attracts the whole universe because Kṛṣṇa is the supreme cause of the universe. All the demigods were afraid of being totally vanquished by suffocation, but the Personality of Godhead assured them that Dhruva Mahārāja was a great devotee of the Lord and was not about to annihilate everyone in the universe. A devotee is never envious of other living entities.

Thus end the Bhaktivedanta purports of the Fourth Canto, Eighth Chapter, of the Śrīmad-Bhāgavatam, *entitled "Dhruva Mahārāja Leaves Home for the Forest."*

Appendixes

The Author

His Divine Grace A. C. Bhaktivedanta Swami Prabhupāda appeared in this world in 1896 in Calcutta, India. He first met his spiritual master, Śrīla Bhaktisiddhānta Sarasvatī Gosvāmī, in Calcutta in 1922. Bhaktisiddhānta Sarasvatī, a prominent religious scholar and the founder of sixty-four Gauḍīya Maṭhas (Vedic institutes), liked this educated young man and convinced him to dedicate his life to teaching Vedic knowledge. Śrīla Prabhupāda became his student, and eleven years later (1933) at Allahabad he became his formally initiated disciple.

At their first meeting, in 1922, Śrīla Bhaktisiddhānta Sarasvatī Ṭhākura requested Śrīla Prabhupāda to broadcast Vedic knowledge through the English language. In the years that followed, Śrīla Prabhupāda wrote a commentary on the *Bhagavad-gītā*, assisted the Gauḍīya Maṭha in its work and, in 1944, without assistance, started an English fortnightly magazine, edited it, typed the manuscripts and checked the galley proofs. He even distributed the individual copies freely and struggled to maintain the publication. Once begun, the magazine never stopped; it is now being continued by his disciples in the West and is published in twelve languages.

Recognizing Śrīla Prabhupāda's philosophical learning and devotion, the Gauḍīya Vaiṣṇava Society honored him in 1947 with the title "Bhaktivedanta." In 1950, at the age of fifty-four, Śrīla Prabhupāda retired from married life, adopting the *vānaprastha* (retired) order to devote more time to his studies and writing. Śrīla Prabhupāda traveled to the holy city of Vṛndāvana, where he lived in very humble circumstances in the historic medieval temple of Rādhā-Dāmodara. There he engaged for several years in deep study and writing. He accepted the renounced order of life (*sannyāsa*) in 1959. At Rādhā-Dāmodara, Śrīla Prabhupāda began work on his life's masterpiece: a multivolume translation of and commentary on the eighteen-thousand-verse *Śrīmad-Bhāgavatam* (*Bhāgavata Purāṇa*). He also wrote *Easy Journey to Other Planets*.

After publishing three volumes of *Bhāgavatam*, Śrīla Prabhupāda came to the United States, in 1965, to fulfill the mission of his spiritual master. Since that time, His Divine Grace has written over sixty volumes of authoritative translations, commentaries and summary studies of the philosophical and religious classics of India.

In 1965, when he first arrived by freighter in New York City, Śrīla Prabhupāda was practically penniless. It was after almost a year of great difficulty that he established the International Society for Krishna Consciousness in July of 1966. Under his careful guidance, the Society has grown within a decade to a worldwide confederation of more than one hundred *āśramas*, schools, temples, institutes and farm communities.

In 1968, Śrīla Prabhupāda created New Vṛndāvana, an experimental Vedic community in the hills of West Virginia. Inspired by the success of New Vṛndāvana, now a thriving farm community of more than one thousand acres, his students have since founded several similar communities in the United States and abroad.

In 1972, His Divine Grace introduced the Vedic system of primary and secondary education in the West by founding the Gurukula school in Dallas, Texas. Since then, under his supervision, his disciples have established children's schools throughout the United States and the rest of the world. As of 1977, there are twenty *gurukula* schools worldwide, with the principal educational center now located in Vṛndāvana, India.

Śrīla Prabhupāda has also inspired the construction of several large international cultural centers in India. The center at Śrīdhāma Māyāpur in West Bengal is the site for a planned spiritual city, an ambitious project for which construction will extend over the next decade. In Vṛndāvana, India, is the magnificent Kṛṣṇa-Balarāma Temple and International Guesthouse. There are also major cultural and educational centers in Bombay and the holy city of Purī in Orissa. Other centers are planned in a dozen other important locations on the Indian subcontinent.

Śrīla Prabhupāda's most significant contribution, however, is his books. Highly respected by the academic community for their authoritativeness, depth and clarity, they are used as standard textbooks in numerous college courses. His writings have been translated into twenty-three languages. The Bhaktivedanta Book Trust, established in 1972 exclusively to publish the works of His Divine Grace, has thus become the world's largest publisher of books in the field of Indian religion and philosophy. Its principal project is the ongoing publication of Śrīla Prabhupāda's celebrated multivolume translation of and commentary on *Śrīmad-Bhāgavatam.*

In the past ten years, in spite of his advanced age, Śrīla Prabhupāda has circled the globe twelve times on lecture tours that have taken him to six continents. In spite of such a vigorous schedule, Śrīla Prabhupāda continues to write prolifically. His writings constitute a veritable library of Vedic philosophy, religion, literature and culture.

References

The purports of *Śrīmad-Bhāgavatam* are all confirmed by standard Vedic authorities. The following authentic scriptures are specifically cited in this volume:

Bhagavad-gītā, 7, 28, 77, 82, 85, 86, 87, 114, 115, 116, 130, 131, 139, 141, 145, 176, 188, 208, 229, 233, 255, 262, 269, 273, 279, 292, 293, 296, 297, 298, 299, 301, 335, 353, 356, 367, 390

Bhakti-rasāmṛta-sindhu, 375

Brahma-saṁhitā, 371, 390

Caitanya-candrāmṛta, 395

Caitanya-caritāmṛta, 288, 333

Hari-bhakti-sudhodaya, 276

Hari-bhakti-vilāsa, 367

Śikṣāṣṭaka, 227

Śiva Purāṇa, 78

Śrīmad-Bhāgavatam, 82, 88, 125, 147, 156, 157, 204, 224, 232, 233, 278, 284, 288

Taittirīya Upaniṣad, 19

Vedānta-sūtra, 75, 297

GENEALOGICAL TABLE

The Descendants of the Daughters of Svāyambhuva Manu

- Svāyambhuva Manu (+ Śatarūpā)
  - Uttānapāda
    - (+ Suruci) — Uttama
    - (+ Sunīti) — Dhruva — (*For the descendants of Dhruva, see* Śrīmad-Bhāgavatam, *Canto Four, vol. 2.*)
  - Priyavrata — (*For the descendants of Priyavrata, see* Śrīmad-Bhāgavatam, *Canto Five, vol. 1.*)
  - Ākūti (+ Ruci)
    - YAJÑA
    - Dakṣiṇā
      - (YAJÑA + Dakṣiṇā): Toṣa, Pratoṣa, Santoṣa, Bhadra, Śānti, Iḍaspati, Idhma, Kavi, Vibhu, Svahna, Sudeva, Rocana
  - Kalā (+ Marīci)
    - Kaśyapa — (*For the descendants of Kaśyapa, see the table in* Śrīmad-Bhāgavatam, *Canto Six, vol. 3, p. 306.*)
    - Pūrṇimā
      - Viraja
      - Viśvaga
      - Devakulyā
  - Anasūyā (+ Atri)
    - Soma
    - Dattātreya
    - Durvāsā
  - Śraddhā (+ Aṅgirā)
    - (daughters)
      - Sinīvālī
      - Kuhū
      - Rākā
      - Anumati
    - (sons)
      - Utathya
      - Bṛhaspati
  - Havirbhū (+ Pulastya)
    - Agastya
    - Viśravā (+ Iḍaviḍā) — Kuvera

The Manus are administrators of universal affairs, and all the members of human society descend from the original Manu. (The word "man"—or, in Sanskrit, *manuṣya*—comes from the name *Manu.*) The Vedic literatures explain that during one day in the life of the demigod Brahmā (4,320,000,000 years), fourteen Manus come and go. Svāyambhuva Manu, the first of the fourteen, is Brahmā's son, and he in turn had two sons and three daughters. This chart delineates the offspring of Svāyambhuva Manu's daughters.

+ indicates marriage ties

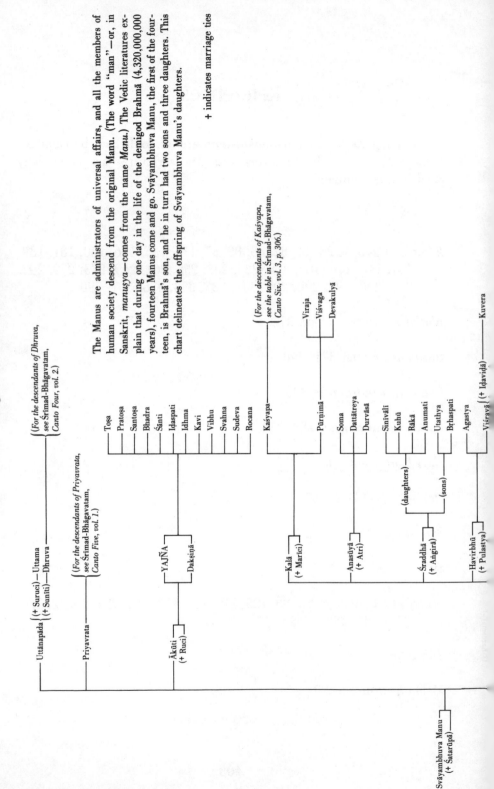

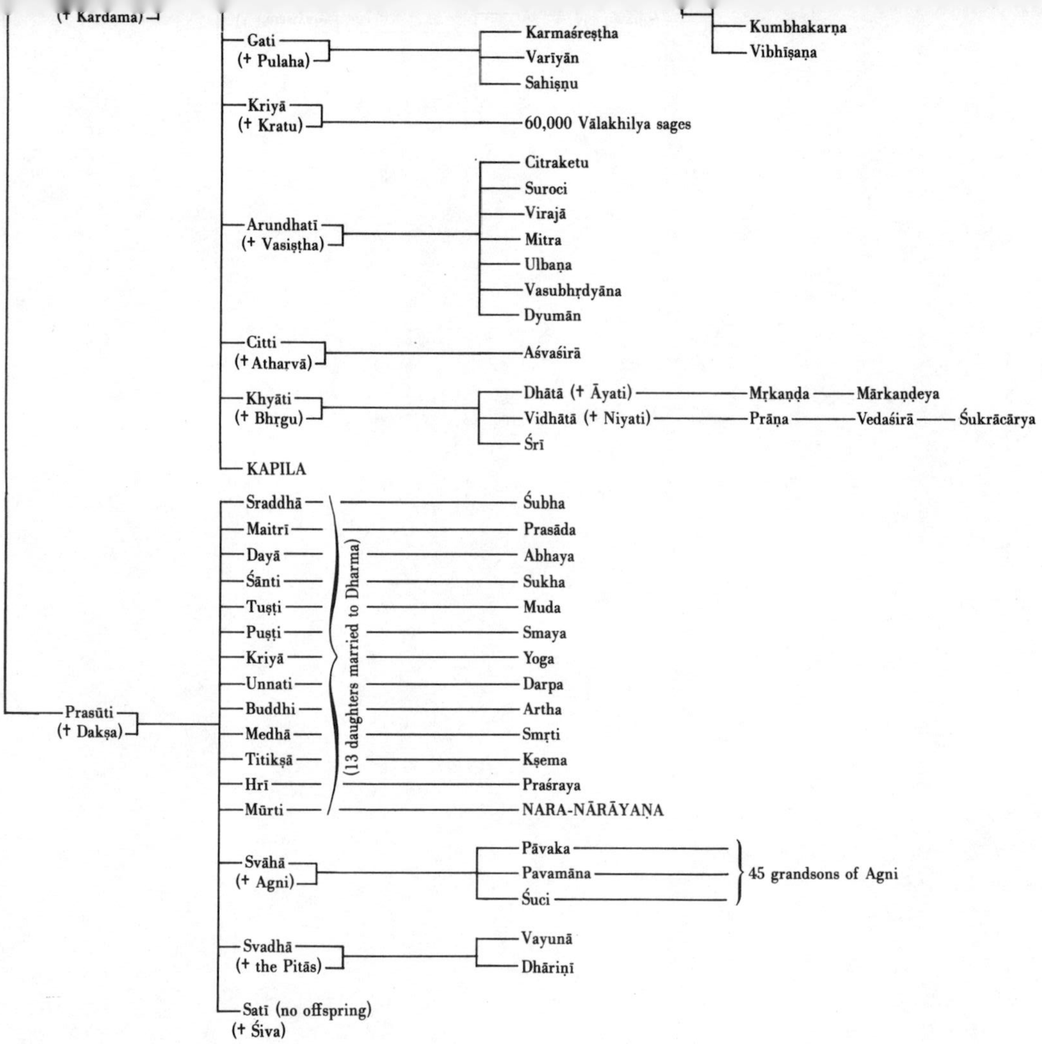
(+ Kardama)
Gati
(+ Pulaha)
Karmaśreṣṭha
Varīyān
Sahiṣṇu
Kumbhakarṇa
Vibhīṣaṇa
Kriyā
(+ Kratu)
60,000 Vālakhilya sages
Arundhatī
(+ Vasiṣṭha)
Citraketu
Suroci
Virajā
Mitra
Ulbaṇa
Vasubhṛdyāna
Dyumān
Citti
(+ Atharvā)
Aśvaśirā
Khyāti
(+ Bhṛgu)
Dhātā (+ Āyati)
Vidhātā (+ Niyati)
Śrī
Mṛkaṇḍa
Mārkaṇḍeya
Prāṇa
Vedaśirā
Śukrācārya
KAPILA
Prasūti
(+ Dakṣa)
Sraddhā
Maitrī
Dayā
Śānti
Tuṣṭi
Puṣṭi
Kriyā
Unnati
Buddhi
Medhā
Titikṣā
Hrī
Mūrti
(13 daughters married to Dharma)
Śubha
Prasāda
Abhaya
Sukha
Muda
Smaya
Yoga
Darpa
Artha
Smṛti
Kṣema
Praśraya
NARA-NĀRĀYAṆA
Svāhā
(+ Agni)
Pāvaka
Pavamāna
Śuci
45 grandsons of Agni
Svadhā
(+ the Pitās)
Vayunā
Dhāriṇī
Satī (no offspring)
(+ Śiva)

Glossary of Personal Names

A

Advaita Prabhu—an incarnation of Viṣṇu who appeared as a principal associate of Lord Caitanya Mahāprabhu.

Ajāmila—a fallen *brāhmaṇa* who was saved from hell by unintentionally chanting the Lord's name at the time of death.

Ākūti—one of Svāyambhuva Manu's three daughters and the wife of Ruci.

Ananta—the Lord's thousand-headed serpent incarnation, who serves as the bed of Viṣṇu.

Aniruddha—a grandson of Lord Kṛṣṇa.

Arjuna—one of the five Pāṇḍava brothers; Kṛṣṇa became his chariot driver and spoke to him the *Bhagavad-gītā.*

Aśvatthāmā—the nefarious son of the great military teacher Droṇācārya who murdered the children of the Pāṇḍavas.

B

Balarāma—Lord Kṛṣṇa's elder brother and first plenary expansion.

Bhaktisiddhānta Sarasvatī Ṭhākura—the spiritual master of His Divine Grace A. C. Bhaktivedanta Swami Prabhupāda.

Bharata Mahārāja—a great devotee of the Lord who because of neglect of spiritual duties took birth as a deer; in his following birth, as a human, he attained perfection.

Brahmā—the first created living being and secondary creator of the material universe; he is born directly from Lord Viṣṇu.

Bṛhaspati—the spiritual master of the demigods.

C

Caitanya Mahāprabhu—the incarnation of Lord Kṛṣṇa who descended to teach love of God through the *saṅkīrtana* movement.

Cāṇakya Paṇḍita—an often-quoted sage whose expert political advice foiled Alexander the Great's plans to invade India.

D

Dakṣa—a son of Brahmā who is a chief forefather of the population of the universe.

Dākṣāyaṇī—a name of Satī.

Dattātreya—a partial incarnation of Lord Viṣṇu who appeared as the son of Atri Muni.

Devahūti—a daughter of Svāyambhuva Manu who was the wife of Kardama Muni and the mother of Lord Kapila.

Droṇācārya—the military teacher of the Pāṇḍavas who was obliged to fight against them in the Battle of Kurukṣetra.

Durgā—the personified material energy and the wife of Lord Śiva.

Durvāsā Muni—a partial incarnation of Lord Śiva, famous for his fearful curses.

G

Garuḍa—the great eagle who acts as the eternal carrier of Lord Viṣṇu.

Gaurakiśora dāsa Bābājī—the spiritual master of Śrīla Bhaktisiddhānta Sarasvatī Ṭhākura.

Govinda—a name of the Supreme Personality of Godhead, who gives pleasure to the land, the cows and the senses.

R

Hare (Harā)—*See:* Rādhā

Hari—a name of the Supreme Personality of Godhead, who removes all obstacles to spiritual progress.

Haridāsa Ṭhākura—a great devotee of Lord Caitanya Mahāprabhu, famous for chanting three hundred thousand names of God every day.

Hiraṇyakaśipu—a demoniac king killed by the Lord's lion incarnation, Nṛsiṁhadeva.

I

Indra—the chief of the administrative demigods and king of the heavenly planets.

J

Jagannātha—a name of the Supreme Personality of Godhead, who is Lord of the universe.

Jīva Gosvāmī—one of the Vaiṣṇava spiritual masters who directly followed Śrī Caitanya Mahāprabhu and systematically presented His teachings.

K

Kapila—an incarnation of Lord Kṛṣṇa who appeared as the son of Kardama Muni and Devahūti to teach Sāṅkhya philosophy.

Kardama Muni—one of the chief forefathers of the population of the universe; the father of Lord Kapila.

Kārttikeya—the younger son of Lord Śiva and Pārvatī; the presiding deity of warfare.

Kaśyapa—one of the chief forefathers of the population of the universe.

Kṛṣṇa—the Supreme Personality of Godhead, appearing in His original, two-armed form.

Kṣattā—a name of Vidura.

Kuntī—the mother of the Pāṇḍavas; an aunt of Lord Kṛṣṇa.

Kuru—the founder of the dynasty in which the Pāṇḍavas, as well as their archrivals, the sons of Dhṛtarāṣṭra, took birth.

Kuvera—the treasurer of the demigods.

L

Lakṣmī—the goddess of fortune and the eternal consort of the Supreme Personality of Godhead Nārāyaṇa.

M

Madhvācārya—a thirteenth-century Vaiṣṇava spiritual master who preached the theistic philosophy of pure dualism.

Maheśvara—a name of Lord Śiva.

Maitreya—the great sage who spoke *Śrīmad-Bhāgavatam* to Vidura; their conversation is recorded in the Third and Fourth Cantos of *Śrīmad-Bhāgavatam.*

N

Nanda—one of the chief personal servants of Lord Nārāyaṇa in His spiritual abode, Vaikuṇṭha.

Nārada—a pure devotee of the Lord who travels throughout the universes in his eternal body, glorifying devotional service.

Nara-Nārāyaṇa—an incarnation of Lord Kṛṣṇa appearing as two sages to teach by their example the practice of austerities.

Nārāyaṇa—a name of the Supreme Personality of Godhead, who is the source and goal of all living beings.

Narottama dāsa Ṭhākura—a Vaiṣṇava spiritual master in the disciplic succession from Śrī Caitanya Mahāprabhu; disciple of Kṛṣṇadāsa Kavirāja Gosvāmī and spiritual master of Viśvanātha Cakravartī Ṭhākura.

Nityānanda Prabhu—an incarnation of Lord Balarāma who appeared as Lord Caitanya Mahāprabhu's chief associate.

P

Pāṇḍavas—Yudhiṣṭhira, Bhīma, Arjuna, Nakula and Sahadeva: the five warrior-brothers who were intimate friends of Lord Kṛṣṇa.

Parīkṣit Mahārāja—the emperor of the world who heard *Śrīmad-Bhāgavatam* from Śukadeva Gosvāmī and thus attained perfection.

Pārvatī—Satī, Lord Śiva's consort, reborn as the daughter of the king of the Himalaya Mountains.

Prahlāda Mahārāja—a devotee persecuted by his demoniac father but protected and saved by the Lord.

Prasūti—a daughter of Svāyambhuva Manu who was the wife of Dakṣa.

Priyavrata—a son of Svāyambhuva Manu who ruled the universe.

Pṛthu Mahārāja—an empowered incarnation of Lord Kṛṣṇa who demonstrated how to be an ideal king.

R

Rādhā—Lord Kṛṣṇa's most intimate consort, who is the personification of His internal, spiritual potency.

Rāmacandra—an incarnation of Lord Kṛṣṇa as a perfect king.

Rāmānanda Rāya—a confidential associate of Śrī Caitanya Mahāprabhu.

Rāmānujācārya—an eleventh-century Vaiṣṇava spiritual master who preached the theistic philosophy of qualified monism.

Rāvaṇa—a powerful demon who was killed by Lord Rāmacandra.

Rudra—a name of Lord Śiva.

S

Sadāśiva—the particular form of Lord Viṣṇu who is the origin of Śiva.

Sanaka—one of the four Kumāras, the eldest sons of Brahmā.

Sanātana Gosvāmī—one of the six Vaiṣṇava spiritual masters who directly followed Śrī Caitanya Mahāprabhu and systematically presented His teachings.

Śaṅkara—a name of Lord Śiva.

Śaṅkarācārya—an incarnation of Śiva who on the order of the Supreme Lord preached impersonalism.

Satī—the wife of Lord Śiva and the daughter of Dakṣa.

Śeṣa Nāga—*See:* Ananta

Śiva—a special incarnation who is in charge of the mode of ignorance and the destruction of the material manifestation.

Sītā—the wife of Lord Rāmacandra.

Soma—the demigod in charge of the moon.

Śrīdhara Svāmī—a Vaiṣṇava spiritual master and commentator on *Śrīmad-Bhāgavatam* in the disciplic succession from Śrī Viṣṇusvāmī.

Śukadeva Gosvāmī—the sage who originally spoke *Śrīmad-Bhāgavatam* to King Parīkṣit just prior to the King's death.

Śukrācārya—the spiritual master of the demons.

Sunanda—one of the chief personal servants of Lord Nārāyaṇa in His spiritual abode, Vaikuṇṭha.

Svāyambhuva Manu—a son of Brahmā who is the original forefather and ruler of the human race.

Śyāmasundara—a name of the Supreme Personality of Godhead, who is blackish and very beautiful.

U

Uddhava—a confidential friend of Śrī Kṛṣṇa in Vṛndāvana.

Uttānapāda—a son of Svāyambhuva Manu and ruler of the world; father of Dhruva.

V

Vāmana—the incarnation of the Supreme Personality of Godhead as a dwarfish *brāhmaṇa* boy.

Varāha—the incarnation of the Supreme Personality of Godhead as a boar.

Vidura—an incarnation of Yama, the god of death, who heard *Śrīmad-Bhāgavatam* from Maitreya Muni.

Vīrarāghava Ācārya—a Vaiṣṇava spiritual master and commentator on *Śrīmad-Bhāgavatam* in the disciplic succession from Rāmānujācārya.

Viṣṇu—a name of the Supreme Personality of Godhead, the creator and maintainer of the material universes.

Viśvanātha Cakravartī Ṭhākura—a Vaiṣṇava spiritual master and commentator on *Śrīmad-Bhāgavatam* in the disciplic succession from Śrī Caitanya Mahāprabhu.

Vyāsadeva—the original compiler of the *Vedas* and *Purāṇas* and author of the *Vedānta-sūtra* and *Mahābhārata.*

Y

Yudhiṣṭhira—the eldest Pāṇḍava, who Lord Kṛṣṇa established as emperor of the entire earth.

General Glossary

A

Ācārya—a spiritual master who teaches by example.
Ārati—a ceremony for greeting the Lord with offerings of food, lamps, fans, flowers and incense.
Arcanā—the devotional process of Deity worship.
Artha—economic development.
Āśrama—the four spiritual orders of life: celibate student, householder, retired life and renounced life.
Asuras—atheistic demons.
Avatāra—a descent of the Supreme Lord.

B

Bhagavad-gītā—the basic directions for spiritual life spoken by the Lord Himself.
Bhāgavata school—the followers of the philosophy of *Śrīmad-Bhāgavatam.*
Bhakta—a devotee.
Bhakti-yoga—linking with the Supreme Lord by devotional service.
Brahmacarya—celibate student life; the first order of Vedic spiritual life.
Brahman—the Absolute Truth; especially the impersonal aspect of the Absolute.
Brāhmaṇa—one wise in the *Vedas* who can guide society; the first Vedic social order.

C

Cāmara—a yak-tail fan used in Deity worship.
Candana—a cosmetic paste made from sandalwood, used in Deity worship.
Cāturmasya—the four months of the rainy season in India; devotees take special vows of austerity during this time.

D

Dharma—eternal occupational duty; religious principles.

E

Ekādaśī—a special fast day for increased remembrance of Kṛṣṇa, which comes on the eleventh day of both the waxing and waning moon.

G

Gāñjā—marijuana.
Gauḍīya Vaiṣṇava-sampradāya—the chain of spiritual masters coming from Lord Caitanya Mahāprabhu.
Goloka (Kṛṣṇaloka)—the highest spiritual planet, containing Kṛṣṇa's personal abodes, Dvārakā, Mathurā and Vṛndāvana.
Gopīs—Kṛṣṇa's cowherd girl friends, His most confidential servitors.
Gṛhastha—regulated householder life; the second order of Vedic spiritual life.
Guru—a spiritual master.

H

Hare Kṛṣṇa mantra—*See: Mahā-mantra*

I

ISKCON—International Society for Krishna Consciousness.

J

Jīva-tattva—the living entities, atomic parts of the Lord.

K

Kali-yuga (Age of Kali)—the present age, characterized by quarrel; it is last in the cycle of four and began five thousand years ago.
Kāma—lust.
Karatālas—hand cymbals used in *kīrtana.*
Karma—fruitive action, for which there is always reaction, good or bad.
Karma-kāṇḍa—sections of the *Vedas* prescribing rituals for material benefits.
Karmī—a person satisfied with working hard for flickering sense gratification.
Kīrtana—chanting the glories of the Supreme Lord.
Kṛṣṇaloka—*See:* Goloka
Kṣatriya—a warrior or administrator; the second Vedic social order.

M

Mahābhārata—the history of the Kurukṣetra war; compiled by Vyāsadeva.

Mahā-mantra—the great chanting for deliverance:
Hare Kṛṣṇa, Hare Kṛṣṇa, Kṛṣṇa Kṛṣṇa, Hare Hare
Hare Rāma, Hare Rāma, Rāma Rāma, Hare Hare.

Mantra—a sound vibration that can deliver the mind from illusion.

Mathurā—Lord Kṛṣṇa's abode, surrounding Vṛndāvana, where He took birth and later returned to after performing His Vṛndāvana pastimes.

Māyā—illusion; forgetfulness of one's relationship with Kṛṣṇa.

Māyāvādīs—impersonal philosophers who say that the Lord cannot have a transcendental body.

Mṛdaṅga—a clay drum used for congregational chanting.

P

Pāñcarātra system—the devotional process of learning to serve the Supreme Lord by serving the Deity of the Lord.

Paramparā—the chain of spiritual masters in disciplic succession.

Prasāda—food spiritualized by being offered to the Lord.

Purāṇas—Vedic histories of the universe, in relation to the Supreme Lord and His devotees.

S

Sac-cid-ānanda-vigraha—the Lord's transcendental form, which is eternal, full of knowledge and bliss.

Śaivites—devotees of Lord Śiva.

Sampradāya—a disciplic succession of spiritual masters.

Saṅkīrtana—public chanting of the names of God, the approved *yoga* process for this age.

Sannyāsa—renounced life; the fourth order of Vedic spiritual life.

Śāstras—revealed scriptures.

Smṛti literatures—supplementary explanations of the *Vedas.*

Śravaṇaṁ kīrtanaṁ viṣṇoḥ—the devotional processes of hearing and chanting about Lord Viṣṇu.

Śruti literatures—the original Vedic literatures: the four *Vedas* and the *Upaniṣads.*

Śūdra—a laborer; the fourth of the Vedic social orders.

Svāmī—one who controls his mind and senses; title of one in the renounced order of life.

T

Tapasya—austerity; accepting some voluntary inconvenience for a higher purpose.

Tilaka—auspicious clay marks that sanctify a devotee's body as a temple of the Lord.

V

Vaikuṇṭha—the spiritual world.

Vaiṣṇava—a devotee of Lord Viṣṇu, Kṛṣṇa.

Vaiśyas—farmers and merchants; the third Vedic social order.

Vānaprastha—one who has retired from family life; the third order of Vedic spiritual life.

Varṇa—the four occupational divisions of society: the intellectual class, the administrative class, the mercantile class and the laborer class.

Varṇāśrama—the Vedic social system of four social and four spiritual orders.

Vedas—the original revealed scriptures, first spoken by the Lord Himself.

Viṣṇu, Lord—Kṛṣṇa's expansion for the creation and maintenance of the material universes.

Vrajabhūmi—*See:* Vṛndāvana

Vṛndāvana—Kṛṣṇa's personal abode, where He fully manifests His quality of sweetness.

Y

Yajña—an activity performed to satisfy either Lord Viṣṇu or the demigods.

Yogī—a transcendentalist who, in one way or another, is striving for union with the Supreme.

Yugas—ages in the life of a universe, occurring in a repeated cycle of four.

Sanskrit Pronunciation Guide

Vowels

अ a आ ā इ i ई ī उ u ऊ ū ऋ ṛ ॠ ṝ

ऌ ḷ ए e ऐ ai ओ o औ au

ं ṁ *(anusvāra)* ः ḥ *(visarga)*

Consonants

Gutturals:	क ka	ख kha	ग ga	घ gha	ङ ṅa
Palatals:	च ca	छ cha	ज ja	झ jha	ञ ña
Cerebrals:	ट ṭa	ठ ṭha	ड ḍa	ढ ḍha	ण ṇa
Dentals:	त ta	थ tha	द da	ध dha	न na
Labials:	प pa	फ pha	ब ba	भ bha	म ma
Semivowels:	य ya	र ra	ल la	व va	
Sibilants:	श śa	ष ṣa	स sa		
Aspirate:	ह ha	ऽ ' *(avagraha)* – the apostrophe			

The numerals are: ०-0 १-1 २-2 ३-3 ४-4 ५-5 ६-6 ७-7 ८-8 ९-9

The vowels above should be pronounced as follows:

a – like the *a* in org*a*n or the *u* in b*u*t
ā – like the *a* in f*a*r but held twice as long as short *a*
i – like the *i* in p*i*n
ī – like the *i* in p*i*que but held twice as long as short *i*

u – like the *u* in p*u*sh
ū – like the *u* in r*u*le but held twice as long as short *u*
ṛ – like the *ri* in *ri*m
ṝ – like *ree* in *ree*d
ḷ – like *l* followed by *ṛ* (*lṛ*)
e – like the *e* in th*ey*
ai – like the *ai* in *ai*sle
o – like the *o* in g*o*
au – like the *ow* in h*ow*
ṁ (*anusvāra*) – a resonant nasal like the *n* in the French word *bon*
ḥ (*visarga*) – a final *h*-sound: *aḥ* is pronounced like *aha; iḥ* like *ihi*

The vowels are written as follows after a consonant:

ा ā ि i ी ī ु u ू ū ृ ṛ ॄ ṝ े e ै ai ो o ौ au

For example: क ka का kā कि ki की kī कु ku कू kū

कृ kṛ कॄ kṝ के ke कै kai को ko कौ kau

The vowel "a" is implied after a consonant with no vowel symbol.

The symbol virāma (्) indicates that there is no final vowel: क्

The consonants are pronounced as follows:

k – as in *k*ite
kh – as in Ec*kh*art
g – as in *g*ive
gh – as in di*g-h*ard
ṅ – as in si*ng*
c – as in *ch*air
ch – as in staun*ch-h*eart
j – as in *j*oy
jh – as in he*dgeh*og
ñ – as in ca*ny*on
ṭ – as in *t*ub
ṭh – as in ligh*t-h*eart
ḍ – as in *d*ove
ḍha- as in re*d-h*ot
ṇ – as r*na* (prepare to say the *r* and say *na*)

Cerebrals are pronounced with tongue to roof of mouth, but the following dentals are pronounced with tongue against teeth:

t – as in *t*ub but with tongue against teeth
th – as in ligh*t-h*eart but with tongue against teeth

d – as in *d*ove but with tongue against teeth
dh – as in re*d-h*ot but with tongue against teeth
n – as in *n*ut but with tongue between teeth
p – as in *p*ine
ph – as in u*ph*ill (not *f*)
b – as in *b*ird
bh – as in ru*b-h*ard
m – as in *m*other
y – as in *y*es
r – as in *r*un
l – as in *l*ight
v – as in *v*ine
ś (palatal) – as in the *s* in the German word *sprechen*
ṣ (cerebral) – as the *sh* in *sh*ine
s – as in *s*un
h – as in *h*ome

Generally two or more consonants in conjunction are written together in a special form, as for example: क्ष kṣa त्र tra

There is no strong accentuation of syllables in Sanskrit, or pausing between words in a line, only a flowing of short and long (twice as long as the short) syllables. A long syllable is one whose vowel is long (ā, ī, ū, e, ai, o, au), or whose short vowel is followed by more than one consonant (including anusvāra and visarga). Aspirated consonants (such as kha and gha) count as only single consonants.

Index of Sanskrit Verses

This index constitutes a complete listing of the first and third lines of each of the Sanskrit poetry verses of this volume of *Śrīmad-Bhāgavatam*, arranged in English alphabetical order. The first column gives the Sanskrit transliteration, and the second and third columns, respectively, list the chapter-verse reference and page number for each verse.

B

C

D

E

G

H

I

J

K

L

M

N

U

General Index

Numerals in boldface type indicate references to translations of the verses of *Śrīmad-Bhāgavatam.*

A

Abhaya (son of Dharma), **40**
Abhyāsa-yoga-yuktena
quoted, 115
Absolute pleasure & pain, 103–104
Absolute Truth, 75
Ācāryas
accept Kṛṣṇa & *Gītā*, 82
accept Kṛṣṇa's deeds, 270–271
See also: Spiritual master
Acintya-bhedābheda-tattva defined, 302
Activities
divisions of, two given, **144–145**
of materialists & renunciants, **144–145**
See also: Karma; Pious activities; Work
Adharma (irreligion), **311**, 313
Adhokṣaja defined, 116, 157
Advaita Prabhu, 217
Agastya (son of Pulastya), **32**
Age of present. *See:* Kali-yuga
Agni (fire-god)
descendants of, **46–48**
descendants of, accept oblations, **46**–47
descendants of, impersonalists worship, **48**
prays to Viṣṇu, **283–284**
Agniṣvāttas (Pitās), **49**
Aham ādir hi devānām
quoted, 297
Ahaṁ brahmāsmi defined, 80,135
Ahaṁ sa ca mama priyaḥ
quoted, 279
Ahaṁ sarvasya prabhavaḥ
quoted, 82, 298
Air of life
controlled by *yoga*, 152
See also: Breathing; *Prāṇāyāma*
Airplanes
of demigods, **94, 100, 205**–206
on different planets, **205**–206
persons on, as unit energies, 393
Ajāmila, 224
Ājyapas (Pitās), **49**
Ākūti
children of, **4, 5, 6**
daughter of Manu, **1, 2**
given to Ruci conditionally, **3**
Alakanandā Lake, **200–201**
Alakanandā River, **202**
Alakā-purī, 201–202
Allahabad, 352
Amāninā mānadena
quoted, 227
Ambikā. *See:* Satī
Americans, 344
Analogies
of airplane & total energy, 393
of bees & highly qualified men, 132
of body & unified existence, **300–301**
of *brāhmaṇa* & law student, 63
of conditioned souls & diseased body-parts, **300–301**
of crows & ritual performers, 147
of Deity form & hot iron rod, 365
of demigods & government servants, 87–90
of demigods & transcendentalists, **143**
of devotional service & electrified copper, 114
of devotional service & heated iron, 114
of devotional service & one with zeros, 107
of Dhruva & elephant, **391**, 392
of Dhruva & snake, **321**
of father & Śiva, 250
of heart & earthen pot, 343–344
of ignorance mode & criminal department, 221
of initiation & transforming bell metal, 367
of jewel on snake & material assets, 106
of Kṛṣṇa worship & watering root, 288
of Lord & building constructor, 25
of Lord & fire, 291
of Lord & lotus, 331
of Lord & root, 88
of Lord & stomach, 88
of Lord & sun, 44

Aṣṭāṅga-yoga
instructed to Dhruva, 353, 354
for meditating on Viṣṇu, 354
purpose of, 354
sitting postures for, 215
Aṣṭottara-śata (108) defined, 114
Asuras
envy of Lord in, 111
See also: Atheists; Demons
Āśutoṣa defined, 190
Aśvatthāmā, 246–247
Aśvinī-kumāra, **238**
Atharvā, **35**
Athāto brahma-jijñāsā
quoted, 75
Atheism, 86
Atheists
associating with, 154
deny *Vedas*, 80, 82–83
envy Lord, 111
Śiva's followers as, **77**, 78, **80**
See also: Demons (*asuras*)
Ātmā
defined, 14
See also: Soul
Ātma-māyayā defined, 116
Atoms, Lord enters, 390
Atri Muni
addressed by deities, **27, 29**
asks about Lord, **24–26**
austerities of, **18, 20**
called for *jagadīśvara*, 25
concentrated on Supersoul, 20
dazzled by deities, **23**
deities welcomed by, **22–26**
desire of, 19
desire of fulfilled, 28, **29**
didn't know God, 19, 25, 28
fire from, **20**
not pure devotee, 19
prays to deities, **24–26**
sons of, **14**
Attachment
for women, 378
See also: Bodily concept of life
Auspiciousness, knowledge as, 135
Austerity
of Atri Muni, **18, 20**
in devotional service, 384–385
of Dhruva, **384, 386–388**
Austerity
elevation by, to serve Lord, 213
needed for success, 326
in Śiva, 212, **213**
Authorities, spiritual. *See: Ācāryas*
Avabhṛtha-snāna bath, **87**
Āvaraṇātmikā-śakti defined, 290
Avatāras. See: Incarnations of God
Avidhi-pūrvakam defined, 87–88
Avyakta defined, 268
Āyati (daughter of Meru), **37**

B

Badarī-nārāyaṇa, 352
Balarāma (Baladeva)
at Aniruddha's marriage, **181**, 182
as Kṛṣṇa's expansion, 288
Banyan tree of Kailāsa, **209, 210**
Barhi, King, 172
Barhiṣadas (Pitās), **49**
Bathing
after sacrifice, **87**
in *aṣṭāṅga-yoga*, 354
avabhṛtha-snāna, **87**
by demigod women, **203, 204–205**
neglected by ignorant beings, 65
persons neglecting, 252
sites for, in Vṛndāvana, 352–353
Beads of Śiva, **215**
Beauty, pride in, **106**
Bees & best men, analogy of, 132
Behavior to superior, equal or inferior, **341**
Beings. *See:* Living entities
Benedictions
on *brāhmaṇa* by Sanātana, 240–241
from demigods, Lord sanctions, 350
devotee's desire for, as honest, 344
in devotional service to Lord, **373**
Dhruva asks, from Nārada, **345, 347**
easy from Śiva, 240
Hare Kṛṣṇa *mantra* as, 240–241
for hearing causes of devastation, **313**
for hearing of Dakṣa's *yajña*, **308**
for hearing of Kardama's descendants, **38**
from Lord, 343, 350–351
from Lord, as beyond expectation, 349
from Lord vs. demigods, 330

Bhṛgu Muni
asks forgiveness from Lord, **267**
Brahmā's request for, **231**
brings demigods to fight, **162**
curses followers of Śiva, **76–84**
descendants of, **36, 37**
discusses illusion of all, **266–267**
goat's beard for, **238**
invites Śiva, **241**
power of, in *mantra* chanting, **161**, 162
power of, vs. Śiva's, 168–169
prays to Viṣṇu, **266–267**
Bhuñjāna evātma-kṛtaṁ vipākam
quoted, 224
Bhūta(s) defined, 84
Bhuvaneśvara, worship in, 303
Birds in Kailāsa, **195, 199, 207**
Birth
forced by nature, 371
by *karma,* 311
pride in status by, 106
See also: Transmigration of the soul
Blasphemy
anger at, 130
dealing with, process for, **140**, 141
death for, **140**, 141
devotee doesn't tolerate, 227
discussed by Satī, **140**
vs. doing duty, **143**
happiness impossible by, **189**
of *Vedas,* 80, 82–83, **84**
Blessings. *See:* Benedictions
Bliss, transcendental
in hearing Lord's pastimes, **274**–275
spiritual pain as, 103–104
See also: Ecstasy
Boar incarnation of God (Varāha), **293**
as transcendental, 371
Bodily concept of life
in *brāhmaṇas* now, 75–76
as contamination, 155, 156
in Dakṣa, 105
in Dakṣa & followers, 71
everyone in, **266–267**
in followers of *Vedas,* 72
forgotten in Lord's service, 155–156
as illusion, 290
Lord not understood in, **267**
offenses to great souls by, **134**–135
purification beyond, 155–156
Bodily concept of life
relationships in, break, 127–128
in Satī, 96, **98–99**
Śiva removes, 135–136
transcending it, 155–156
in *Vedas,* **72**
See also: Illusion; Materialism; *Māyā*
Body, material
attained by Satī, 156
consciousness apart from, 243
dead, decoration of, **276**
dead, society compared to, **276**
eating to maintain, 384–385
fit in spiritual life, 152
forced on living beings, 371
given by *karma,* 371
human, as chance for liberation, 289, 290
human, illusory attraction in, **289**, 290
human, perfection via, 289, 290
identifying with. *See:* Bodily concept of life
obeisances to Lord in, 100–113
Satī ashamed of, **148, 149**
soul keeps fresh, 152
as temple of Lord, 111, 112, 113
temporary, 289–290
yoga for health of, 152
Bondage by work, 233
See also: Karma; Work
Boys, training of, 344
Brahmā, Lord (demigod)
addressed by Śiva, **236–238**
addresses Atri Muni, **27, 29**
addresses Śiva, **220–232**
advised marriage of Śiva & Satī, **65**
advises demigods, **189–192**
afraid of Śiva, 219
angered by Kumāras, 211–212
asked Dakṣa to stay, 68
Atri as noticed by, 20, 21
avoided Dakṣa's sacrifice, **188**
behavior of, as scandalous, 267
in bodily illusion, **266**, 267
born from Viṣṇu, 100, 297–298
cause of, Viṣṇu as, 297–298
celibate sons of, **309**–310
in charge of materialists, 65
as created being, 81–82
created good & bad both, 311
as creator secondarily, 2
criticized by Dakṣa, 66

Brahmā, Lord (*continued*)
devastation at sleep of, 286
didn't author *Vedas*, 81–82
directed by Vāsudeva (Supersoul), 20, 21
discusses bewildered materialists, 226, 228
discusses blasphemy, **189**
discusses injured parties, **231, 232**
discusses Śiva, **190–192, 222, 223**
discusses Śiva & sacrifice, **230–231, 232**
discusses Śiva's status, **220, 221, 229**
empowered by Lord, 314
exalted by Lord's mercy, **325–326**
independent of Lord never, **300**
inferior to Śiva, 139, 220
instructed by Lord, 82
kuśa grass symbol of, **22,** 23
Lord may take part of, 139, 314
Lord of, Viṣṇu as, 257
as Lord of universe, 28
neglected by Dakṣa, 91
as nondifferent from Lord, **297**–298, **300, 301–302**
offers Viṣṇu obeisances, 257
one with & different from Viṣṇu, 302–303
as plenary expansion of Lord, 314
prays to Viṣṇu, **268**
as qualitative incarnation of Viṣṇu, 299
respects Śiva, **138,** 139
Śiva born from, 212
Śiva's obeisances to, **218**
smiling at Śiva, **219**
Soma as incarnation of, **14,** 16, **30**
son of, Svāyambhuva Manu as, **314**
sons of, bad group of, **311, 312,** 313
sons of, celibate group of, **309**–310
as *svayambhū*, 100
swan carrier of, **22,** 23
Vedas not authored by, 81–82
Viṣṇu Lord of, 257
Viṣṇu may be, 139
Brahma-bandhu(s)
Dakṣa as, 247
defined, 159, 247
less intelligent, 4–5
Vedas inaccessible to, 4–5
Brahma-bhūtaḥ prasannātmā quoted, 335
Brahmacārīs, 309–310
Brahmacarya system
benefit in, 309–310
as division of life, 339
Brahmajyoti. See: Brahman effulgence
Brahman (impersonal Absolute)
basis of, Lord as, 389–390
brāhmaṇas should know, 75
defined, 389
devotees realize, 265
devotional service on level of, 114
everything as, 298
as expanding unlimitedly, 389
gradations of, among beings, 15–16
humans should know, 75
knowledge of, as incomplete, 135–136
knowledge of, Śiva gives, 135–136
meditation on, as difficult, 356
meditation on, vs. on Lord, 356
taught by *Vedas*, 80
See also: Brahman effulgence
Brahmānanda (*brahma-nirvāṇa*) defined, 137, 217
Brāhmaṇas
abandon duty now, 75–76
absent nowadays, 163
afraid of Dakṣa, 126–127
alone hear *Vedas*, 63
Americans trained as, 344
animals sacrificed by, 125
argue scripture, 125
bad food eaten by, 75–76
benedicted by Sanātana, 240–241
birth doesn't qualify, 4–5, 75, 76
blaspheming them, 80
blasphemy if heard by, **140,** 141
bodily concept of, 75–76
born from Lord's mouth, 248
brahma-bandhu defined, 159, 247
brahma-bandhus, 4–5
Brahman known by, 75
Caitanya's principle on, 76
caste *brāhmaṇas*, 365
chanting of *mantras* by, 125, 365
charity & preaching for, 248
contrasted to *kṣatriyas*, 344
creation of, in present Age, 163, 344–345
criticize brahminical candidates, 75, 76, 365
criticize chanting of *praṇava*, 365
criticize Śiva's followers, 294
cursed by Nandīśvara, **75**
curses by, 76–77
at Dakṣa's sacrifice, **124**–125, 128–129
describe Viṣṇu as sacrifice, **291**
as *dvija* (twice-born), 132
elevation to status of, 75, 76

D

E

Human beings (*continued*)
benefit by Śiva, 64–65, **136–137**
best relief work for, 264
in bodily concept, 99
as boys, training for, 344
can't imitate Śiva, 143
can't imitate transcendentalists, 143
classes of, according to desire, 342
classes of, demons & devotees as, 255
classes of, materialists & salvationists as, 137
compared to ass or cow, 99
control of senses for, 248
dangerous position of, **263–264**
degraded by tongue, 259
delivered by devotees, 226, 229
demoniac. *See:* Demons
in different modes, 65
don't accept Lord's acts, 270
envy in, 111, 226
etiquette in meetings among, **341**
four kinds of activity for, 377
four kinds of spirit in, 344
four principles of life for, 137
frustrated, attempt liberation, 137
greatness in, as finding good, 132–133
in ignorance, Śiva benefits, 65, 137
illusory attraction in, **289,** 290
interpret *Śrīmad-Bhāgavatam,* 270
life as, as *arthadam,* 289
life as, as chance for liberation, 289, 290
life as, general conception of, 339
life as, perfection via, 289, 290
life as, principles for, four given, 137
life as, spirituality at end of, 339
malicious kind of, 107–108
materialistic. *See:* Materialists
meant to know Brahman, 75
meetings among, etiquette for, **341**
offenses to great souls by, **134–135**
protection for, by surrender to Lord, 267
sacrifices necessary for, 232–234
spirit in, four kinds of, 344
surrender by, 357
twice-born, defined, 132
See also: Kali-yuga; Society
Husbands. *See:* Marriage
Hymns. *See: Mantras*

I

Iḍaspati (son of Yajña), **9**
Iḍaviḍā (wife of Viśravā), **32**
Identity. *See:* Self-realization; Soul
Idhma (son of Yajña), **9**
Ignorance
in everyone, **266–267**
of God's name, 19
material education as, **73**
in material happiness, 72
in ritual performers, **262**–263
Śiva removes, 135–136
of Vedic followers, **72**
See also: Bodily concept; Ignorance, mode of; Illusion
Ignorance, mode of
as auspicious, 221
compared to criminal department, 221
vs. goodness, 168–169
persons in, Śiva benefits, 64–65
Śiva incarnation of, 221
Śiva in charge of, 103
Illusion
of accepting world as real, 99
dissatisfaction as, **335**
everyone in, **266–267**
happiness in, in abominable life, 290
material world as, 99
by *māyā*'s influence, 290
as neglect of spiritual identity, 289, 290
See also: Bodily concept; Ignorance; *Māyā*
Impersonalist philosophers (Māyāvādīs)
can't know Lord, 269
consider Dhruva merged in Lord, 396
consider Lord mundane, 269, 370, 371
consider Lord's acts unbelievable, 270
consider Lord woman, 359
contrasted to personalists, 269
curse regarding, 78
followers of Śiva as, 78
meditation by, 369
monist's vision, 279
offensive to Lord, 371
opposed to scripture, 78
"unification of soul" idea of, 396
worship fire-god, **48**
Impersonalist philosophy
Śiva taught, 78
See also: Oneness

J

K

Kṛṣṇa consciousness movement
Americans in, 344
brahminical training in, 344
in Caitanya's footsteps, 264
criticized by Indians, 366
Deity worship in, 365–366
to deliver envious, 226
for everyone, 366–367
as greatest relief work, 264
preachers in. *See:* Kṛṣṇa consciousness, preachers of
purifies consciousness, 239
purpose of, 290
regulative principles in, 385
universal work of, 366
Kṛṣṇa-kathā defined, 274, 366
Kṛṣṇaloka (Goloka)
beyond material qualities, 280–281
desire trees in, 206
Kṛṣṇas tu bhagavān svayam quoted, 288
Kṣatriyas
Americans not, 344
as "arms" of society, 345
blasphemy if heard by, 141
boys trained as, 344
contrasted to *brāhmaṇas*, 344
defined, 83
Dhruva as, **333–334**
discussed by Nārada, **333–334**
family spirit kept by, 334
fight at marriages, 182
as part of Lord's cosmic form, 222
permanent class of, 83
pride in, **333–334**
qualifications for, two given, 334
spirit in, vs. *brāhmaṇas*, 344
See also: King(s)
Kṣema (son of Dharma), **40**
Kṣīrodakaśāyī Viṣṇu, 28
See also: Supersoul
Kuhū (daughter of Aṅgirā), **31**
Kumāras, the four
angered Brahmā, 211–212
as *brahmacārīs* (celibate), **309,** 310
refused to marry, 211–212
Sanaka, **285, 293**
sitting with Śiva, **211**–212
Kumbhakarṇa, **32**
Kuṅkuma, **204–205**
Kuntīdevī, 106
Kuśa grass of Brahmā, **22,** 23
Kuvera
abode of, **206**
parents of, **32**
sitting with Śiva, **211,** 212

L

Laborer class. *See: Śūdras*
Laghimā-siddhi defined, 363
Lake of Satī (Alakanandā), **200–201**
Lakṣmī (goddess of fortune)
always serves Lord, **329,** 330
always with Lord, 6, 277
born with Yajña, **5–7**
demigods worship, **329,** 330
incarnation of, as Dakṣiṇā, 6, 8
Lord not attached to, **273**
on Lord's chest, 256
as Lord's feminine feature, 359
as Nārāyaṇa's wife, 8
as worshiped for opulence, 330
Lakṣmī-Nārāyaṇa, 8
Lamentation
soul beyond, 335
as useless, 322, 336
Law(s)
on giving daughter for son, 3
of Manu on punishment, 189
punishment by, as good, 189
Vedic, transcendentalists surpass, **143, 144,** 145
Leaders. *See:* King(s); *Kṣatriyas*
Learning (education)
compared to jewel on snake, 106
pride in, 106
in service to Lord, 106–107
See also: Knowledge
Liberation (*mukti*)
by associating with devotees, 154
beyond happiness & distress, **340**
beyond pain & pleasure, 335–336
by chanting about Lord, **289,** 290
defined, 211
desire absent in, 374–375, 377
devotee gets, 223–224, 350–351
devotional service beyond, 375
devotional service from level of, 374–375

M

Mahārāja . . . *See name following title*
Mahātmā
Dakṣa as, 176
defined, 176
Mahātmānas tu māṁ pārtha
quoted, 176
Mahat-tattva
defined 390
includes all material entities, 390
Mahā-Viṣṇu, 28
Mahīyasāṁ pāda-rajo-
quoted, 134
Maitreya Muni
desired to describe piety, 316
heard from Uddhava, **307**
narrative arrangement by, 314
Maitrī (daughter of Dakṣa), **40**
Malicious persons, **107–108**
Mama māyā duratyayā
quoted, 229
Māṁ ca yo 'vyabhicāreṇa
quoted, 114
Mām eva ye prapadyante
quoted, 77, 229
Maṇimān, **123, 179**
Mankind. *See:* Human beings
Man-manā bhava mad-bhakto
quoted, 111
Mantras
airplanes run by, 205
animals rejuvenated by, 125, 272
Bhṛgu's use of, **161,** 162
for *brāhmaṇas* only, 365
brāhmaṇas' power in, 161, 162
chanted at Dakṣa's sacrifice, **124,** 125
chanting of, impossible now, 161, 162–163
chanting of, rules for, 365
in Deity worship, 369
devotees (Vaiṣṇavas) may chant, 365
disciplic succession needed for, 363, 365
given by spiritual master, 363, 365
Hare Kṛṣṇa *mantra. See:* Hare Kṛṣṇa *mantra*
as meant to please Viṣṇu, 284
must be via disciplic succession, 363, 365
must be via spiritual master, 365
for oblations to Śiva, 128–129
for offering oblations, 128–129
oṁ namo bhagavate vāsudevāya, worship of Lord by, 372
Mantras
praṇava (*oṁ*)
for *brāhmaṇas* only, 365
rules for chanting, 365
for Vaiṣṇavas (devotees), 365
for protecting sacrifices, **161**
qualification for chanting, 365
Ṛbhu demigods called by, **161,** 162
requirement for receiving, 363, 365
for sacrifices, 284
for seeing flying beings, **363**
svāhā, 128–129
tested on animals, 125, 184, 272
worked wonders, 161, 162
worship of Lord by, 372
Manu (Svāyambhuva)
daughters of, **1, 11**
descendants of, as pious, 314
desired Lord as son, 3
as first mentioned in *Bhāgavatam,* 2
gave daughter for son, **3**
got son of Ruci (Yajña), **6**
knew Lord would appear, 3
law of, cited on punishment, 189
as son of Brahmā, **314**
sons of, **315**
worship of Lord by, **327**
Manu defined, 217
Manu-smṛti, cited on family duty, 378–379
Marīci
chief of sages, **9**
descendants from, **9, 13, 14**
Marijuana (*gāñjā*), 78, 79
wives' property sold for, 97
Mārkaṇḍeya Muni, **37**
Marriage
according to status, 66
bodies shared in, 122
decorated wives attend, **92, 94**
divorce in, 122
dowry system for, 97
giving daughter in, for son, 3
as "home" life, 310
ideal life in, 8
kṣatriya fighting at, 182
Lakṣmī-Nārāyaṇa ideal in, 8
parents' duty to arrange, 66
pleasing wife in, 8
satisfaction in, 8
of Śiva & Satī, Brahmā advised, **65**

N

R

S

Spiritual life
life culminating in, 339
women check, 99
See also: Devotional service to the Supreme Lord; Kṛṣṇa consciousness; Self-realization
Spiritual light. *See:* Brahman effulgence
Spiritual master
all people should accept, 367
all should become, 290
as *aṣṭottara-śata* (108), 114
birth status unimportant for, 76
boys trained by, 344
caitya-guru, 355
devotee of Kṛṣṇa as, 76
disciplic line necessary for, 367
duty of, to engage disciple, 349
gives *mantra*, **363, 364**
as Lord in heart, 355
Lord sends, 333, 355
as Lord's representative, 382
obeisances by, to disciple, 112
perfection by following, 383–384
as *prabhupāda*, 382
Śiva as, for all, **54**–55
in *śuddha-sattva* (*vasudeva*) state, 114
tests disciple, 337, 339
within & without, 355
Spiritual world
attaining to. *See:* Liberation
beings in, 208
beings in, vs. material world, 394–395
beyond material qualities, **280**–281
chanting in, 208
contrasted to material world, 103–104, 394–395
demons absent in, 255
devotees always in, 255
devotees attain, 223–224
devotees candidates for, 223–224
glorification of Lord in, 208
inhabitants of, 208, 394–395
material world reflection of, 99, 103–104
quality in, 281
as reality above illusion, 99
sex insignificant in, 208
women in, 208
See also: Internal energy of Lord
Śraddhā (wife of Aṅgirā), **31**
Śraddhā (wife of Dharma), **40**
Śrī (daughter of Bhṛgu), **36**
Śrī-Bhāgavata-candra-candrikā, cited on Satī's lake, 201
Śrīdhara Svāmī, cited on *viṣṇu-prasāda*, 304
Śrīmad-Bhāgavatam
author's commentating on, 1–2
cited on pleasing Lord, 233
cited on *saṅkīrtana* (chanting), 284
cited on Śiva's worshipers, 147
Fourth Canto of, 2
materialist's view of, 270
as principal book on Kṛṣṇa, 289–290
quotations from
on chanting in this Age, 88
on decorating dead body, 276
on devotee's accepting difficulty, 224
on Kṛṣṇa as God, 288
on Lord's inspiring Brahmā, 82
on Lord within, 297
on pilgrimage sites, 204
on purification via Lord, 156
on real satisfaction, 157
on *saṅkīrtana* (chanting), 125, 233, 284
unqualified commentaries on, 5
Śrīvatsa defined, 358
Straw mats, use of, 214
Strī defined, 96
Striyo vaiśyās tathā śudrāḥ quoted, 141
Śubha (son of Dharma), **40**
Success, **326**
Śuci (son of Agni), **46, 47**
Śuddha-sattva
defined, 114–115
Lord revealed in, 114, 115
not in material world, 169
spiritual master in, 114
Sudeva (son of Yajña), **9**
Śūdras
Americans as, 344
blasphemy if heard by, 141
as *brāhmaṇas*, 75, 76
defined, 83
as "legs" of society, 345
less intelligent, 4–5
part of Lord's cosmic form, 222
permanent class of, 83
as spiritual masters, 75, 76
unfit to hear *Vedas*, 4–5, 63
women as, 141
See also: Varṇa & āśrama system

V

W

DATE DUE